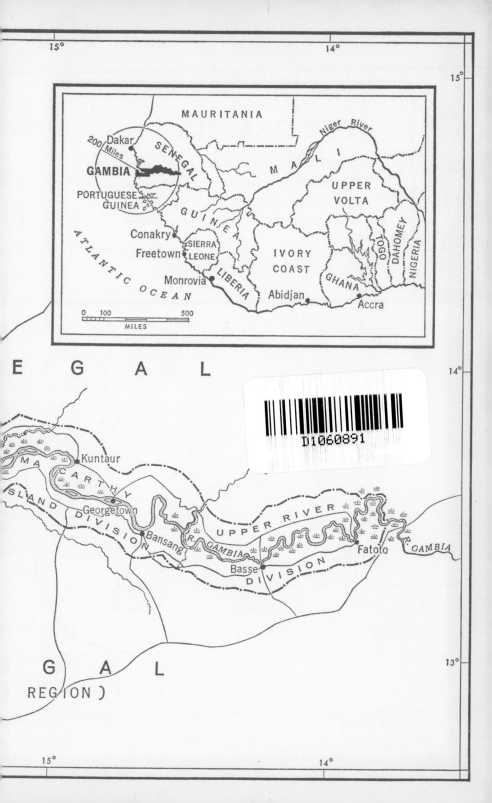

# Enter Gambia

## THE BIRTH OF AN IMPROBABLE NATION

# ENTER

by Berkeley Rice

# GAMBIA

the birth of an improbable nation

ILLUSTRATED WITH PHOTOGRAPHS BY THE AUTHOR

HOUGHTON MIFFLIN COMPANY BOSTON

1 9 6 7

*To Edward Engberg*

I wish to thank
the Philip M. Stern Family Fund
for assistance in doing the research
on which this book is based.

# CONTENTS

# ILLUSTRATIONS

# INTRODUCTION

SINCE FEBRUARY 18, 1965, Gambia has been independent. This fact has escaped general notice because few non-Gambians know where or what Gambia is, and little about it is on a scale likely to attract attention. A tiny enclave jutting into Senegal, on the West African coast, Gambia is Africa's smallest and poorest new independent nation. It has no railroad, no daily paper, no university, one airport and one city. Its population of 320,000 is roughly equal to that of Oklahoma City, Toledo or Rochester, N. Y. Its 4,000 square miles encompass only the Gambia River and a few miles of relatively dry river bank on either side. Slightly smaller than Connecticut, Gambia does not loom very large on the continent of Africa. Mapmakers, in fact, sometimes forget to include it. This annoys the few Gambians who look at maps.

Gambia has few economic advantages to offset its size. There is only one cash crop — peanuts — which accounts for 95 per cent of the country's exports. Until independence, industrial development was limited to two small peanut oil mills. The only natural resource in plentiful supply is fish, and Gambians have never been interested in fishing. British, French, Lebanese, Indian and Mauritanian businessmen handle most of the exports

and local commerce. The only significant source of income besides peanuts is smuggling to Senegal.

The great majority of Gambia's Negro population are Moslem
tribal villagers, who farm their peanuts with a small wooden hoe
called a "coop-coop." The five major tribes are Mandinka, Fula,
Woloff, Serahuli and Jola. There are also assorted Manjagos and
Balantos from Portuguese Guinea, Bambaras from Mali, Sereres
from Senegal, Yalunkas from Guinea, and Mauritanians from
Mauritania. Since 1963, these friendly, easygoing people have
been under the moderate and capable leadership of Prime Minister David K. Jawara, a shy, bespectacled, former veterinary
officer. Assisting him are about 50 British advisers, a relatively
efficient civil service, and six Gambian Ministers, one of whom
went beyond high school.

Though the government's annual revenues of $6.5 million run
about a million behind expenditures — England makes up the
difference and contributes another $2 million or so for develop-
ment projects — no one can accuse Mr. Jawara of extravagance.
His administration makes do with a two-man foreign ministry,
a four-man foreign service and a 150-man army. Mr. Jawara receives an annual salary of $8,400, while Baboucar Ousman Sem-
ega-Janneh, the mayor of Bathurst, the capital and Gambia's
only city, receives none. The Bathurst City Council meets about
once a month in a crumbling World War II Quonset hut, and
Parliament gathers from time to time in the ballroom of the
former British social club.

Despite its independence, England's first and last colony in
West Africa remains a member of the Commonwealth and is
distinctly British. Faded pictures of the Queen hang in Gambian
homes throughout the country. Senior government officials and
well-to-do citizens spend their vacations in England, and, when
able, send their children to British private schools. Bathurst

youths dressed in spotless whites still play cricket at MacCarthy square, and Bathurst elders still gather at the Reform Club to play darts, "snooker" pool and draughts, and down pints of Guinness stout.

These virtues led Queen Victoria, who never visited her colony, to call it "that dear, loyal little place." Sir Richard Burton, who did, described Bathurst as nothing but mud, mangroves, malaria and miasma." Conditions have improved considerably since then, and today Bathurst is one of the more pleasant cities on the coast. During the seven-month dry season the days are warm and the nights cool. The summer rainy season is hot, with a humidity admitted by the British tourist guide to be "trying." Upriver temperatures run considerably higher — up to 140° in the sun — but there is no dank, dense jungle as in Tarzan or the Congo. The interior is flat and sandy, with low, sparse vegetation. Wild game is limited to baboons, monkeys, wild pigs, stray hyenas and occasional crocodiles and hippopotamuses.

Officially, this country's name is "The Gambia," acquired in the days when it was only thought of as the Gambia River. Through successive Franco-British treaties it came to include both river banks, nearly cutting surrounding Senegal in half. This geographic oddity frequently inspires flights of descriptive fancy. The Senegalese call Gambia "an arrow pointing at our heart," and "a knife plunging into Senegal's side." John Gunther, in a flurry of similes, said it "looks like an earthworm and fits around the Gambia River like a long, tight, wrinkled sleeve." Another American reporter spoke of the "Gambian hot dog in the Senegalese roll."

Until recently, no one ever expected Gambia to be a country at all. In 1661, the first British settlers, a group called "The Royal Adventurers of England," thought of it only as a convenient trading post for slaves and other commodities. In the nineteenth century, when its commercial value had diminished, the Colonial Office tried repeatedly to exchange it with France (which owned surrounding Senegal) for Gabon, a slice of Guinea, and various other parts of France's African empire. The French refused. Still, everyone always assumed that Gambia would eventually become part of Senegal. The idea of independence was out of the question. One former governor called Gambia "a geographic and economic absurdity." In 1953 an American journalist described it as "broke but happy." Just seven years ago, a *New York Times* reporter wrote confidently from Bathurst, "Gambia could never stand alone as an independent nation. Everyone here knows this."

Despite such opinions, Gambia has become Africa's 36th independent state, and the 115th member of the United Nations. Reactions to this event differ. One ex-governor told a recent visitor, "You can't really live in Gambia unless you have a good sense of humor. It's a wonderful country, and a lot of fun, and it should be taken that way." Outgoing Governor-General Sir John Paul took things more seriously. Noting Gambia's reputation for friendliness, tolerance and tranquility, he prayed that "God may help preserve and prosper this small settlement of peace and sanity in a world which, in many regions, so sadly lacks these qualities."

This is the story of Gambia's independence — a year in the life of a small country.

## AUTHOR'S NOTE

THE STATISTICS used in this book are not to be relied upon. They are approximations based on the best available figures in Gambia, which conflict with each other, and are gathered under conditions that would drive any reputable statistician insane. The same is true for spellings of Gambiana. There are no definitive grammars for Mandinka or Woloff, and any similarity between the spelling of proper names in this book and those used in Gambia is purely coincidental, for Gambians themselves rarely agree on the spelling of their own names and villages. "Woloff," for example, can also be spelled Wolof, Wolloff, Wollof, Joloff, Jolof, Jolloff, Jollof, Djolof, Jaloff, Joluff, Galofe, Yolof, Yaloff, Yuloff, Ioloff, Ouolaf, Oloff, or Oualofe. Most Woloffs do not worry about spelling.

# Enter Gambia

## THE BIRTH OF AN IMPROBABLE NATION

# 1

## BATHURST

PLATO SUGGESTED that 50,000 people was the ideal population for a city. A citizenry of this size, he felt, was large enough to produce all the goods and services necessary for the city's welfare, and small enough to allow everyone to participate in its government. While Bathurst has only 30,000 people, and has never managed to produce all of its required goods and services, it is charmingly small enough to keep its governmental, commercial, social and cultural affairs on a distinctly personal level. Though it is Gambia's capital, only city and only seaport, it gets along comfortably with two restaurants, two high schools, one bank, one bookstore and one fire engine. Health services, though not extensive, are easy to find — there is one hospital, one pharmacy and one dentist. While these facilities may satisfy Plato's ideal, they are not everyone's cup of tea. One American visitor who spent a few days in Bathurst after an extended trip about the continent, sighed, "If there's an Endsville in Africa, this is it."

Because of its unflamboyant virtues, Bathurst attracts few visitors. Those who do arrive generally wait until the end of the rainy season before driving down from Dakar, the capital of surrounding Senegal. By October, the rains have ended, though the air is still heavy. The sun is oppressively hot, the countryside is lush, and the ground is soft and steaming. There are two possible routes, both winding through miles of window-high bush grass in southern Senegal. The shorter one takes about four to five hours, depending on how much a driver cares about his car. It consists of a rutted, orange, dirt road with a laterite rock base that gives it the consistency of a washboard. The longer and gentler route takes about six hours, via a hard-surfaced Senegalese road pockmarked by potholes and the Trans-Gambian Highway.

Though brief, the Trans-Gambian is noteworthy as one of Gambia's few paved thoroughfares. If you drive along it at a reasonable speed you might miss the one-room Gambian customs post set off the road on the left. The staff — one officer and one guard — are usually sitting out front on a wooden bench, playing cards. A few miles further you come to the Gambia River and the Bambatenda Ferry. Though the crossing itself takes only about fifteen minutes, getting across is not that easy. Asked when the ferry leaves, the attendant replies, "Whenever we get enough cars, oh yes." Under this system, if yours is the last car on board, the ferry leaves as soon as you get there. If it's the first, you may wait up to two hours.

Therein lies the reason for the rows of corrugated tin stalls lining the road at both ferry landings. They offer the waiting traveler plastic hairpins, candy, soap, matches, costume jewelry, liver pills and other necessities. There are also bottled sodas called "mineral water" cooled to a tepid degree in kerosene refrigerators. These come in a variety of flavors, such as peach, banana, mango and pineapple — all flat, sweet, and tasting exactly alike.

Shortly after leaving the river bank, the route to Bathurst leaves the paved highway and turns west onto a dusty laterite road heading for the Atlantic coast. It winds through lush, green mangrove swamps and past clusters of thatch-roofed mud-brick

huts. The villagers smile and wave at passing cars. Some yell
"Hello!" and others clap. As dusk settles, the driving becomes
hazardous, for the road is strewn with dogs, cattle, goats, children, women with baskets on their heads and men with hand-
made seven-foot rifles. When cars approach them, the women
and men melt into the thick bush grass which crowds the road on
either side. The children and animals remain in the road. In the
swampy areas, toads jump out in front of the headlights and
make soft "plops" as the tires roll over them.

Arriving in Bathurst, the exhausted, dusty visitor heads for the
Atlantic Hotel. Experienced travelers say about most African
capitals that "there is really only one hotel," by which they mean
only one worth staying at. Until independence, however, there
really was only one hotel in Gambia, and before the Atlantic was
built in 1958, Bathurst's infrequent visitors had to put up with
friends or make do at a government rest house offering a few
cots and no meals. The Atlantic is an attractive, pastel, 50-room
complex on the edge of the Gambia River mouth. By the standard of other African hotels it is well run; the rooms are pleasant,
the food is quite good, and one can swim at the beach out front.
Service on the dining terrace is often erratic, since few of the
waiters are proficient in English. Guests order from the menu by
the number, not the dish. Though this system decreases the potential confusion, there is always some doubt that the correct
dish will arrive. October is not the best time of year for a visit to
either Gambia or the Atlantic Hotel. In the muggy evenings, the
lights on the dining terrace attract swarms of mosquitoes and
more elaborate flying insects. They congregate around the tables
and sample the various dishes. During the day, lizards and toads
compete with guests for a place in the sun on the terrace.
Closets in the chalet rooms are likely to yield a variety of small
exotic reptiles that make sleep difficult for the faint-hearted.

Never was there a city with less of the atmosphere of a city than Bathurst. With paint peeling from its hundred-year-old buildings, and creaking wharfs along the waterfront on the verge of giving in to the river, it has the seedy charm of a down-at-the-heels Mississippi River town, brightened by frangipani, bougain-villaea and jacaranda. Buxom Woloff women amble about in elaborate neon-hued dresses like bulky birds of paradise. Mad-men, mystics, blind men and beggars drift back and forth along the edge of MacCarthy Square, mumbling to themselves. Ragged little boys follow visitors about with cries of "Gimme penny mistah?" but they are not as persistent as in other African capi-tals, and are just as pleased with a few words of greeting.

On the sidewalks of Wellington Street, the main shopping center, traffic is heavy but slow: Serahuli petty traders with huge bolts of cloth for up-river shops; Bathurst women with baskets of vegetables from Albert Market on their heads; mysterious Mau-ritanians in white robes like unpressed sheets, carrying cartons of cigarettes to their little shops in the city. While the Gambian ambles, the Mauritanian glides as though on secret mission. A young man passes, wearing a T-shirt that proclaims PAMNASTIC — *World's Best Emulsion Paint.* Government officials slip out of their offices to shop during the cool of the morning. People stand at corners, rubbing their gums intently with chewing sticks (the toothbrush of West Africa) and gazing at the passing scene. Everyone stops often to chat with friends, for everyone knows nearly everyone else. The greetings are in many languages: Eng-lish ("Morning, morning. How de morning?" — "Fine, fine"), Arabic ("Salaam Aleikum" — "Aleikum Salaam"), Woloff ("Jambagam" — "Jambarek"), Mandinka ("Sumolay" — "Ibid-jay"). Every greeting goes through a long series of traditional ex-changes, for these are friendly, courteous people, with plenty of time.

To a visitor from the United States, Europe or even Dakar, one of the most charming surprises in Gambia is the informality of its government. At the crumbling Secretariat quadrangle, citizens lounge peacefully in corridors and outside offices, waiting for nothing in particular. Government messengers in khaki colonial uniforms amble from one office to another with files still bearing the British royal coat of arms, and marked "On Her Majesty's Service." Down below in the courtyard, uniformed chauffeurs slowly polish their ministers' black Zephyr sedans.

A government that runs at such a leisurely pace can offer personal service unrivaled in more prosperous and bustling countries. The visitor who stops his car to ask directions from one of the bicycle-mounted police officers may be escorted to his destination and receive a salute upon arrival. Gambians who have business with the government officials often wait till they happen to catch them shopping on Wellington Street, or relaxing in the lounge of the Atlantic Hotel. Unless some unforeseen problem arises, one can often call and make an appointment to see the Prime Minister the same day. One issue of the government's official *Gambia News Bulletin* instructed "the person who left a pair of sun glasses in the Prime Minister's office recently to please collect them from the Information Office." Shortly after I arrived, I stopped in at the Survey Department to buy some maps, and found myself with only a £5 note. The unruffled official there dispatched a messenger by bicycle to the bank for change. Five months later, while strolling down Wellington Street, the same official stopped to give me my receipt.

Though the government occasionally stands on ceremony, as all governments must from time to time, it does so with distinctively Gambian grace. When a new wooden ferry built by the Marine Department was to be christened, the Minister of Public Works, a devout Moslem, christened it with a bottle of locally brewed lemonade. A visiting American official, invited to dinner at Prime Minister David Jawara's home, was shocked when the

P.M. rose from the table and said, "Excuse me, I must go and relieve myself." He invited his guests to follow him and walked outside to the bushes at the edge of the garden. The American was unaware of the traditional British colonial custom called "going to see Africa," which dates back to the times when plumbing facilities at the best of colonial residences were too meager to accommodate the needs of a large assemblage. The practice is continued today in many ex-colonies partly out of nostalgia, and seems to have no ill effects on the flourishing gardens of the Prime Minister and the Governor General.

Commercial affairs in the city keep in step with both the pace and style of the government. Gambian women do most of their shopping either at the tiny neighborhood shops run by the Mauritanians, or at Albert Market, where despite the apparent bustle, they generally manage to spend several hours happily negotiating the purchase of a few onions, rice, peppers and a fresh bonga fish. European women who don't wish to buy their provisions at the open stalls of the market choose from the more sanitary, if less exotic, shelves of Kingsway, Chellerams or Maurel & Prom, the three stores that cater to their needs. Selection is often limited, for the stores receive their supplies only every few weeks by ship. Every six weeks, on the morning after the arrival of the *Apapa* from England (the only passenger and mail vessel stopping at Bathurst) British housewives line up early at Kingsway to get first crack at the frozen meats. Some of the goods in the shops have obviously been dropped off by mistake, though this does not seem to bother anyone. A visitor who noticed a television set on the counter of a dry goods store was startled, since Gambia has no plans for television in the near future. Asked whether the set was for display purpose only, the Gambian clerk replied, "Oh no, sah. He be for sale."

"Do you have television here in Gambia?"

"Oh no, sah, but he go come small time, with independence."

The shops and people who advertise their goods and services in *The Gambia News Bulletin* do so with a combination of British reserve and Gambian innocence that would horrify a Madison Avenue professional, but which suits perfectly the taste of their clientele. Actually, "Nice Things at Nice Prices at Vezia Fancy Shop" tells the reader everything he really needs to know. The open-air Verro Cinema out at Serrekunda advertised *The Bells of St. Mary* with this message: "Will you please come and see this wonderful film." One issue of the *Bulletin* announced the formation of Mr. Moses G. Leigh's New Age Construction Company, specializing in homes, graves and tombstones. "Mr. Leigh hereby informs the general public that he is now a licensed building contractor for the living and the dead." An ad in December informed "all ladies in Gambia" that "Wadad's Beauty Saloon has started work for hairdressing, setting, curling, stretching, dyeing and all treatments. Saloon opens all day at 3 Leman Street. Telephone 462. Please wash your hair at home until the pipes are ready."

Like the government, commercial services in Gambia function at a pleasantly informal level. To hire a taxi alone is both difficult and expensive. But if you are willing to wait until four other passengers arrive, you can make the 10-mile run out to Bakau or Serrekunda for only one shilling (15 cents). There is little reason to hurry, for things do not change very quickly here, and if someone has gone, they can not have gone very far. The taxi drivers, like most private entrepreneurs in Bathurst, make few long range plans, buying only one gallon of gas at the outset of each round trip.

The visitor who is alarmed when told there are no barbershops in the city is eventually delighted to discover that tonsorial service is more accessible than in any large metropolis. Most Bathurst barbers set up their mobile shops on the sidewalks around Mac-Carthy Square. Their shops consist of a few rusty implements and a folding stool. While these men cater mostly to the Gambian trade, a few barbers with more extensive equipment or experience go about the government and commercial offices to render more personal service to Europeans. When you see one of them pass by, you can call him up to cut your hair in your own home for a mere three and six-pence (50 cents). At the Atlantic Hotel, Kemo the barber appears every few days about noon, and sets up shop under a mango tree in the garden.

Facilities along the waterfront are in keeping with the rest of the city. At the ferry terminal for the 40-minute trip across the river, Gambians with produce from the market stand patiently in line, while Europeans fret at the ferry's haphazard schedule. If the ferry captain wishes to take a nap, or grab a bite to eat, everyone waits. At the Customs Wharf, only one freighter can tie up at a time. Other ships either wait at anchor in the harbor or continue down the coast, dropping the cargo for Bathurst off at the next port. There it sits until picked up by the next ship heading up the coast with space in its hold. Work on the quay proceeds at a leisurely pace partly because that is the normal pace of all work in Gambia, and partly because of the lack of mechanical assistance. A few years ago, when a new fire engine tender fell off the quay, it sat on the river bottom for six weeks until a large enough block and tackle arrived from England to pull it up.

\*

Bathurst social life may not equal that of Africa's more cosmopolitan capitals but it does have its carefully delineated rituals and customs. The Reform Club, founded in 1912, calls itself the oldest social club on the coast. Its members gather in the cheerful ramshackle hall each evening to play "snooker" pool, checkers, or darts, and stand over pints of cool Guinness or Tennants, trading the news of the day. As one of the city's oldest landmarks, as well as an institution of considerable political influence, it is honored by many visiting dignitaries, and by occasional visits from the Prime Minister and the Governor. Though ostensibly open to all Gambians, the Reform Club consists mostly of Akus, the light-skinned descendants of the freed slaves resettled in Freetown, Sierra Leone, around the turn of the nineteenth century. Until quite recently, because they were generally better educated than other Gambians, Bathurst's 3,000 Akus dominated the city and held most of the senior government positions open to Africans. As a small minority, however, they lost much of their political power with self-government and the extension of the franchise to the provinces, but they still hold many of the top civil service posts, and represent a cultural and social aristocracy.

Between their liberation and repatriation, many of the Akus' ancestors had worked for a time as footmen and valets in England, where they acquired habits difficult to continue upon their later return to Africa. Today's Akus still exhibit traces of their British heritage, and speak an English filled with such Victorianisms as "Don't humbug me, man." Aku elders stroll about town in formal black or soiled white double-breasted suits, black ties and battered Panama hats. They bear names like A. B. Able-Thomas, Horace Monday, William Small and Rosamond Fowlis. (Sierra Leone's Governor-General is an Aku named Sir Henry Lightfoot-Boston.)

Out at Serrekunda, ten miles from Bathurst, the Lebanese merchants and their families gather at the Cedar Club, while the British socialize at the Bathurst Club. Each institution has a few Gambian members. Despite the existence of the other two clubs, and to the slight annoyance of their members, the British refer to theirs simply as "The Club." Besides a bar, it has facilities for light meals, jukebox dancing, ping-pong, bridge and darts. Behind the club, along the Atlantic coast, a nine-hole golf course offers a challenging variety of sandy fairways and greens. Those who hook or slice into the adjoining swamps generally play another ball rather than contend with such occasional hazards as cobras and crocodiles. On the other side of the Club, a crumbling but playable squash court lies nearly hidden in a tangle of underbrush, like the ruin of an ancient civilization.

Despite these amenities, most of the 200 or so British living along the river's edge in Bathurst or on the coast out at suburban Bakau find the social life rather cramped. Many of the wives have little to do all day, since their houseboys, cooks, or garden boys do most of the work, and their children are generally at school in England. Bachelors spend much of their leisure time downing large bottles of Heinekens and Carlsburg at the lounge of the Atlantic Hotel. Faces at cocktail or dinner parties are always familiar, and there is considerable well-mannered rivalry over invitations to the Governor's occasional receptions at Government House. Guests invited to parties are informed in advance that there will be either "small chop" or "big chop" — hors d'oeuvres or dinner. On weekends the British sail, take picnic lunches to the fine beaches on the coast or go bird-watching. Bird fanciers in the colonial service consider Gambia a choice post, for it is a major wintering and passage region for more than 400 species, including such feathery exotica as bar-tailed godwits, long-tailed shags, buff-backed herons, spur-winged plovers, blue-cheeked bee-eaters, Abyssinian rollers and Barbary shrikes.

While the Reform, Cedar and Bathurst are the only visible clubs, the city abounds with others, whose members meet from time to time in various locations, hold dances and issue mimeographed bulletins. There is the Friendship Builders Society, Baah

Yai Social Circle, Women's Corona Society, Aljamiatu Hariatu Society, Congress Youth Wing, Tonya Youth Council, Kombo United Circle, Gambia Griots Society and Guinean Friendly Society, to name just a few. Their most common function seems to be holding dances, for every weekend there are usually several large public dances to choose from. When the Moslem holiday Tobaski approached, hand-printed posters appeared all over town, announcing:

> ATTENTION ATTENTION — Linaen Sports and Social Club, Chief Patron Kebba Foon Esq., and under the auspices of the GSSC — A GRAND DANCE to be held at UAC Tennis Lawn on Tobaski Day, between the hours of 9 P.M. and 4 A.M. Music will be supplied by the famous Eagles Jazz. This is surely going to be the DANCE OF THE YEAR. Please prepare to win the pachanga and twist medal prizes and also the best dressed gentleman.

Some clubs have more serious purposes, providing various services for the community. According to one issue of *The Gambian News Bulletin*, "A large group of members of the Women's Corona Society recently had an interesting afternoon at the Wellingara Ox-Ploughing School when the Director of Agriculture took them on the Farm Walk." Other groups sponsor dramatic and musical events. In April 1965, the Gambia Music Festival Society presented a concert of performers from all the schools of the city. Featured on the program were "Now is the Month of Maying," by the Senior Choir, a recorder solo by Saihou N'Jie, Percussion Band and Traditional Songs, by the Methodist Preparatory School, Scottish Country Dances, performed by students of St. Augustine's and St. Joseph's, a harmonica solo by Charles Jallow, and the Intermediate Choir singing "A Dairymaid was Milking."

Music is highly popular throughout the country, and any occa-

sion is sufficient to schedule drumming and dancing. In Bathurst, Beatles records sell briskly, and listeners to Radio Gambia
regularly write in requests for their favorite songs. Shortly before
independence, Gambia's Top Ten, as published in the *Bulletin*,
were "Kano," "Massanneh Ceesay," "Oubil Ma Ya Boi," "Mali-
gundo," "My Boy Lollipop," "Salimito Mina Lahda," "I Need
You," "Merengue Heartbeats," "Julietta" and "Tiemseng." Six
months after independence, students of Gambian culture noted
that "My Boy Lollipop" and "I Need You" were no longer
among the Top Ten.

Along with club activities, young Gambians lead an active social life. So active, in fact, that Bathurst is beset by some of the
problems normally associated only with more developed countries. While teen-age morals seem to be a problem everywhere
these days, and Bathurst's are probably no more critical than
other cities', for some reason a rash of articles and letters appeared on the subject around the time of independence. *The
New Gambia*, organ of the ruling People's Progressive Party, ran
the following letter in October:

> It has been observed that the immoral behavior of some of our
> girls especially in Bathurst is becoming rampant. Nowadays girls
> are not out for better Education or thinks of their future, but
> rather engage in collecting money by living a prostitute life. Bath-
> urst is too small for such a thing to happen and even though if
> it is a large town, is a thing that should not be encouraged.
>
> Mr. X, as by a correspondent, he now have a prostitute home
> for young girls between the age of 15 to 19, where a man could go
> and have a go for 10 shillings [$1.40] and pay an extra 10 shil-
> lings for his duty as manager of the affair. This is a thing that
> cannot be tolerated in Bathurst, and I will strongly recommend
> to the, say, Commissioner of Police to see that such a thing is
> stop before it becomes widen. . . .
>
> — CORRESPONDENT

*The New Gambia's* editors assured readers that "more facts on this will appear in our next issue. Let's beware less what happen Sodom and Gomorah befalls us."

Few visitors would think Bathurst's nightlife worthy of divine wrath. Besides the peaceful lounge of the Atlantic, there are only a few informal jukebox bars like the Black Star and Louisette's, generously referred to as "night clubs." Somehow, though, they managed to stir the ire of *The New Gambia's* editorialist:

> The Gambia Police Force is actually busy these past nights raiding Bars and pubs, raking out teenage girls. At these Bars, some mean men with money in their pockets to spend on drinks despite the fact that they have a lot of bills to settle, lay wait like a crocodile, their prey the young girls to exploit their virtues. The society now has some officious and forward-looking girls whose regard for prestige and their person is non-existent.

When asked about this problem, one student at Gambia High School said it all starts with the dating system. "Many girls, when you ask them to a dance, will insist that you buy them a dress. Some girls get gifts of money from competing suitors. The boys give them a pound or so whenever they can. A very popular girl can make up to ten or twenty pounds a month. I know one girl who got a fridge, a tape recorder and a radio from different men."

A bright young Woloff teacher said the problem was peculiar to girls of his tribe:

> These girls who get in trouble are all Woloff girls. They do these things more than any other. These immoral practices are not part of the Mandinka girls, and the Aku girls don't go to these jazz dances. They are under very strict parental control. They could never come home with a new dress like the Woloff girls do.

These things start at the dances. After the dance, you take the girl to your compound and do what you like with her. Many mothers in this town, if I give her five pounds, I can sleep with her daughter in her compound.

One reason why moral standards are shaky is that, like many cities in the world today, Bathurst has been absorbing an increasingly large influx from small villages and towns in the interior. These people arrive with tribal and regional customs of their own, and little knowledge of those of the city. Many of the customs of the village are unworkable in the city, and money takes on an importance unknown in the village. Faced with confusion, villagers and townsmen who arrive in Bathurst generally try to find homes in compounds shared by fellow villagers, townsmen, or at least tribesmen. Young men return to their former villages or towns to choose their wives, partly through custom, and partly through ignorance and fear of the rituals and expense of urban courtship.

*

Along with looking after the morals of teen-age girls, Bathurst's courteous and relatively well-trained policemen busy themselves with the routine duties of law enforcement common to all cities. The great majority of crimes involve petty theft or embezzlement, for Gambians in general have not yet acquired a taste for alcohol or narcotics, and their normally placid nature makes violence a rarity. Criminals at large rarely remain at large for long, for unless they leave Gambia they can not go far. Bathurst is small enough to make seclusion difficult, and strangers are quickly noticed in any up-river village or town.

Backing up the police in case of riots (rare) or parades (frequent) is the Gambia Field Force, a 150-man group that specializes in close drill, performs at most public ceremonies and guards

Government House. The men of the Field Force fought during World War II in Ethiopia and Burma, but their only action in recent years was a riot in Bathurst in 1961, which most observers called a draw between the Force and the ragged rioters. The Field Force musketry team sees action more regularly, competing in the annual East and West African Police Rifle Shooting Competition — which it won in 1962 — and launching occasional campaigns against Gambia's prolific bush pigs.

Except in serious criminal cases, when the Solicitor General may step in, police officers or constables handle the prosecution in most trials. This system has some defects, according to one high official: "Ten years ago, the Superintendents or Assistant Superintendents, who had some legal training, used to handle most of the prosecutions. Now they're all bloody field marshals, and you can't get anyone with a 'pip' on his shoulder to show his face in court. They send in bloody sergeants or corporals who are not particularly learned in the law. In fact many of them are barely literate."

Along with cases arising in the city itself, Bathurst courts also review and hear appeals from up-river cases held before Division Commissioners and the "district Tribunals" run by the chiefs. Such review is frequently necessary, for the chiefs and village elders often render judgments at variance with accepted judicial procedure. In one rape case, for example, a district tribunal ordered the rapist to pay fines of ten shillings to the offended girl, ten shillings to the girl's father for "damages" and thirty shillings to the owner of the house whose door the impetuous youth had broken down in his precipitous entry. Upon review by the magistrate in Bathurst, the fines were termed "nonsense," and the case retried.

When sentenced to jail terms, convicted criminals enter a prison two miles outside Bathurst known as Mile Two. Here, the 90-100 inmates while away their time planting vegetable and flower gardens, and doing occasional odd jobs of manual labor. They receive a stipend of two shillings (28 cents) a month for their efforts — one for cigarettes and the other to be banked toward their departure. Like most public institutions in Gambia, Mile Two is an informal affair. Prisoners drift casually about the attractive grounds on both sides of the wall, and admittance can be gained simply by knocking on the prison gate. Escapes are rare, for many of the inmates are better off than they were "on the outside." They receive three meals a day, have decent quarters, and the work is not strenuous. For the most part, they find life at Mile Two pleasant, and their main regret is that their families are not able to join them.

As a rule, prisoners at Mile Two are courteous, friendly, and well above average in education, being mostly commercial clerks or minor government officials in for embezzlement (known as "fiddling"). Their unofficial leader is a good-looking, charming fellow named Andrew, who, because he is more literate than many of the prison staff, and has spent more time there, assists in its administration. He also serves as a guide for visitors and acts as spokesman for his colleagues. He is an excellent auto mechanic, an ability so rare in Gambia that prison officials and other government employees regularly bring him their cars for repairs.

On a visit to Mile Two, I found life there quite tranquil. A Mauritanian in for attempting to bribe a policeman was watering the prison yard. A huge black Woloff from Senegal, who had stolen some cloth from a shop, was shadowboxing against the prison wall. There was a clerk from the Ministry of Local Government, the executive secretary of the Brikama Area Council and an official of the Gambia Workers Union, all in for "fiddling" with funds. Doudou N'Jie, a dock worker, was serving four years for stealing from a ship, and Falla Aliou was serving three for stowing away on one. A gentleman named Aliou Jobe announced proudly, "I am French. I'm from Dakar. I am here only on a little vacation." Asked how he happened to choose Mile Two for a vacation, he replied, "Well, there was this little affair about a bracelet, and they arrested me." A bright young man named Saihou Ceesay asked whether I thought he should study economics at Harvard or Moscow's Friendship University, upon his departure. When I asked what training he had had in economics, he said he had been a clerk at the Bank of West Africa in Bathurst, and was serving time for embezzlement. He was sure the warden would recommend him for a scholarship. An old man named Moise said, "Before I come here I be trader. I buy 'em plenty goods in Senegal and sell 'em in Gambia. Den I buy goods here in Bathurst and sell 'em in Senegal. I buy 'em and I sell 'em." Moise wound up at Mile Two because one time he forgot to buy 'em.

Communicating with the citizenry of a town the size of Bathurst might not seem much of a problem to an outsider, but there are limitations peculiar to this city. Few Gambians can read, although the percentage is much higher in Bathurst than the 5 to 10 per cent literacy for the country as a whole. Since inexpensive Japanese transistor radios have spread more rapidly than literacy, and have far greater appeal than school to a youth newly arrived from the provinces, Radio Gambia has an immense importance in the dissemination of news and the education of the public. For this reason, the government recently increased the station's broadcasting time from two to three hours daily. Any more would stretch beyond their capacity the station's human and technical facilities. This became evident recently, when the Gambian station director (who serves under the guidance of a British adviser) had to turn down a study grant from the United States because there was no one to take his place.

During the day, transistors tune in to Radio Senegal, from Dakar, which carries mostly French and Arab music. On a typical Tuesday evening Radio Gambia offers the following program: 5:20, Juke Box; 6:00, BBC World News Bulletin; 6:10, National News in English, Woloff and Mandinka; 6:45, Group "Jamma Baah Chi Rew"; 7:15, Cleanliness; 7:30, Serahuli and Fula music; 8:00, BBC World News Bulletin; 8:10, Gambia Crackers.

For those who can read, or who do not have radios, *The Gambia News Bulletin*, which appears three times a week, prints the same news heard on Radio Gambia. Visitors know they are far from home when they find foreign affairs under the heading, "News from the Outside World." The government uses the pages of the *Bulletin* to announce appointments, vacancies, auctions, ministers' tours up-river, sailings of the river vessel *Lady Wright* and various other messages of public interest. During the Christmas season, a notice informed readers that "Drumming during the Christmas holidays will be permitted after 8 A.M. up to 12 o'clock midnight on the following days . . . No drumming will be allowed near any place of worship or the Royal Victoria Hospital." In the spring, when a mango glut flooded the city, the public was "requested not to throw discarded mango peel on the footpath or roads, but to dispose of it in refuse bins, etc. Not only is the indiscriminate disposal of mango peel disgusting, but it can involve the danger of accidents to pedestrians and vehicles, particularly to cyclists."

The *Bulletin* also serves as the city's lost and found center, informing the public that "Mr. I. A. Jarboh of Serrekunda village lost a Mauritanian sheep, white in color with black mark on the back," and that "a second-hand refrigerator has been found at No. 6 Rankin Street, Bathurst. Will the owner please report to the Bathurst Police Station." Occasionally, the journal's editors seem doubtful about the literacy of their readers. When the Gambia High Commission in London moved to its new quarters, the *Bulletin* ran the following announcement: "THE HIGH COMMISSIONER FOR THE GAMBIA, LONDON — New Address — The High Commissioner for the Gambia, London, has a new address. It is: — The High Commissioner for the Gambia, London, The Gambia House, 28 Kensington Court, London, W. 8, England."

As an official government publication, the *Bulletin* carries no editorials. The PPP's mimeographed weekly, *The New Gambia,* does, but never attacks the PPP-ruled administration. Shortly before independence, a new four-page monthly appeared, called *The Nation.* Along with urgent appeals for donations to help continue its existence, it ran several editorials and letters attacking government policy. The editorials were strident, left-of-center, and given to the upper case when discussing MORAL ISSUES. In succeeding numbers, *The Nation* recommended improvements in various ministries, and urged the government to "launch a massive illiteracy campaign on a small scale." Along with these publications, there is also *The Gambia Echo,* a six-page, poorly printed weekly with a circulation of several hundred copies, depending on the state of its finances. Front page articles in a recent issue gave the results of a Ladies Cycling Club race and described the Bathurst City Council's new coat of arms. Ads for patent medicines featured prominently throughout the paper, and half the front page was devoted to an ad for "Antepar," a roundworm expeller "proved safe and effective by millions of healthy and successful people throughout the world."

Besides newspapers, radio and word of mouth — called "bush telegraph" — there is one other form of communication which seems to be on the increase: writing on sidewalks, streets and walls. Anyone possessing a piece of chalk and political opinions unsuitable for more formal publication can easily spread them about the city with an hour's work at night. Such opinions customarily run along the lines of JOHN PAUL GO HOME or D. K. JAWARA GO BACK TO YOUR OWN COUNTRY. These scribblers have competition from high school students who, because of a lack of space and light at home, often study in the evenings under the street lights. Also lacking paper, they do their addition and subtraction on the pavement. Then there are those with less lofty aims, such as the person who scrawled in yellow crayon on the walls of the Methodist Bookshop: ASSAN CHAM IS A BASTER.

## ENTER GAMBIA

As INDEPENDENCE drew near, the government busied itself in equipping the country with the usual accouterments of nationhood. It offered prizes of £50 ($140) each in contests for a national flag, a coat of arms, and a national anthem. The winning design for the flag, selected from more than 400 entries, called for horizontal stripes of red, blue and green. A draftsman with the Survey Department submitted the winning design for Gambia's coat of arms, which was then prepared by England's College of Heralds. It shows two rampant lions leaning against a shield, looking angry, and standing on a banner which reads: PROGRESS PEACE PROSPERITY. Each carries in one paw a local all-purpose agricultural implement known as a coop-coop. Two of these crude ax-like instruments are also crossed upon the shield. Above the shield sits the usual visored helmet, but instead of the usual bent plumes, the helmet is topped by a peanut plant.

Mr. J. F. Howe, a former British administrative officer, wrote the new Gambia National Anthem, with lyrics by Mrs. Howe. He took the music from a popular Mandinka song, "Foday Kabba Dumbuya." Foday Kabba is revered by Gambians as a powerful nineteenth-century Mandinka ruler, while British historians describe him as a ruthless marauder whose fervor for the new Muslim religion led him to forcibly convert or ravage pagan villages.

The words of the new anthem are:

> *For The Gambia, our homeland*
> *We strive and work and pray,*
> *That all may live in unity,*
> *Freedom and peace each day.*
>
> *Let Justice guide our actions*
> *Toward the common good,*
> *And join our diverse peoples*
> *To prove man's brotherhood.*
>
> *We pledge our firm allegiance*
> *Our promise we renew;*
> *Keep us, great God of nations*
> *To The Gambia ever true.*

This entry by Mr. Howe won out over such contenders as the following, written by The Reverend J. C. Faye, a Gambian political leader, Anglican cleric and former High Commissioner to London:

> *Thy river gently flows,*
> *Palms feath'ry fronds do wave*
> *Small thou art, small may be.*
> *Bless'd thou art! For from thee*
> *Days gone by greater lands*
> *Bless'd were they through thy toil.*
>
> *Gambia Good-will land,*
> *O Koras sweetly ring:*
> *Gambia: Gambia: God bless our Fatherland.*

While Bathurst's educated citizenry quickly learned their new anthem, the rest never quite mastered the words. A simpler independence song spread spontaneously among these others, with neither prize nor publicly acknowledged composer. A merengue, it has only one verse, in Woloff, which is repeated indefinitely. As roughly translated by a Gambian hotel steward, it goes:

> Make him God bless Gambia go front./ David Jawara, you trying very hard your own part get Gambia independent.

One item among the independence trappings for which the government did not have to run a contest was a new name. Some of the other emerging African nations have dramatized their independence by discarding their European names for African ones — i.e., Nyasaland, which became Malawi. Gambia has always been Gambia, give or take a bit of variety in pronunciation (Gambo, Gambra, Gamboa, Gambea) as the Portuguese, Dutch, Spanish, French and English successively altered the original African version. A problem did arise over names early in 1964, when the administration learned that Northern Rhodesia, which was about to become independent, planned to adopt the name "Zambia." Foreseeing confusion, colonial officials in Gambia wrote to their counterparts in Northern Rhodesia suggesting as tactfully as possible that they consider a different name. The effort got nowhere. Ever since, mail for Radio Gambia has gone to Radio Zambia in Lusaka, and packages for Zambia Airways have wound up in Bathurst at the Gambia Airways office.

While Gambian officials did not have to find a new name, they did have to make one unpopular change. Upon independence, as in other Commonwealth countries, the House of Representatives would become the House of Parliament, and all Members of Parliament other than cabinet ministers would cease to be addressed as "The Honorable . . ." and would instead be addressed as "Mr.————, M.P." Although each Member received instructions explaining the reasons for the change, many of them resented losing their "Honorable" titles. One senior

British adviser commented, "It will reduce their credit down-town by 50 per cent." With characteristic adaptability, however, Gambians adjusted to the ruling by ignoring it, and continue to call all Members "Honorable."

The administration had much more trouble with the invitations to the various independence ceremonies. Rabid nationalists complained that British officials were organizing all the festivities, and spread a false rumor that three quarters of the invitations would be going to non-Gambians. Uninvited Gambians and British swamped the officials in charge of invitations with phone calls and letters pleading for or demanding special consideration. One evening, a senior Gambian official walked into Prime Minister Jawara's home, demanded a drink, and complained that although a bachelor, he deserved two invitations so that he could bring his mistress. Three weeks before the ceremonies began, an anonymous reader sent a protest to *The New Gambia*, the PPP's paper, claiming that "this occasion is for the Gambians and Gambians only should therefore have best part of the invitations for all ceremonies."

> There is a massive body of opinion quarrelling about the exclusion of notable Gambians and inclusion of men who had not contributed even an iota of effort in the National struggle towards INDEPENDENCE. The people now struggling to swamp and take a leading part in all the ceremonies were born free and had had their own days, and there was no fuss-making on the side of the Gambians to eclipse them . . . The Leaders we have no doubt will look into this matter with a view to regularise the situation.
>
> GAMBIA FOR GAMBIANS

The invitations to other countries caused a good deal of turmoil because the normal delicacy of diplomatic protocol was compounded by Bathurst's meager housing capacity. With only one small hotel, the government was forced to limit state invitations severely. First in priority came Gambia's fellow members of the Commonwealth: Australia, Canada, Great Britain, New Zealand, India, Pakistan, Malaysia, Ghana, Nigeria, Sierra Leone, Kenya, Tanzania, Malawi, Uganda and Zambia. Next came some of Gambia's West African neighbors: Senegal, Mali, Mauritania, Morocco, Guinea and Liberia. After these, the invitations seem to have been distributed with a long hard look at potential sources of foreign aid — West Germany, France, Israel, Italy, Russia, United Arab Republic and the United States — plus a glance at diplomacy: Ethiopia (a leader in the Organization of African Unity); Lebanon (Gambia has a sizable Lebanese merchant community); and the Vatican (you always invite the Vatican to such affairs).

Along with these countries, each of whom sent at least two people, representatives also came from the United Nations, the World Health Organization, UNICEF, the UN Food and Agriculture Organization, United Africa Company, Elder Dempster Lines, British United Airways and the Bank of West Africa, Ltd. Among the government's most distinguished guests were five of Gambia's former governors. Many private guests appeared also, some of them invited. The government commandeered the Atlantic Hotel for the entire week, turning out its half-dozen long-term residents to fend for themselves. With more than thirty state delegations arriving, along with the Duke and Duchess of Kent and many other official guests, the fifty rooms of the Atlantic were hardly sufficient. Though Kamal Milky, a Lebanese merchant, rushed his new Adonis Hotel to completion, the government still had to "request" senior officials with spare rooms to put someone up during the festivities.

Much of the burden of such problems fell upon the man in charge of the celebrations, Deputy Governor Paul Gore, a tall,

lean, moustached veteran of seventeen years in the colonial service in Uganda and Mauritius. "It's going to be simply frantic,"
said Gore. "Very, very difficult. We have to do the whole business on a shoestring." He explained that the total budget for the
celebrations was $140,000, one half of which was a grant from
Great Britain. Asked how he decided which countries to invite,
he replied, "Well, we went through the list of countries and tried
to cut the number down to a workable lot. Then we — the
Gambian government, I mean — sent out the invitations. The
trouble is, some of the African nations are not averse to inviting
themselves, or requesting invitations. We tried to keep each of
the smaller countries to one delegate only, but some of them
have written back to say they'll be bringing their wives, their secretaries, and other officials. Really, it's impossible!"

Gore explained that upon independence, Gambia would
change from a self-governing colony to a "Constitutional Monarchy" — an independent state recognizing the nominal authority
of the Queen, represented by a Governor-General. According to
custom, the present Governor, Sir John Paul, would assume the
title of Governor-General. Asked what Sir John's current duties
were, Gore replied, "Well, as the personal representative of Her
Majesty, he wears feathers in his hat, opens bazaars, and attends
parades. You know, all that sort of thing. Theoretically, he tells
them what they can do, and what they can't do. If they decide
to declare war on the United States, he'll tell them, 'No, you
can't do that.' Of course, after independence, they can do as
they please. They can even declare war on the United States."
This prospect amused Mr. Gore.

While the government was busy making official preparations,
individual Gambians did what they could to get ready. The government worried a bit about this, for prior to the self-government
celebrations in 1963, there had been a few unfortunate incidents.

In some villages, PPP supporters with odd notions about the meaning of self-government had run amok, burning huts and attempting to appropriate farms belonging to United Party supporters. Some had even come down to select compounds in the capital, unnerving Bathurst residents who found them peering intently into their homes. This time, however, calm prevailed. The only incident that caused trouble was the sudden appearance of fresh coats of white paint on hundreds of small Bathurst houses. Officials traced the paint to the Public Works Department, which reported fifty gallons of whitewash missing. The culprit turned out to be the municipal sign painter, but he was not arrested. "What could we do?" said one British officer. "We still have dozens of 'ladies' and 'gentlemen' [public rest rooms] to paint up around town for the celebrations. And he's the only man we've got."

Nearly every woman had to have a new dress for the ceremonies, many of them buying the new Gambian Independence cloth that began to flood the local market. This printed material, in a variety of gay colors, displays the benign features of Prime Minister Jawara, along with appropriate Gambian scenes and inscription such as GAMBIAN INDEPENDENCE 1965 or PEACE PROGRESS PROSPERITY. Men and women alike sported apparel made from this cloth. Up-river, crafty traders with unused stocks from previous African independence celebrations sold grateful Gambian villagers dress material bearing the faces of Sékou Touré of Guinea, Kenneth Kaunda of Zambia, and the late Patrice Lumumba of the Congo. A New Yorker who had visited Gambia a few months before received this letter from a boy he had met briefly on the street in Bathurst:

I have the greatest pleasure to write you this letter asking you Whether you can buy me two shirts and one short for our Independence celebration in the gambia in 18 eighteen of February

1965. please If I can have it, please will you Reply to me. Because I think you all are in home safely I think nothing strange at
home. I am giving all my Compliment to all the families at
home.


Prisoners at Mile Two got up a petition to the Prime Minister for a general amnesty upon independence. "Now that the
country is independent," said one inmate, "everyone should be
free." While there was some talk in government circles about an
amnesty for political prisoners, only one inmate seemed to qualify on political grounds, and his was a doubtful case. He had set
fire to the Speaker's chair in the House, and was picked up the
following evening playing with matches outside Government
House. Uncertain of his sanity or motives, the court decided his
political activities could be more safely supervised at Mile Two.

Every evening, in the lounge of the Atlantic, the old Africa
hands among the British commercial community discussed
Gambia's imminent statehood over peanuts and pints of cold
beer. "They've gone bloody balmy with this independence
business," said one gnarled veteran of two decades on the coast.
"We've nearly lost control at the firm. You can't get anything
out of them any more. If you say anything to them they tell you
to watch your step, 'cause independence is coming."

"The educated Gambians in Bathurst don't want independence," said a companion. "It's the illiterate people out in the
bush who want it. [Neither statement was true. This gentleman had acquired most of his opinions on the subject from
equally ill-informed colleagues who had little contact with Gambians from either Bathurst or upriver.] They've been promised
jobs and money by the PPP when independence comes, and
they'll be lining up at the bank the next morning, waiting for the
vault to open. They just don't understand. Some figure they

can't be any worse off than they are now, so they're for it. I was for it myself, three years ago, but not now."

When an American visitor brought up the possibility of foreign aid to help Gambia get started, the first Englishman broke in: "You American blokes or the Russians can come in and do all you want. You'll never civilize these people. Maybe three out of every hundred you can do something with. The rest are bushmen, and they'll always be bushmen."

An up-river British colonial official who had joined the group said that the Americans did not have to worry, for England would most likely continue to pay the foreign aid bill. "You know, these people still expect us to pay them back for what we did to them hundreds of years ago. None of them here now were around then, and none of us were either. But it's a good way for them to extort money out of us."

"What do you think about the prospects for independence?"

"I don't know. You see, this is a never-never land. The boys I worry about are the twenty-five pound [$70] a year farmers. They're a good lot, and I'm very fond of them. I wouldn't give tuppence for these half-baked politicians here in Bathurst. They've just dropped down out of the trees and they want to Gambianize everything."

*

In January, three weeks before independence, the government called a special session of Parliament to pass new laws on citizenship, immigration and naturalization, and to provide the Administration and other Members of the House a public opportunity to voice their sentiments at this historic moment. In reading the new laws, Attorney General Philip Bridges, the only British Member of the Cabinet, apologized for their complexity, and summarized them as simply as possible for the impassive faces before him. Only once was he interrupted by a question from the floor, when he mentioned that the new immigration law would prohibit the entry of "prostitutes or people living from such practice."

"How are we going to know when someone is a prostitute?" asked one Member.

"The Honorable Member has no cause for anxiety," replied Bridges. "It will be up to the discretion of the Principal Immigration Officer. If he carries his investigation too far, it would be considered indiscretion."

The first speaker of the evening was Howsoon Ousman Semega-Janneh, former Minister of Agriculture, who had a word of "advice" for the commercial firms in Bathurst which, he assumed, were planning to make independence gifts to the government. From the United Africa Company, whose local British manager sat across the hall, Mr. Janneh hoped for "at least £50,000 [$140,000] in cash or kindness. Such a wealthy firm should set an example for the others." To the five French trading firms operating in Gambia, he said, "We do not want just a saucer with De Gaulle's photograph." For the Lebanese firm of S. Madi Ltd., owners of the Atlantic Hotel, Gambia Construction Company, the larger of the two peanut oil mills and many other local enterprises, Mr. Janneh also had a word of advice: "I know the Lebanese — they are broad-minded people. Let their gift be one that will be remembered by generations of Gambians yet unborn."

Kalilou Singhateh, a left-of-center PPP Member from Lower Baddibu, proclaimed that "free from the shackles of imperialism and colonialism, we shall join the free nations of the world." He felt that most of Gambia's problems were due to English misrule: "The legacy that the British government has left in this country is not a good one, not honorable at all." In view of this, he lamented what he took to be the fact that 300 Englishmen had been invited to the Independence State Ball and only 35 Gambians. He was joined in this complaint by Momodou Cham, who at 27 was the youngest Member of the House. "It is Gambia's independence!" yelled the Honorable Mr. Cham. "Gambians should have priority. All these expatriates are invited to all these functions. This should not be. It is Gambians who should be at the center of things. We have been so long under colonialism that these things are now insults."

In reply to these complaints, Prime Minister Jawara explained that the majority of the guests at the State Ball would be Gambians. He pointed out that "three hundred thousand Gambians can not come to the State Ball. Do we want to have the celebrations by ourselves? We would then miss the significance of the ceremony. It would detract from the celebrations if outsiders did not come and take part. Remember, we will be judged not by the measure of our jubilation, but by the energy we bring to solving the problems of independence."

Mr. Alphonso Demba, Member for suburban Bakau Constituency, drew laughter from the audience — whose reactions were unpredictable throughout the session — by attempting a "quote from Christian Bible. Jesus say . . ." Mr. Demba unfortunately forgot what Jesus had said. Some time before, he had written his thoughts about approaching independence to an American official who had stopped briefly in Bathurst:

As is known by the World news, our constitutional advance was successful by attainment of Full internal self government. Gambia was backward but will be perhaps one of the most advance places in Africa for the good hope we have and determination of purpose. For its size and population many many thinks it is so forth. However, the inhabitants of the country are naturally

unique by most human level. I do not bother into details but
even the English whose rule the Gambia is perhaps do not fully
well know this people. I can better conceive of something than
what I should express in this letter.

This evening, standing before the House, Mr. Demba was still
unafraid of Gambia's independent future: "We should have
confidence in ourselves. We have been well-schooled by our colonial rulers." Mr. Demba did have one final request to make of
those rulers:"Can not Great Britain give us something that
could, in one or two years, bring us to equal development with
the rest of the developing countries?"

The next speaker was the Honorable M. D. Sallah, former
headmaster of Armitage School (the only secondary school up-
river). Mr. Sallah is noted for his long-winded, florid ramblings
and effusive praise of the Prime Minister. He began by thank-
ing the P.M. for guiding the country to independence, pointing
out that "the Almighty God chose the Honorable Prime Minister." Then, launching into his main discourse, he said, "In just
over twenty days, this country will *emerge*. We are going into
independence with a deficit in our budget and with great dependence on the United Kingdom. We must fill this gap." He
offered no suggestions on how to do this other than exhorting his
countrymen to "work harder."

As Mr. Sallah began to warm up, he gave the impression that
his speech might well be a lengthy one. Sensing this, the
Speaker of the House, A. Sam Jack, declared the House in recess
until after dinner. When the session reopened later, Mr. Sallah
launched into a detailed analysis of the Cold War, and gave a
highly imaginative view of Gambia's role in it. Referring to the
speech of a colleague who had urged the country to cease its dependence on the West and turn to the East, Sallah claimed,
"When all is said and done, the West are our best friends. I

think we should throw in our lot with the West, not the East."
(As yet, no nation from "the East" has made any attempt to
woo Gambia and its steady budget deficit away from "the
West.") In a nimble appeal to every shade of Gambian nationalism, Sallah said that he had "no room for expatriate officers
who are redundant, but most are honest and we want them to
stay, at least for the time being." He quoted a passage from Lincoln's Gettysburg Address, and concluded, "Let us not go into
independence with any bitterness of the past. We deserve it,
and we are getting it."

The question of British ex-colonial officials serving as advisers
to the government drew considerable heated comment. One
Member felt "it is high time we replaced all expatriate officers,"
while others urged caution. Minister of Education, Paul Baldeh,
the only M.P. besides the Prime Minister with a university degree, said that too many expatriates were still taking up jobs that
should go to Gambians. "Every suitably qualified Gambian has
a right to be employed in this country. In short, we should make
Gambianization a reality, a practice." Prime Minister Jawara
rose and cautioned the advocates of rapid Gambianization, saying, "Unless we have enough qualified Gambians to go around,
we should not be in a hurry to replace expatriates."

Several Members of the House felt that with independence
" 'round the corner" the government should explain what it
means to the villagers up-river via Radio Gambia. One of them
said, "Many in the provinces think independence means sitting
down on the 'bantaba.' " (A bantaba is a raised wooden platform on which village elders recline in moments of leisure.)
None of these members offered their own explanations of what
independence meant. One also insisted that the government
make its stand quite clear on the Congo without stating his
own. In reply, the Prime Minister stated, "we don't know

enough about what is going on in the Congo to have a position
on it."

As a succession of Members recommended numerous ways in
which money should be spent on their districts, the audience
began to drift out. By 10:00 P.M., those remaining were either
dozing or feigning various poses of somnolent attention. Up-
river Members generally complained that the government neglected the provinces in favor of the glittering capital. One of
them grew excessively irate as he considered the injustice of it all,
which he attributed vaguely to the continuing colonial influence.
"I am not crazy," he said. "I am talking something very sensible. Each time I ask questions, always 'No funds.' I think funds
will be available after independence."

P. S. N'Jie, the Woloff leader of the Opposition United Party,
rose with a page of notes full of red and blue doodles, twisting his
multi-colored pen in his hand. He promised that the United
Party would cooperate fully with the Administration during the
forthcoming celebrations. "Entering into independence is entering into the unknown," he said. "There will be fear, especially
among our cousins in neighboring countries." Although he was
glad to see the end of colonial rule, he warned against "exchanging one set of masters for another," concluding, "The old order
changeth, yielding place to new."

About 11:30, Prime Minister Jawara rose to give the final
speech of the evening. "Each one of us knows that there is a lot
to be done in the fields of development — education, agriculture, communications, housing, medical services, et cetera.
With the continued help of the British government, and of
other friendly countries, we shall hope to find the means to improve the lot of all our countrymen. As I have said, the task will
not be easy. Independence brings with it new complex problems
which henceforth we shall have to resolve on our own. But we

shall be sustained by the goodwill of friendly nations, and for this reason I look forward to the future with confidence." He urged every carpenter, mason, farmer, civil servant and daily worker to work harder, now that Gambia was to be independent, and hoped that "in time, Gambia will prove that a small country can stand on its own feet, and play its own part in world affairs by providing an example of stability and progress and good sense."

*

Reporters and photographers began drifting into Bathurst the weekend before things got underway. The "foreign press" consisted of correspondents for the Associated Press, Reuters, *The New York Times*, *Newsweek*, London's *Daily Express*, *Daily Telegraph*, and the weekly, *West Africa*, plus camera teams from CBS and BBC television. The Eastern bloc was represented by gentlemen from Czechoslovakia's and Hungary's state news agencies. Rumors circulated during the week that two men from Peking were in town, but if so, they remained well hidden. There were assorted correspondents for various African publications, and several Gambians of the local journalistic community. Since the Atlantic Hotel was already booked to well over capacity, the government arranged to house the press downtown in "Madi Flats," a small, temporarily vacant apartment building on Wellington Street. By the time the thirty-odd journalists had been crammed into it, the building resembled a pre-game college locker room. The Europeans and Americans, accustomed to more lush quarters, spent their first moments here in a state of shock, unwilling to believe that Bathurst had only one hotel. Depression was temporary, for soon they scared up a few dirty tumblers and broke out the Scotch. The veteran Africa hands exchanged gossip about colleagues in the Congo, and compared notes on who had attended the most independence celebrations.

Several of the Africans who arrived late, and were given cots in the crowded outer rooms, made threatening noises about discrimination, but nothing came of it.

Late Sunday afternoon, George Peters, the government's Information Officer, called a press conference. Known locally as "Capt'n Peters," he is, by general agreement and his own admission, one of Gambia's characters. A jovial, rotund, teddy bear of a man, Peters first came to Gambia early in World War II as a supply officer with the Royal West African Frontier Force. After the war, he stayed on as Information Officer and editor of the government's *Gambia News Bulletin*, a post and function he had performed steadily for nearly 20 years. According to local legend, he once brought fame to himself and Gambia by riding home to England on a motorcycle.

This Sunday afternoon, Capt'n Peters stood in the new Information Office, briefing the press. He diagrammed on a blackboard the routes and layouts of various processions and events, and passed out sheets of mimeographed instructions and background information about the Duke and Duchess, the "P.M.," the Governor and members of the Cabinet. He said that the major event of the following day would be the Civic Welcome for the Duke and Duchess at Gambia High School. "We have no town hall, you see. It's a couple of huts. So we use the next best building we've got — that's the high school. The band will play, and that sort of thing, and H.R.H. [His Royal Highness] will make a speech. Catch him before he opens his mouth if you please, you photographers. He's a bit chinless, and he tends to leave his lower jaw hanging open."

When several reporters asked for advance copies of the Duke's speech, Peters informed them that "higher authority" had decided against advance copies of any speeches during the week's activities.

"That's ridiculous!" said Lloyd Garrison of *The New York Times*. "There's not an independent state in all of Africa that's done that. What's the reason for the policy?"

"In case there's a change from the text," replied Peters.

"But that's exactly why we want advance copies. If we don't have them we won't know."

"The point's well taken. I'll see what I can do."

Walter Martens, a German free-lance television cameraman based in Lagos and here for BBC-TV, asked if someone could guard his cameras and equipment at the high school while he was out at the airport covering the arrival of the Duke and Duchess. Capt'n Peters told him he didn't have enough people for that, but that he might be able to have a policeman "keep an eye on them." When Martens protested that his cameras were worth $8,400, someone said they had better assign two policemen, one to watch the other.

Reggie Lancaster, a tall, red-headed photographer from the *Daily Express*, asked when he would have a chance to get shots of the royal couple "with real people — you know, *people* people." When Peters started to explain that positions for the press had already been worked out by the Police officials, Lancaster jumped to his feet. "For your interest," he yelled, "we've been to dozens of these things before. We can't use any more formal handshaking and bouquet-giving."

"I realize there's not much human interest," said Peters, trying to calm him. "I'll admit it's all ceremony that's been done before."

Peters then announced that invitations to the Tuesday afternoon Garden Party at Government House were "in the hands of higher authority. I've submitted the names of those whom I think should be invited. It's all on the basis of what papers and things you represent."

"Now wait a minute, George," said Norman Smart, the florid-faced foreign manager of the *Daily Express*. "We've come 3,000 miles here at their express invitation. God knows we didn't ask to come. *They* asked *us*. Now I think it would be damned asinine if we were not invited to this garden thing. We *are* invited guests."

"Now Norman," said Peters, "I don't think there's any point in jumping into the pond before it's necessary."

A few more "Now Georges" and "Now Normans" settled this issue for the moment.

The next dispute arose over where the cameras would be during the Tuesday evening "parade of traditional lanterns" on Wellington Street. Capt'n Peters said that the balcony of the press quarters would be an excellent vantage point. Reggie Lancaster objected, pointing out that Madi Flats was on the same side of the street as the royal party's reviewing box, and that he must face them to get his shots. He asked about using the roof of Police Headquarters, directly across the street.

"No," said Peters. "That's reserved."

"For whom?"

"The Police."

Norman Smart broke in. "I think it should be pointed out that the Duke and Duchess of Kent are the central figures in this story. Everything should be arranged so that we can be facing them." One of the Americans argued that he "couldn't care less about Their Royal Highnesses, since the American public wouldn't know the Duchess of Kent from the Sheriff of Nottingham." The press briefing nearly broke up over this Anglo-American conflict. Peters attempted to calm the group by telling what he considered an uproarious story about his father's having told him he'd "make a better co-respondent than a correspondent." No one laughed.

Angus McDermott, a top BBC-TV reporter, and the dean of the foreign journalists present, was worried about getting his film and tapes off on the Wednesday morning British United Airways flight. "George, you must get the top officials to do something about that. Get the real top men, I mean. I'm not just giving you a line. The whole thing will be worthless without it. We'll charter a plane from Dakar if necessary."

Capt'n Peters assured him that he would speak to the BUA officials; he added that the government would provide minibuses to take the press to and from each event. McDermott asked about hiring a taxi.

"There won't be any," said Peters.

"Well then, I'll hire one for the week."

"You can't. The government has hired twenty of them and there's nothing left."

"Well, I'll just wave a few ten pound notes around and see what happens. I've been caught in these bloody royal processions before without transportation."

For the Duke's "Speech from the Throne" at Friday morning's opening of Parliament, "higher authority" had decided that no television cameras would be allowed. "We don't want a lot of noisy cameras and things mucking everything up," said Peters.

"Now just a moment, George. There are five million viewers who want to see this . . ."

"Your cameras make too much noise."

"No! No! No noise at all."

This issue led to a squabble over which networks had the most viewers and which papers the largest circulation.

Peters next outlined a few visits the royal couple would make during their stay. "The Duke's visit to the oil mill won't be much. Just the mill pressing a lot of groundnuts (peanuts), and 'H.R.H.' mucking about. Now the Duchess will be visiting the maternity clinic at Royal Victoria Hospital. That's the human interest thing — the Duchess with a lot of babies." Capt'n Peters then wished everybody luck, and closed the press briefing. As the correspondents, reporters, cameramen and photographers left, there were mutterings of "cable the desk in London and have them put pressure on the Colonial Office . . . call the Governor . . . never seen anything like it." During the week "higher authorities" and the press continued to exchange flak over such issues as whether the sun should be in the Duke's eyes or the cameramen's lenses. Harried government officials were heard speaking of "a bloody bunch of prima donnas."

*

Early Monday morning members of the press rode out to the Yundum Airport in three new minibuses just purchased by the government. This expedition was under the direction of the Government Security Officer, A. Sidney Edwards, known in Bathurst as "Security Sid." A massive Englishman with a square black moustache, Edwards has served in Gambia even longer than Capt'n Peters. Before starting out, he issued instructions to the Gambian drivers to stay forty yards apart. Once outside Bathurst the three buses promptly lost sight of each other. As they passed the Gambia High School, someone pointed out Walter Martens' $8,400 worth of equipment, sitting unguarded in the school courtyard. The entire route to Yundum was blocked off, and no other cars were on the road. The normal contingent of stray cattle, sheep, goats and dogs, either uninformed or unconcerned about the occasion, wandered as usual across the road. Policemen stood at intervals along the route, one of them urinating against a bamboo fence. At one point the press buses swung off the bumpy road to allow the royal car, an elegant black Austin Princess, to pass by. "The trouble with that car," said Peters, "is there's no springs. If it goes fast over this road they'll go through the roof."

Out at Yundum Airport, a large crowd watched the royal plane land and saw the Duke descend in a gleaming white uniform, followed by the Duchess, his equerry and her lady-in-waiting. The Duke of Kent, then 29, is tall and slender, with a pale, bland, boyish face. Christened "Edward George Nicholas Paul Patrick," he is a cousin of both the Queen and the Duke of Edinburgh. He graduated from Sandhurst and holds the rank of Captain in the Royal Scots Greys. A press release described him as having "enjoyed rowing at Eton," "captained his regimental ski team," and being a "keen horseman" and "fond of polo." Though young, the Duke is no stranger to the world of diplomatic ceremony. Representing the Queen, he has attended independence celebrations in Sierra Leone and Uganda. Also standing in for Her Majesty, he has welcomed to England President Tubman of Liberia, who presented him with the Order of the Star of Africa, Grand Band, and the King of Nepal, from whom he received the Order of Tri Shakti Patta, First Class, with Chain.

The Duchess, the former Katharine Worsley, is nearly three years older than her husband, but no one who sees her could be churl enough to bring the matter up. Though a "commoner," she is a charming radiant young lady whom Central Casting would unhesitatingly use in the role of a fairy princess. After completing finishing school, the press release says, Miss Worsley "had thoughts of making teaching her career, . . . but gave this up in order to help her mother in the management of Hovingham Hall," the Worsley home. This might well be a considerable task, for her father's estate sprawls over 4,000 acres of Yorkshire countryside. She and the Duke were married in 1961 and have two children, the Earl of St. Andrews and a daughter.

The Governor and Lady Paul, with Prime Minister and Mrs. Jawara, greeted the royal party and conducted them along a newly built cement walkway to a thatched-roof reviewing stand, where a few hundred government officials were seated. The Duke reviewed the 150 troops of the Gambia Field Force while the Field Force Band played appropriate tunes. Then the dignitaries climbed into their limousines and headed back to Bathurst. Along the way, they passed crowds of schoolchildren lining the roads, who cheered every passing car, including the blue press minibuses. Most villagers along the way cheered and sang and waved and beat lustily on calabashes, but one group stood silently as the procession rolled by. "That must be the opposition," said Edwards.

On the way into Bathurst, one of the American reporters asked Capt'n Peters, "What other Dukes and Duchesses do you people have around to use for this sort of thing?"

"Well, there's Princess Margaret and Tony, the Queen Mother, and the Duke and Duchess of Gloucester — he's Kent's uncle. That's why we breed them so fast, so we'll have enough to go around."

Another reporter asked what a lady-in-waiting does.

"She'll just come in and go straight to Government House and start laying out the royal laundry."

At the Civic Reception at Gambia High School, local dignitaries and their wives sat outside in folding chairs, awaiting the royal couple. The mid-morning sun blazed down on the women's flowing gowns, shimmering in pastels of lilac, peach, citron and lavender. One particularly buxom lady billowed into the courtyard like a ship under full sail, the numerous folds of her body enveloped in layers of sequined organdy. Protruding from her ample lips was a large brown chewing stick with which, from time to time, she explored her nether dental regions.

When the Duke and Duchess, Mr. and Mrs. Jawara, and Governor and Lady Paul had taken their places, a city official offered a brief speech of welcome, in which he made "so bold as to ask Your Royal Highness to convey the very loyal greetings of Bathurst to Her Majesty the Queen." The Duke then presented the Royal Charter by which Queen Elizabeth granted to Bathurst "the status and dignity of a City." Despite the speed and altitude of the plane in which he had arrived, the Duke said, "As I flew over your city an hour ago, I saw exciting possibilities of development that lie ahead."

Mayor Baboucar Ousman Semega-Janneh, formerly head of the Survey Department, thanked the Duke for this honor, and presented him with a silver key to the city. He told the Duke that the people of Bathurst "are confident that we shall, by steadfastness and constant endeavor, prove equal to the formidable tasks that lie ahead of us."

That afternoon the City Council held a reception at the high school, where the Duke met the members of the reception committee, signed the visitors' book, and, as reported by *The Gambia News Bulletin*, "moved among the guests." Next day at noon, there was a small reception at Government House to allow the press to meet the Duke and Duchess. The press concluded unanimously that the Duchess was charming. In the afternoon, Sir John Paul held the Garden Party at Government House, at which the state delegates met the royal couple.

Along with a five-man Parliamentary delegation England had dispatched the Home Fleet cruiser H.M.S. *Lion* to show the flag. With 649 men aboard, the *Lion* not only showed the flag to little Bathurst, it nearly took the city over. British residents, happy to see new Anglo-Saxon faces from "the outside," organized an intense round of social and athletic activities for the ship's officers and crew. While white-uniformed officers with dangling swords and golden shoulder boards graced formal receptions, hundreds of young "ratings" descended upon the lounge of the Atlantic and less seemly watering places. The crew brought a healthy glow to selected quarters of the local economy, and provided Gambia's Boy Scouts an opportunity for their finest hour. During the days, these slender lads in shorts and broad-brimmed hats guided the sailors about Bathurst's points of cultural interest. Later, in the evenings, they could be seen in staggering pairs, coaxing overly festive salts back to the ship.

About ten o'clock Tuesday evening, after a formal dinner at Government House, Their Royal Highnesses, along with others of suitable rank, sat in a box overlooking downtown Wellington Street and watched the parade of "fanals." Fanals (Portuguese for "lanterns") are intricate and highly accurate models of old sailing ships, some as long as sixteen feet, made from strips of white paper as one cuts out paper dolls. They have candles inside, lighting up the lace-like filigree paper, and colored paper lanterns hanging from the wooden yardarms. The custom of fanal parades dates from the days of the sixteenth-century Portuguese coastal settlements. They are now held at Christmas time only in Bathurst and down the coast in Bissau, Portuguese Guinea. Local boys clubs spend several weeks making their fanals, and compete for prizes. In the parade a half dozen or so will carry their fanal, while their friends dance along behind to the sound of drums and whistles. The joy of this evening was so contagious that several Western journalists held their own celebration on the balcony of Madi Flats, throwing empty Scotch bottles down onto Wellington Street.

On Wednesday morning, everyone assembled out at Brikama, 22 miles from Bathurst, for a "Mansa Bengo," or gathering of chiefs. This tradition — found throughout Africa — dates back to unrecorded history, when chiefs of a region would gather periodically like feudal lords to pay tribute to their king with speeches or more convertible currency. During the colonial era, British and French administrators continued the practice as a means of uniting newly carved territories and propagating new policies. Gambia's chiefs and area councillors from every district had been ferried down the river on the country's only passenger vessel, the *Lady Wright*. Chiefs, officials and invited guests now sat in thatched-roof reviewing stands. A layer of peanut shells covered the dusty grounds. "Looks like a bloody circus," observed one English reporter.

Speaking for his fellows, a senior "seyfu," or chief, read a speech of welcome to the Duke in English, which an interpreter then rendered into Mandinka and Woloff for the other chiefs. The prose of this speech, and the speaker's apparent unfamiliarity with it, indicated that it emanated from the same government offices in Bathurst that produced several others during the week. "On this proud and happy occasion," read the seyfu, "when we take up our grave responsibilities, it gives us confidence to know that as a Monarchy within the Commonwealth of Nations, we are members of that family of which Her Majesty the Queen is the Head."

The Duke thanked the seyfu for this intelligence, and expressed his awareness of "the many problems which will confront you and the great responsibilities that you will have to bear after independence, but your proud record over the past years enables you to look forward to the future with every confidence." Speaking of the flag-raising ceremonies to be held that evening, he told them that "this will be a moving occasion for us all, but to you who have worked so hard and looked forward so long to the attainment of independence, this will be a moment of special pride and satisfaction."

When the speeches were over, the chiefs went up one by one and shook hands with the Duke, as their retainers put on brief displays of dancing and yelling. Some of the chiefs were accompanied by "kankurang" dancers — acrobatic men who leap wildly about in suits of green leaves. Many of the chiefs were undoubtedly meditating upon the significance of independence, since their own power could only decrease with the end of colonial rule. They realize that the "new Gambians" in the PPP consider the chiefs an anachronism better suited to colonial days than modern African statehood.

That afternoon the Prime Minister held a reception at the Atlantic Hotel which, according to a *New Gambia* reporter, "was the largest reception ever thrown in the Gambia. The guests were over 500, comprising all tribes and creeds of the Gambia . . . The service was superb. Drinks and refreshments were in galore." Drinks were indeed in such galore that one official of the Gambia Workers Union became excessively demonstrative in his joy, and had to be dragged out of the lounge.

By five o'clock, Gambians began gathering at MacCarthy Square cricket grounds for the Independence Eve flag-raising ceremonies, high point of the week's festivities. Several thousand had come from up-river districts by truck, bus, taxi, boat and foot. By nine o'clock the Square and surrounding streets were filled with crowds later estimated at 10,000 to 20,000. A Royal Marines drill team from the H.M.S. *Lion* opened the evening's program with a display of precision marching. They were followed by more lively, if less precise, tribal dancing by Mandinkas, Woloffs, Yorubas, Fulas, Sereres, Jolas, Sussus, Bambaras, Serahulis and Tukulors. The dancers performed such diversions as the kumpo, ogoogoo, makalo, kankurang, bolor, piti and the Bambara debool. After the dancers came a gymnastic display by Bathurst schoolchildren. Then the Gambia Police and Field Force marched by the reviewing stand in slow and quick time, giving the Royal Salute. A detachment of Royal Marines took up a position across from the Field Force.

At 11:57, the Union Jack was lowered for the last time in

Gambia, while the band played "God Save the Queen." The crowd was silent. There were tears in the eyes of some British officials. At midnight, the new red, green and blue Gambian flag was unfurled atop the pole, lit by a single spotlight. It hung limp in the breezeless night. The crowd broke into a long cheer, churchbells rang, and the band struck up the Gambian National Anthem. This time there were tears in Gambian eyes. The delegate from Mali turned to his neighbor and said, "Well, now the real problems begin." The reporter from *The New Gambia* felt stirred to a more dramatic outburst:

> This was the most sensational and pathetic moment in all the ceremonies, when we, at last, come to realise that the shackles were not only about our wrists and ankles, but also round our necks, waist and everywhere, but have by God's grace been broken and shattered, and we now are as God intended us to be in the continent in which he had placed us.

The evening ended with a fireworks display. This caused some concern among officials, since a few years before, a similar festive evening was spoiled when all the fireworks went up at once, burning a few attendants. This evening's fireworks went off without any serious mishaps. A few misdirected roman candles headed for Government House, with no apparent ill effects, and one landed still sputtering next to the Captain of the Marine Guards from the *Lion*. He did not budge. The fireworks ended with a fixed display at the far end of the field. Its glowing sparklers portrayed the features of Prime Minister Jawara, complete with cap and spectacles. As the sparklers fizzled out, the face slowly disintegrated.

*

The next morning was February 18, Independence Day, and the crowds gathered again at MacCarthy Square. The Chief Justice swore in Sir John Paul as the first Governor-General of the Gambia. The Duke of Kent read a message from the Queen in which she looked back with pleasure to her visit to Gambia in 1961, and then read a speech of his own. He said that this day "marks the culmination of the peaceful and ordered evolution of the Gambia to full Nationhood, ending Britain's colonial responsibilities in West Africa . . . Gambia may not be large, but its people are renowned for their ability to live together, for their natural friendliness and dignity and for their innate common sense and good humor. These are the attributes which many large and more prosperous countries have good reason to envy."

The Duke presented Prime Minister Jawara with something called the "Constitutional Instruments," formally marking Gambia's independence. In reply, the Prime Minister said that Gambians were honored that Her Majesty the Queen had been graciously pleased to mark this great and historic occasion by appointing the Duke as Her Representative. Mr. Jawara was also pleased to hear that Her Majesty could look back with pleasure to her visit to the Gambia.

We are very conscious that the task which lies before us is formidable; and, this being so, we are the more determined to strive relentlessly to overcome the difficulties that make the task so considerable . . . We are a small nation, who like to think that the orderly nature of our people can contribute something to the peace and stability of this Continent . . . With the Gambia's characteristic tolerance, understanding and friendliness, we intend to align ourselves on the side of the world's peaceful forces.

"Thank heaven for that," commented one foreign reporter.

The P.M. then addressed the crowd in both Mandinka and Woloff. Prayers were offered by the Imam of Bathurst, the General Superintendent of the Methodist Mission, the Vicar-General of the Anglican Mission, the Roman Catholic Bishop of Bathurst and the head of the Ahmaddiya Movement of Islam.

The schoolchildren sang traditional songs and everyone joined in on the Gambian National Anthem. The Duke and Duchess closed the ceremony with a drive around the field in an open Land Rover, leaving the car to walk among some of the children.

That evening, a glittering State Ball took place on the grounds of Government House. The tennis court served as a dance floor, and music was supplied by the Royal Marine Band from the *Lion* and the Eagles Jazz Band from Bathurst. Lloyd Garrison of the London *Times* stirred up considerable comment among the heavily bemedalled guests with a maroon and blue decoration sash he wore diagonally across his chest beneath his white dinner jacket. Garrison, who had covered the Congo from time to time, explained modestly to those who inquired that he had been awarded the "Patrice Lumumba sash" for some vague act of heroism. Actually an Ivy League belt, it had been awarded earlier that evening by a group of festive colleagues.

Friday morning there were more speeches, as the Duke formally opened Gambia's first Parliament. This is a complex traditional ceremony, the significance of which was lost on most of the audience and the press. The high point of the affair was the Duke's reading of the "Speech from the Throne," similar to a State of the Union Message. Though read by the Duke, the speech was actually written by the Prime Minister and his advisers. The speech professed Gambia's intention to "maintain close links of friendship and good will" with England, the United Nations, Senegal and other African nations. While assuring the world that "The Gambia has quarrels with no one," it mentioned a defense treaty with Senegal. It told of the Government's desire to improve the economy and the general efficiency of the country, and to mobilize and exploit all resources. The speech did not include any specific proposals designed to achieve these goals.

The Prime Minister thanked the Duke for reading the speech

and promised that "the Parliamentary democracy that has been bequeathed to us by our British friends shall be maintained by tolerance, goodwill and the common goal of the common good." Speaker of the House A. Sam Jack announced: "It is His Royal Highness' pleasure to take his leave," which ended Gambia's first independent Parliament. Everyone then marched over to Clifton Road, where the P.M. made a speech, cut a ribbon, unveiled a commemorative stone and renamed the street "Independence Drive." This brought the week's official celebrations to a close.

*

In between the various ceremonies, the thirty state delegates had greeted Prime Minister Jawara and bestowed on him gifts from their countries. State delegations were led in most cases by the country's nearest diplomatic representative, usually based in Dakar, Senegal, or Lagos, Nigeria. Among those who paid greater tribute was the United States, which sent from Washington G. Mennen Williams, Assistant Secretary of State for African Affairs. By far the tallest delegate, Mr. Williams stood out at every ceremony, his gray crew cut and polka dot bow tie clearly visible above the crowd of fezzes and skull caps. He was also a tireless worker. Almost every evening, after days filled with exhausting ceremonies and meetings with Gambian officials, Mr. Williams was out in the streets joining buxom Woloff women in energetic street dances. At the State Ball and the Miss Independence Dance, he waltzed or high lifed with the wife of nearly every important Gambian official. While British observers looked askance at what they considered such blatant diplomacy, the Gambians were obviously delighted. The truth is that Mr. Williams has the gift of enjoying himself at such occasions.

His bluff, gregarious manner made a distinct impression on many Gambians. On Wednesday, at a hotel luncheon with the

Minister of Finance and other officials, Williams leaned over to
the Minister, put his hand on his shoulder, and asked, "Well,
what are you gonna do now that you're independent?" The startled Minister smiled and made no reply. During the Prime Minister's reception at the hotel that afternoon, Williams walked
over to a tiny African who stood enveloped in a flowing brown
robe. Grasping him firmly by the shoulders, Williams shook him
briskly, and with a big smile, bellowed "Malawi!"

The little man look up at Williams, smiled nervously, and
shook his head.

"Aren't you from Malawi?" asked Williams, still holding the
African firmly by the shoulders.

The little man shook his head.

"Weren't you at the independence in Malawi?"

The man not from Malawi shook his head again, beginning to
look a bit frightened.

"Well, you havin' a good time here at independence?"

The little man nodded uneasily. Williams let go of him and
walked away to greet other acquaintances.

On Independence Day, Mr. Williams had an audience with
the Prime Minister, and made a brief speech upon presenting the
independence gift from the United States: "It is a great pleasure
to be here at this historic time of Gambia's independence. The
United States is always gratified to see progress toward freedom
and self-determination throughout the world. I am delighted to
join with you on this memorable occasion, and to have the privilege of bringing you the warm personal greetings of President
Lyndon B. Johnson and the hearty salutations of the American
people." Williams assured Mr. Jawara that the gifts "reflect
American friendship for the people of Gambia and our deep interest in your economic and social progress. With them go our
most sincere wishes for your future progress and freedom."

America's gifts to Gambia consisted of one heavy-duty loading crane for Bathurst's port facilities, one heavy tractor for land clearing, and twelve rice-hulling machines. To those who wished to make comparisons — and many Gambians wished to do so — the $100,000 value of these gifts compared favorably with other expressions of friendship received that week although a few ungrateful souls felt that such a wealthy country might have given more.

Along with its more than $3 million in annual aid, and a special grant of $70,000 for half the cost of the independence celebrations, Great Britain announced gifts of a $224,000 river launch for the Head of State, a new Speaker's chair and some furniture for the Cabinet Room. A problem arose when West Germany announced that it too planned to give an executive river craft, along with six scholarships to German universities. At last report, England was planning to withdraw in favor of West Germany. A dispute also arose over the Speaker's chair, for Speaker A. Sam Jack, who had designed the present chair himself, let it be known that he was quite happy with it. The issue grew more muddled when Bathurst's Nigeria Welfare Association announced that they too were giving a new Speaker's chair. Before the government could suggest a substitute, the chair arrived — a seven-foot ornate throne with canary-yellow upholstery and carved fleur-de-lis. It sat for a week outside the P.M.'s office, while the administration tried to decide what to do with it. One British official privy to the affair of the chair later discussed the Nigerian model: "They ran through four alternatives. They could use it to enthrone new chiefs, but the chair would never survive the trip up-river in a Land Rover. They tried to give it to the Speaker, but he likes the one he has very much, thank you. They thought of giving it to the Mayor, since he's tall enough, but then someone suggested giving it to Gambia High School as a prop for amateur theatricals."

Israel offered 25 scholarships, India gave Mrs. Jawara a shawl and a handbag, the delegate from Pakistan presented a silver salver, Australia gave an oil painting and a desk set, Canada gave two projectors and film, and France caused considerable grousing with a Sèvres vase. Nigeria made what many felt was relatively the most handsome gift from any country — $28,000 for development projects. Alongside this sum, Ghana's carved mahogany box, Kenya's silver tray and Zambia's lampstand struck some as slack. Senegal, however, provoked the loudest outcry, when midway through the celebrations a Senegalese fishing boat, presumably acting on the part of the government in Dakar, dumped five tons of assorted fresh fish on the Bathurst wharf. Although the purpose was ostensibly to help in feeding the independence crowds from up-river, most Gambians considered the gift an insult, particularly in that the fish were probably caught in Gambian waters.

As gifts continued to pour in, *The Gambia News Bulletin* published periodic lists, including their approximate value. This practice contributed to a running public debate over the degree of generosity involved in each case. Intimidated by the publicity, local commercial firms grew touchy about discussing their gifts. The Bank of West Africa and Elder Dempster Lines each gave $14,000 and the United Africa Company, $28,000 for educational purposes. Compagnie Française de l'Afrique Occidental, the largest French trading firm in town, gave $6,160 to the Agriculture Department. The other four French firms together gave Victoria Hospital a sterilization unit. S. Madi Ltd., the largest Lebanese firm, gave the Prime Minister a Chrysler Imperial convertible, plus several thousand dollars' worth of dinnerware engraved with the Gambia crest. British Petroleum, which is exploring for offshore oil along Gambia's coast, gave a compressor for the Technical School. Shell Oil gave Gambia High School a set of reference books. Mobil Oil gave 20 wall thermometers and 600 ball point pens.

One week after independence, an anonymous reader wrote to *The New Gambia* with a critique of these gifts. While complimenting the firms which, in his opinion, had acquitted themselves with distinction, he offered a word of advice to the others:

> I cannot keep silent over some of the gifts made to the Gambia Government after over 50 years of establishment by some firms in The Gambia. First and foremost, it is a shock and it is very disappointing too, to Gambians, to see five French Firms which have been long established in The Gambia, after exploiting all that we had and sending all to France to develop their own country and enjoying the huge profits of this loyal, peaceful and lovable land (The Gambia) for years cannot donate something worth the while, but only £600 each . . . I do not intend to force anyone to give what they do not want to give but I feel attention should be drawn to the paucity of the gifts given . . . Their gift is not to the mark we expected . . . *The managers of these firms should really reconsider their gifts.*

Along with the gifts, congratulatory telegrams arrived from capitals around the world. Most of them, from such countries as South Korea, Albania and Formosa, cited the historic ties that have bound them to Gambia in friendship over the centuries, and foresaw a rosy future ahead for this newest addition to independent Africa. From East Germany, which had not been invited to the celebrations, came a typical message which said, in part:

> Now all fetters which limited free development of Gambia have been thrown off once and for all, the road is clear, it leads into a bright future of prosperity, happiness and security for all citizens of Gambia.

*

The story of Gambia's independence week is not complete with an account merely of official ceremonies, gifts and messages of goodwill. Unofficial Bathurst was just as active as the government. Receptions were given by the Co-operative Central Bank, Gambia Labour Union, PPP Women's Society, Gambia Oil-seeds Marketing Board, Elder Dempster Lines, Nigeria Airways and the Methodist Boys High School. The Methodist Girls High School Ex-Pupils Association held a buffet and dance at Masonic Hall, and the St. Joseph's Secondary Ex-Pupils Association held a dance at St. Mary's School. The Gambia Drama Festival Committee presented a special performance of *Antigone* at the High School, and the Gambia National Drama Association organized a concert at Crab Island School. The Vero Cinema put on special showings of *Maciste Against the Monsters* and *Thalus, Son of Attila*. Shyben Madi presented special wrestling matches at his arena at Half Die. The Guinean Society, Berending Y.F.C. and the Grant Street Kanylengo performed traditional dances at Box Bar Stadium, while the Metta Youths Society sponsored a Miss Independence Dance at Bathurst Tennis Court. The Young Rising Society held tribal dancing on Fitzgerald Street, the United Party held Woloff dancing in Anglesea Street, and the PPP held drumming and dancing in Hagen Street. The only function that did not go off as scheduled was a facetiously named "Opposition Party," planned for the night of the State Ball by a group of British residents not invited to it. A menacing phone call from edgy "higher authorities" led them to cancel the party, under an implied threat of deportation.

As with most other significant social or political changes in Africa, Gambia's independence took some time before moving up-country. Village headmen, district chiefs and Members of Parliament organized celebrations in Provincial villages and towns for several weeks after the Bathurst festivities had ended. Nearly 10,000 people gathered at Bansang for kankurang and seruba dancing, after which they settled down to feasting on seven bulls. At Georgetown, celebrants fired 300 shots in salute.

At Chamen village, in the Nianija District, three hunters fired 61 gunshot salutes, 13 dancers competed in a kankurang contest, and Jainaba Cham was elected "Miss Nianija." The PPP leaders of Sami District held an impressive affair at which some 4,000 people consumed ten bulls and twenty sheep. There were 26 kankurang dancers and Samba Joss gave a display of acrobatic cycling.

Although some observers had expected the complex arrangements for the Bathurst celebrations to end either in chaos or a grinding halt, the orderly precision of the ceremonies surprised and impressed everyone. This was due mainly to the efforts of British administration officials and development officers who had been taken off their normal jobs or pulled in from the provinces and assigned to different tasks with an almost military concern for strategy. For weeks they had rehearsed the various MacCarthy Square ceremonies. Rabid Gambian nationalists, who had strenuously objected to the "colonialists" running what they felt should be a purely Gambian affair, were heard the following week pointing out how smoothly Gambians could run things.

There were, of course, minor indignities and calamities. The *Lion's* arrival on Sunday morning was nearly marred when some bags of cement split open on the freshly hosed-down wharf during Saturday night. By morning the wharf was covered with a layer of rapidly congealing gray mud. Bathurst's lone fire truck rushed to the scene and barely cleared the mess up before the *Lion* docked.

Fifth Formers at Gambia High School, described by one staff member as "an intelligent lot, but extremely bolshie," presented their British teacher with a wooden chopping block labeled: "For White Heads." Occasional delegates were reportedly lost or left behind at various ceremonies. One of the hotel stewards fussed a bit over a Ghanian ten shilling note (unacceptable and non-convertible outside Ghana at that time) left him as a tip by the delegate from that economically troubled nation. Food flown in specially for the State Ball canapés was somehow lost for several hours on the day of the Ball. A tank truck struck the gate as it left the oil mill one evening, spilling seven tons of peanut oil onto the main road. This made driving a bit sticky until it was covered with a layer of peanut shells. Commissioner Gordon Edwards' white Rolls Royce was driven off the road into a swamp.

The working press also suffered a few near-catastrophes. One afternoon, BBC's Angus McDermott discovered that an urgent cable he'd sent that morning to London, for broadcast that evening, was still sitting in the cable office, unsent. Angus could be seen muttering to himself frequently during the week's festivities. The CBS-TV crew sent one load of films and tapes to New York via a carefully arranged series of flights through Dakar and Madrid, with CBS contacts checking the shipment through at each airport. The films and tapes never reached Madrid, but after several hours of frantic cabling, they finally arrived on time, direct from Frankfurt. Reggie Lancaster gave up trying to develop his films in the hectic Information Office, and set up a makeshift darkroom in the bathroom at Madi Flats. Returning there one evening to process the day's film, he found that the cleaning boy had tidied up the bathroom, pouring his developing fluids down the drain.

Despite these troubles, correspondents managed to get their stories out to the rest of the world. African papers hailed the occasion, welcomed Gambia to their midst, and damned Great Britain for having left it in its present condition. Senegal's *Dakar Matin* predicted that now with independence, Gambians would certainly choose to become part of Senegal. *Flamingo*, an African magazine published in London, also saw such a union as "the only course open to little Gambia." The influential British weekly, *West Africa*, called Gambia "the worst example . . . of the carving up of Africa in which European powers have indulged." It said the tiny enclave "passes none of the tests that would have been applied not so long ago to a country's readiness for independence." Congratulating Gambia for having "no illusions, even at this heady stage," the magazine quoted Finance Minister Sherif Sissay as saying that Gambia "simply can not afford to live other than extremely modestly." *The Manchester Guardian Weekly* said that "Gambia ought never to have occurred," but that "it deserves a few cheers for its pluck." Norman Smart, in the *Daily Express*, called Gambia a land of hope. "Hope they must have," he wrote, "for if you tried to float a company in the City of London with a prospectus based on what they have here, you would get a visit from the Fraud Squad."

In the United States, where Gambia is less well known, many papers ignored its independence, or buried the story on page 17; most, having no correspondents in West Africa, had to rely on the wire services. *The New York Times* called Gambia "the most overlooked and unwanted state in Africa." *Time* cautioned its readers that Gambia was "not to be confused with Gabon or Zambia." (A columnist in Singapore's *Malay Mail* did mistake it for Zambia.) *Newsweek* felt that "in a more rational world Gambia would simply not exist as a separate entity." Complimenting Gambia's financial moderation in contrast to some of its extravagant neighbors, the magazine quoted Governor-General Sir John Paul: "We have the enormous advantage here of never having had much money." Concluded *Newsweek*: "And it looks as though Gambia will go right on having that advantage."

A sample of Gambian reactions to independence appeared in a special issue of *The Nation*, a sporadic four-page Bathurst monthly. Gathered by a staff reporter in street interviews, some of the comments were obviously translated from Woloff or Mandinka. Mr. Alfred Bell, a merchant, felt that independence would "improve the nation enormously with big developments, betterment of relations and progress, regardless of colour, race or creed." Mr. Yoro Khan, a Head Laborer with the Public Works Department, told the reporter, "I am really happy about independence because other sister countries have it and therefore the Gambia should have hers as well." Mrs. N'Goneh M'Boge, a shopkeeper, expected "improvement in agriculture, health, education and housing for all sections of the community during independence." This feeling was shared by Mr. G. M. P. Val-Phatty, Secretary of the Gambia Employers' Association, who expected "new industries to provide more employment for all. I am quite sure conditions will be better because the Government will be in our own hands." Madam Kumajar, a street merchant, was happy that "independence is at close quarters and although a seller on the sidewalk, I am hoping that all will be well so that getting a stall at the Albert Market after independence should not be a problem." The one note of caution among the interviews came from "T. K.," a school teacher:

> Personally, I hope independence will prove a happier period for everybody. I contemplate a drastic change in the affairs of the State so that we may cautiously crawl a step forward, through the maze of political strategy and the clinging network of international development, towards the goal of universal peace, prosperity during independence . . . I will not be bamboozled into thinking that an independence of rosy promise lies before me. As a matter of fact, the thought of it smashes me to fragments with harder tasks of individual responsibilities ahead.

Capt'n Peters, writing in *The Gambia News Bulletin*, rose to a commendable degree of emotion in summing up the independence week:

And so came to an end, an historic week for the Gambia, with all its drama and colour which will be long remembered. And now, on to the broad uplands of the future.

By the end of the week, everyone had left — the Duke and Duchess, the state delegates, the official and unofficial guests, the 649 men from the *Lion*, the reporters and photographers. The permanent residents of the Atlantic had moved back in, and business at the lounge was back to its normal sedate pace. Walking the empty streets of Bathurst on Sunday morning, with dead leaves, streamers and torn paper decorations blowing about, a young British-trained Gambian engineer said to a friend, "You know? It's as if nothing had really happened. Everything's the same as it was."

## THE WAY THINGS WERE

THOUGH MANY GAMBIANS feel that nothing ever really happens, everything is not the same as it was centuries ago. Learning what it was like then is difficult, for the rest of the world has never known much about Africa. Europe's ignorance, rather than Africa's jungles, caused it to become known as "The Dark Continent." Unlike most other ancient civilizations, the tribes of Black Africa never produced a written language, and as a result, historians have had to rely mainly on the records of traders and travelers, plus their own speculations. Since traders and travelers kept few records, there is much room for speculation. Because of this scarcity of source material, most Western histories still skim briefly over the centuries prior to the arrival of the Europeans, and refer to the "discovery" of Africa as though it had not existed before they came. This annoys Africans who read histories.

In the absence of written records, Gambia offers the modern historian two other sources of information — one meager and enigmatic, the other rich but untrustworthy. Hidden in the underbrush up-river are a series of ancient stone circles which bear a striking resemblance (though much smaller) to those constructed by the Druids at Stonehenge, in England. While

Stonehenge was built about 1800 to 1400 B.C., archeologists set the probable date of the Gambian circles somewhere between 1400 and 1600 A.D. Each circle enclosed the grave of a chief, who was buried with pottery, spears and copper bracelets. Though local villagers refer vaguely to a curse on anyone who disturbs the burial sites, they have no traditions associated with them and show no interest.

Less puzzling than the stone circles are the "griots," the traditional caste of musicians in Senegal and Gambia whose function is the preservation of tribal legends. Like medieval minstrels, each is attached by custom to one family of chiefs, and is responsible for recounting to music the tales of that family's greatness. In the days of yore, when chiefs were generally out marauding the countryside and destroying villages, there was plenty to sing about. As the central government took over more and more of the chiefs' former powers, however, tribal life diminished and glorious exploits became rare. The griots have thus fallen on hard times. A British sociologist who studied them recently wrote that "for a few coppers a griot will sing one's praises. For six-pence or one shilling his voice will be louder and his praises more elaborate, while for two shillings or four shillings a man can be made to feel that he is one of the bravest and most generous men in the Gambia."

From the songs of the griots, the tales of Arab traders and their own speculations, historians have been able to piece together a hazy approximation of the origins of today's Gambian tribes. From the earliest recorded times, traders, adventurers, thieves and slave raiders had journeyed westward from the Nile Valley, across the Sudan to Lake Chad and the Niger River. Whole tribes followed this route, settling around the upper Niger, near Timbuctu, where they found a flat country onto which the river overflowed each year as in the Nile Valley.

About the time the Jews were driven out of Egypt, tribes of Hamites made the journey west, where they found another Hamitic tribe called the Wangara already settled beyond the Niger. Their offspring were known as the Wakore, and anthropologists feel they were the ancestors of Gambia's Mandinkas.

Another branch of Wakore offspring — the result of intermarriage with Berber tribesmen from the north — was the Serahuli, whose descendants live up-river in Gambia today. The Serahulis founded the Ghana Empire (not to be confused with modern Ghana) which lasted for several centuries and extended from the Sahara to Senegal. On the direct trade route from the Mediterranean to the gold regions in the south, Ghana became a prosperous commercial center. Moors from the desert brought salt, silks, dates and figs in exchange for gold and ivory. Traders had to pay the emperor a tax of gold dust on all the goods they brought into and took out of the Empire. More than 200,000 foot soldiers and 40,000 archers and horsemen defended the Empire and saw to it that the traders paid their taxes. The emperors thrived. By 1000 A.D., however, the power of Ghana began to decline, and in 1076, Mohammedan Almoravids from North Africa conquered the Empire. According to custom, they killed all the inhabitants.

Meanwhile, the Mandinkas, or "Mandingos," as they were known until recently, had settled in the Futa Jallon mountains in present-day Guinea. Over a period of several centuries, the Mandingos joined the Susus to overthrow the Songhois, who had overthrown the Almoravids, who had overthrown the Serahulis. At first, the Susus ruled the Mandingos. Hoping to become king of the Mandingos, Sumawuru Konteh, the Susu king, killed eleven of the Mandingo king's twelve sons. He spared the twelfth son, Sunjiata Keita, because he was a cripple. This proved to be a costly display of mercy, for Sunjiata grew up to be a cruel and powerful king (with the aid of a pair of golden legs, according to the griots) and eventually, in 1235, defeated Sumawuru and the Susus.

Sunjiata Keita founded the Mali Empire, which included the old Ghana Empire, the Futa Jallon region, Senegal and Gambia. Despite nearly constant wars, he introduced cotton and weaving, and encouraged agriculture. In 1307, a powerful Mandingo king named Gongo Moussa enlarged the Mali Empire, and its fame began to spread to Europe and the Middle East. A good Moslem, Gongo made one triumphal pilgrimage to Mecca, accompanied by 60,000 retainers. Not wanting to be caught short on the trip, he brought along eighty sacks of gold dust weighing more than eighty pounds each, and had 500 slaves walk in front, each bearing a five-pound bar of gold. As one might imagine, Gongo made a great hit in Cairo and Mecca.

After Gongo Moussa's death in 1352, the Empire began to break up. Under seige from the Arabs, Songhois and Susus, the Mandingos gradually withdrew to their old homeland in the Futa Jallon mountains. Here, for the next three centuries, they held sway over the Casamance, Senegal and Gambia. (They are still a major tribe in Senegal, Mali, Sierra Leone and Guinea.) During this period, the Woloffs — about whose origin little is known — had formed several minor kingdoms in Senegal, extending South as far as the Gambia River. Here, they fought one another and defended themselves against invasions from what is now Mauretania. In the 1670's Moorish marabouts (Islamic priests, pronounced "maraboos") who circulated freely, urged the Woloff tribesmen to overthrow their kings, promising that in return, they would make the millet grow without planting by their prayers. Since planting was a strenuous task, the people of Walo and Kayor killed their rulers. When the millet failed to grow, and famine set in, they drove the marabouts away and re-elected kings from the royal families.

This then was West Africa before the arrival of the Europeans — empires and kingdoms rising and falling; tribes migrating, merging and scattering again; and always the din of destruction, massacre, conquest, and rebellion. Tribal warfare was not a pretty thing in those days. If a beseiged village refused to surrender, the attacking tribe would burn it to the ground, sell the prisoners into slavery, and carry off the women. Fortunately, such activities ceased each year during the rainy season, when villages stopped to plant their crops. Besides, the muddy ground was unsuitable for fighting.

Until the fifteenth century, there was little outside contact with West Africa, and records are scarce. About 600 B.C. Phoenicians sailed around the African continent, and since they generally kept close to shore, they may have explored the mouth of the Gambia. A century later, a Carthaginian fleet under Hanno sailed along the West African coast. Some of his crewmen stopped at the mouth of a river that might have been the Gambia and killed several monkeys, bringing their skins back to Carthage. About 300 B.C., a Greek merchant captain described one river on the coast that was full of crocodiles and hippopotamuses. Since he named the river "Bambotus," historians surmise that it may have been the Gambia, for the Mandingo word for crocodile is "bambo."

In the fifteenth century, Portugal's Henry the Navigator began sending out maritime expeditions to explore the Africa that Arab geographers and cartographers had described. As his captains reached points further and further down the West Coast, he began to hear reports that the banks of the Gambia River were rich with gold (a rumor that has not yet died out among Gambians). He therefore dispatched a Venetian named Luiz de Cadamosto to explore the river. Cadamosto, upon setting out in 1455, described himself as "young, well fitted to sustain all hardships, desirous of seeing the world, and things never seen before by our nation, and I hoped to draw from it honor and profit." Joined by two other ships under a Genoese named Antoniotto Usodimare, Cadamosto reached the mouth of the river and proceeded up about four miles. There they met several native canoes. After the two groups had stared at each other for some time, the Africans attacked the Portuguese ships with spears. The Portuguese responded with crossbows and cannons and drove the canoes off. In hopes of finding friendlier natives, Cadamosto and Usodimare decided to sail further upstream, but their crews refused. Faced with a potential mutiny, the captains returned to Portugal.

Undaunted, Cadamosto and Usodimare refitted and set out for the Gambia again the following year. This time they reached an island twenty miles upstream without incident. When a sailor named Andrea died of fever, Cadamosto buried him there and named it "Isola di Sancto Andrea," or St. Andrew's Island. Proceeding a bit further upstream, Cadamosto encountered some friendly natives who promised to take him to their leader, Battimansa. ("Mansa" in Mandingo means "chief.") He reported that the natives were amazed by his ships and "were of the opinion that the portholes in the bows were really eyes by which the ships saw whither they were going over the sea." Cadamosto was surprised to find the natives clothed, since those he had seen on a previous visit to "Senega" had been naked. The natives were equally surprised at the Venetian's garb which, though elegant, was unusual dress for the sweltering tropics. Cadamosto described it as "after the Spanish fashion, a doublet of black damask, with a short cloak of gray wool." The natives were also fascinated with the odd color of his skin. "Some touched my hands and limbs, and rubbed me with their spittle to discover whether my whiteness was dye or flesh. Finding that it was flesh, they were astounded." Sixty miles further upstream, the ships reached the village of Battimansa, who gave them a warm reception. They exchanged presents, concluded a treaty of friendship, and bartered for gold and a few slaves. After eleven days with Battimansa, Cadamosto took his leave, and eventually sailed back to Portugal. This trip seemed to drain his thirst for hardship and adventure, for he returned to Venice, married a wealthy woman, took over the family estates, engaged in commerce, and eventually held high office in the local government.

In 1458, Prince Henry fitted out another three caravels under the command of a Portuguese captain named Diogo Gomez. Gomez traveled up the Gambia River past St. Andrew's Island. In his talks with chiefs, tribesmen and traders, Gomez heard tales of fabulous gold mines in the interior. During a visit with a chief named Nomimansa, he entered into a theological dispute with the local Mohammedan priest. According to Gomez, he argued so well, and dispensed wine so lavishly, that Nomimansa ordered the Mohammedan to leave the country, begging Gomez to baptize him a Christian. A devout Catholic, Gomez protested that while he could not perform this service himself, he would prevail upon Prince Henry to send out a priest from Portugal. Disappointed, Nomimansa settled for adopting the name Henry, while his nobles took the names of Gomez and his sailors. Upon his return to Portugal, Gomez honored his promise, and Prince Henry dispatched the Abbot of Soto de Cassa to instruct Nomimansa in the Christian faith. During the time between the departure of Gomez and the Abbot's arrival, however, Nomimansa's fervor had apparently waned, for there is no record of any conversions by the good Soto de Cassa. Gomez later returned to West Africa and heard that a Spaniard named De Prado was selling arms to the Moors in Gambia for use against the Portuguese. Gomez intercepted De Prado's ship on its return voyage and carried the Spaniard off to Portugal where he was burned as a heretic.

The Spaniards evidently had a more callous attitude toward

trade with the Africans than the Portuguese. Without even
bothering to arrange treaties of goodwill, one Andalusian expedition to Gambia bundled a native king and one hundred of his
subjects off to Spain. Concerned about this blatant breach of
regal honor, Spain's Ferdinand V ordered the native king returned to Gambia. He allowed the 100 subjects to be sold as
slaves.

As commerce with West Africa increased, a few Portuguese
traders and missionaries settled along the banks of the Gambia
in the sixteenth century. But the harvest of gold proved far
smaller than their expectations, and the settlements never
caught on. Most traders and settlers preferred the more prosperous Gulf of Guinea to the fever-ridden banks of the Gambia.
Those who stayed and survived gradually intermarried with the
local African population. Their decline may be due to the fact
that they were not exactly the flower of Portuguese society. One
voyager described them as "banished men or fugitives, for com-
mitting the most heinous and incestuous acts; their life and conversation being disagreeable; and they are of the basest behaviour
that ever we have seene of these nations in any other countrye."

Richard Jobson, an Englishman who arrived in 1620, wrote:

> They call themselves Portingales, and some few seem the same;
> others of them are Molatoes, between blacke and white, but the
> most parte as blacke as the naturall inhabitants. . . . all are mar-
> ried, or rather keepe with them the countrey blackewomen, of
> whome they beget children . . . It doth manifestly appeare that
> they are such as have beene banished or fled away from either of
> Portingall or the isles belonging unto that government . . . The
> conditions they live subject unto, under the blacke kings, makes
> it appeare they have little comfort in a Christian countrey . . .
> still, [they preserve] carefully the use of the Portingall tongue,
> and with a kinde of affectionate zeale, the name of Christians,
> taking in great disdaine, be they ever so blacke, to be called a
> Negro.

Historians do not judge the Portuguese harshly for their activities in Gambia. Though they dabbled in slaves, they taught some Gambians the rudiments of seamanship. They also introduced oranges, limes and papaya from their colonies in Brazil, and brought something that is now the basis of the entire Gambian economy — the peanut.

*

Until late in the middle of the sixteenth century, the English and French did not interfere with the Portuguese trade in West Africa because they were not yet great maritime powers, and because they were too busy fighting each other. Also, Pope Alexander VI had issued the Bull of Demarcation in 1493 dividing all the lands in Africa and the New World between Catholic Spain and Catholic Portugal. As late as 1562, Queen Elizabeth instructed her captains, when sailing along the African coast, to confine themselves to those parts where the King of Portugal "hath not presentlie dominion, obedience, and tribute." Eventually, however, the English and French began competing, and encountered stiff resistance from the Portuguese. Portuguese power in West Africa began to decline rapidly when a chaotic struggle over succession to the throne led Spain's Philip II to press his claim by marching into Portugal with his army, and having himself crowned. One of Philip's rivals was Antonio, Prior of Crato, an illegitimate son of a Portuguese royal prince. Finding himself in poverty and exile in England, he raised spending money by granting trading concessions of dubious authority to British merchants for trade to "Guinea," as the West African coast was then known. These concessions formed the basis for England's eventual claim to the River Gambia.

The first English ships to enter the Gambia in 1587 returned with a fine cargo of hides and ivory, but succeeding expeditions met with resistance from Portuguese settlers who questioned the Prior's claim to the Portuguese throne. Queen Elizabeth settled the issue by "absorbing" the Prior's rights to the Guinea coast, and began selling concessions herself. There were few takers at first, for the cautious British merchants were unwilling to risk their funds in dangerous and highly speculative expeditions. Sir Francis Bacon urged the Queen to grant concessions to "noblemen and gentlemen" rather than merchants, because the latter "look ever to present gain," instead of the long-range benefits to England. The Queen took Bacon's advice, and in 1598 gave exclusive trading rights to the River Gambia to Charles, Earl of Nottingham, and Sir John Stanhope, Treasurer of the Chamber. These gentlemen proved no more foolhardy than their commercial predecessors, however, and sent no ships to the Gambia.

By this time, Dutch, French and Hanseatic merchants also began outfitting trading voyages to the Guinea coast. In 1612, the Chevalier de Briqueville led a large French expedition to erect a fort on the banks of the Gambia, and establish a colony. The climate and diseases proved too much for the Frenchmen, however, and the survivors returned home. In 1618, James I of England revived interest in the Coast by granting a patent to a group of businessmen who formed the Guinea Company and dispatched a vessel laden with £1,856 worth of cargo to trade in Gambia. Most of the crew of this ship died from fever or were killed by a native attack instigated by Portuguese settlers. The survivors eventually made their way back to England, but despite the disaster, their report led the Guinea Company to send another ship to the river. Under the command of George Thompson, the second voyage also proved fruitless. Thompson sent the ship home, and with a few men proceeded further upriver in a small boat. His companions did not relish the idea of heading into the unknown stretches of the river, and during an argument with Thompson, they killed him.

Unaware of Thompson's fate, the Guinea Company sent two more cargo-laden ships to Gambia in 1620. Apparently, a large part of the cargo consisted of spirits. According to a passenger, the master of one vessel, "after our passage from Dartmouth, which was in October, untill the middle of March after, about which time he died, was never twenty dayes sober." The residents of Gambia apparently favored alcohol as much as this captain, for the expedition managed to make friends everywhere. At a village called Mangegar, the Englishmen presented gifts to the local king, who "dranke himselfe with his consortes so drunke that the customs were deferred till the next day." Going on to Jarakunda, they found that the chief there was "a perpetual drunkard." At Oranto, they met Chief Suma Tumba, who "made haste to drown his wits in the aquavitee and good liquor we brought him." At Tenda, they found an African trader named Buckor Sano who "liked our drinke so well, he suckt it in."

When he recovered, Buckor Sano was of great assistance to the Englishmen. He introduced them to local chiefs, arranged for them to buy ivory and cloth, and reported on trade in the interior. Richard Jobson, a company agent on this expedition, was one of the first Englishmen to record carefully the life of the natives he encountered:

The men for their part do live a most idle kind of life, imploying themselves (I mean the greater part) to no kinde of trade nor exercise, except it be only some two months of the yeare, which is in tilling and bringing home their countrey corn and graine, wherein the preservation of their lives consists, and in that time their labor is sore. All other times of the yeare, they live wandering up and downe, from one to another, having little understanding, either to hunt in the woods or fish in the waters; . . . In the heat of the day, the men will come forth, and sit themselves in companies under the shady trees to receive the fresh aire, and there pass the time in communication.

Despite Jobson's otherwise glowing account of the expedition, the Guinea Company, finding itself £6,000 in debt after three voyages, decided against another. Besides the lack of profit, they were beginning to have trouble finding crews. Few of the crewmen had returned from these voyages in particularly good health, and many had not returned at all.

It was not until thirty years later, in the reign of Oliver Cromwell, that the Company again sent out ships to the Gambia in search of the legendary mountain of gold rumored to be at the source of the river. For the first time, the company also ordered its agents to buy slaves for shipment to Barbados, where a burgeoning sugar crop demanded more laborers. This 1651 expedition met with a series of misfortunes. When they arrived in the river, they found that all but three men were dead out of a company that had remained behind upon an earlier voyage that year. The heat was stifling. One crewman awoke with a terrible thirst at night, drank a bottle of ink in the dark, and died. A company agent destroyed the town in which part of the ship's cargo and the purchased goods were stored when he bent over a chest of gunpowder while smoking a pipe. While the ships were loading for the return voyage, three raiders entered the river under the command of Prince Rupert, who laid claim to the English throne upon the execution of Charles I. Though his claim meant little in England, Rupert enforced it on the high seas as the self-titled "Lord High Admiral of the Royalist Fleet," and demonstrated it in Gambia by capturing the ships of the Guinea Company. After this affair, the Guinea Company gave up trading in the River Gambia.

In the seventeenth century, there was a prosperous Baltic Duchy known as Courland, which later became Latvia and Lithuania and today has been absorbed by Russia. The Duke of Courland who succeeded to the duchy in 1640 wished to make his mark on the world, but was hampered by the size of his tiny country. He therefore decided that Courland must become a great mercantile power, and dreamed of establishing an overseas empire. Unfortunately, the Duke had few ships, crewmen or spare subjects to settle any colonies. But he did have money, so he hired them. Since his godfather, King James I of England, had given him the Caribbean island of Tobago as a christening gift, the Duke decided to establish a colony on the River Gambia to supply slaves for his island plantations. He sent an agent to Gambia, who easily purchased St. Andrew's Island from the Mandingo King of Barra. The Duke was unaware or unconcerned that this monarch did a thriving business of selling this island as frequently as possible.

The Duke dispatched a small group of Courlanders under a Major Fock to settle St. Andrew's. The Major built an excellent fort, but neglected his water supply. Over the centuries, this proved to be a serious military defect, for the fort's defenders always had to depend on friendly relations with the fickle Kings of Barra to insure a steady supply of fresh water from the opposite shores. A devout Christian, the Duke also sent out two missionaries, Gottschalk Eberling and Joachim Dannefeld, to look after the Courlanders and "especially to see that the heathen souls are brought to a true and right understanding of God."

In 1652, hearing of the mountain of gold at the head of the river, the Duke decided to send out a major expedition. Since he had run out of Courland mariners, he hired a Dutch sea captain named Jacob du Moulin, a disreputable, roving type who had recently left Denmark in great haste. Unaware of the Dutchman's reputation, the Duke made him his Governor in Gambia, gave him three ships, and commissioned him to hire crews and settlers in Denmark and Norway. Du Moulin reached Copenhagen in October, and managed to recruit 140 settlers before the

Danish government demanded that they be put ashore. When the Duke sent him $2,000 (rix) to pay the members of the expedition, Du Moulin used most of it to pay off his personal debts in Copenhagen, selling part of the ships' cargo to outfit the ships.

At the end of December, with the ships still resting peacefully in the harbor at Copenhagen, Du Moulin ordered one of them to proceed to the West African coast, promising to follow later himself. Its captain refused. In March, the three ships set sail for Norway, but the crewmen of two of them mutinied when they received no pay, and brought their ships back to Courland. The Duke had Du Moulin thrown in prison, but released him upon his promise to repay the misused money. There is no record of such repayment.

Apparently a slow learner, the Duke hired another soldier of fortune, this time a Dane named Lieutenant-Colonel Philip von Seitz. A friend of Du Moulin, Von Seitz had arrived in the Courland capital of Mitau and approached Duchess Louisa Charlotte. Through her mediation, the Duke named him Governor of Gambia. After Von Seitz had sailed for Africa, the Duke heard rumors that he planned to turn St. Andrew's Island over to the Spaniards, and wrote letters trying to stop him. He need not have worried. Von Seitz sailed only as far as Hamburg, where he ran the Duke's credit up to $15,000 (rix) and sent the ships back to Courland.

After this experience, the Duke decided to try a Courlander, and picked Captain Otto Stiel. Stiel proved a worthy choice, but the Duke's misfortunes continued. War broke out between Holland and England, and though the Duke remained neutral, both countries found it profitable to seize the ships of Courland. Under Otto Stiel, the Courland settlement on St. Andrew's Island flourished, trading salt, iron and brandy for indigo, coffee, ebony, wax, spice, hides, ivory and gold. Stiel maintained excellent relations with the local chiefs and their people, which proved a valuable investment. By this time, Courland had virtually established commercial control of the river, and with Tobago prospering, the future of the Courland Empire looked bright. Then misfortune struck again. By long tradition, Courland recognized Polish suzerainty. Though relatively meaningless, this arrangement was sufficient to make Courland a legitimate prize when Charles X of Sweden declared war on Poland. One of the first victims of the war was the Duke, who along with his family was captured and carried off into exile for two years. This cut off the Courlanders in Gambia from their source of supplies and money.

Learning of this situation, the Dutch West India Company offered to protect and supply the Courland settlement in exchange for the commercial rights to the river until such time as the Duke was able to look after his own affairs. A Courland agent in Amsterdam accepted this offer without bothering to inform the Duke or the settlement. When the first Dutch ship arrived at St. Andrew's, in 1659, Otto Stiel refused to recognize its authority. When the Courlanders in the fort heard of the Duke's condition, however, they clapped Stiel in irons, handed the fort over to the Dutch, and returned home on the Dutch ship.

The Dutch did not last long. Less than a year later, a French privateer in Swedish service surprised the fort at night, expelled the Dutch garrison, and plundered the island. Hearing this news, Otto Stiel rounded up a ship and some soldiers, and sailed back to reoccupy the island. Three Dutch ships arrived a few weeks later and threatened to bombard the fort. With only a handful of defenders, Stiel had to surrender, and was taken prisoner again. At this point, his friendship with the King of Barra paid off. Seeing the Dutch takeover the fort without any regard to his royal pleasure, the King seized a Dutch water party on the shore, and sent word that he would not release them until Stiel was again in command of the island. Faced with a vast force of hostile natives, and the prospect of no fresh water, the Dutch commander removed all the goods and provisions, destroyed the fort, and handed it back to the Courlanders, threatening to hang Stiel upon their return. Once again, the flag of tiny Courland flew over the Gambia.

In his diary of October 3, 1660, Samuel Pepys recalls overhearing the Duke of York "speak of a great design that he and my Lord of Pembroke have, . . . of sending a venture to some parts of Africa to dig for gold there . . . But I do not find my Lord [of Sandwich] do much like it." Pepys did not invest in this scheme himself, but later, as Secretary of the Admiralty, he followed the affairs of the resulting company, The Royal Adventurers of England Trading into Africa. Behind the new company was Prince Rupert, who had returned to England upon the Restoration, and told his noble companions of the wealth that lay waiting in Gambia. The new company had few worries about competition from England, since the Royal Adventurers had a royal charter and were promised ships from the Royal Navy. Never one to waste the profits accruing from a royal charter, King Charles II himself invested in the company, along with the Queen and many courtiers. No one seemed concerned about the Duke of Courland's claim. The company's purpose was mainly to supply slaves from the Gambia — "from whence a plentiful harvest was rationally to be expected" — for the plantations in the West Indies and the colonies in America, where they would fetch about £17 a head, or a quantity of sugar.

The fleet of the Royal Adventurers reached the mouth of the river in 1661, under the command of Major Robert Holmes, whom Pepys described as "a rash proud coxcombe, . . . though a stout and cunning fellow." At Dog Island, a few miles up the

river, Holmes "caressed and entertained [the natives] very civilly
to gaine their friendship to our people and interest." In his journal, he tells of a visit to the King of Kombo, who lived about 10
miles from the river. Holmes took along two boatloads of soldiers "in case the blacks should prove false for us."

It was a very hott day — no breath of wind stirring. The king
accommodated me with the only horse that was there to be hadd,
but being young and strong, and Captain Stokes old, fatt, and
burley, I let him ride and I walked, which was one of the hardest
taskes that I ever undertook, the sun shineing so very hott, and
all our way upon dry sand. It was soe very hott that our chirur-
geons mate, whom I took along with me for fear of any accident
. . . fell down dead upon the way, and soe did a greyhound I
had with me. Nay, one Mr. Fowler, walking along with me,
carrying a gun upon his shoulder, the excessive heath of the sun
fired it upon his shoulder. [After returning to the ship] I was 3
or 4 daies so dazed in my head that I thought I should never have
recovered.

Upon recovering from what must have been sun stroke,
Holmes decided to deal with the Courlanders on St. Andrew's
Island "by faire or fowle means." By this time, disease had reduced Otto Stiel's company to seven — including women. Hoping to give the impression of a well-armed fort, Stiel fired on two
advance English frigates before they came in range. The wily
Courlander also sent word to his friend, the King of Barra, that
the English had come to enslave him and his people. Holmes
sailed with the entire fleet to within cannon range of the island,
and sent a lieutenant ashore "to let the Governor know that he
had behaved himself verie uncivilly to His Majestie of Great
Brittaines shipps to fire at them for coming peaceably to fetch
water . . . I would have him quietly surrender [the fort] into
my hands; otherwise I would have it by force, which I hope his
prudence would prevent."

After some negotiation, Stiel realized he had no hope, and surrendered the fort for the third time. On March 19, 1661, the seven Courlanders marched out of the fort, while a party from one of the ships raised the British flag and renamed the settlement James Island. For twenty years, the Duke of Courland tried by means of letters, audiences and bribes to regain his rights to the island. England's Charles II replied with promises of consideration, occasional "investigations" of the Duke's claim, and more promises. The Duke finally died in 1681, his dreams of a Courland empire reduced to increasingly apologetic requests for the return of a crumbling fort on a barren island in the River Gambia.

*

For nearly a century, trade in the River Gambia was in the successive hands of the Royal Adventurers, The Gambia Adventurers, and the Royal African Company. (The latter flourished about the same time as the Hudson's Bay Company.) Except for occasional attacks by the Dutch, business was relatively peaceful, if not always profitable. Trade on the river yielded about 500 slaves annually (at a cost of thirty bars of iron each), plus fourteen to fifteen tons of ivory and wax, and 10,000 hides. Ships of every size and every maritime nation sailed up the river — frigates and sloops, shallops and snows, schooners and brigs, pinks, pinaces and caravels. Much of the competition came from private English "interlopers." While both they and the Royal African Company dealt in slaves, the Company, desirous of maintaining good relations with the local chiefs, objected to some of the practices of the interlopers.

> Few or none of them had any consideration in view than barely the ready disposal of all such cargoes as they carried along with them (no matter to whom or which way) and the speedy

procuring of negroes, or any other commodities, which they could get on the coast, whether by purchase or otherways, so as not to stay long there; for accomplishing which design they stuck at nothing, but were too frequently guilty of such sinister practices, as proved not only very injurious to the private interest of the Company, but likewise disgraceful and pernicious to the British interest in general among the natives . . .

The Company's agents on the island also had occasional difficulties with the natives, sometimes caused by the greed of the chiefs and at other times by the callousness of the agents. In 1686, for example, agent Alexander Cleeve had an altercation with Gennow Sonko, Chief of Barra.

> The king . . . arose from his place to come and commune with the said agent concerning the matter, and coming to the town of Jillefree, sent the agent word he was coming to speak with him, but the agent returned answer . . . that if the king would speak with him, he should make haste, for he would depart with the next high water. At which the king . . . went to the agent's pallisadoes, and there sat down at the foot of a great tree to await his master Cleeve's approach, who was no sooner come into the king's presence, but with a great deal of impudence said, "How now, old Gennow, how is it?"
> But one of the grandees, by name Sambalama, taught him better manners by reaching him a box on the ears.

There were also occasional slave rebellions and troubles with pirates who poached on the heavily laden and lightly armed coastal shipping. In 1683, a pirate named Anderson entered the river with a small pink of seven or eight guns, and found the fort at James Island in sad condition — 22 men of the garrison had died of fever within seven months, two had been killed by natives, and one had drowned. Six of the Company's men joined

Anderson's crew while he helped himself to such tackle and provisions from the Company stores as he required.

In the latter part of the seventeenth century, the French replaced the Dutch as England's major competitor on the West
African coast. They captured all the Dutch forts on the coast of
Senegal, and in 1678 established a small post on Dog Island, in
the Gambia River. This installation, like a Dutch one some
years before, ended abruptly when natives from the mainland
surprised and massacred the garrison. As the French moved
through Senegal, the native chiefs happily signed treaties with
them — as they did with anyone else who showed up bearing
spirits or gifts. They enjoyed the pomp of diplomatic negotiation and loved to sign impressive documents pertaining to lands
over which they had only the vaguest of claims. The possibility
that these treaties might conflict with others they had signed
with representatives of other powers either did not occur to the
chiefs, or did not bother them. Such unconcern was reasonable
according to their traditions, for few of their tribal pacts had ever
lasted more than one season. Much of the confusion at negotiating tables in Europe during this period was due to their pleasant
if haphazard attitude toward treaties.

Through such treaties, the French eventually laid claim to the
North Bank of the Gambia. For a monthly payment of four bars
of iron, they obtained from the King of Barra the right to build a
trading post at Albreda — directly across from the English fort
at James Island. As more and more French ships began trading
openly in the river, the agents of the Royal African Company,
who were powerless to do anything about it, sent numerous complaints to London. Their home office did not feel it could afford
to send the reenforcement necessary to drive the French off. At
this time, morale on the tiny island was at a low ebb, and English
prestige among the chiefs had been seriously damaged by the

blatant flaunting of British authority by French ships. The fort was in sad disrepair, ammunition and supplies were low, and the garrison was riddled by disease. French ships began stopping and seizing English ships they found trading along the coast. Before any action was taken on either side, war broke out in Europe between England and France that was to last almost uninterrupted for 25 years.

Along the West African coast the war was generally an affair between gentlemen. The crews of captured ships and the garrisons of captured forts were allowed honorable surrender and safe passage home. When the first attack on the island came in 1695, it proceeded in a most dignified manner. The French commander, Monsieur de Gennes, sent Monsieur de la Roque ashore to open negotiations for the surrender of the fort.

> Monsieur de la Roque was regaled magnificently and the healths of the King of France and the King of England were drunk several times to the sound of artillery. When the meal was finished, Monsieur de la Roque returned on board with three English officers, whom Monsieur de Gennes treated with reciprocal magnificence.

Later that day, the fort replied, "We are resolved to wait for you and to fight you until death, before we surrender, and we do not doubt that we shall meet an honourable enemy." The next morning, after the French had fired two shots, the fort surrendered.

For the next two decades, duty at the fort was a short-term affair as it repeatedly changed hands between the English and the French. Dishonest or incompetent agents allowed the fort to deteriorate and ruined the affairs of the Company. Soldiers died off like flies, and the average life span on the island was not much more than a few years. The Company always managed to find replacements, for few men ever returned from service on James Island to tell about it. One Company advertisement read:

ALL SUCH PERSONS *That are desirous to serve* THE ROYAL AFRICAN COMPANY As souldiers in GUYNE upon the following Terms, may repair to the *African House* in *Leaden-Hall-street London* & find entertainment, VIZ EACH Souldier shall receive as a free Gift (before he proceeds the Voyage) Forty Shillings, also a Bed, Rugg, & Pillows the Company pay his Passage over to *Guyne,* upon his arrival there to enter into pay, at Twenty Shillings *per Month,* the Company finding Diet and Lodging. His wages to be duly paid every Month.

Though this salary was relatively good (an able seaman in the Royal Navy received about the same wage) these ads usually attracted the dregs of London's taverns. The Company's own agents were of a similar breed. One visitor who found the fort "in a ruinous condition," described the agents as "unqualified, knavish, sottish and ignorant persons, who basely cheated the Company."

When the war ended in 1713, with the Treaty of Utrecht, the African Company sent out a new expedition under William Cooke to rebuild the fort at James Island. Cooke's letters complain of inefficient subordinates, English privateers, French, Dutch and Portuguese traders, troublesome chiefs and the unreasonable demands of his employers. His soldiers and artisans were constantly deserting or dying of fever — 22 died within the first seven months. In February, ten of them went off in a Company pinnace. In June, three more went off in a canoe. A month later, two took service with a private trader. Cooke's opinion of the competence of those who remained was so low that he sent two of them back to England:

Wee have sent you in this ship James Irish, said to be a bricklayer, and Richard Shapland, said to be a carpenter, by which your honors may partly see how wee can carry on your business; and, were it not to have countenance of so many white faces, wee might have sent four parts of the five parts of those that remains, for they are rather objects of charity than anything else.

Cooke's troubles came to an end later that year when he died of gout.

By 1719, news of the garrison's weakness began to attract pirates who normally sailed the Spanish main. One named Edward England captured five ships belonging to private traders and a Company sloop in four days' work. A former apprentice to Mr. England, named Howel Davis, appeared a few weeks later, and after a brief show of arms, captured the fort. While he was busy looting the island's stores, half the fever-ridden 14-man garrison decided to join him, preferring life under the Jolly Roger to living like vermin in the stifling, barren fort.

In 1721, fearing that the French, Dutch or Portuguese might try to take over the virtually abandoned fort, the African Company decided to reestablish a permanent settlement there. It dispatched a military governor with 165 persons, including eighty soldiers, twenty women and children, accountants, artisans, a surgeon and a chaplain. This five-ship expedition was plagued with misfortunes. The chaplain left the fleet at Madeira, having suffered "abuse" from one of the captains. Another ship proved unseaworthy and had to turn back. The H.M.S. *Weymouth* ran aground upon entering the river. Arriving at James Island, the newcomers found that the French had demolished the fort, and were forced to live in huts on the mainland with neither "due care, provision nor lodging suitable for any Christian." Within seven months, sixty men and all but one of the women and children were dead. One ship's crew mutinied, seized the ship and sailed away to take up piracy.

While the Company's agents were generally a rough lot who

lived hard, drank deep and died early, there were exceptions, like Francis Moore, a scholarly young man who arrived at Fort James in 1730, as an accounts clerk. Unlike his fellows, who passed their leisure time with rum or brandy, Moore rode, hunted, fished, walked about the country, drew sketches of the animals and birds, and learned Mandingo and the local Creole Portuguese. In his journal, he wrote:

> The Natives are, really, not so disagreeable in their behaviour as we are apt to imagine; for when I went through their Towns, they almost all came to shake Hands with me, except some of the Women, who having never seen any White Men, ran away from me as fast as they could, and would not by any Means be persuaded to come near me. Some of them invited me into their Houses, and brought their Wives and Daughters to salute me, and sit down by me, always finding Things to gape and admire, such as Boots, Spurs, Gloves, Clothes or Wig, each of them being to them Subjects of Discourse or Admiration.

As for the women in the villages close to the island, Moore found that they were considerably different from those further up-river:

> The Girls would have People think they are very modest, especially when they are in Company; but take them by themselves, and they are very obliging; for if you will give them a little Coral or a Silk Handkerchief, you may take what Liberty you please with them . . .

Assigned to an up-river trading post, Moore had to endure the King of Barsally's insatiable thirst for brandy. Moore reported that this monarch occasionally led raids on his own villages, burned them, seized the fleeing people and sold them into slavery in order to raise money to buy brandy. When low on funds, the King was given to raiding the Company post in search of his favorite beverage. One evening he arrived and found a case containing six and a half gallons of brandy that belonged to Moore and a colleague named Harrison. The King ordered Harrison to open the case, but the agent refused, saying it contained nothing but Company papers. "The King was too well acquainted with Liquor Cases to be put off, so he ordered some of his men to hold down Mr. Harrison in bed, rifled his breeches pocket of the key and took out all the brandy contained in the case." While such habits made the King and unwelcome visitor, he usually had the decency to invite the two agents to join him when consuming the Company's brandy.

During the middle of the eighteenth century, conditions in the river changed with each new conflagration in Europe — the War of the Austrian Succession, 1743–48, and the Seven Years War, 1756–63. In time of war, England and France seized each other's ships on various flimsy excuses. The French fort at Albreda was rebuilt, destroyed, rebuilt, burned, rebuilt, overrun and rebuilt again. At one point, the French abandoned the fort completely, leaving only "two black butlers there to hoist their colours every Sunday." Despite the periodic destructions, relations between the two forts remained quite friendly. Cannonades ceased nearly every day to allow the British to fetch water on the mainland, and to permit both sides to try their hands at fishing in the river. Between wars, the officers of each fort would invite their opposite numbers over for as sumptuous a banquet as conditions allowed. Accompanied by artillery salutes, they would toast the healths of both kings till late into the night, the guests returning by canoe.

Despite these banquets, life in the two lonely garrisons was hardly a pleasant existence. A British merchant calling at James Island in 1750 reported that the garrison's original thirty men "were reduced to five or eight, by which means a common soldier had succeeded to the command of the troops." He found the remaining residents of both forts "labouring under fluxes or fevers." A visitor to Albreda found "only one Frenchwoman, all the men except her husband being dead, and he was gone up river trading; and while I was there, she heard that he was dead and all the white men with him, which was a very common case, for she had five husbands in three years."

By this time, the affairs of the Royal African Company were in such a state that Parliament eventually created the Crown Colony of Senegambia, with a governor at St. Louis, on the mouth of the Senegal River, and a lieutenant-governor at James Island. This arrangement proved awkward, for the settlement in Gambia now had to conduct all its affairs with London via St. Louis. The problem was particularly acute because the Governor at St. Louis had "an overmastering aversion to correspondence." A military man who took little interest in administrative affairs, he largely ignored Fort James, using it chiefly as a penal settlement for convicted felons from St. Louis.

When the American colonies rebelled against Great Britain in 1776, the officers at Fort James were instructed to seize the American slave ships that frequently traded there. The French sided with the rebel colonies, which allowed them once again to attack British merchantmen in the river. In 1778, they captured the British fort at St. Louis and reduced Fort James to rubble. This time, the French did the job so well that James Island never again figured prominently in the history of Gambia. In the nearly two centuries since then, the river has slowly eaten away at the island, while the sun, rain, wind and weeds have taken command of the ruins. Today, vines grow over the walls, and rust-covered cannons lie in the water or tilt wildly at the sky. Tourists from Bathurst come up by launch on Sundays to picnic among the ruins and search among the pebbles on the shore for old trading beads. From time to time they find bits of green glass from the rum bottles that helped to while away the lonely hours for the garrisons of the past.

*

In the Treaty of Versailles, in 1783, England ceded to France the fort at St. Louis, in exchange for the rights to the River Gambia. This virtually ended the short-lived province of Senegambia. In view of past commercial and military difficulties in the Gambia, the British government was not anxious to try again, and began to think seriously of turning it into a penal colony. For some time, the jails in England had been dangerously overcrowded, and the "secession" of the American colonies cut off what had been the largest outlet for convicts. For £374 15s, the Crown bought Lemaine Island (now MacCarthy Island), about 100 miles upstream from Fort James. Mr. Evan Nepean of the Home Office urged Parliament to send to Lemaine 200 convicts — "the worst of both sexes." This would save the government a great deal of money, even if "all the settlers should live." A few weak souls spoke up about the inhumanity of sending human beings unaccustomed to the outdoor life to an uninhabited and unpromising island in tropical Africa, but they were shouted down. Parliament finally rejected the proposal on the grounds that "the outcasts of an old society cannot form the foundation of a new one."

A few years later, the Society for Promoting the Discovery of the Interior Regions of Africa sent a young Scottish physician named Mungo Park to learn if trade could be opened between Gambia and the upper reaches of the Niger, and possibly Timbuctu. Arriving in 1795, Park spent his first six months in a village called Pisania, just above Lemaine Island. There he gathered information about the region, learned Mandingo, and fought off the fever. In his journal, Park described "the tedious hours during that gloomy season

when the rain falls in torrents; when suffocating heats oppress by
day, and when the night is spent by the terrified traveller in listening to the croaking of frogs (of which the numbers are byond
imagination) the shrill cry of the jackal, and the deep howling of
the hyaena; a dismal concert, interrupted only by the roar of such
tremendous thunder as no person can form a conception of but
those who have heard it.

The country itself, being an immense level, and very generally
covered with woods, presents a tiresome and gloomy uniformity
to the eye; but although nature has denied to the inhabitants the
beauties of romantic landscapes, she has bestowed on them with
a liberal hand, the more important blessings of fertility and
abundance. A little attention to cultivation procures a sufficiency
of corn; the fields afford a rich pasturage for cattle; and the natives are plentifully supplied with excellent fish.


Though the fort at James Island was no longer used at this
time, many European traders were operating flourishing trading
posts along the river. The slave trade had become so profitable
that ships from England, France, America, Portugal, Spain, Denmark and Prussia crowded into the River Gambia for their black
cargo. In one year, about 3,700 slaves left Gambia for the New
World.

Though Queen Elizabeth had condemned slavery as "a detest-
able act which would call down the vengeance of heaven upon
the undertakers," her compunctions did not prevent her from
investing in the first British slave voyage, in 1562, in which Sir
John Hawkins brought 300 slaves to the West Indies. By investing in the various "royal" companies that subsequently carried
on the trade, the royal family continued to draw considerable
profit from it. While the companies gained the protection of the
Crown and the Royal Navy from this arrangement, the Crown
was protected from embarrassment by the companies' private
status. Between 1680 and 1786, English merchant ships out of
Bristol, Liverpool, London, and Lancaster carried 2,130,000

slaves to the British colonies in America and the West Indies. The British were not alone. By 1790, only fourteen of the forty slave depots on the coast were British. With blessings, tacit approval or silence from Popes and monarchs, few merchants or traders bothered to concern themselves with questions of humanity.

The question is a sticky one. Contrary to the belief of most educated Africans today, the Europeans did not introduce the practice of slavery in Africa — they merely refined and enlarged the marketing system. Africans had practiced slavery long before the arrival of the Europeans, and in fact continue to engage in it to some extent today. In 1620, when the trader Richard Jobson was offered some slaves by an African trader in the Gambia, he refused, noting that the English "were a people who did not deale in any such commodities; neither did we buy or sell one another, or any that had our owne shapes." Even as the trade grew, there were some misgivings. The agent, Francis Moore, recounted how every petty misdemeanor was used by the chiefs as a pretext for selling a man into slavery:

> In Cantore, a Man, seeing a Tyger eating a Deer, which he had kill'd and hung up near his House, fir'd at the Tyger and the bullet kill'd a Man; the King not only condemn'd him, but also his Mother, three Brothers and three Sisters to be sold. They were brought down to me at Yamyamacunda; it made my Heart ake to see them, and I did not buy them; upon which they were sent farther down the River, and sold to some separate Traders at Joar.

As European slave ships increased the demand, the supply changed from a by-product of tribal warfare to its purpose. A Swedish traveler in 1787 described the result:

> The Wars which the inhabitants of the interior parts of the country . . . carry on with each other, are chiefly of a predatory

nature, and owe their origin to the yearly number of slaves which the Mandingoes, or the inland traders suppose will be wanted by the vessels that will arrive on the coast . . . The publick Pillage is, of all others, the most plentiful source, from which the slave trade derives its continuance and support. The Kings of Africa . . . incited by the merchandise shewn them, which consists principally of strong liquors, give orders to their military to attack their own villages in the night.

By 1807, anti-slavery sentiment in England had become so strong that Parliament was forced to pass an act that declared slavery "utterly abolished, prohibited, and declared to be unlawful." Though some hard-headed businessmen called the abolitionists "a pack of snivelling Quakers," the ships of the Royal Navy dutifully proceeded to enforce the act, attacking the slave trade as energetically as they had formerly supported it. Though one English historian ranked his country's crusade against the slave trade "among the three or four virtuous pages comprised in the history of nations," Lord Palmerston, writing in 1844, was less inclined to praise: "If all the crimes which the human race has committed from the creation down to the present day were added together in one vast aggregate, they would scarcely equal . . . the amount of guilt which has been incurred by mankind in connection with this diabolical Slave Trade."

Summing up the first 250 years of British contact with Africa, another British historian concluded that "the effects were almost wholly discreditable. On the coast itself, they contributed virtually nothing to any political or administrative advance. Their only influence on the local ways of life was to change them for the worse."

*

While the suppression of slavery pleased the abolitionists in England, it did not please the Mandingo chiefs in the Gambia.

Unable to understand the change of heart that caused those who had formerly purchased their slaves to now suppress the trade, they retaliated by attacking British ships that tried to seize the foreign slavers. Though America also passed an act in 1807 prohibiting the importation of slaves, crafty Yankee traders out of Providence and Boston continued to thrive by sailing under Spanish colors. Until 1815, American-owned vessels, along with those of France, Spain and Portugal, managed to carry off thousands of slaves from the River Gambia, no longer hampered by British competition. As the Royal Navy became increasingly diligent, however, the trade grew riskier, the profits grew higher, and the men who engaged in it became increasingly unsavory. Such were the types who crammed Africans into the holds like animals, and pushed shiploads of slaves overboard when under pursuit by one of His Majesty's frigates.

Unable to patrol the coast effectively enough to stop the slavers, the Secretary of State, Lord Bathurst, instructed Governor Charles MacCarthy in Senegal to establish a fort either on James Island, or at some more suitable site. In 1816, MacCarthy dispatched Captain Alexander Grant to the Gambia River with fifty men of the African Corps and twenty-four artisans to construct a new fort. Realizing that James Island was strategically defective, Captain Grant decided to erect the fort instead on Banjul Island, a sandbar commanding the river mouth. The King of Kombo agreed to cede the island (renamed St. Mary's) in exchange for British protection and an annual payment of 103 bars of iron. Grant quickly constructed a barracks for the soldiers, and a battery of six twenty-four pounders. (Except for some continued French activity, these guns effectively ended the slave trade on the river.) To encourage settlers, Grant offered them free lots in the new settlement. Many British traders operating up-river and in Senegal took up this offer, along with many Woloff petty traders from St. Louis and Gorée, an island off the coast of modern Dakar. Though Lord Bathurst approved the site of the new fort, he noted that it should be merely a defensive outpost, and cautioned that "you are not to consider yourself authorized to incur any expense, which may have for its object a permanent establishment." Despite the Lord's qualified blessing, it was decided to name the new town "Bathurst."

Because of the protection offered by the presence of the British troops, the new colony grew rapidly. By 1819, there were 700 civilian residents, including thirty Europeans. By 1825, the population had doubled. Nearly forty ships put in at Bathurst in 1817, and within six years, the revenues from trade increased from £500 to £3,500. Captain Grant laid out streets and built many of the public buildings that still stand today, including the Secretariat and Government House. Under his command, the new settlement prospered, the merchants thrived, and relations with the surrounding natives remained excellent.

Grant deserves a great deal of credit for accomplishing his mission so well, considering the quality of his men. The rank and file of the Royal African Corps were recruited mainly from the prisons of England and the discards of other military units. They lived in such miserable conditions that they looked on their assignment to Bathurst as tantamount to a sentence of death. For many, it was. In May, 1825, a ship arrived with 199 fresh recruits. Since there was insufficient accommodation, only 108 landed, and the rest remained on board ship. By the end of that rainy season, 87 of the new men were dead. Since that meant more room, the remaining 91 disembarked. Within three months, 73 more had died. The following March, 200 replacements arrived from Sierra Leone, described as "men of the most desperate character." By August, only 116 of them were left, 93 of whom were in the hospital under the care of a solitary acting assistant hospital mate. By 1827, the authorities in London belatedly decided that Bathurst was unhealthy for British troops, and replaced the garrison with units of the West India Regiment, composed largely of ex-slaves.

As the town grew, its several sections acquired separate names. The soldiers lived in Soldier Town, the Woloff (or "Joloffs") from St. Louis and Gorée lived in Joloff Town, and the mixed-blood descendants of earlier "coasters" occupied Portuguese Town. (All mulattoes were generally referred to as "Portuguese.") Among the British traders lived an African named Thomas Joiner. Born a Mandingo, he had been kidnapped as a young boy and carried off to America as a slave. His talents eventually won him his freedom, and he returned to Africa to set up as a trader. He became one of the wealthiest traders in Bathurst, and dwelled in one of the largest houses in town. Next door, in a smaller house, lived a mulatto trader named Robert Aynsley, the man who years before had sold Joiner to the captain of an American slave ship.

The town's several residential units were separated by strips of open land designed for cultivation to sustain the settlement. By 1844, the sandy island still had forty such acres under cultivation, but one visitor described them as "patches of ground on which labour has been lavished, where some sickly vegetation seems to be doing violence to the poverty of the soil." Grant, by then a Major, purchased some land out on breezy Cape St. Mary as a convalescent station for Bathurst's crowded hospital, and also to serve as a site for a navigation light for ships entering the river. For years, the "lighthouse" there consisted of a lantern hung on a prominent palm tree.

Though floods, fever and humidity made life in the new settlement a curse for many, some managed to fight off such discomforts with a flourishing social life. Any visiting ship or official was grounds for a round of festivities. As Reverend Thomas Poole wrote after visiting Bathurst for a few weeks, "dinner parties and excursions succeeded one another without intermission." The dinner parties "commence about two o'clock, and are kept up till the guests find neither time nor inclination to do anything but arrange some plan for the next day's amusement . . . Happier days I had not known since I last left Old England."

As trade on the river increased, Major Grant established a fort on MacCarthy Island to protect up-river traders. Another reason for spreading out was the growing number of liberated slaves arriving in Bathurst. British cruisers which captured foreign slave ships generally brought the cargoes to Freetown, Sierra Leone, which transferred many to Bathurst. Repatriation seemed out of the question, since many of these ex-slaves came from far into the interior. Some were unable to tell what their "country" was, and others would most likely have been re-enslaved had they returned. Most were in poor health after being crammed into the slavers' holds, and were unable to fend for themselves. Officials in Bathurst attempted to find work for them as apprentice artisans, and many of them thus merged into the local African community. The officials purchased nearby Deer Island as a haven for some of them, but had to abandon the project when they learned that Deer Island was under water during half the year.

In better physical condition than the freed slaves, but even less able to fend for themselves in the African bush, was a group of 351 ex-slaves who had been working in relative comfort in England. In a burst of ill-considered energy, the Society for the Abolition of Slavery gathered these men up in 1787, and shipped them off to Freetown, a colony they had established for this purpose. To assure the permanence of the new settlement, they also sent along sixty women "swept up from the gutters of London and Portsmouth." One historian commented on this venture: "There surely could never have been so strange a band of pioneers. A number of the men had been servants of the wealthy in Britain — footmen, valets and the like — used to the second-hand luxury and perquisites of such callings. Here they were, deposited in good faith on the edge of that brooding forest land from whence their forefathers had come, in a country still peopled by wild and naked tribesmen." Through the nineteenth century, some of the light-skinned descendants of this group, known as "Akus," moved up the coast to Bathurst, where, because they spoke English, they managed to find work as assistants to traders and shopkeepers.

In the early years of the settlement at Bathurst, British missionaries who attempted to look after the settlers and the freed slaves suffered as high a mortality rate as the soldiers. In 1823, the Society of Friends sent a mission to Bathurst under a fifty-year-old leader named Hannah Kilham. Though she and her co-workers established a mission, translated bits of the Bible into Woloff, and trained some natives in agriculture, all but one returned to England suffering from fever. The one who remained "succumbed to the climate." The same fate befell the early members of the Wesleyan Mission and two French Sisters of Charity.

The oldest Christian group in Bathurst is the Wesleyan Methodist Mission, established in 1821 at the invitation of Governor MacCarthy. Thirteen years later, Reverend William Fox opened the present Wesley Church on Dobson Street with a membership of 300 souls. Later transferred to the settlement of liberated slaves on MacCarthy Island, Reverend Fox found his flock rapidly increasing:

> To-day I united in marriage thirty couples of liberated Africans, the female part of whom had only recently been rescued from the slave-ship by His Majesty's cruisers. There may be an evil in this wholesale system of marrying; but when there are two

evils prudence dictates that we choose the least; and believing this to be the least of the two, I perfectly concurred with the governor in the propriety of thus uniting them in matrimony. The courtship, though of short duration, was mutual; the man having "popped the question" as in other lands, he almost immediately received an answer in the affirmative from the female; and so they were married, and duly and properly registered; and it is to be hoped that all parties will attend to the vows they have now made. At all events, I did my duty, though it was with some difficulty that I maintained my accustomed gravity during a part of the service.

With the local population, spiritual progress was considerably slower. In 1833, for example, when Bathurst's Reverend and Mrs. William Moister crossed the river to pay a social call on Chief Burungai Sonko, King of Barra, the results were not encouraging.

His sable majesty was not seated upon a throne; but reclining upon a couch, in a state of intoxication. With the assistance of his councillors, he raised himself up to receive us with true African etiquette. He was incapable of much conversation; and we had not been long in his presence before I saw him put his hand under the couch and take out an old English tea-kettle. This was the King's decanter, in which he kept his rum. He first drank from the spout himself; then poured a quantity of the "fire-water" into a calabash and offered it to us; but we respectfully declined the favour.

During the first few decades of the settlement, relations with the surrounding native population were generally friendly. Both soldiers and natives, however, would occasionally take too much rum, and insult the other, but apologies — requested or demanded — usually ended the matter. As each new chief assumed office, he had to make a reasonable show of defiance to the British to demonstrate to his people that he was not one to be pushed around. On the few occasions that disputes led to hostilities, British efforts were frequently ill-considered or embarrassing. One edgy officer at MacCarthy Island read the Riot Act to a band of unruly Mandingos who spoke no English. When they did not disperse, he ordered his men to fire. In another incident, a party of soldiers and members of the River Fencibles, a Bathurst civilian militia, were routed when they attempted a punitive assault on a village across the river in Barra. A superior force from the village chased them back to their boats, killing 23 men. Four months later, with the help of British and French reinforcements, the "rebellion" was put down.

For many years the French remained active at Albreda. French men-of-war visited it from time to time, usually neglecting to salute the British flag over Bathurst — a breach of international etiquette. Extensive diplomatic correspondence would flow between London and Paris upon each violation. A British Governor who visited Albreda in 1843 called it a "paltry, miserable settlement," and the French must have agreed, for in 1857 they ceded it to England. This did not end French trade on the river, however. A later Bathurst official was galled to report that "while I write, I count thirty tricolours, six stars and stripes and but one union jack flying in the port of Bathurst."

As punitive expeditions against unruly tribes began to raise the expense of the Gambia colony about midcentury, some Members of Parliament in London advocated ceding it to France. They argued that the French already controlled all the surrounding territory and most of the trade on the river; the garrison at Bathurst was costing £20,000 a year; the settlement's revenues were precarious; and the fort no longer had any strategic value. These M.P.'s spoke of the "hopelessness of extending civilization among the peculiar people which surrounds and composes the bulk of the settlement." These sentiments naturally drew protests and petitions from Gambia's British merchants, African traders (who considered themselves British subjects), the Wesleyan mission, liberated slaves and local chiefs. Along with loyalty to England, many of these protests were based on much more practical considerations. The merchants stood to lose a profitable trade; the Wesleyan missionaries would be swallowed by the French Catholics in Senegal; the chiefs and headmen would have to begin all over again to court a new protector; and the educated Africans would lose the one social and economic asset that set them apart and above their more primitive brethren — the ability to speak English. A letter of protest from one chief began, "I Tomani Bojang, King of Kombo, thank the Queen for all past favours." He reminded the Queen that "when your subjects required a piece of land, for farming or building purposes, I have never refused . . . My reason for so doing is because I love the British people and like their friendship . . . Even Bathurst, which your Majesty is about to give away to strangers, was given to you by my grandfather." Chief Bojang added that in case the Queen went ahead and ceded the settlement to France, "I would rather you return my territory back to me as an act of friendship."

In their negotiations with England, the French offered to exchange their posts on the Ivory Coast for Gambia. (Ivory Coast now has the most flourishing economy of any country in Black Africa.) Later they offered the Gabon coast instead. (Gabon is now one of the world's major suppliers of uranium.) The British declined both offers. Several other sections of the West African coast were suggested, but reluctance to give up part of the Empire, protests from Bathurst, and the outbreak of the Franco-Prussian War in 1873 ended the negotiations. The issue arose again, later in the century, but never gained much momentum.

*

Referring to kings and kingdoms in Gambia is somewhat mis-
leading, for the kingdoms of Barra and Kombo were hardly
comparable in size or power to the ancient Kingdom of Mali, or
even the contemporary Kingdom of the Ashanti in Ghana. Barra
and Kombo and the other kingdoms of nineteenth-century
Gambia were relatively small, loosely organized regions, governed
by petty chiefs who could claim the allegiance only of the villages
in their region. Because the tribes intermingled more in Gambia
than elsewhere, the chieftainships became territorial, rather than
tribal, and therefore less stable. Many of the "royal" districts,
particularly those in the upper river regions, were so fragile that
their chiefs rose to and fell from power with awesome rapidity.
However short the term of office, chiefdom was hereditary,
passing from father to son, brother, cousin or nephew. Pagan
beliefs invested these chiefs with quasi-divine status. The rest of
tribal society was divided into distinct social castes — nobles,
warriors, farmers, artisans, tradesmen, musicians, household slaves
and captured slaves. These castes were also hereditary, and
except for warriors and captured slaves, they still exist today.

In the nineteenth century, traditional pagan beliefs came
under serious pressure from Islam. For centuries, Moorish
traders and holy men called "marabouts" had traveled about
West Africa, spreading the word of the Prophet, although there
were still few Moslems in Gambia by 1800. In the nineteenth
century, the marabouts increased the pressure, and the new faith
began to spread rapidly through the African trading communities
and the lower Mandingo castes. Most of the chiefs and the
higher castes looked on Islam as an evil from the north that
could endanger their power, for devout Moslems might eventually choose between the authority of their king and the Koran.
(They did.) As Islam gradually established itself in Gambia,
two sects arose — the Marabouts, or devout Moslems, and the
Soninkis, who refused to abstain from liquor, as prescribed by the

Koran, and were generally more concerned with tribal than religious customs.

Until the middle of the nineteenth century, the Marabouts were still a minority, and as a result, they suffered persecutions at the hands of the Soninkis. Like the Jews in Egypt and the early Christians in Rome, they gained strength and unity from these persecutions, and began to gather in their own "Morokundas," or holy cities. By 1850, the Marabout villages began to band together in loose confederacies. At the same time, Moorish holy men began preaching a "Jehad," or holy war against the unbelievers. Fighting broke out with surrounding Soninki villages, mostly done by traditional Serahuli and Serrere mercenaries. Raids and retaliatory raids eventually involved the British, who felt bound to defend the loyal Soninki chiefs with whom they had signed treaties. In the first serious outbreak, in 1855, troops of the West India Regiment and the Bathurst Militia attacked a Marabout village in the Kombo. The Marabouts, trained and led by a Moor named Omar, repulsed the attack and killed or wounded more than a quarter of the British troops. For a time, nearly defenseless Bathurst feared an attack, but the Marabouts withdrew to their village. Eventually, a combined Anglo-French force from Gorée and Sierra Leone came to the rescue, aided by some loyal natives from Barra and Kombo, and successfully stormed the heavily stockaded village.

In the 1860's a Marabout leader known as Maba or Mahaba overran the kingdoms of Baddibu and Sine Saloum in another holy war. Soninki prisoners had the choice of shaving their heads, renouncing drink, and becoming Moslems — or being killed. In this way, Islam spread rapidly through Baddibu and Sine Saloum. The military commander at Bathurst described Maba's style of attack in this report to the Duke of Newcastle:

> On approaching a town he intends to destroy, he dismounts from his horse, orders his praying carpet to be spread, and calls

for writing materials. A staff of blind Marabouts now surround him, repeating in a low chaunt that God is great and that there is only one God and Mahomet is his prophet. Mahaba then most earnestly writes grees, or charms, which he hastily distributes to his warriors, who, as they now imagine themselves doubly armed, rush to victory or heaven. It is said that Mahaba has never yet been seen under fire or even been known to carry a weapon.

Encouraged by Maba's success, Marabout leaders in other parts of Gambia began to take up arms. Though their battles were called "religious wars," many of them degenerated into brutal raids on defenseless villages. Pillage and plunder proved as satisfying as converting the heathen.

As the rule of the traditional hereditary chiefs became increasingly fragile under the attacks of the Marabouts, many chiefs turned into petty war lords. Traditional forms of rule broke down, leaving disorder and chaos. Villagers who merely wanted to be left alone to tend to their farming did not dare to venture out into their fields. Dozens of beleaguered headmen offered to cede their villages to the British in exchange for protection against the Marabouts. On instructions from the Colonial Office in London, which wanted the least possible involvement in native affairs, the commanders at Bathurst had to refuse all but temporary protection in emergencies. Fortunately for the exhausted British troops and the average African villagers, fighting stopped briefly each year during the rains, when everyone returned to their own villages to plant their crops. To add to the turmoil of these times, several thousand Fula warriors from the interior swooped down into Gambia each year, attacking both Marabout and Soninki villages with no evident spiritual purpose. Bakari Sardu, one of the Fula chiefs, had the benefit of a French education, and had been awarded the Legion d'Honneur. Perhaps because of this cultural heritage, Bakari Sardu only attacked villages in British territory.

By 1864, the Marabouts of the Kombo had gathered around the town of Gunjur, under the command of a young man named Fodi Kabba, whose organizational talents enabled him to form a confederacy of all the Marabouts in the middle and lower river kingdoms. In a letter to the Administrator at Bathurst, he once wrote: "I beg to say I have nothing to do with groundnuts. . . . Ever since I knew myself to be a man, my occupation has been a warrior; and I make it my duty to fight the Soninkis, who profess no religion whatever." In his annual report, that same Administrator described Fodi Kabba as "a curse to the neighborhood. He lives by slave hunting and robbery . . . he naturally attracts to himself all the idle and worthless ruffians, who prefer living on the industry of others to doing any honest work for themselves."

Frequently the Marabouts' work was easy. The Soninki village of Manduari, for example, fearing a raid from nearby Gunjur, stockpiled its gunpowder and placed it in the charge of the village headman. This worthy promptly sold the gunpowder and fled to the Marabouts at Gunjur. There, he underwent a rapid conversion to Islam, and led an attack on Manduari. By 1875, the Marabouts controlled most of the Kombo, and the remaining Soninkis withdrew to the edge of British-held territory near Bathurst. A small remnant under Chief Tomani Bojang erected a stockade within 400 yards of the colony, hoping for protection. The British offered to resettle Chief Bojang across the river, but rather than leave the land of his ancestors, he finally surrendered to the Marabouts. The last of a dynasty which had ruled the Kombo for more than two centuries, old Tomani Bojang was forced to shave his head and profess himself a Moslem.

Wars continued off and on for another 25 years, disturbing trade and frustrating the attempts of the average villager to simply plant and harvest and be left alone. In 1901, the last major battle took place when a massive Anglo-French expedition went after Fodi Kabba, who though seventy years old, was still stirring up considerable mischief. Troops from the Third West India Regiment, the Second Central African Regiment, marines from three British ships, French troops and a band of Fula warriors finally defeated Fodi Kabba at his stockade at Medina. For some reason, perhaps to prove that he could take it with him, the old warrior had locked his 40 wives in a room over the powder magazine. Shortly after the attackers opened fire, the powder and his wives exploded.

Along with Fodi Kabba, the Administrators at Bathurst had to contend with various other disturbances. African traders up-river continued to deal in slaves, carrying them to Senegal, where the French continued to allow slavery. In 1859, a yellow-fever epidemic killed all but ten Europeans at Bathurst. A few years later, more than one-fourth of the settlement's 4,000 residents and thousands more along the river died in an outbreak of cholera. In this manner, another section of Bathurst acquired its name — Half Die.

> The first thing every morning, Mr. Fowler [the Colonial Secretary] went round to collect the dead in the streets, lifting the bodies with his own hands into the carts, as sufficient men could not be obtained for love or money. . . . So many natives have been struck down whilst engaged in this work, it is only by the free use of brandy that one or two can be prevailed upon to take the risk of supplying their places . . . The natives are given up to despair and drink, and it is a work to distinguish the dead from the intoxicated; . . .

A later visitor to Bathurst described another problem:

> During the rains the chief part of the town is overflowed, and the people catch fish in the middle of the streets. Occasionally a

crocodile from the creek makes its appearance, affording the natives considerable amusement, . . . Other natives enjoy the Venetian pastime of rowing up and down the streets in boats . . .
Luckily these floods soon subside, the muddy soil covered with a
great coat of sand, under which the water stagnates, and becomes
prejudicial to health from the air being overloaded with evil
odours.

Somehow, despite all these problems, the settlement remained relatively prosperous. Ships continued to call at the river
to pick up peanuts, hides, wax and other products the traders
brought down from their up-river stations. Soldiers, crews,
traders and merchants supported many grog shops — or "estab-
lishments for the promotion of civilization." The major administrative problem for the settlement was its status as a kind of
province of the British Colony at Sierra Leone. All legislative
and judicial matters had to be approved by the Governor, 500
miles down the coast in Freetown, before Bathurst could take
action. One Governor complained to the Secretary of State
about this arrangement, noting that "it would be easier for the
general officer at Cork to take charge of the Barbadoes."

Finally, in 1888, with the prospect of cession to France no longer at issue, Gambia became a separate colony. A joint Anglo-
French boundary commission marked off the borders between
Gambia and Senegal, but since there were few distinguishing
natural boundaries, the border was — and still is — much clearer
on maps than it was to the villagers who lived near it. The headman of Suwarrakunda, thought to be in Senegal, was informed
that henceforth his village would be considered part of Gambia.
The shrewd headman, who would have to live there after the
members of the boundary commission left, told a British official
that he would like to see some evidence of England's authority
over his village before he ignored that of France. "If Your Excel-

lency sees a woman with her husband, and you like her for wife, you are to drive away her husband before you get her for wife."

In 1901, after signing treaties with all the chiefs of the Gambia for protection against Fodi Kabba and the Fula raiders, England finally organized the up-river districts into the Protectorate. With authority over the entire country, the administration in Bathurst suddenly found itself with 150,000 people spread over 4,000 square miles along the river, instead of 14,000 isolated in about seventy square miles near the coast. In governing the new colony, England applied a policy of "indirect rule" that Lord Lugard had established in Nigeria. It meant administering a country through the existing chiefs and headmen, instead of replacing them — as the French did — with Europeans. In this way, the British managed to rule great areas and populations in Africa with very few white administrators, while the French had to create a vast network of local French officials. The British system turned many native rulers into creatures of colonial power who later stood as a reactionary force in the way of the movement to independence. While the French attempted to create native Europeanized elites in the cities, the English were content to let the Africans remain Africans, perhaps because they would be easier to govern.

The government in Bathurst passed laws regulating trade and prohibiting slavery, but left most other matters to the chiefs and headmen. Traveling Commissioners went out to instruct the villagers in the new laws, and help settle disputes. Even in the twentieth century, this was still a hazardous occupation. Of the first twelve Traveling Commissioners, three died on duty, two were killed and one was disabled. But they did their job well. After centuries of tribal warfare, the guns were still. The villagers planted in peace, and prospered.

When war broke out in Europe in 1914, more than 400 Gambians fought with the Royal West African Frontier Force against the Germans in Cameroon and East Africa. One Frontier Force song emerged from these campaigns:

> *Fine, fine soldier,*
> *Fine, fine soldier.*
> *Some are dere, some are dere:*
> *When he go to war, first-class he go,*
> *Second-class he go, German war over.*

Of the men of the Gambia Company, Brigadier-General F. G. H. Cunliffe wrote:

> They have been called upon to take part in a great struggle, the rights and wrongs of which they can scarcely be expected dimly to perceive. They have been brought through the, to them, extremely novel experience of facing an enemy armed with modern weapons and led by highly trained officers. Their rations have been scanty, their barefoot marches long and trying, and their fighting at times extremely arduous. Yet they have not been found wanting in discipline, devotion to their officers, or personal courage.

Between the two World Wars, several schemes were put forth for developing Gambia, but the Colonial Office was reluctant to spend any money. Advisers came and went, and made reports. Officials in London discussed the reports and shelved them. Badly needed drainage schemes were turned down, and for a short time, to save funds, the government abolished the post of Medical Officer of Health.

During World War II, the dispute was closer to home, for the colonial officials in neighboring Senegal sided with Vichy France. The Allies attacked Dakar, only ninety miles away, and Gambia lived under intermittent threat of invasion. Hundreds of Gambians volunteered for service in the Field Force, and the Gambia

Regiment saw honorable service in Burma. Thousands of miles from Gambia, they sang this song:

> *When shall I see ma home?*
> *When shall I see ma native land?*
> *I shall nebber forget ma home;*
> *I leave my fader,*
> *I leave my modder,*
> *When shall I see ma home?*

One resident of war-time Bathurst observed the training of the Gambia Regiment:

The young African starts off with one natural bent towards Army life — he likes doing things in company. On the other hand, he is a democrat; before taking action of any kind, he likes to sit and discuss it with all his friends, sleep a night on any decision taken, and then do the opposite of what he had decided on the day before. British NCO's, used to raw recruits in England, felt baffled; the Englishman, having had it carefully explained what he was to do, made some attempt, however bungling, to do it. The African listened with bland inattention to their orders and did, in a vaguely amiable way, what he felt inclined to do. True, they were enthusiastic soldiers, and on occasion their enthusiasms would coincide with the wishes of their superior officers.

During the war, thousands of British military personnel poured into Bathurst, turning it into an armed military camp and a major naval and air base. A group of British, French, Lebanese and African wives formed the Gambian Women War Workers, and met regularly at Government House. General de Gaulle passed through the city twice on his way to rally the forces of Free France in Africa. President Roosevelt stopped off after his 1942 meeting in Casablanca, but reportedly did not like it much.

The observer quoted above recorded his impressions of war-time Bathurst:

Wages quadrupled, apart from the many pickings available to the ingenious. Rackets grew up, flourished, were closed down and started elsewhere. Pubs and canteens abounded. Free enterprise came into its own; broken down Syrians living in broken down shops became leading capitalists; rich Africans lost every penny they had attempting impossible contracts; a recreation centre, run at an annual loss . . . was converted into a house of ill-fame.

Vast quantities of military stores were lying around, awaiting disposal by the relevant department. But the relevant department was never so quick as the indigene. Great parks of military vehicles would be assembled and boards of survey held. But the stocks melted away . . . On a dark night, it was a poor man that could not remove a couple of staff car Humbers . . . or strip a lorry of every portable part in twenty minutes. All over the country a transport and building boom began. Houses were roofed with the wings of Sunderlands, strange vehicles built of Bren carriers lumbered along the roads; engines from Air-Sea Rescue launches, like race horses in a farm wagon, drove launches in the less frequented creeks. At night . . . the quiet was broken by a monotonous rattle, as hundreds of Wolofs and Mandinkas and Fulas wrenched and tore and hammered at the surplus stores.

*

Among the many distinguished visitors and guests of the government during the week of independence, were five of Gambia's former governors: Sir Arthur Richards, Sir Hilary Blood, Sir Andrew Barkworth Wright, Sir Percy Wyn-Harris and Sir Edward Windley. All but Sir Percy arrived on a special charter flight from London. He had come some weeks earlier on his 35-foot sloop, the *Spurwing.* This was typical, for in his nearly 10-year reign, from 1949 to 1958, he established himself as by far the most colorful of Gambia's recent governors. Sir Percy ruled Gambia at a time when the governor still governed, and was not merely a ceremonial appendage. Despite the seven years that have passed since his rule, he is still extremely popular. Everywhere he goes, either in Bathurst or up-river, Gambians rush up to greet him with cries of "Hello Pa," and he often responds with their first names. He is popular partly because his term as Governor was particularly long, and partly — his critics say — because he spent little of that time in Government House attending to dull paper work. Sir Percy himself proudly points out that he spent half his time up-river, nosing about unexplored creeks, and even during this visit, he stopped only briefly in Bathurst, before making a two-week trip up-river in the *Spurwing*. A veteran Gambian riverman said, "Dat Pa Wyn-Harris, he know de ribba better past all Gambia man."

Gambians today still tell of Sir Percy's numerous feats and eccentricities. Upon taking over the Governorship, he found that his predecessor, Blood, had been accustomed to importing expensive French vintages for table wine at Government House. He immediately ordered a few barrels of cheap Portuguese wine and had it served in ornate glass decanters. "No one ever questioned it," he says. "The French stuff was a bloody waste of money." During a tour of an up-river rice project, he startled a native chief by wading fully dressed into the rice paddies to examine the crop. The chief, in billowing robes and brocaded finery, could not afford to be upstaged by the white master. He followed Sir Percy into the paddies, his robes floating at waist level and an attendant struggling to shade him with his parasol. Once, when the government wharf seemed in a particularly bad state of disrepair, the Marine Department decided to send a diver down to examine the pilings. The Department unearthed an ancient patched diving suit, but found no one willing to don it. When word reached Government House, Sir Percy volunteered. "I got into the thing and went down," he says, "but the water was so murky that I didn't have a clue about pilings. So I mucked about for a while, then came up and told them the wharf was fine and would last another five years. And it did."

Percy Wyn-Harris was born in 1903, and graduated from Cambridge University. After working for a time in his family's iron foundry business, he joined the Colonial Service as a District Officer in Kenya, at an annual salary of about $840. An excellent mountaineer, he made one of the early ascents of Mt. Kenya, and took part in the 1933 Mt. Everest expedition. During his 23 years in Kenya, he served in various parts of the country, and eventually became Chief Native Commissioner. In 1949, he was knighted and named Governor of The Gambia. "I hadn't the foggiest idea where the place was," he says now. Although he retired at fifty-five, Sir Percy immediately took up a series of Colonial Office special assignments in Nyasaland (now Malawi), Cameroon, and other points in Britain's diminishing empire. Finally, in 1963, he retired completely, and now spends most of his time cruising about the world in his sloop. This present voyage had taken him to Athens and Gibraltar before coming down to Gambia, and just after independence he set sail for the Bahamas.

My first sight of Sir Percy came a few weeks before independence. He had moored only that afternoon, and a group of Englishmen in blazers, puffed ascots and old-school ties were sitting in the lounge of the Atlantic Hotel awaiting him. They had been waiting with increasing impatience for nearly an hour when Sir Percy burst in from the terrace, his soggy suit dripping water on the lounge floor. "Sorry I'm late," he said. "We motored up from the mooring in the dinghy, and swamped as we tried to beach it out here. There's a pretty heavy surf." He then sat down and fished some wet cigarettes out of a tin.

Two weeks later, during the celebrations, Sir Percy appeared again at the hotel, after his trip up-river, wearing the same rumpled gray flannel suit. He has the face of a ruddy cherub. His sparkling gray eyes, wind-reddened cheeks, and large sun-burned nose are capped by an unruly shock of white hair. Stocky and barrel-chested, he stands just over five feet. He invited me out to see his boat, and we drove down to the dockyard in an old, battered, gray Rolls Royce, the pride of Ali Jacobs' car rental stable. On board the *Spurwing*, I mentioned that there had been a great deal of talk about the "ravages" or "yoke" of colonialism during the week's many speeches, and in the local press. I asked Sir Percy what he felt about such talk. "I, for one, am not ashamed of our Colonial Service," he said. "When I came out to Kenya, in 1926, they hadn't even come to the wheel. Disease was rampant everywhere. No man was safe from raids from tribes like the Masai. But it was great work. You had a tremendous number of African friends, and you also had African enemies, but at least it was worth living. You've got to be jolly tough to work in Africa. If you start ten things and even one succeeds, you're damned lucky. What I think is astonishing is that we were able to accomplish so much."

"What about the implications of racial discrimination in some of the talk about colonialism?"

"If one lives in an African community, many of one's friends are African, of course, but there's still a social distinction. In my time there were never many Gambians of sufficient financial standing to come to the Bathurst Club. Many of the chiefs today would be quite uncomfortable at a Government House reception. In Kenya we never thought of inviting Africans to dinner. It would have been incongruous. This has nothing to do with color. While there was a color bar in Ghana and Nigeria, there has never been one here. It's so small that the British and Gambians had to get along together. There was a wonderful warmth and affection between many of them. When Ben Leese, the Chief Commissioner, died, four thousand Gambians came to his funeral. Things have always been very relaxed here. When I first arrived, the prisoners who worked at the docks unloaded my baggage. They rushed up the steps of Government House and welcomed me. We shook hands, and they hoped I'd have a pleasant tour."

"Did you ever have any serious troubles when you were Governor here?"

"Troubles? No, not really. The real trouble in Gambia is the lack of education."

"But many Gambians feel the British Colonial administration was responsible for this problem."

As he poured two cups of tea, Sir Percy broke in sharply. "The function of government in the last century was keeping the peace. This was true in Gambia, Kenya and also in England and America. The idea that the government is somehow responsible for public education did not become current until well into this century. In Kenya, in 1926, the government had just decided that it should do something about education. As for Gambia, you have no idea what a lack of money and teachers there was. People who talk about education have no idea of the difficulty of starting with no money and no teachers. The worst thing has been the lack of a literate populace to start with. Even with money and teachers, the government still has the problem of illiterate homes. It was only seven years ago that the chiefs issued the order to get girls to school. And they are today's mothers.

"And then much of the education has been misdirected — all aimed at government office jobs, and no agricultural training. We can't even get any Gambians who want to be Commissioners up-river. They think they're destined for better things. Many of today's elected officials had risen no higher than third grade clerks, and never gave an order in their lives."

"Why didn't the British Government foresee some of these problems? Why didn't they make better preparations for independence?"

Sir Percy smiled. "As for independence, neither the Africans nor the Colonial governments recognized the possibility until after World War II. When I left here, only seven years ago, no one was talking or even thinking about independence. The wheel of education was just beginning to turn, and economically Gambia was still living on its hump. You see, it's an incredibly expensive operation, running a country."

As I climbed into the dinghy to head back to shore, Sir Percy stood on the deck of the *Spurwing*, squinting into the sun. His shock of white hair blew in the breeze. "Remember," he yelled, as I pulled away, "you can't really live in Gambia unless you have a good sense of humor. It's a wonderful country, and a lot of fun, and it should be taken that way."

## GORDON EDWARDS

One February afternoon, shortly before independence, a
white Rolls Royce pulled up to the Atlantic Hotel. A Gambian
chauffeur in white livery, cap and gloves stepped out smartly and
opened the rear door. Out climbed a big man, dressed in a white
suit, white shoes and socks, and a white tie on a dark shirt. All
this was embellished by black sunglasses, black pipe and a black
wood walking stick with a carved African head for a handle.
This, friends in the lounge informed me, was Gordon Edwards,
Commissioner at Basse for the Upper River Division. They described him as "a book in himself" — a wealthy eccentric throw-
back to the old colonial days, ruling Gambia's most distant outpost with a firm paternal hand. A forty-year-old veteran of the
Colonial Service, Gordon served twelve years as a District Officer
in Ghana before coming to Gambia three years ago. Over six
feet tall, and weighing about 200 pounds, he has a boyish face,
curly gray hair and a scraggly beard that looks as though he hasn't
quite decided whether to really grow one or shave the thing off.
He joined us in the lounge for a drink, and after some polite
conversation invited me to return with him the following morning to spend a few days at Basse. When he raised his glass, I
noticed he wore a white watch strap.

Along with their official duties, Gordon Edwards and his Development Officer, Peter Tremayne, an Englishman, are noted for their impromptu dramatic presentations whenever minor foreign officials and visitors come to Basse. The wife of a newly arrived United Nations official was standing in Gordon's office once when Tremayne walked in. In a parody of the exhaustingly extended traditional African greeting, the two exchanged a long series of shouts in front of the startled lady: "Tremayne!" "Edwards!" "Tremayne!" "Edwards!" . . . etc., etc. Their greeting concluded with three hearty clasps and a joint cry of "Ballocks!" Upon their return to Bathurst, visitors to Basse often spoke ominously of up-river officers who have been "out here too long," or who are "going bush."

Edwards and Tremayne used to while away their leisure moments devising schemes to confound or amuse colleagues in Bathurst. One favorite gambit was to send in complaints to various Ministries from fictitious Gambians. Serious students of Gambiana consider their letters superb imitations. Their most famous coup concerned a "Greek vase" discovered by one "MoUSTAPHA tOURAY, Acedamician," who wrote the following letter to Capt'n George Peters, the editor of *The Gambia News Bulletin:*

Dear Mr. Information Officer,
 Can you spare the time esteamed SIR to assist myself in enlitening my goodself on a little problem.
 This is it, when my pupils were diging in the bushes for a perpose which they probably are understanding they fell on earthenwaring urn. I think myself it is Pfoblematicaly of *Greek* or latin origination but because my father is a poor man I have not been vouschafed the dignity of HIGHER EDUCATION. Notwithstanding as you can see I am not doing so friteningly badly.
 On the side of this Urn is a INSCRIPTION in less than ex-

cuse me to say well polished finnish. It reads (open invertin commers) ITI SAPIS SPOTANDA TINONE (close them).

Perhaps kindly SIR you can sea your gracious way to printing this INSCRIBTON inside your famous *Bulletin* — even perhaps God granting unto us his divine Providence someone among your learning readers can forward asistance in telling your esteamed servant what this can be meaning. Knowing your kindness to fellow Gambians i am fealing certain you will not spare to sea the way to helping myself with this.

Having the glorious honour to be your fallow worker in the name of INSCREWTABLE PROVIDENCE

MoUSTAPHA tOURAY

British officials in Bathurst who had undergone the rigors of public school Latin recognized the inscription as an old schoolboy joke. With a few letters moved a bit, it reads: IT IS A PISS POT AND A TIN ONE.

When Gordon came by the next morning, he had switched to beige attire for the journey — beige bermuda shorts, beige shirt, beige shoes and socks, and a beige watch strap. Metal plaques on the Rolls bumper proclaimed membership in automobile clubs in Norway, Ghana and Southern California. As we set off, the chauffeur put a forty-five rpm record into a dashboard machine. A jazz version of "Bless This House," it was the theme song of a popular British television police thriller, "Z-Cars." It was also Gordon's current theme song. "I used to have several records of it," he said. "This is my last one."

He apologized for the air conditioner's being out of commission and for the deep rumble coming from the engine. The muffler had dropped off on his trip down from Basse. These and other minor defects were to deprive me of the sublime pleasure of driving through the African bush in the deep leather seats of an air-conditioned Rolls Royce. "I'm trading it in for a new Mercedes when I go on leave in the spring," said Gordon.

At a friend's house just outside Bathurst, we left the Rolls and switched to the lesser luxury of a battered government Land Rover. Gordon's official Land Rover had followed him down from Basse, but it too had broken down. Because of the condition of most Gambian roads the average life of a car is not much more than two years. Up-river officials who make the trip to Bathurst in their own vehicles are generally followed by their Land Rovers. Our present one had already logged an impressive 60,000 miles, and jarred as though it should be followed itself. At Brikama, twenty-two miles from Bathurst, we stopped to speak to Commissioner Reid of the Western Division. Reid, at forty-seven, is a rugged, sun-reddened veteran of the India Service, who sports a shock of white hair and a knobby walking stick. (These sticks, like a chief's staff, were partially as symbols of authority.) While Gordon chatted with Reid, a faded blue Jaguar sedan came wheezing and rattling up, gave a final gasp, and stopped. Out stepped Commissioner Arthur Ward, the thirty-year-old Commissioner of the Lower River Division at Mansa Konko. (Both Reid and Ward are British.) "Poor old Arthur," said Gordon. "He bought that Jaguar a year ago at a ridiculous price, and he couldn't get a penny for it now. I'm surprised he got this far [92 miles] from Mansa Konko. He has to fill up with water every ten miles, or else it boils over."

Commissioner Ward came up and asked Commissioner Reid if he could leave his exhausted Jaguar at Brikama. "My driver is following me in the Land Rover, if you could have somebody flag him down."

"I'll have one of the boys catch him when he comes by," said Reid. "You go over to the house and get a cold drink."

As we prepared to leave, Ward said to Gordon, "Will you be stopping in Mansa Konko for lunch? I've told Lamin to lay on something for you."

February is a pleasant month for a drive through the Gambian bush. The mornings and late afternoons are cool, and even at midday the temperature rarely gets above 100 degrees. When one speaks of "bush" in West Africa, Americans weaned on National Geographic and Tarzan generally have the wrong idea. This is not jungle, but low, sparse vegetation, growing in relatively sandy soil. During the dry season, when the roads are in good condition, the passing scene is dull green and brown. Scrub brush and shoulder-high bush grass dominate the landscape. Occasionally coconut or rhun palms and cotton silk or baobab trees rise above this low bush. The hoary massive baobabs seem to be growing upside down, their gnarled twisted branches sticking up like roots in the sky. Africans compete with monkeys for the tart white pulp encased in the shell-covered baobab fruit. From time to time, the road passes anthills ranging from a few feet in height to a towering twenty feet or more. The ants construct them in a complex series of towers reminiscent of Mad King Ludwig's castle in the Black Forest. The rains beat the anthills down, and change the architecture, but the ants build them up again to bake to a rock-like hardness in the hot sun of the dry season.

While Gambia's sandy soil offers insufficient sustenance for lush vegetation, it is ideal for peanuts. February is the end of the harvest season, and farmers everywhere were pulling their last peanut plants from the ground and thrashing the nuts from the stalks. Women and children stood on raised wooden platforms and poured baskets of peanuts out into the breeze. This ancient winnowing process enables the peanuts to drop in a pile below, while the breeze blows the lighter stalks, leaves and dirt further away. Along the road to Mansa Konko many of the fields were singed and smoking from recent fires. "They burn it down to get rid of the old peanut plants," Gordon explained. "Makes it easier to cultivate and plant the next crop."

"Doesn't it also get rid of the topsoil?"

"Oh yes. It ruins the soil. That's the scourge of West Africa. They do it everywhere."

"Has the government tried to point out the dangers of burning the fields to the farmers?"

"God yes, for a donkey's age. They've tried passing laws too, but they've had no effect."

After stopping for lunch at Commissioner Ward's house at Mansa Konko, we set out on the toughest stretch of the trip, a narrow, winding, rutted track through the bush from Mansa Konko to Georgetown, headquarters of the next division. Its eighty-one miles take between three and four hours, depending on the age of one's car and how much the driver cares about it. (A new unpaved road has since replaced this one.) We averaged about twenty miles per hour, and even at that speed our Land Rover bounced as if it had square wheels. In the rainy season this road is frequently closed. The parallel road on the North Bank of the river is closed throughout the entire rainy season.

During the eighty-one miles from Mansa Konko to Georgetown, we passed only two Land Rovers (one of them broken down) and one tractor. As we passed a few ox-carts in the fields, Gordon said, "That's considerable progress. They only started using them two years ago. Most still plow by hand. There are now about twenty or so ox-plowing schools in Gambia. Both the oxen and the handlers have to be trained."

"Do the bulls breed well in this climate?"

"Oh yes. There's no problem with their breeding. There's no problem with that among any of the species in Africa."

We passed through innumberable small villages of thatched-roof mud-wall huts: the huts of more prosperous villages had frames of rhun palm branches, with walls made of plaited bamboo called "crinting." Crinting fences separated compounds of huts from each other and from the road. Bony dogs, asleep, exhausted or dead, lay motionless in the sandy village roads, regardless of how close our Land Rover came. By three o'clock the work day was over, and the villages were crowded. Village elders sat on benches in front of their compounds, or strolled as elegantly as Roman senators in the Forum in their long toga-like Moslem robes. They stared blankly at us as we passed. Women ground millet (called "coos" in Gambia) in large wooden bowls, or carried water from the village wells in hollow calabash gourds balanced on their heads. Every child waved, including one in the process of urinating against a baobab tree. Groups of men sat or reclined on the village "bantabas" — low wooden platforms that allow the cooling air to circulate beneath. Bantabas are generally built under the central shade tree, and are the traditional gathering place for village gossip, affairs and festivities. "The groundnuts are mostly harvested by now," said Gordon. "Between February and June, when they plant again, the men don't do much except repair fences and huts, clear the land, and sit on the bantaba. Mostly they sit on the bantaba."

Between villages, as the road wound through the bush, boys and men walking in our direction turned and waved half-heartedly for a ride.

"Do they really expect us to stop and pick them up?"

"No, it's just a habit. Government vehicles are not supposed to pick up any unofficial passengers, but most of them do. I give my drivers hell when I catch them doing it, but it doesn't do any good. Half these people along the road are their relatives." It seemed unfair to pass by heavily-laden Gambians in our relatively empty Land Rover, as they trudged along the sandy road under the glaring afternoon sun. Besides, there was almost no public transport on this particular road. But government officials — British and Gambian — feel that they can not afford to have their few precious vehicles take a greater beating than they already do on Gambia's roads. They have found that there is no such thing as picking up "just a few" Gambians.

Around dinnertime we pulled into the Catholic Mission at Fula Bantang, where we would spend the night. Fula Bantang is a village of the Fula tribe ("bantang" is Fula for "big tree"). The mission is run by Father Brown, a cheerful energetic man who has served in Gambia for ten years, and in Fula Bantang for the past two. He is a member of the Holy Ghost Fathers, the Irish Catholic missionary order operating in Gambia. I found Father Brown in a shed, bending over a balky generator. It was 7:30, and time for the compound lights to go on. He and his Gambian assistant, Francis, were having trouble getting the generator going. After about twenty-five tries at the hand crank it finally sputtered and caught, and the grounds lit up. As we walked about the grounds, Father Brown told me about the mission. The school normally has about sixty boys, including twenty boarders from distant villages. The rest come from Fula Bantang and surrounding villages each day on foot. Attendance fluctuates widely with the seasons, planting, work about the family compound and Moslem holy days. The Fulas see no spiritual conflict in sending their children to Christian mission schools and keeping them out to celebrate Moslem and tribal rites. Like many tribes in Africa, they have the spiritual generosity to embrace several religions simultaneously, and combine the disparate observances with equal joy and fervor.

When I asked Father Brown if I could observe classes in the morning, he replied that there would not be many children, because most of them were out for Ramadan, a month-long semi-fast similar to Lent, in which Moslems do not eat or drink from sunrise to sunset. "As a matter of fact, several of them from Fula Bantang are out in the bush now, beyond the village, going through their tribal initiation and circumcision ceremony.

They've been out there three or four weeks now. Would you like to go out and see them?"

We climbed into Father Brown's little Renault, and drove across the fields under the dim light of the rising moon. With no road to follow, Francis had to guide us through the bush grass, using the baobab trees as sign posts. "Very often several villages join and have one big ceremony," said Father Brown, "but this time Fula Bantang is having one alone. The boys come out here about the beginning of Ramadan and are circumcised on the second day. The man who used to do the job was the village blacksmith. He used to cut wood and tobacco with the same knife. Now many of the boys go to the government clinic at Bansang. That's some progress I suppose."

About a mile from the mission we came to a small bamboo hut in a clearing beneath a baobab tree. In back of the hut five boys, from nine to eleven years old, sat before a blazing fire, dressed in a kind of white bloomers. Near them stood a wizened old man, appointed by the village elders to supervise the boys' tribal education. The old man greeted the priest warmly, and they spoke together in Fula. We asked if the boys would sing us one of the tribal songs they had learned, and the old man turned to the boys and gave them a sharp command. Each one picked up two small sticks and began beating rhythm on a log lying in front of him. The oldest boy sang verses, and the rest joined in on the chorus. They seemed to enjoy demonstrating their new talents. The light from the fire flickered on their bare chests and shiny eyes. Their adolescent voices cut sharply into the still evening.

Behind the youths, an older boy violently twirled a flat wooden stick on the end of a string. It made an eerie "whirring" noise disturbingly like the growl of an angry animal. "That's to frighten off the small boys of the village who are still uncircum-

Government Secretariat in Bathurst

Bathurst City Council chamber and City
Councillor Alasan N'Dure

Government House

Perseverance Street, Bathurst

The Albert Market, Bathurst

Bathurst Shop

The Atlantic Hotel

Bathurst Woman Selling Fruit

Bathurst Woman
in Festive Costume

Blind Beggar

Woman in Independence Dress

A Group of Chiefs

Bathurst Women

INDEPENDENCE

A Chief and His Attendants

Up-River Women

CELEBRATION

The Duke of Kent and the Mayor of Bathurst

cised," explained Father Brown. "These fellows stay out here for about a month, learning tribal songs and rituals. When they come out they all wear clean white half-robes. During the entire month they never change and never take a bath. Then when it's all over, they race to a pond in the rice fields and jump in. The first one in is said to have killed an elephant. When they return to the village there will be a big ceremony. They will then be full members of the village and the Fula tribe."

Father Brown's enthusiastic interest in the non-Christian rituals of his flock showed a healthy spiritual adjustment to the realities of tribal life — an accomplishment not attained by many Bathurst Gambians. Problems can develop from such an adjustment, however. A few months before, Sam Jones, the Aku Director of Education, came through Fula Bantang on an inspection tour, and looked in on Father Brown's mission school. "He turned in a sharp report, mentioning that he saw one boy in his birthday suit. I suppose he considered this shocking. There's nothing I can do, however. The boy's father simply won't get him any clothes until he's circumcised.

"I've been trying to get the schoolchildren to wear decent clothes for several years without much success. The Fulas usually spend their money on themselves quickly, and forget about their children. This is the time of year to catch them, at the beginning of the trade season, when they've got money and haven't spent it yet. So last week I went out and bought a lot of blue cloth at a low price for school uniforms. Then the other day I went out and sat at the village bantaba and sold it to the parents. Now we're going to get a tailor to make up all the uniforms at a reduced price."

Back at the mission house, after we showered off the dust of the day's drive, Father Brown emerged in a fresh white cassock and black sash. The living room of his house was crowded with bare wooden furniture and a few cushions. Scattered about the walls were several pictures of Christ, a crucifix, assorted religious illustrations and a picture of a Swiss chateau. Out on the back porch sat a shiny new bathtub in lonely splendor, unconnected to any pipes. "I had an electric pump connected to the well for a while," said Father Brown, "but I had to stop. They would let it run all day and the well nearly went dry. Now the cook uses the tub for washing clothes."

\*

Next morning we were up at 7:00. Out back, a group of mission boys turned a circular hand pump at the well. They were filling watering cans to water the mission's small but flourishing vegetable garden. "I try to teach the boys a bit about gardening,"said Father Brown, "because the Fula men traditionally stick to raising cattle, and their diet is not what it might be."

We bid Father Brown good-by, and set out for Basse. Soon after leaving Fula Bantang, we came upon a large herd of cattle ambling peacefully across the road, stopping now and then to nibble the grass at the edge. "Those are Fulas," said Gordon, pointing to the men driving, or rather, following the cattle. "The Fula are the cattlemen of Gambia. They raise most of the cattle in the country and they generally herd those owned by Woloffs and Mandinkas. There's only one thing wrong. The government can't get them to sell their cattle. They use them in marriage settlements and celebrations, but not many are sold for chop — only when they specifically need something. Fula cattle are prestigious rather than economic. It's their visible form of wealth, and they hate to part with it."

I had noticed a good deal of coverage in *The Gambia News Bulletin* about government-sponsored cattle auctions, along with advice to cattlemen ("It pays to sell your surplus beasts."). But since few Fulas read the *Bulletin*, and because they have more confidence in their cattle than in money, the government's program was proceeding as slowly as the Fulas were now driving their cattle across the road.

After the turn-off to Georgetown, the road improved. It was still bumpy, but we could now drive at 40-50 miles per hour. Gordon pointed out a village called Bakadagy. "We had to close a school here. No pupils. Parents just wouldn't send them. Hard to find any place in the Upper River Division good for a school. The missionaries have the same trouble. The people here just don't seem to be interested in education." One explanation for this is that the Upper River Division has remained less affected by the progress in the distant capital than the nearer provinces. As a result, it now offers less prospects for those with an education. It also has the largest population of Fulas and Serahulis, more primitive tribes than the Woloffs and Mandinkas.

I asked Gordon if there were any distinguishing characteristics of geography or vegetation by which one could recognize the Upper River Division. "There's no sure way of telling," he replied, "but if you notice, the sheep here all get up on their hind legs and salute as I go by."

We reached Basse shortly before noon. The last town of any size on the river, Basse is a trading center of 1,639 people, boasting a cinema and a makeshift nightclub called the "Tropicana." Basse is actually two towns. Huddled down near the river bank is the dry season business district of Lebanese trading shops, a market and other buildings known as "Basse Wharf Town." With the summer rains, the river rises as much as thirty feet, pouring over the steep banks and flooding the Wharf Town. During this period, the traders and townsmen withdraw a few hundred yards to an alternate town of rainy season shops and markets, known as "Santosu," Mandinka for "high compound."

To avoid any possibility of flooding, the Commissioner's head-quarters is located about two miles out of town, near the village of Mansajang. When we arrived at Gordon's house, he yelled "Kebba!" and a white liveried Gambian houseboy appeared to take our bags. Gordon told him to "take this master to the guest room," and left me to rummage about the house while he went over to his adjacent office to do some paper work. Known as "the second best digs in the Gambia" (after the Governor's mansion in Bathurst), the Commissioner's residence at Basse reminds an American of an impoverished Southern plantation. The grounds are dense with lush bougainvillaea, jacaranda and over-hanging mango trees. Vine-covered lattice arbors shade the winding ce-ment walk from the midday sun. A garden boy walks about the grounds, sweeping up loose leaves and twigs from the ground. Across the road, a cement tennis court swelters in the sun. The house itself is a large, rambling, two-story building with several connected out-buildings for the servants, laundry and cooking. It boasts pillars, balconies, French doors and a veranda. On the hall table lay the latest issues of *Playboy, Time, The Saturday Evening Post, The Economist,* several automotive jour-nals and assorted British newspapers. Glaring down on those who enter the hallway was an imposing portrait of Gordon's grandmother. The well-appointed living room contained shelves of Wedgewood china, pewter mugs and plates, glass goblets, and dozens of souvenirs of Gordon's years in Ghana.

When Gordon returned from his office, we lunched on canned tongue, imported like most of his food directly from Fortnum and Mason in London. The meal was served by Kebba, the head boy. Gordon's numerous domestics illustrated Gambia's contin-uing melting pot: there was Kebba, a Jola, another Mandinka houseboy, a Woloff driver, a Fula laundress and an old Bambara garden boy from Mali.

Later that afternoon we walked over to the Catholic mission, where two of Father Brown's colleagues, Fathers Corrigan and Fleming, also run a small school and church. Standing on their porch, I watched three cows grazing in the front yard. "We tried fencing them out for a while," said Father Corrigan, "but finally gave it up."

"There's a cow in a nearby village that has three horns," Father Fleming interjected.

"We've got everything up here in Basse," said Father Corrigan. "You just ask for it."

Over tea, conversation turned to a non-Catholic spiritual crisis troubling Basse. This was "Koriteh" ("Id el Fitr," in Arabic), the Moslem holy day marking the end of Ramadan, and celebrated with prayers and feasting. The government, by decree of the Prime Minister, had declared it a public holiday and ordered all government and commercial enterprises closed. The decree was based on strict Moslem custom, which stipulates that the moon must be visible the night before Koriteh. The Moslem spiritual leader, or "Imam," traditionally renders this astronomical judgement. The previous evening, however, the sky above Bathurst had been overcast. Worried government officials, who had made extensive plans for a public holiday on Wednesday, hurriedly telephoned to Dakar and learned that His Eminence, the Imam of Dakar, had caught a glimpse of the moon. Aided by this news of his colleague, and by pressure from Gambian officials, Bathurst's Imam managed to perceive a faint glimmer through the clouds that night. In the morning, the Ministry of Local Government phoned all divisional headquarters, confirming the holiday and instructing the Commissioners to spread the word to all government employees.

It was then that the crisis came to light. The venerable Imam of Basse, because of variable climatic conditions, poor eyesight or stubbornness, announced that he had been unable to locate the moon in the firmament that night, and refused to accept the word of the Imam of Bathurst. He sent messages to the faithful of Basse and vicinity to proceed about their affairs as usual. He would inform them if he observed the moon over Basse this night, whereupon they would celebrate Koriteh tomorrow. This left the government workers of Basse in a bind. When they attempted to go to their jobs this morning, officials told them to go home and celebrate. There was a bit of a scuffle down at the Public Works Department, where the gates had to be locked to keep the workers out. The acting Commissioner, in Gordon's absence, announced that anyone not reporting for work the next day, regardless of the Imam of Basse's observations, would be docked a day's pay. The Imam countered by refusing to hold the customary rites of Koriteh. Some of the younger men, more firmly attached to the temporal world than the spiritual, traveled twelve miles down to Wellingara, in Senegal, to celebrate with their relations there. The elders stayed at home, grumbling.

Father Corrigan drove us back to the Commissioner's residence in his battered Citroën "deux-chevaux." Gordon remained without a vehicle during my stay in Basse, since his Rolls was being repaired in Bathurst, his official Land Rover had broken down on the way in, and the spare lent to him for the trip back to Basse had already returned to Bathurst. Without the Rolls, I was deprived of several rituals reported by other travelers to Basse. Gordon was customarily driven down to the town each evening at exactly six o'clock. There he took a half-hour stroll along the river's edge, watched the Union Jack lowered at exactly 6:30, got back into the Rolls and was driven home. On shopping excursions across the border to Wellingara for French cheeses and wines, Gordon lowers the windows of his Rolls and drives into the sleepy town with the "Colonel Bogie March" blaring from the dashboard record player, and a small Union Jack flapping from the fender.

Another customary diversion for visitors to Basse is Gordon's movie on *The Life of a Commissioner in Gambia*. Produced and directed by Gordon, this film shows him performing the daily rituals in his life at Basse, including the afternoon stroll and flag-lowering at the river. It also shows him setting off on a tour of his division in his official motor launch. As the boat pulls slowly away from the Basse wharf at sunset, Gordon stands on the stern, a Union Jack flutters in the breeze, and the dubbed-in sound track offers a stirring rendition of "Rule Britannia."

While these rituals may strike the casual visitor as eccentric, Gambians in the Upper River Division are reportedly enthralled by them. They are proud of a ruler who surrounds himself with symbols of his power, as their kings did in ages past. The British understand this better than many of the new educated leaders in Bathurst. Thus Governor-General Sir John Paul, when touring the provinces in his white uniform, medals, plumed hat and sword, will often outdraw the Prime Minister, who dresses in a dark suit. A Basse youth put the idea quite simply: "Commissioner Edwards, he be fine, fine, Commissioner. He get big white car. All de Basse people, dey like him too much."

\*

The air was chilly next morning, as we walked over to the Commissioner's two-room office. The cement walls displayed maps of the Upper River Division's four districts and ten-year-old photos of the Queen and Prince Philip. Gordon sat at a long green wooden desk with trays labeled "In," "Out," "Correspondence" and "Trek Files." Across the room, Assistant Commissioner Davis, a Bathurst Aku, sat at a smaller desk.

The chief clerk came in and announced that the Imam of Basse had seen the moon last night, and since there had been no ceremony yesterday, the office staff wanted today off to attend Imam's prayers. As government offices were theoretically open today, Gordon compromised, and told him those wishing to pray should be let off at noon. He then picked up his phone to make a call to Bathurst, but was unable to get the Basse operator. He flicked the lever irritably a few times, and slammed the phone down. Mr. Davis reported that his Land Rover had broken down. This left the headquarters of the Upper River Division dependent for transport on a bicycle belonging to one of the clerks.

While Gordon busied himself with paperwork, I leafed through some statistics on the Upper River Division. Its four districts (Falladu East, Kantora, Sandu and Wuli) contain 58,000 people, spread over 790 square miles on both sides of the river. There are 19,000 Mandinkas, 17,500 Serahulis, 14,000 Fulas, and about 5,000 Gambians of various other tribes. The foreign population includes about 1,200 Senegalese, 1,000 Guineans, 500 Malians, 100 Portuguese Guineans, 23 Sierra Leoneans and 8 Mauritanians. Basse has a dozen Lebanese traders, and a few British missionaries and officials. The furthest of Gambia's four provinces from the capital, the Upper River Division is relatively isolated. To reach Basse, one has a choice of a full day's Land Rover trip over 257 miles of jolting laterite rock and dirt, or a meandering three-day trip up the river on board the *Lady Wright*, the ancient creaking steamer which makes the round trip every ten days. Verbal communication is limited to a five day river mail service, and a sporadic single telephone line.

While this isolation gives Gordon considerable autonomy, it also gives him occasional headaches. The line between his office and the telecommunications center at the Basse Post Office is

generally out of commission. When calls come in — many of
them inconsequential — the switchboard operator must send a
messenger by bike two miles out to Mansajang, and Gordon
must then drive into town to receive the call. This procedure
could easily fray the most steady nerves. Recently Gordon decided to do something about it. "I'd gotten bloody tired of
getting up from a meal, driving two miles down to the post office,
only to find that someone wanted to book reservations for the
government rest house here. So I gave orders to the Post Office
that I wouldn't accept any calls unless they were from my
superior, Henry Oliver, the English Commissioner for Local
Government. Well, last week, a Gambian Minister called me up
from Bathurst, and the Basse operator told him 'Commissioner
Edwards does not speak to Ministers — only to Henry Oliver.'
The Minister was furious, and turned in a report to the P.M.
saying that the Commissioner at Basse had refused to talk to him.
I got a rocket the next day from my Ministry."

"How often do you get around your domain?"

"Oh, I visit the four district chiefs every so often, when something comes up. In general the chiefs are a pretty good lot. We
have two chiefs here in the Upper River Division who are excellent. One is mediocre, and another is totally useless. [The latter
chief was removed from office by the central government a few
months later.] I get out to Fatoto [the last sizable village on the
river, about twenty-six miles away] whenever I feel I haven't had
a look for some time. Nothing ever goes wrong in Fatoto, but
then nothing ever goes right either. Very few emergencies come
up. This year, a crazed hyena attacked a few people in Sara Bojo.
A fisherman at Diabugu caught a 27-foot crocodile. They had to
finish it off with a shot gun, and needed a lorry to pull it onto the
bank."

While we were talking, a short, stout Gambian with large

rheumy eyes entered the office. Mr. Davis introduced him to me as the Honorable Numakunda Darbo, Opposition Member of Parliament for Upper Fulladu West. Mr. Darbo told Gordon that his Land Rover had broken down near Basse. He wanted Gordon to authorize the Basse workshop of the Public Works Department to do some welding repairs on it — gratis. Its immediate repair was vital, he explained, "because I must transport some of my close supporters." Gordon rose wearily, and said, "We'll have to call P.W.D. in Bathurst for that. I can't authorize labor from another Ministry on a private vehicle." Mr. Darbo groused a bit, but hastily told Gordon not to bother calling Bathurst.

The Honorable Numakunda Darbo's Land Rover is worth special mention, for it has a fascinating history. When the People's Progressive Party came to power, in 1963, one of its first acts was to pass a bill enabling Members of Parliament and other senior officials to borrow $1,540 from the government for the purchase of personal vehicles. The seven Members of the Opposition, including Mr. Darbo, objected strenuously to the bill, labeling it a blatant political maneuver. When the bill passed, over their objections, one of the first applications for credit came from UP Members, who purchased an official Land Rover for the Party. A few weeks later, the new UP Land Rover ran into a herd of cattle, killing six of them, and reportedly setting a new record. The PPP's *New Gambia* quickly informed its readers that the United Party Land Rover, purchased with government credit under the new law opposed by the UP, had been involved in an accident on the Cape Road, killing five cattle. In the next issue, *The New Gambia* ran a correction, stating that the UP Land Rover, purchased with government credit under the new law opposed by the UP, had not killed *five* cattle, but *six*. Soon after this incident, the UP sold the vehicle to Mr. Darbo. Due to the six cows, and subsequent misfortunes, the fenders of Mr. Darbo's Land Rover are now distinctively laced to the body with odd bits of wire.

When he had finished his business with Gordon, I asked Mr. Darbo what he did for a living, in addition to serving as M.P. Since M.P.'s meet only ten to fifteen days each year, most supplement their annual $1,344 salaries by farming, trading or running small transport services. Mr. Darbo smiled, showing two front teeth missing and said he did nothing else. On prodding from Assistant Commissioner Davis, however, he recalled that he was slightly involved in "the transportation business." He was forced into this activity, he said, because of the meager salary he received as an M.P. "We Members of Parliament should live in a better style. After all, the new Labour Government in London just voted an increase for M.P.'s. Here, they keep tell us they get no money."

About ten o'clock, Gordon announced that it was time for the Upper River Division's weekly traffic court. In a town with little other organized entertainment, the Commissioner's Court at Basse, with two performances weekly — traffic and civil cases — generally draws a sizable crowd. About twenty-five people were already waiting out at the courtroom, a small open cement building behind Gordon's office. Gordon, sitting as Magistrate, and his clerk-interpreter sat at a bare wooden table at one end of the room, up on a dais. The prosecutor, an Aku police inspector from Bathurst, sat facing them at another table in the middle of the room. There were no defense attorneys. Casual observers stood outside, looking in over the shoulder-high walls. More serious spectators shared several wooden benches inside with the morning's defendants.

In the first case on the morning's docket, the clerk called to the cement defendant's box the Honorable Numakunda Darbo,

M.P. Mr. Darbo pleaded not guilty to charges of transporting passengers in an unlicensed taxi — his Land Rover — operated by an unlicensed driver. Inspector Nicol called a police constable as the first witness. He testified that on the morning of January 5, he had come upon Mr. Darbo's car broken down on the road from Georgetown to Basse. Determining that both the vehicle and driver were without licenses, the constable had collected fares totalling two pounds nineteen shillings from the passengers himself. Inspector Nicol now turned the money over to Gordon as Exhibit A.

Mr. Darbo crossed to the other side of the room and took the witness stand in his defense. After swearing on the Koran to tell the truth, the whole truth, and nothing but the truth, he stated that on that morning of January 5, "I left my vehicle under repair at Bansang, and went to Georgetown to renew my license. When I returned to Bansang, I see the car missing and I ask my wife where vehicle. She say one Kebba Susso took it. [Throughout his testimony, Mr. Darbo showed a familiarity with legal phraseology such as "one Kebba Susso" that indicated considerable courtroom experience.] I am not give instruction to anyone to take my vehicle from Bansang to Basse."

A surprised murmur rippled through the audience at this last statement. A Gambian on my left explained that Mr. Darbo regularly used the Land Rover as a taxi between Bansang and Basse, and that Kebba Susso was his regular driver. Inspector Nicol asked Mr. Darbo how the vehicle could have made the trip to Basse if it was undergoing repairs in Bansang, and why he had not reported its disappearance to the police. Mr. Darbo was unable to answer. The inspector then told the court that the vehicle's license had not been renewed until several days after the arrest.

Gordon, who had been painstakingly recording all the testi-

mony in a large leatherbound court record, continued to write
for some time after Inspector Nicol finished his case. Then he
looked up and read the court's decision. He found the defendant, Numakunda Darbo, guilty on both charges, and fined him
ten shillings ($1.50) on each, or three days in jail. Inspector
Nicol smiled. Gordon continued, declaring that since Mr.
Darbo's vehicle had transported the passengers to Basse, their
fares rightfully belonged to Mr. Darbo. At this, the Inspector
frowned. Mr. Darbo smiled. This still left him with a profit of
nearly two pounds on the trip.

The second case on the docket was that of Kebba Susso, Mr.
Darbo's unlicensed driver. A young man, Kebba Susso had formerly been a driver for the police department, but had been dismissed for "inefficiency." He wore a leather jacket, black trousers and a thick woolen ski-cap. He also sported a moustache
and red fingernail polish. (The latter adornment on Gambian
males does not carry the implication it might in certain Western
societies.) Since Mr. Susso spoke little English, the interpreter
translated the proceedings into Mandinka for him, and rendered
his testimony into English. Mr. Susso testified that on the day of
January 5, he had "left his license behind." Asked if he had the
license with him now, he produced it for the court. It was dated
January 18. Inspector Nicol then produced police records showing that Kebba Susso had been driving without a license for two
years. Faced with this gap in his defense, Mr. Susso clutched his
woolen cap and glowered at the floor. Gordon fined him two
pounds for driving without a valid license for two years, and one
pound for operating an unlicensed vehicle. This seemed a rather
stiff sentence, until my neighbor pointed out that since Susso
was his driver, Mr. Darbo would end up paying these fines also.

The next case involved an overloaded taxi, which had been
stopped while carrying fifteen passengers inside, sacks of peanuts

on the roof, and more people sitting on the peanuts. Because of the danger to the passengers, Gordon fined the driver five pounds. The next defendant, one Sidibeh, had driven a Public Works Department Land Rover with faulty steering into an electricity pole. Since Sidibeh had been driving under P.W.D. orders, Gordon found him innocent, and said he would send a "stern note" to the Basse P.W.D.

The clerk next called Safio Baldeh. When he did not appear in the courtroom, the police yelled his name three times out in the compound. Someone in the audience said that Safio Baldeh was home sick. Gordon put his case over till the following week. The clerk then called Safio N'Saneh, who also failed to appear. After some confusion, it turned out that Safio N'Saneh was home sick, whereas Safio Baldeh had been sitting in the courtroom dozing. (The non-appearance of defendants is quite common in Gambian courtrooms. This is not due to any disrespect for the law, but to normal casualness. They forget. Some remember, but send in letters of apology instead of appearing. One defendant wrote a Commissioner a long explanation of how his violation had occurred, and begged to be let off, concluding, "Please forgive me until next time.") The clerk read the charges against him as "pedaling a bicycle without reasonable considerable." Inspector Nicol rose and told the court, "On this day, the defendant was seen riding the bicycle without his hands on the handle grips. He was also observed knocking a woman and a baby down." Gordon fined him one pound.

The last case of the morning involved Alpha Mani, a seventeen-year-old lad from Bansang, wearing shower clogs on his feet, and a leather ju-ju bracelet on his wrist. Mani was charged with driving an unlicensed taxi. The owner — the Honorable Numakunda Darbo — rolled his frog-like eyes at the mention of his name. (Alpha Mani had apparently become Darbo's driver after

Kebba Susso's arrest.) Asked if he had passengers in the car when stopped by the police, Alpha Mani replied in Mandinka, "Yes, but I did not invite them." The court held that people in the car would be classified as passengers. Mani claimed that it was a private car, and that the people were "friends, not passengers." One of the arresting constables testified that while he was writing up the ticket, he observed Mani collecting fares from the "friends." At this, Mani said nothing. He leaned against the defendant's box and picked his nose. Gordon declared the court in recess for ten minutes.

During the recess, Inspector Nicol discussed the finer points of each case with his constables and the defendants. Darbo and Kebba Susso sat in a corner, arguing over who would pay Susso's fines. Inspector Nicol walked over to Darbo and told him that his other driver, Alpha Mani, was lying. Mr. Darbo told Nicol that being unable to speak Mandinka, he had been unable to follow Mani's testimony. Nicol yelled that Darbo spoke Mandinka better than Mani. Just then, Gordon returned, and the clerk called the court to order.

Inspector Nicol called police Corporal N'Jie to the witness stand. N'Jie, off duty, wore shorts and a T-shirt. He stated that when he had asked the defendant at the station about not having a license for the Land Rover, Mani had replied, "This is not my look-out. I act under orders from Mr. Darbo." The clerk, who had removed his plastic slippers, translated this into Mandinka for Mani, while scratching his feet. Mani now claimed that he had asked Darbo whether the vehicle was licensed to carry passengers, and that Darbo had said no, but to ignore this. Darbo himself took the witness stand, and told the court that the vehicle was a private car he used in his constituency to transport his "close supporters." Gordon thought it odd that Mr. Darbo's close supporters should make the same trip from Bansang to

Basse each day, and that the driver should collect money from them. He fined Mani seven pounds, and then declared Basse Traffic Court closed. Darbo went up to Inspector Nicol and asked when the fines had to be paid. Nicol said today. Darbo asked if he could sign a note, Nicol said no. Darbo walked out in a huff, and appealed to Gordon. Gordon agreed to give him two days to raise the money.

Back in Gordon's office, we found another Member of Parliament, the Honorable Demba Jagana, from Jimara. Mr. Jagana was here to receive a sentence rendered a week before, when he had failed to appear in court. Gordon had fined him one pound on each of two charges: operating an unlicensed taxi (also purchased with government credit) and having an unlicensed driver. Neither Mr. Jagana nor Mr. Darbo impress one as the criminal type, or even as corrupt bureaucrats. They are rather simple, engaging rascals, who go about their petty illegalities with the same bumbling innocence they bring to bear on the nation's legislative affairs.

When Mr. Jagana had left, I asked Gordon if he had many serious crimes — robbery, murder or rape. "Oh, we get a bit of petty thievery from time to time, and occasional fights, but we don't have many violent crimes. As for rape, there's no such thing here. It just means a fellow forgot to ask. The only time the charge is brought is when the girl's parents don't agree on a settlement. It's just like the law that says no one shall have carnal knowledge of a girl before she's sixteen. Why there's not a bloody one of my parishioners who hasn't had carnal knowledge of a girl under sixteen.

"They're a peaceful lot, the Gambians. A bit shiftless, perhaps, but good-natured, friendly and honest. Compared to the Ashanti, in Ghana, the Gambians are wonderful. The Ashanti are a twisted tricky people. They're born twisted and they die twisted. If anyone can administer the Ashanti, I guess he could administer any people on God's earth."

Though a bit eccentric and opinionated, Gordon Edwards is a highly competent administrator. But God's earth is quickly running out of call for competent colonial administrators. England is divesting itself as rapidly as possible of its remaining colonial bits and pieces, while her ex-colonies, despite their discouraging lack of experienced administrators, are divesting themselves just as rapidly of men like Gordon Edwards. The Africanization of jobs such as Gordon's has taken longer than it has for the other British-filled positions, because few African public servants share Gordon's desire to serve the public in upriver bush country. But ready and willing or not, Africans will eventually replace all the British. This leaves men like Gordon Edwards with a bleak future. Few companies back in England need men with fifteen years experience as an administrator in the African bush. Africa does, but it doesn't want white men. Though he knows he will not be needed in Gambia much longer, Gordon Edwards wants to stay on. "I like the work here, and I like the people. I go on leave in April, then back here, I hope. I told them in Bathurst that I'd come back without pay if they'd give me Basse."

## ARACHIS HYPOGAEA

THAT AFTERNOON I joined Robin Mulholland, a young British Agriculture Officer who had stopped by the Commissioner's office on an inspection tour of the Upper River Division. Described by Gordon as "one of the hardest-working people in the country," Mulholland came to Gambia in 1961 after receiving a degree in Tropical Agriculture from Cambridge University and training at an experimental agriculture station in the West Indies. At thirty, he is one of the new breed of well-trained, industrious young specialists who are replacing the older colonial officials whose duties encompassed many fields.

As we drove off in Mulholland's Land Rover, the conversation turned to a subject about which I had heard a great deal from colonial officials in Gambia and neighboring countries — the African's alleged laziness. According to Mulholland, such talk is nonsense. He thinks much of it is a confession on the part of the man who uses it that he has been unable to work with Africans. Europeans frequently call Africans lazy because they will not work long at something of whose benefit they are unconvinced. Such unwillingness is quite reasonable, since no one works willingly on any project until he is convinced of its value. Mulholland pointed out that what infuriated white supervisors was not so much that Africans wouldn't work, but that they wouldn't work hard. He felt the explanation for this is simple. "Their standards of nutrition and health are so poor that their idea of a hard day's work is much less than ours. They'll avoid anything requiring heavy work. That's why groundnuts have been so successful here. It's the easiest crop in the world to grow. The work is light and there are few diseases."

As we bounced along the rutted sandy road, through the drab, dry bush, Mulholland told of recent changes in agricultural policy. "In the early days, in the twenties and thirties, colonial officials used to do all their work and demonstrations at their agriculture stations. There was very little transfer of knowledge, and even less acceptance. Now we do all the demonstrations on the farmers' land itself or at the Agriculture Department's twenty-two mixed farming centers around the country. The government supplies all the materials to build the centers, plus masons and supervisory help. The people build them themselves, on a community development basis. That way they think of them as their own. The new policy began in 1956, and since then we have been concentrating on only four things: oxenization of cultivation, insecticides, seed storage, and fertilizer. Recently we have begun three new programs on a small scale — oil palms out near the coast, tractor-plowing in the rice fields in MacCarthy Island Division, and improved cotton in the Upper River Division. This afternoon we're going to look in on two Fula villages where we've experimented with the new cotton. The Fulas are traditional cotton growers, as well as cattlemen. They have always grown cotton in this area, but it's a crude local variety that is not very good — certainly not good enough for export. The Agriculture Department has introduced a Nigerian cotton seed that is of better quality and more resistant to disease."

About a half-hour's drive up-river from Basse, we stopped at

Wallibakunda, where we left the Land Rover at the edge of the village and walked across a field to the compound of the headman, Alkali Saidou Jawo. The Alkali's hut was large, with a conical thatched roof, mud-clay walls and floor, and wooden doors — a mark of prosperity. We were ushered in by the Alkali, an old man with a white robe, yellow Moslem cap, rimless glasses, and a face creased with age. We sat down on wooden stools, surrounded by the Alkali's wives and relatives, who squatted on straw mats. The women's gold earrings flashed in the darkness of the hut. Children crowded at the doorways to peer in at the "toubabs" or white men.

Drameh, Mulholland's driver-interpreter, went through the customary five-minute exchange of formal Fula greetings with Alkali Jawo, inquiring minutely into the health of the Alkali, his wives, sisters, brothers, children, grandchildren, the village elders and the cattle. To each question, the Alkali enthusiastically gave the standard reply. Eventually Drameh edged around to the state of the weather, and finally the crops. Mulholland told him to ask whether there had been any insect damage to the cotton. The Alkali said no, but there had been some damage from the rains. Because the new seed had not been delivered until late in the previous June, the villagers had not had time to  plant it before the first rains. The Alkali sent someone to fetch a bit of the cotton, and when it arrived everyone peered intently at the little white tufts. Then we all went out to examine the cotton field, followed by most of the villagers and a griot who sawed at a gourd violin. Several of the young men sported western cowboy attire, including Levis, studded shirts, and cowboy hats. Mulholland walked about the field examining the soil and the stalks. He told Alkali Jawo the cotton was coming along fine, but to be sure not to neglect the groundnuts. At this advice, the Alkali drew himself up and said, "We are Fula. The groundnut is our meat and our soup. We will not neglect it."

We thanked the Alkali for his hospitality and turned to leave. Drameh gave six pence to the griot — standard procedure — and one-and-six-pence to the Alkali. Surprised by the last gift, I asked Drameh why he did it. "To encourage him," said Drameh. "Sometimes I bring him a bit of tobacco or sugar. It pays to keep him friendly." Along with such tokens of friendship, village headmen receive 10 per cent of the taxes collected in their village — which normally ranges from about $140 to $420 — plus the proceeds from their own crops, usually planted on choice ground and farmed by young men of the village. Many headmen supplement their income with a share of whatever other financial activity takes place in the village. When an Alkali dies, the village elders meet and decide upon his successor, generally a brother or son, and always someone of the same family.

Our second village on that afternoon's tour was Sambakunda, a few miles away. When we arrived, we found the entire village gathered in festive dress for the traditional ending of the circumcision ceremony. Five young boys sat on a straw mat, holding long beaded sticks from which coins and other flashing objects hung. Dancing around the boys was the man in charge of the initiation rites, wearing a leather outfit topped by a headdress of fur tails. When the ceremony was over, and we had given a few coins to the boys and their mentor — again, customary — we took the Alkali aside and asked him how the cotton was doing. He had been somewhat difficult to find, and now that we had him he seemed unable to look Mulholland in the eye. He said that the new cotton seed was bad, and would not grow. After much palaver, and consultation with several village elders, we learned that no one had fenced in the cotton, and that goats and sheep had trampled and eaten it. The Alkali looked sullen, and shuffled his feet in the dust.

The next morning I joined Mulholland for a trip along the

North Bank, heading back toward Georgetown. As we left the Commissioner's compound at Basse, we saw a crowd gathered behind the office around a wizened old man in a white robe and burnoose. They were giving him money. Drameh explained that this was the "senior marabout" in the Upper River Division. He was passing through Basse to visit the faithful and to give them an opportunity to increase their stature in the eyes of Allah by contributing to his own estate here on earth.

We drove down to the Basse ferry landing to cross over to the North Bank. The Basse ferry is a large, sideless wooden barge which crosses the river — about 250 yards wide at this point — by means of a hand-operated cable stretching from one bank to the other. Despite such exhortations as "Full Ahead" from the vessel's quartermaster, and varying numbers of passengers — all of whom customarily lend a hand at the cable — the ferry's velocity never seems to vary. This situation can be explained by a basic law of African labor — the time necessary to complete certain jobs is a constant, and does not vary with the number of men assigned to it. Since passengers on the ferry are almost never in a hurry, they contribute only that much individual effort which in total will propel the ferry across the river in its customary time. "This ferry is a vast improvement over the last model," said Mulholland. "It was a paddle wheel job. With a strong breeze you were likely to end up in Kowsemar, the next village down the river. The new motorized ferries are always breaking down, but the cable ferry is reliable. Not much can go wrong."

At Madina Koto, we stopped to look in on a Cooperative "secco," a fenced-in mountain of peanuts awaiting sale and shipment down-river. "The co-ops have been very successful," said Mulholland. "They're gradually getting the farmers out from under their credit ties to the traders. The traders extend credit during the rainy season [formerly known as "the hungry season"] when the farmers have used up all the money they earned in the fall. The credit is generally in the form of rice, sardines, tomato paste, sugar, salt and possibly some cloth. This credit is extended on the basis of their personal relationship with the farmers. Some farmers try getting credit from several traders. No matter how much money they have, they still want to get credit from the traders. They like to be able to go in and have a big palaver with the trader and get credit. It's a kind of prestige."

From Madina Koto we drove to the village of Jacunda. There, out in an open plain, a pleasant young extension worker named Jassy ran one of the Agriculture Department's mixed farming centers. Though an up-river boy, Jassy's apparel clearly showed the cosmopolitan effects of Bathurst life and a year's training in Nigeria. He wore black pegged pants, and a neon-blue shirt. As a check on the fruits of Jassy's education, Mulholland asked him if he remembered the order of crop rotation. Jassy said it was coos (millet), peanuts, then fallow. Mulholland told him the proper order was peanuts, coos, then fallow. Jassy said he had not read that part of his manual very carefully. Mulholland then asked how the coos collection was working. (Villagers can purchase plows and oxen from the centers and pay for them with coos from the next harvest.)

"Not well," said Jassy.

"What do you mean, 'not well'?"

"There has been none collected."

"Why not?"

"Well, you see, I did not know about coos collection. No one told me about it. Did you tell me about it?"

Mulholland looked dejected. "Have you read your manual at all?"

"Yes."

"Doesn't it tell you about coos collection?"

Jassy shrugged, and scuffed his shiny black Italian-style shoes in the dust. Mulholland told him to go and get the manual. Jassy left, and returned a few moments later with empty hands and a hangdog look. "Well, you see, it's not here. I left it in Basse."

When Mulholland sent Jassy off to fetch the village headman, I mentioned that the extension worker seemed unsure of himself. "He'll do all right," said Mulholland. "He's very young and just getting used to the job. We've just gotten underway with the extension worker program, and we're only just beginning to get the assistants out in the field. Yundum College [a Gambian teacher-training institution that also offers a brief course for prospective agricultural extension workers] trains about fourteen each year. Seven go out in the field and seven go on for further training in Nigeria or the U.K."

In about twenty minutes Jassy returned in the Land Rover with the Alkali of Jakunda and a village elder in back. These two gentlemen climbed gingerly out to meet Mulholland. The Alkali is an ancient, bent patriarch with a white goatee and a white Moslem skull cap. Since the midmorning heat was approaching 100 degrees in the sun, everyone moved over to a thatched shelter at the edge of the clearing. Jassy brought out a faded canvas camp chair for the Alkali, who sank into it with a deep sigh. It held him a half inch off the ground. Mulholland straddled a chair; the rest of us sat on sacks of coos. With Jassy interpreting into Mandinka, Mulholland tried to explain to the Alkali that his people must build Jassy a house. The local Area Council had voted the funds for the house, and surrounding villages were supposed to help, but Jakunda must get it started. "Tell him I am counting on him to get the other Alkalis to help. Get the Seyfu [district chief] and the area councillors to help also." The old man's rheumy eyes showed no expression. He seemed to hear everything as though it was a foreign language, coming to him from a great distance. He may have been asleep. Jassy was skeptical about the prospects of community support to build his house. "These people have not awakened. They will not come unless they are forced. They think why should they work when we are being paid and they are not. They are not convinced." Jassy himself seemed unconvinced of his ability to convince them.

Hoping to win the Alkali's support for the project, Mulholland asked him how things were going in the village. The old man thought about this for a long time, then mumbled in a nearly inaudible voice. Jassy somehow interpreted. "He says the boys in his village who are out in the bush for circumcision have used up all their chop, and they still have a few more weeks to stay out. He wants you to give him something for the boys out in the bush." Mulholland gave the old man four shillings. The Alkali thanked him and promised to say a prayer for him. It looked to me like a smooth shakedown.

*

When the Alkali had left, I asked Mulholland if he really expected Jassy to win the support of the village. "Oh, yes. Things will work out. One trouble is that we've had to put all our young assistants into villages far from their own, or else their relatives will latch onto them. We do put them into villages of their own tribe, however. The main trouble here is that the headman is acting bolshie because he doesn't think he can get his villagers to work at the center."

I mentioned that the morning's meeting had taken quite a bit of time for what seemed like dubious results. "Oh, no," said Mulholland. "At meetings with headmen, Seyfolu or village elders, you have to let them have their say. Even if your business is completed and there's general approval, you don't get up and leave. Each one will speak his piece. It may have no relevance to anything discussed, but that's the way you do business here. Everything takes time.

"One problem here is that the other villages are annoyed that we've built the center in Jakunda, and therefore they aren't anxious to work on it. We've got to convince them that it's designed to serve the whole area, and that we only chose Jakunda because of its location. The Cooperative movement has the same trouble selecting sites for its cooperatives, each of which will serve several villages. These village rivalries can be very petty. If we drop off some lindane [a peanut insecticide] for an area in one central village, sometimes another village of the same size feels slighted and won't come and get their share. Each time something like this happens, you have to go and talk to the Alkali of that village."

"Are there ever conflicts about what land belongs to which village?"

"No. All land in theory belongs to the District, and is distributed locally by the Alkali. Traditionally, though, when a man clears a plot of land for the first time, it belongs to him and his children. There's really not much of a problem about it, because there's not much land pressure yet in Gambia. There's always plenty of uncultivated land. When the soil around a village gets worked out, the village just ups and moves to another site."

If a son's portion of the family plot gets too small to support him and his family, he sometimes becomes a "strange farmer," going to another village or district and contracting to work a few days a week for a large landowner in exchange for a portion of the man's land to farm on his own. Each year, about 30,000–35,000 Senegalese arrive to work as strange farmers in Gambia while some Gambians go to Senegal's Casamance region. They usually get room and board from the landowner, plus seed nuts to get them started. Some strange farmers stay for only one season, while others will come year after year, hoping to save enough money to buy land in their own village.

As we headed down-river to Mulholland's headquarters at Yoroberikunda, near Georgetown, he told me more about the mixed farming centers, the cornerstone of the Agriculture Department's attempt to improve farming methods. Each center has sixteen local trainees, aged from sixteen to thirty, sponsored by their own villages and supervised by a trained extension worker like Jassy. Each trainee must bring two bulls — which, when castrated, will become a team of oxen — and 200 pounds of coos to feed them. At the center, they learn crop rotation, animal husbandry, and how to plow. While training, the young men receive a daily allowance of one pound of rice and one shilling, to help support their families. When the planting season starts in June, they return to their villages with their oxen, a plow loaned by the center, and seed nuts and fertilizer for their own farms. They plow village land for a nominal charge of ten shillings an acre, turning the proceeds over to the center. When the centers close in November, each trainee receives a share of this money, usually amounting to approximately $12. With this money, plus the profit from his own farm, he is expected to buy or make a downpayment on a new plow, which costs about $45.

The average Gambian farmer now earns about $84 a year, a figure limited mainly by his use of the traditional hand hoe. Since land is not a problem, the increased use of plowing should allow an increase in the size of each man's farm. On this prospect rests the long-range hopes of the Agriculture Department. Along with fertilizers and insecticides, ox-plowing may bring about a small revolution in Gambia's agriculture within the next generation. This may seem like a long wait, but in a land where any kind of progress is cause for joy, most officials consider the wait worthwhile.

While the Agriculture Department is constantly thinking of crop-diversification, Gambia's economy is likely to remain for many years based primarily on the peanut — or "arachis hypogaea," as it is known to botanists. As one-crop economies go, Gambia is rather fortunate, for while such commodities as sugar, coffee and cocoa have suffered fluctuations and declines of late, playing havoc with the economies of many countries of South America and Africa, the world market for peanuts has remained relatively firm.

A small percentage of Gambia's peanuts are consumed domestically by the Gambians themselves and by the patrons of the Atlantic Hotel's lounge, whose thirst they are used to stimulate. (While Americans are accustomed to eating peanuts, the British are not. In England, the British feed them only to animals at the zoo, and refer to them as "monkey-nuts." Gambians do not like the overtones of this phrase.) Most of Gambia's peanuts are decorticated and pressed for their oil, which is used to make soap, candles, margarine, and — some say — olive oil. The pulp left after the pressing is known as groundnut "cake" or "meal," and serves as an excellent cattle feed. One Agriculture official told an American visitor that "all would be jolly if an ice cap would descend on Western Europe, permanently wiping out cultivation of that despicable crop, the olive. You Americans tend to look upon these primarily as vehicles for what I believe you term martinis. It may not have occurred to you that the oil of the olive and of the groundnut, when completely refined, are identical both in color and in taste, more accurately in lack of taste. When cold weather ruins the Spanish and Italian olive crops, our groundnut oil is featured both in the barber shops and in the salad dressings of those countries. When Latin skies are sunny, we must rely upon the greed of baseball fans and zoo animals and the enthusiasm of young Saxons for that disgusting spread known as peanut butter."

From the time the Portuguese first brought peanut plants from Brazil until the nineteenth century, Gambians cultivated them for local consumption only. In 1830, they exported 100 baskets of peanuts. Five years later, the figure was forty-seven tons, rising steadily to 8,636 tons by 1848. Along with their benefits to the economy, peanuts had two other historical virtues — they helped to end slavery and contributed to the decline of tribal wars. The Annual Report to London in 1848 pointed out that the potential of peanut farming was having an "effect in inducing native proprietors of slaves to retain them for the fruits of their labour instead of being anxious to dispose of them." As villagers gradually learned that they could earn more by growing peanuts — under considerably safer working conditions — than by tribal warfare, they became less and less willing to fight.

Under increasingly peaceful conditions, the Gambia colony's revenues — based primarily on a tax on peanut exports — rose from £13,000 in 1887, to £50,000 in 1902. In the following decades, however, irregular rainfall and wildly fluctuating world market prices caused havoc among the farmers. Since by nature they have always had the outlook of the grasshopper rather than the ant, they never saved enough in good years to support themselves in the bad ones. (A local proverb advises that "A quick penny is better than a slow shilling.") In this way, improvident farmers gradually went into debt to the traders who advanced them credit on food and supplies when they had no money. When one bad year followed another the government would have to step in with loans to tide the farmers over. Other farmers became entangled with local money-lenders called "Julamen," who cheerfully extended credit at interest rates of 100 per cent and up. Occasional near-famines forced villagers to pawn their clothes and jewelry, and live on wild berries and roots.

To try to end the cycle of debt, the government began storing seed nuts at each harvest, to be loaned next spring to those farmers who had none. This system encouraged abuse, and soon few of the farmers saved any seed nuts, happily depending on the government issue. By 1921, farmers owed the government about $140,000, and the government issues ceased. Since then, under a more enlightened system introduced by the Agriculture Department, each village sets aside a portion of its harvest to be used as seed nuts the following year. Local cooperative societies, one of the most successful recent innovations in the economy, have enabled many farmers to get out from under their burden of debt to the up-river traders.

Since its creation in 1924, the Agriculture Department has concentrated on improving the quality of Gambian peanuts, in order that the farmers can earn the highest possible price per ton. In recent years, the introduction of fertilizers and ox-plowing have been largely responsible for an impressive gain in the annual crop. From an average of 65,000 tons a few years ago, the figure has risen steadily to 73,000 tons in the 1963-64 season, 92,000 in 1964-65, and 118,000 in 1965-66, thereby providing a greatly needed boost to the economy. As with most rapid gains in Africa, however, the increase in Gambia's peanut crop raises problems. Agriculture officials worry that the increasing acreage means a progressive deterioration of the soils through overuse. As villages move to new land, they clear uncultivated bush, stripping the country of its few trees. Unlike peanuts, which mature in one season, the trees require a lifetime. Also, concentration on peanuts as a cash crop through the nineteenth century caused Gambians to ignore the planting of food crops, leaving them dependent on imported rice. One reason this situation continues is that the men look after the peanuts, and the women look after the rice. As one Governor's report noted: "Groundnut cultivation is light work, and consequently, after the manner of the people, it has been appropriated by the men, who gallantly leave the heavier and more laborious work of rice and corn planting to the women."

The most pressing problem resulting from the growth of the peanut crop is a bottleneck in the transportion system. While everyone has been busy improving the peanuts, no one has done anything about the creaking hulks that carry the nuts downstream to the "seccos" and from the seccos to the decorticating station at Kuntaur and the oil mills at Bathurst. These decrepit old "groundnutters" are sadly out of date, but there just doesn't seem to be any money around for new vessels. Motorized boats or trucks are out of the question because of repair problems, and because the shipping season is too short to make their purchase a reasonable investment.

To learn what new plans the Agriculture Department has in mind, I visited the headquarters out at Cape St. Mary, about ten miles from Bathurst. "Cape Station," as it is known, supplies all the up-river agricultural stations, and builds the wooden ox-carts that the Department is trying to introduce along with ox-plowing. On a tree outside the main building, a poster in English and Arabic, signed by Agriculture Minister Amang Kanyi, announced: ATTENTION ALL FARMERS. Select your Best seed Now. Thrash Early and stack Separately. Apply lindane Early. Remember Next Year! Be Truly Independent!!

The Director of Agriculture is a placid, forty-year-old Englishman named Hector Davidson, who has been serving in Gambia since 1953, and who will soon be replaced by a Gambian. Both studied agriculture at Cambridge. I found Davidson in his office, puffing on a curved-stem pipe, and looking at plans for a small, one-cylinder tractor he would like to introduce in Gambia. "We now have about 2,000 ox-drawn plows in the country," he said, "and this should be the next step. We feel that if we don't get this small tractor in use very soon, they'll be coming in with large ones. That's the mistake they've made all over Africa."

In a report that he and a UNESCO Technical Adviser prepared, Davidson outlined several reasons why conventional tractors are unsuitable for Gambia: they cost two to three times more than the mini-tractor, and are thereby out of the reach of farmers who never have much money. Because of their price, only groups of farmers could afford them, but since the planting time lasts only a few weeks, they would all want the tractor at the same time. Also, the fragmented pattern of land-holding would make such groups difficult to organize. Since Gambia has pathetically few trained mechanics, keeping such tractors in repair would require extensive service facilities, supervised by foreigners. Breakdowns or extended repairs on such machines would be disastrous in a growing season that lasts only a few months.

"What we need here is a simple machine that is Gambian-proof," said Davidson. "One that needs few repairs, and that is easy to fix. In a short farming season, timing is critical. The rains only last a few months, and the plowing must all be done in the first few weeks. If a tractor is out of commission for two weeks, the poor farmer is finished. If a chap goes out in the rain to weed by hand, and catches lumbago, his family is going to be hard put to get through the year. These new tools can make a farmer independent of seasonal variations."

When I complimented Davidson on the year's successful peanut crop, he said, "We can push groundnut production up to 150,000 tons or more, as we get them using more fertilizer and give them plows. The locals all tell me we should be concentrating on a second cash crop, but it's not that simple. The country needs money badly, and groundnuts are the easiest way to get it. The first thing we have to do is get some money in the farmer's hands so he can afford to take a chance on new crops. The Gambian farmer is a reasonable, conservative chap, and he isn't going to give up groundnuts when they are supporting him and his family. He risks this security every time he takes the advice of a young extension worker, or one of our up-river officers. Changes here don't take place overnight. It will take fifty or sixty years before we have a major second crop. The important thing now is to concentrate on the things we know well here. As a small producer, we must concentrate on improving the quality of our nuts. It's the one way we can withstand changes in price and marketing.

"As for second cash crops, there are any number of possibilities — limes, avocados, pawpaws [papayas], bananas, cashew, tobacco. We have shown that they can grow well here. You can see them over at our experimental station at Yundum. The problem is in transportation and marketing. We don't have anyone around who knows how to market these crops. You can't just grow them, and wait for someone to come and buy them. When you're as small as we are in Gambia, it's hard to get any of the freighters to stop off here. It's just not worth their while unless we can produce in quantity, as we do with our groundnuts. We have enough trouble now, just getting them down the river. I could grow potatoes on the top of Ben Nevis [a craggy peak in Scotland] but it wouldn't be an economical crop."

"What do you feel about the Gambians who say that the British are responsible for the country's dependence on a single crop?"

"Oh certainly. You can criticize the British. The reason they're not developed here is because the colonial officials neglected agriculture. They didn't even have an Agriculture Department till 1924. But we can say we've given them what they want. Up to now, all education centered in Bathurst. The Akus and the Bathurst Woloffs were the educated ones, and they were the men on the consulting bodies. They were the ones who gave 'local opinion' to expatriate advisers. Their education led them to believe that farming was something dirty. They wanted new schools, roads and hospitals — not experimental farms. You can't blame the U.K. for this.

"If we had opened agricultural schools twenty or even ten years ago, no one would have gone to them. Children were sent to school by farmers so that they could get out of farming. As a result, we now have a vacuum — almost no educated Gambian agricultural specialists. When I joined the Department over ten years ago, you were jolly lucky if you could get a man with a Standard six [about 6th grade level]. There was a stigma about being associated with the Agriculture Department. Mind you, some of them were jolly good chaps. But things have changed. When we tried to get extension workers, we used to get the village idiot. Now we're getting the best.

"You see," said Davidson, drawing on his pipe, "we're in competition with the social services — Health, Public Works, Education. Everyone's in favor of increasing Agriculture, but are they willing to take a cut in their own ministries? This is the problem in all developing countries. They've got to get their priorities right. Our purpose in Agriculture is to create a psychological and economic revolution. Up till now, the farmers have been apathetic, because no one bothered to show them they could do better. Now they see a ray of hope."

## GAMBIANIZATION

ALTHOUGH MOST of Black Africa is now independent, nearly every country has retained former colonial officials on contract to assist the new governments, and at the senior administrative level, the Europeans are still very much around. Senegal's President Leopold Senghore, for example, has six Frenchmen serving as "Conseilleurs personnels," many of his Ministries have French advisers, and the Minister of Finance is a Frenchman. In other countries — even those like Zambia, Guinea and Mali, whose relations with their former colonial ruler are frigid — Europeans hold similar positions, although their euphemistic titles may hide the fact. While most of the Europeans theoretically work in advisory capacities, some of them, particularly those at technical levels, are doing the work themselves. This is not a matter of neo-colonialism — it is a matter of pragmatic necessity.

African leaders can blame the French and British for the lack of skilled native administrators and technicians, but this does not solve the problem. The British and French claim that no one — including most African leaders — seriously considered the prospect of independence until about fifteen years ago, and they feel they have done well, considering the available time and raw material. The French are more grievously at fault than the British, for in addition to leaving few trained African administrators behind, they also left their colonies the dubious heritage of the French bureaucracy.

The lower, non-technical levels of government have been filled and often flooded by Africans. Throwing out the colonialists meant replacing them — ready or not — with Africans. The new political leaders all have friends, and particularly in Africa, extended families. In the new impoverished nations, government jobs are the only form of patronage available for these friends and relations. At the same time, the secondary schools are beginning to pour out thousands of graduates prepared for nothing but minor clerical positions — the one place they are not needed. Under all these pressures, the new governments have developed a virulent case of Parkinson's Law. Ministries enlarge, new departments appear, payrolls and paperwork increase, and work slows down. Compared with increasing agricultural or industrial production, the new rulers have found it remarkably easy to produce more jobs. At the end of the first year of its Four Year Plan, Senegal was on schedule in only two or three categories. One of them was something called "Administrative Infrastructure" — a euphemism for government employees. In one year, this category had surpassed its four year target by 280 per cent.

At the senior levels of the civil service the quality and standards are generally quite high. But as the United States A.I.D. mission chief in one country said, "A thin layer of top-level people here are damned good men, and work like hell. The rest are worthless." This thin layer is extremely thin, and thus far these men have been unable to transmit their energy and devotion to the lower levels. Another problem is that many of these graduates of London and Paris are reluctant to work outside the capital. Even this existence they endure grudgingly, whisking off to international gatherings at the least opportunity.

Today's lower level African bureaucrats lack not only training,

but something more subtle and more difficult to acquire — pride
in their work. Time alone will help supply the necessary training, but there is no reason to assume that it will instill this pride.
The new leaders hope that nationalist fervor will help, but while
they speak endlessly of the need to work harder now that they
are independent, government workers secure in the civil service
remain outrageously casual. In too many capitals, officials arrive
at work an hour late, take three-hour lunch breaks, leave an hour
early, and spend much of their four-hour work day chatting with
friends and relatives. In Senegal's gleaming new Administration
Building, known among Dakar's Western embassies as the "Pal-
ace of Sleep," it often takes a few days and several phone calls to
reach an official in his office. When one arrives for a scheduled
appointment, the official is frequently "not yet arrived," "somewhere in the building," or "just left." While most colonial administrators would not have tolerated such behavior, the present
African leaders seem loathe to do more than complain about it in
speeches. When foreigners express dismay over the casual attitude toward work, Africans reply that it is merely the African
way of doing things, and that critics should not try to impose
Western standards.

Then there is the problem of corruption. Though much has
been written about rampant corruption in African bureaucracies,
it is actually no more shocking than in many other parts of the
world, both underdeveloped and developed. The difference is
mainly that the Africans are less skillful at covering their tracks.
Like the lack of training and pride, corruption is certainly not
peculiar to Africa. But while more developed areas of the world
may be able to afford untrained, inefficient, callous or corrupt
bureaucratic jungles, Africa cannot.

*

In its government, Gambia is both more and less fortunate than its larger neighbors, for its size and poverty have been mixed blessings. When Governor-General Sir John Paul said, "We have the enormous advantage here of never having had much money," he meant that there was never enough to waste on luxuries or useless expansion of the civil service. The 1963 census, for example, illustrates the benefits of such poverty. "We had to choose between an election or a census," said one official, "since they use the same administrative machinery. We could only do it during the dry season, and only after the trade season had ended. That left only April, May, and part of June. It had to be held during the school holidays because we used high school lads as the census takers. We sorted the returns in empty beer cartons. I'd say it was the cheapest post-per-head of any census ever done in the world."

Gambia's civil service is one of the best and most efficient in Africa. This, of course, is not much of a compliment, but it does make life easier for the administration. Though there were only a dozen or so well-trained Gambian administrators upon independence, the country can almost get along with that many. While the civil service performs admirably, the leadership is another matter. However poor their training, those now at the top of the civil service have at least the benefit of experience. Most of the Ministers have had neither. The reason for this is simple. The up-river electorate vastly outnumbers the voters of Bathurst, and they therefore elect most of the M.P.'s — from whom, according to the British Parliamentary system of government, the Prime Minister must choose his Ministers. Unfortunately, the Provinces did not vote until 1960, and thus did not participate much in government. Few of the up-river candidates have had the benefit of training and experience. Also, as in far more developed countries, the electorate are frequently unimpressed by training and experience.

For these reasons, it is understandable that several of Mr. Jawara's Ministers did not complete high school, and only one has a college degree. Most of them were village school teachers, minor clerks or petty traders before entering politics. Fortunately, under the Parliamentary system, most of the ministries are actually run by their senior career civil servants, many of whom are excellent. Few of the M.P.'s, on the other hand, went beyond primary school, several have prison records, and despite regulations to the contrary, several are illiterate. One of them, who defeated a highly qualified Bathurst accountant, had failed the exam for the lowest grade of the civil service. "Considering what the P.M. had to choose from," says one British adviser, "the old boy's done bloody well."

At forty-two, the "old boy" is one of the younger heads of government in Africa, and despite his age and the size of his country, he has already acquired a reputation as one of the continent's most effective and stable leaders. (For such virtues, he was recently knighted by Queen Elizabeth.) A shy, quiet, extremely courteous man, Prime Minister Jawara is hardly a reporter's dream. He has a round, generally expressionless face, and does not laugh or smile easily. He takes his position and his work seriously. He dislikes small talk, replies to most questions with three words or less, and outside of his formal speeches, rarely discourses at length on any subject. Correspondents who interviewed him during the independence celebrations left his office shaking their heads.

These characteristics are hardly marks against the P.M. In a continent where chiefs of state customarily speak in monologues of harangues, this careful, moderate man is refreshing. Some hardened British colonial officials who generally have little complimentary to say about Africans, consider Jawara "a good bloke." They do not mean by this that he "knows his place," but that he is a competent, industrious administrator in a land where such virtues are extremely hard to come by. As Britain's Colonial Secretary said, "It is, above all, his wise leadership during the past two years which has made it possible for the Gambia to achieve independence, despite all the practical obstacles which nature and circumstances have placed in her path."

"D. K. Jawara," as he is commonly known, was born in 1924 in the up-river Mandinka village of Barajally, where his father was — and still is — a relatively prosperous trader and farmer. Of his six children, the father chose David to send to school in Bathurst. He arranged for the boy to live with a Bathurst trader, who enrolled him in the Mohammedan primary school, and later, the Methodist Boys High School, then the only one in Bathurst. "Jawara was always number one in every class," recalls one of his former classmates. "He won many prizes." Upon graduation in 1945, young Jawara joined the Medical Department, serving as a male nurse for two years at Royal Victoria Hospital. He won a scholarship to study veterinary science for a year at Ghana's Achimota College, going on later to Veterinary School at Glasgow University. After six years of study, he qualified as a Member of the Royal College of Veterinary Surgeons. While at Glasgow, he began to give evidence of his political instincts, taking active part in the African Students Union there, and eventually becoming its president. He was also a member of the "Forward Group," a student advisory committee to the Labour Party.

In 1954, Dr. Jawara returned to Gambia to work as a veterinary officer with the Agriculture Department. For the next six years, (except for one, when he returned to Glasgow to earn a diploma in Tropical Veterinary Medicine), he trekked across the country, inspecting and inoculating cattle, and teaching farmers how to improve their breeds. (He reportedly told a recent interviewer, "There's not a cow in the Gambia that doesn't know me personally.") "He was not just a good veterinary surgeon," says a colleague. "He was an excellent veterinary surgeon." During this time he married Augusta Darling Mahoney, the youngest daughter of Sir John Mahoney. This was quite an achievement for the son of an up-river Mandinka farmer, for the Mahoneys are perhaps the most prominent and cultivated family in Bathurst. Sir John was then a member of the Legislative Council, and was later appointed Speaker of Gambia's first House of Representatives, in 1960.

That same year, David Jawara resigned from his post as Chief Veterinary Officer — a considerable sacrifice, since few Gambians, and particularly Mandinkas, had risen that high in the civil service — to lead his newly formed Peoples Progressive Party in the country's first nation-wide elections. When the PPP won ten seats, Governor Sir Edward Windley offered Jawara the Ministry of Education; when the Governor later appointed the UP's P.S. N'Jie Chief Minister, however, Jawara resigned in protest. In the 1962 elections, the PPP won eighteen seats to the UP's thirteen, and David K. Jawara became Chief Minister and later Prime Minister.

The Jawaras live in a large house next to Government House, facing the river. Two of their five children attend school in England. The Prime Minister has little time for hobbies, spending most of his spare hours in an office at home, studying government affairs. His wife, Augusta, makes up for his withdrawal, presiding over or participating in numerous women's and charitable organizations. She once ran unsuccessfully as a PPP candidate for Parliament from Bathurst, and has written a play about Mandinka marriage customs.

Though Mr. Jawara is not a gifted orator or a flamboyant crowd-pleaser, his speeches on public occasions are models of earnest good sense — a quality notably lacking in the speeches of many of his counterparts elsewhere on the continent. His most dominant theme is that Gambians must have no illusions about the fruits of independence. "Independence is not a magical formula which will transform your groundnuts into diamonds," he tell them. "Independence does not mean an overnight change from poverty to wealth, or that leisure will replace hard work. It means facing the fact that we shall be on our own, and that by our own efforts we must earn our keep."

While the Gambians are busy earning their keep, their government has the assistance of a few dozen British advisers, one of whom spends a great deal of time assisting the Prime Minister. His name is K. J. Winton Lane, M.V.O., O.B.E. During World War II, Lane served for a time as British liaison officer at the Pentagon, and was awarded the Legion of Merit by the United States government. He later served at the United Nations, and spent ten years in the Colonial Service on the island of Mauritius. A small, lean, precise man, Lane has been Permanent Secretary to the Cabinet and the Prime Minister since 1963. As such, he is probably the most important and effective adviser in the country. Though his name rarely appears in reports of official proceedings, he is involved with the affairs of every ministry. Some ultra-nationalistic Gambians consider him a kind of Machiavellian puppeteer, toying with the Prime Minister, and secretly controlling the government. This view gives insufficient credit to the P.M. and too much to Winton Lane. His position is actually that of a trusted and experienced personal adviser who channels the flow of the P.M.'s work, protects him from unnecessary concerns, and gives valuable advice. Because everything of any significance seems to go through Winton Lane's office, Western embassy officials in Dakar often refer to Gambia as "Wintonia." This amuses neither the P.M. nor Winton Lane.

Along with Winton Lane (who in 1966 became United Nations adviser to the Gambian government), there are still forty to fifty British officials serving on contract in various departments, including the Chief Justice, Attorney General, Registrar General, Senior Magistrate, Director of Cooperatives, Commissioner of Income Tax, Director of Marine, Commissioner of Police, and the senior engineer in Public Works. Up-river, there are still British Commissioners and Development Officers. Outside the government the situation is the same. All the large commercial firms are run by non-Gambians. The senior staffs of the Bank of West Africa, Cable and Wireless and Yundum Airport are all British. The principals and half the staffs of Yundum College and Gambia High School are British. An Indian now fills the Prime Minister's old post of Principal Veterinary Officer.

This may be neo-colonialism, but there is not much Gambia can do about it. There are simply no Gambians qualified or available to fill most of these positions. The administration is touchy about this fact, and issues frequent reports on the progress of Gambianization. As independence approached, officials made a special effort to find even semi-qualified Gambians to fill many positions — with questionable results. "The Gambianization of the government increased so rapidly over the last six months," reported one official, "that the civil service was on the verge of cracking up. We've had to slow down." A colleague remarked, "If you took away all the British administrative secretaries, advisers and senior aides, they'd be jolly well hard put."

With a university degree and years of experience, a Gambian can rise to the top of the civil service, and earn as much as $5,600 a year in base salary. This is a very long and strenuous path, however, and many of the brightest young Gambians consider politics more attractive. With a bit of luck, little experience and less education, a man may become a Member of Parliament. Though a Member's salary is only $1,344 the position opens up many opportunities of extra-curricular remuneration. With a bit more luck, and some political agility, the young politician might be named a Minister. At this level he has left his colleagues in the civil service far behind, with a salary of $7,560. The Prime Minister earns $8,400, plus several extras including a house and entertainment allowance. Many officials feel that their salaries should be higher, referring to Senegal, where Ministers earn $12,000 and the President, $15,000. Gambia, however, just doesn't have that kind of money. They also resent the fact that British officials on contract earn much more than Gambians at the same level. (They forget that the expatriates generally have much more education and experience than their Gambian counterparts.) A senior British adviser, for example, may earn about $400 in base salary, plus housing and another $3,000 or so in bonuses and hardship allowances. Gambians find the necessity of the latter payment particularly galling.

Despite the government's modest salaries, Gambia's senior public officials have not been driven to the corruption that seems regularly to scandalize many neighboring countries. There are several possible explanations for this. One is that Gambians are more honest. Another is that there is simply not much money around to steal. Momodou Cham, the young United Party M.P., offers a third explanation: "In Senegal, each department head is like a separate trader. He gets a certain amount of money each year, and he can do with it almost as he likes. In Gambia, the director of a department has no access to the money. He just fills out the paper work and sends it through channels to the Treasury or the Accountant General."

At the lower levels of government, the record for financial scrupulousness is somewhat spotty. An up-river official, commenting on the fact that five out of nine candidates for M.P. in his Division had prison records, said, "There isn't much we can do. They're the only people who can read and write. They've all been treasury scribes of clerks with the Cooperatives or the Area Councils, and they were picked up for filching funds. Same thing with three of my clerks. So many clerks dealing with funds end up in jail. It's not that they are all corrupt. They really don't think it's wrong. They just can't seem to keep their hands out of the till. Yet farmers leave their groundnut stacks out in the fields unguarded, and no one touches them."

Despite such gloomy analyses, visitors from neighboring countries generally judge Gambia's civil service one of the best on the Coast. Whatever faults it has are even more common in the larger countries. As for Gambianization, it is simply a matter of time. Many Gambians would like to see all the British leave immediately, regardless of whether or not there are qualified Gambians to replace them. Most British officials feel that if they can remain for another few years, until the government has a chance to train some replacements, the country will be the better for it. Nationalistic Gambians consider this argument a last ditch effort of colonialism, denying that these officials care about more than their own jobs.

A collision of these two views occurred shortly before independence, when a British Commissioner at Basse named Addis was sacked because of a letter he had written to the magazine *Encounter*. In the letter, he took issue with an article that had advocated speedy dismantlement of Britain's remaining fragments of empire, and a withdrawal of all colonial officials. Addis had excellent credentials for defending colonialism. His grandfather had served in India, and his father had been Governor of the Seychelles. He himself was an accomplished linguist who spoke fluent Mandinka, and had the reputation of being one of the best and hardest-working Commissioners in the Gambia.

Prime Minister Jawara, under pressure from the radical wing

of his Party, removed Commissioner Addis. Addressing Parliament, he said that Addis "has expressed his unreserved and, I do not doubt, sincere apologies for his action, and for the expressions which, as he now sees, can be read as a slur on the Gambia and its government. I must regard his action nonetheless, as completely unacceptable conduct in a senior Civil Servant, and Mr. Addis' request to retire — which he submitted at the government's invitation — has been granted."

In his letter to *Encounter*, Addis wrote that he was "left with the inescapable belief that Mr. MacInnes [the author of the article] must be joking. No thinking man in this day and age could seriously be both quite so naïve and so irresponsible."

> I am (dare I say it?) a Colonial Administrator — a member of an extinct species, a fossil interred in the "now long gone" empire. I actually work in a British Colony in West Africa . . . an area from which our withdrawal is still incomplete. I am one of those wicked colonial practitioners who, through torture, violence and the suppression of democratic will, are, by immutable law, tending to endanger the social life and corrupt the power of Britain. Having spent a number of years and considerable energy, under conditions which I should like Mr. MacInnes to share with me, in trying by every means to awaken ideologically my subject people, I can assure him that no amount of force will persuade the British Government to hold on to the territory for one minute longer than they have to. The territory has, in fact attained full internal self-government just as soon as it asked for it, and rather sooner than it was ready for it. It will similarly . . . attain Independence just as soon as it wants it, and a little before it can have any real meaning. Under its rosy cover, Britain will continue for some time to come quietly to balance the country's budget, pay for its development works, and provide the technicians and administrators which it still so sadly lacks. The freely elected Government of the country now has the power to dispense with the services of the likes of me.

Mr. MacInnes may fondly imagine . . . that there will be a wholesale banishing of the sun-helmeted imperialists and a stepping into their highly polished mosquito boots of the downtrodden subject peoples, at last claiming their birthright. It is a whimsical picture, and one often painted in cadmium yellow and cardinal red at anti-colonialist meetings of those who know the colonies through any medium barring firsthand personal experience. Strangely, the picture is inaccurate. The down-trodden peoples are not yet ready to take over our functions and responsibilities. Not only this, but the elected Government know they are not, and are asking, nay, urging us to continue to occupy our own shoes.

## ELECTION

In March, the government startled local political observers by announcing the "retirement" or dismissal of seven chiefs and calling elections for their replacement. This was surprising because, except for rare cases, chiefs traditionally hold office until they rot away. Neither age, infirmity nor moderate incompetence and corruption have usually been sufficient grounds for removal. While theoretically the government has always had the power to dismiss unruly chiefs, it had rarely done so.

Before the Europeans came to Africa, chiefs were relatively autonomous, with a feudal dependence on the king of their region only for military protection. Otherwise, the kings did not meddle with their administration of local affairs. In establishing their colonies, the British and French reacted differently to this system. The French destroyed the power of the chiefs completely, placing Frenchmen or loyal Africans in every district as local administrators. The British policy was to break the autonomy of the chiefs, but to allow them to continue ruling their people as agents of the central government. Today, in Nigeria, Ghana and Sierra Leone, some of the chiefs are well-educated officials who have risen to senior positions in the government. In Gambia, few of them have had much formal schooling, and

many do not speak English. One of the few who had risen to
national prominence, Seyfu Omar M'Baki, of Sami District, was
one of the men dismissed in the present purge. He had served
for fourteen years on the old Governor's Executive Council, and
later became a cabinet minister in the administrations of both P.
S. N'Jie and David Jawara.

Through a rigid caste system, chiefs and village headmen always come from the same few families. When a headman ("Alkali" or "Alkalo") dies, the village elders simply meet and decide
upon one of his brothers or sons as the next headman. When a
chief ("Seyfu") dies, candidates are usually picked from among
the families of the headmen of the villages in that district. Only
yard-owners or compound heads vote for a new chief. Though
they constitute only about 5 per cent of a district's population,
they are more conversant than most with the customs of the district, and therefore more qualified to decide upon a largely ceremonial position.

Chiefs' salaries range from $420 to $1,540, depending on
the length of their service and the amount of revenue from
their districts. The government also gives the chiefs small
allotments to employ "badge messengers," traditional retainers
who carry the chief's word about the district, and act as unofficial
policemen. In the good old days, chiefs had as many as forty or
more badge messengers. Today they have only two to six, depending on the district. Most of them are simply relatives or
cronies whom the chief wants on the payroll. One of the modern trappings of chieftancy that most Seyfolu consider an improvement over the good old days is the government pension.
However, it is also a handy tool for the central government,
since a chief does not receive a pension if he is dismissed — only
if he retires. The government can thus wield the pension as a
club over those whom it feels should retire. In the current purge,

five of the seven chiefs involved, when faced with a loss of their pensions, decided it was time for a rest.

Even opposition leaders had to admit that the purge was not blatantly political, since only two of the seven chiefs were supporters of the United Party. Most were dismissed for abusing their powers. One ran a financially shaky transport service. When the bank refused to extend him further credit, he put pressure on the farmers' cooperative society in his district for a $280 loan to repair one of his trucks. Somehow, he never got around to repaying the loan. Another of the chiefs had collected nine wives (Moslem law allows only four), and spent much of the rest of his time concocting schemes to relieve his Fula tribesmen of their cattle.

The chiefs "relieved from office" were Kantara Juwara of Wulli District and Omar M'Baki of Sami. The government "approved the retirement" of Seyfus Saikuba Jarjusey of Jarra West, Kebba Leigh of Fulladu West, Famara Singhateh of Lower Baddibu, Jundu Turey of Kombo South and Sainey Biagi of Foni Bintang. Speaking on Radio Gambia, Sherif Dibba, the Minister for Local Government, denied allegations that the move represented "an intention of destroying the institution of chieftancy." He referred to the chiefs as "the traditional link between the government and the people." He insisted that "when acting impersonally and in harmony with government policies, and providing fair and proper administration, they constitute a very valuable adjunct to the general peaceful life and well-being of the people in the provinces."

Shortly after the announcement of the purge, I paid a call on Mr. Dibba in his office at the old Secretariat building on MacCarthy Square. After climbing the rickety wooden stairs to the third floor, I entered the outer office of the Ministry of Local Government. The room was filled with piles of files heaped on

wooden tables and dusty shelves. Several tired-looking clerks
waded slowly through the piles, occasionally shifting a file from
one pile to another. A government messenger in khaki uniform
and pith helmet entered, took six cigarettes from his pocket,
gave them to the chief clerk, and left.

Ushered into Mr. Dibba's office, I found him speaking on the
telephone, with a paperback copy of *Economic Aid to Underdeveloped Countries* open on his wooden desk. Though only
twenty-eight, Sherif Dibba is particularly well-qualified to discuss
the status of chiefs in Gambia, since his father, a farmer in Sa-
likeni, recently became Chief of Central Baddibu District.
Dibba gave two reasons for the Administration's action in re-
moving the chiefs. "First, nearly all of them were out of touch
with the people. This was a great obstacle to the central government. Second, some of them were completely against the government. In this country the government and the Party are two
different things. We are not asking the chiefs to support the
Party, but we insist that they support and carry out the policies
of the government. They must not overtly act against the government whose policies they are supposed to implement. This
man, Omar M'Baki, when he left the Cabinet, the majority of
the people in his district didn't like him. He was known to have
serious anti-government grievances, and he didn't hide this at all.
The Seyfu of Bansang, Kebba Leigh, was a loyal supporter of the
Government, but he accepted bribes. He suppressed the people
in ways that our grandfathers did, and engaged in fraudulent
practices. The P.M. and I have had several complaints about
him. The people are extremely happy that these steps have been
taken."

Next door to Sherif Dibba's office is that of Henry Oliver, his
British adviser and Commissioner of Local Government. A veteran of twelve years as a police officer in India, Mr. Oliver lost his

right eye to an ax-wielding demonstrator in the Hindu-Moslem riots in Kashmir, upon the declaration of India's independence. He came to Gambia in 1949, and served fifteen years as an up-river Commissioner before rising to his present position, in which he supervises the work of the four Division Commissioners. Although he is an old hand at colonial rule, Oliver's views on local government are decidedly modern. "People here in Gambia don't much like the old school of Commissioners and Chiefs. Power has shifted from such one-man rules to the Area Councils and the central government. Of course, you get these old die-hards who cling to a power that's no longer theirs." As he talked, Oliver carefully polished the left lens of his eye glasses. "Originally, you became a chief by having the biggest stick — or if your brother was chief you poisoned him. Then you surrounded yourself with trusties who were usually members of your family. Under colonial rule, if a chief was acting in an odd manner, an inquiry was held by the Governor's Executive Council. If he was judged guilty, they went up to him and said, 'Look here, old man, you're not performing very well are you?' He'd say, 'No, I'm not.' 'Well then, what about your brother?' He'd say, 'Jolly good,' and that was that. With the coming of independence, all that sort of thing is finished. Now the government — or really the P.M. — can sack whomever they like without an investigation."

When the elections were held in May to replace the purged chiefs, I discovered that the "head boy" at the Atlantic Hotel, Souri Fatty, was related to Karamo Fatty, one of the three candidates in Lower Baddibu. As head boy, Souri is a force to be reckoned with in Bathurst, for the hotel is one of the city's largest employers. ("Boy" is a job classification rather than an age description in Africa. Many "boys" working in private homes in Bathurst are in their fifties or sixties. A relic of colonial days, the word has carried over to independence despite the distaste for it among educated Africans.) Souri carries his responsibilities as head boy with an air of calm dignity, enhanced by a wrinkled, yet ageless face. No one seems to know his age, least of all Souri. Of his service at the hotel, he says, "This month he go be ten years." The closest he can come to a determination of his age is that "during the war time I be small picken like this."

The exact relationship between Souri and Karamo Fatty is confusing, for Souri refers to Karamo as his father, while the other boys at the hotel say that "Karamo Fatty not Souri's propah fadda. He be small fadda. Souri's real fadda be old pa. This be his brudda." Translated, this means that Karamo and Souri are stepbrothers. They both have the same father, who is now the headman, or "Alkalo," of Kerewan, the main village in Lower Baddibu. Karamo is the son of an early wife, Souri of a much later one. Because of the loose polygamy practiced throughout much of Gambia there is always a great deal of confusion when it comes to determining ancestry and family relationships. The situation is further clouded by the indiscriminate use of words like brother, father and uncle, as illustrated by Souri. Speaking of his stepbrother, Karamo Fatty, he said, "Karamo be big countryman, but first time he go try for chief. Always, since we come in de world, Fatty people be Alkalo in Kerewan, since de beginning, but we no get chief. De ol' chief of Lower Baddibu was Saba man [Saba is a village near Kerewan] name Famara Singhateh. He be ol' pa, maybe eighty years. Now de government sack him for make palava."

"Did Karamo Fatty go to school?" I asked.

"No. He learn in de army. He get long time in de army. He go Burma an' get sergeant. When he come back dey give him messenger job at Kerewan, den Mansa Konko. Den dey make him interpreter an' transfer him Basse. Now he back at Mansa Konko."

"How do you become a candidate for chief?"

"Well, you must get twenty people from de country [district]. Not de small picken. Dey must be old pa, yard mastah. You try to get mix people because one nation [tribe] can no support you. You get some Joloff, some Mandinka, some Fula. If you get de twenty people, it left to de government to certify you for get [ballot] box. De Commissioner, he go talk to you, ask you why you want to be chief. You know de person who be chief, he s'pose to be straight man. When two people come to you, make palava, you have to talk straight between de two people. If de government certify you, you get box. If de people like you, you win. If de people no like you, you no win."

\*

To reach Kerewan, you must cross the Gambia River on the Bathurst-Barra Ferry, a forty-minute trip, then drive for an hour on a rutted road to the Mini Minium Bolon (creek). If you blow your horn and yell very loud, and if the ferry man on the other bank is awake, he will slowly pull his hand-operated cable ferry across the creek to pick you up. If you have come by taxi, which will leave you off on the bank and return to Barra, the ferry man will send his son for you in a two-foot-wide dugout canoe. When burdened with a passenger and luggage, this vessel sits about an inch out of the water.

The one sandy road that runs through Kerewan is closed during the rainy season, and few vehicles use it the rest of the year. There are not many reasons why one would come to Kerewan. It is not a river port or a trading center, and except for a few huts selling kola nuts, cans of sardines and warm bottled soda, there are no shops. Although there is a population of 1,500, the nearest school or store is seven miles away. Kerewan's one claim to distinction is that it is the headquarters of Assistant Commissioner Malcolm Clark, who administers the affairs of the North Bank of the Lower River Division.

Clark is one of the government's bright young men, a new breed of university-trained administrators who will replace the British Commissioners. A tall, well-built, handsome Bathurst Woloff, Clark is so thoroughly Europeanized that it is difficult to think of him as an African. After graduating from Bathurst's Methodist Boys High School in 1954, he worked for four years in the Treasury Department. Then, as a private student, he spent four years at Queens University, in Belfast, Ireland, graduating with a degree in economics. Clark is a rarity, for few university-trained Africans are willing to serve "in the bush." He misses his student days — "I used to travel every year to the Continent, usually Scandinavia" — but finds his job interesting. "I like the work here very much, but at times it is very lonely. The people here are all Mandinka, and I speak only Woloff. If I want to speak to anyone — I mean have a real conversation — I have to drive seven miles over to N'Jawara. There are some Woloff teachers at the primary school there."

The morning I arrived, Clark was just going off on an inspection of Lower Baddibu's three polling stations for the following day's election. We piled into his Land Rover and headed for Saba, a village two miles away.

There, we drove through a maze of alleys out to a clearing at the edge of the village, where the polling booth, constructed of bamboo, straw and palm fronds, nestled under a huge cotton silk tree. An old villager named Kebba, who had built the booth, stood proudly by, watching Clark examine it. Clark told him it would have to be moved. Kebba had built it so that it would be in the tree's shade during the afternoon. The election would take place in the morning. As Kebba and Clark tried to pick a proper site, villagers gathered about and offered their advice on the probable angle of the sun the next morning. A lengthy and meticulous discussion ensued, involving diagrams in the sand and gesturing at the sky. Everyone present offered an opinion — Clark's driver, the local interpreter, the village headman, the village elders and a rapidly growing crowd of children. Clark calmly allowed the debate to flourish for some time, then pointed to a spot and told Kebba to build it there.

Five miles from Saba, we came to N'Jawara, where the polling booth was also under a cotton silk tree, this one in the center of the village. A much more sophisticated construction than the one at Saba, it was made entirely of woven straw. Though smaller than Kerewan, N'Jawara is the main peanut-buying center for Lower Baddibu. Most of the large firms in Bathurst maintain agents and stores there, and the district cooperative society has its "groundnut secco" there. At the Maurel & Prom shop, managed by a Gambian, we bought cans of pineapple and peaches, both imported from South Africa. At another store, run by a Lebanese merchant, we bought beer. There we found the faculty of N'Jawara's primary school sitting on crates, playing checkers. Two transistors blared Arab music from Dakar. The shelves of the shop were lined with transistors for sale.

Back at his residence in Kerewan, over a lunch of rice and meat, Clark spoke of preparations for the election. There had been eighteen candidates originally, of whom fifteen managed to come up with the necessary twenty supporters. Each of them had given a brief speech on why he wanted to be chief. Clark had recorded their particulars, checked for police records, and sent the material down to Bathurst. From the fifteen candidates, the Ministry of Local Government had chosen three to run in the election: Karamo Fatty; Foday Singhateh, the headman of Saba; and Sherif Janko Kinteh, treasurer of the Kerewan Area Council and son of a former chief from Kintekunda village.

"The candidates are usually pretty sure of their own villages," said Clark. "For that reason you won't see Karamo Fatty campaigning here in Kerewan, and you noticed that Singhateh, the

Alkali of Saba, wasn't at Saba." According to Clark, Fatty had
the advantage of coming from Kerewan, the biggest village, with
about ninety yard-owners. Saba has seventy yard-owners, N'Jawara fifty, and Kintekunda thirty to forty. Many smaller villages
also vote at the three polling stations. Although Sherif Janko
Kinteh was from the smallest village he had the advantage of his
brother's being the Alkali of N'Jawara. Since none of the candidates was from N'Jawara, they had been spending most of their
time campaigning there. The political scene in N'Jawara is complicated by the fact that half its residents are Woloffs, and therefore probable supporters of the United Party, while all three candidates were PPP men and Mandinkas. Another problem is that
because N'Jawara is almost on the Senegalese border, nearly half
its yard-owners are Senegalese citizens, and therefore ineligible to
vote.

"Another point to remember," said Clark, "is that chiefs generally favor their own village. Both the Kintehs and the Singhatehs have been chiefs before, so there is some opposition to them
in the other villages. The Fattys have always been the headmen
of Kerewan, but they have never been chiefs. They have the advantage of not having had the opportunity of making enemies.
However, the chiefs aren't as important today as they used to be.
They used to have great power. They were feared and respected.
Today, they are no longer feared, and they get little respect from
the younger generation or from the Party."

After lunch I dropped in on the Fatty compound and found
Souri inside resting. "I be up all last night see people in N'Jawara and Kintekunda. I no sleep all time."

"How did you campaign in N'Jawara?"

"I come each compound and say, 'I going to take your part.'
Kinteh man, him brudda be Alkali of N'Jawara. His people
come same compounds, say same thing."

Soon the little mud-brick hut filled with Souri's relatives. There were two wrinkled old women, several children, and Souri's father, Kemo Fatty, Alkali of Kerewan. He had white hair, a white goatee and yellow, rotting teeth. As he talked, he fingered his Moslem prayer beads. Souri translated the old man's mumbled Mandinka into English. "He say all dis country [Kerewan] is PPP. Small picken, old man, woman — all be PPP." The old man seemed so emphatic on this point that I feared he thought I was some official from Bathurst, checking up on his loyalty to the Party. The recent purge must have made all the traditional rulers uneasy.

Old Kemo Fatty rose to leave, pressed my hand in his, and made me promise to help the Fattys win the next day. He said that if his son Karamo won, I must come and sit with him on the village bantaba, where he would make big prayer for me. Souri and I then left to stroll about Kerewan. At every compound he stopped and exchanged long Mandinka greetings with the yard-owners. "You see?" he said. "I smile all de time now, and talk with everybody." We also bought kola nuts to distribute among the village elders. These small red nuts, about the size of chest-nuts, are immensely popular both up-river and in Bathurst, and are used as gifts to mark the successive stages of marital and other formal negotiations. Their popularity is due in large part to the fact that they are a mild stimulant, appealing to Gambia's Moslems, whose faith prohibits the use of alcohol.

Back at the Assistant Commissioner's compound, Clark and two assistants were gluing photos of the candidates to the sides of blue insecticide barrels that would serve as ballot boxes. The candidates' names appeared under the photos, but since few of the voters can read, each candidate had his symbol attached to the tops of his barrels — kerosene lanterns for Fatty, machetes for Singhateh and wooden hand hoes for Kinteh. Candidates and voters attach great significance to these symbols, and occasionally squabble over who shall have which symbol. These barrels represent a major improvement over the old system of casting paper ballots. Many voters used to stuff the ballots into their pockets instead of casting them in the ballot boxes, and then sell them outside to the highest bidder. This man would then cast all the ballots he had managed to buy, along with his own, for the candidate of his choice. Because the ballots booths were screened off, local election officials had no way of checking such abuses. The booths are still screened off now, but the new system seems to be foolproof. Each insecticide barrel has a length of pipe sticking through the top, like a periscope. Attached to the bottom end of the pipe, inside the barrel, is a bicycle bell. Instead of paper ballots, voters receive marbles. When dropped into the pipe in any barrel they ring the bell on the way down. Since each voter receives only one marble, and the voting supervisors who sit just outside the booth can hear the sound of the bell, Gambian officials feel their new system is a major step forward in insuring democracy.

Later that afternoon, a Land Rover from Division Headquarters at Mansa Konko pulled up with John Bishop, a British Development Officer, and Hardi Fye, another young Gambian Assistant Commissioner. They were both serving as supervisors at the polling stations. Like Clark, Hardi Fye is a tall, bearded Bathurst Woloff, who sports a curved stem pipe and a strong Oxford accent. Fye attended Queens University, majoring in political science, and then went on to study public administration at Oxford. Though a Woloff, he speaks Mandinka because he was born up-river.

We all went up to the terrace of Clark's house, which overlooked a blaze of bougainvillaea. Like many up-river government quarters, the house is built on stilts, which serve the double purpose of cooling the house and keeping animals and insects away. Over well-chilled bottles of Heinekens, Bishop, a former police officer in the colonial service in India, explained some of the problems of voter registration in Gambia. "A lot of these people give their nicknames or titles when they register," he said. "Or they give their mother's name as their surname. They don't care much one way or the other about the order of their names. They switch them around from time to time, and sometimes just change them completely. Then when they come to vote, we don't find their real name on the list and say 'Sorry.' They get furious. For example, a 'Lamin Cham' will be known to his friends by the nickname 'Doudou.' When he comes up to vote he will give his name as Doudou Cham, and we have him down as Lamin Cham. The problem is far more serious during the regular elections, when everyone votes, for we may have dozens of Chams in a village."

To illustrate this point, we went through the yard-owner lists for Lower Baddibu and found that Kerewan had thirteen "Fattys," Kintekunda had eleven "Kintehs," and Saba had twenty-one "Singhatehs." (On the regular voting list for a village near Basse, there are 52 Dukureys, 37 Jakitehs, 40 Kabbas, 50 Kamaras and 136 Tuncaras.) Many of these people have the same first names, so to avoid as much confusion as possible, the registration lists record the voter's first name, surname and mother's name. This still leaves room for confusion.

*

Next morning, Clark and I went to inspect the polling stations just before the voting began. Clark's driver was a Mandinka named Sajo Jawara, and like most Commissioners' drivers he was indispensable. Since Clark spoke little Mandinka, Sajo served as interpreter in this predominantly Mandinka region. He was also a jack-of-all-trades useful to a Commissioner, providing expertise on local agriculture, customs, genealogy and rumors. As he drove, Sajo announced that he was very excited about the election because he was a cousin of Karamo Fatty. "But I call him brudda. My fadda, his mudda get same mudda, fadda. So he be my brudda [i.e., cousin]. Last night my wife bring me chop, I no eat 'im. I get too much for election. She tell me 'You got to chop. Your brudda win, he no win, you no die. Got to chop.'"

As we drove from Kerewan to Saba to N'Jawara, we passed groups of village elders striding across the fields in single file behind their Alkalis, heading for the polling stations. They wore colorful embroidered ceremonial robes and caps, and carried multi-colored golf umbrellas as sunshades. At N'Jawara, they gathered in the shade of a crinting fence and waited to be called up village by village. One by one, they went up to the supervisor's table, checked their names against the ones on the list and received their blue marbles. Many, after long disputes, turned out to be unregistered, and were sent away.

As each voter entered the booth, we could hear the marble drop down the pipe, "ping" off the bell and fall into the barrel. A problem arose when a blind man, led by a friend, came up to vote. He passed inspection, but his friend turned out to be unregistered. One of Karamo Fatty's agents offered to lead the blind man into the booth, but the expression on his face showed that even he did not expect his offer to be accepted. Finally, the supervisor called a police constable over, who led the blind man into the voting booth. When they emerged, I asked the constable what he had done. "I asked him which man he wanted, and he said Karamo Fatty. I asked him what Fatty's symbol is, and he said a lantern. I put his hand on the lantern and asked him what it felt like. He said it felt like a lantern. So he put his marble in that barrel."

Heading back to Kerewan from N'Jawara, we passed Sherif Janko Kinteh, roaring along the sandy road on an old black motorcycle, with an old black voter sitting behind him. This is apparently how they "get out the vote" in Lower Baddibu. Kinteh is a dark-skinned demonic-looking fellow, with deep-set piercing eyes, bushy black hair, handlebar moustache and Van Dyke beard.

Back at Kerewan, a dispute was in progress at the polling station, set out beyond the village under a cotton silk tree twice as large as those in Saba and N'Jawara. John Bishop, the supervisor, could not find Alkali Kemo Fatty's name on the list of registered yard-owners. While Bishop looked through the lists, the old man stood before the table, trying to maintain his dignity before his assembled villagers. The issue, which was confused by having three "Kemo Fattys" on the list, narrowed down to the Alkali's mother's name. She had apparently gone by two different names — "Tida" and "Karafa." Since the lists did show a "Kemo Fatty Karafa," and since he was the village headman, they finally agreed to let the old man vote. He gathered up his robes in a huff, took his blue marble, and stalked away to the booth. "Because they make up the lists of yard-owners themselves," said Bishop, "Alkalis often forget to put their own names down."

On our next swing around the three polling stations, near the end of the morning, we met Gavin Dudley, the British Commissioner at Mansa Konko, who had just come over in his Land Rover. When Clark told him things were nearly through at Kerewan, Dudley said, "You'll have to keep the polls open till one o'clock, as announced. Even if they say everyone has voted, you never know. Some old pa may be wending his lonely way across the trackless wastes, coming to exercise his centuries-old franchise."

We all drove over to Saba, where we found the candidate Foday Singhateh, Alkali of Saba, sitting in state under the cotton silk tree in a chair brought by his villagers, and holding a rainbow-colored golf umbrella over his head. His head, like that of many strict Gambian Moslems, was shaved, accentuating his skeletal face. Sherif Janko Kinteh stood nearby, clutching a blue plastic brief case. Commissioner Dudley shook both their hands, wished them luck, and spread his arms to the sky. "It's in the hands of Allah now." Singhateh and Kinteh nodded impassively.

Over at N'Jawara, we found the Gambian supervisor named Jallow sitting alone at his table. All the voters had left for their homes or headed over to Kerewan to await the final results. Jallow reported that only 82 out of the 110 eligible voters had shown up. "Some are out of town, trading in Farafenni or Bathurst. Some are sick, some are dead. One man from Suarakunda village died the day after he registered." Since most men are getting on in years before they become compound heads and yard-owners, such casualty rates in the voting lists are normal.

By noon, the temperature was 90 degrees in the shade, and about 120 in the sun. Because the climate in March is very dry, this heat, though intense, was not particularly uncomfortable. Gavin Dudley passed around a thermos of cold lemon squash, a popular British drink made with fruit syrup and water. "All I ask for is my squash," said Dudley. "I could go anywhere, in any heat, as long as I had my squash — across the Sahara."

When we returned to Kerewan, at 12:30, most of the registered yard-owners had voted. One old man, who lived only a few hundred yards away, was sick, and they sent a police Land Rover to fetch him. More than a hundred village elders lay reclining in the shade of the giant cotton silk tree, as a dry hot wind blew across the open field. After 1:00, the polling station closed, the police loaded the barrels into the Land Rover, and we all went over to Clark's office to await the barrels from Saba and N'Jawara. A crowd of several hundred gathered outside the office, and the police had to clear them away from the open doors and windows. A loud sputtering announced the arrival of Sherif Janko Kinteh on his motorcycle. Soon Jallow and Hardi Fye drove up and brought their barrels in. The little tin-roofed cement office was now jammed with seventeen people — officials, police, candidates' representatives and observers. A Mobil Oil thermometer on the wall pointed to 98 degrees — inside.

Clark and an assistant first opened the Singhateh barrel from N'Jawara. They broke the seal, took off the top, and tipped the barrel upside down. A shower of dust fell out, along with ten marbles and a rusty nail. Singhateh's Saba barrel produced 62 marbles. Fifteen more in his Kerewan barrel gave him a total of 87 votes. As predicted, most had come from his own village of Saba. Karamo Fatty's three barrels yielded 119 marbles, 93 of them from Kerewan. Clark placed each candidate's marbles in a tray similar to a Chinese checkers board. The thermometer now read 99 degrees. Sherif Janko Kinteh polled 56 marbles from N'Jawara, where his brother was Alkali, 57 from Saba, which surprised everyone, and 47 from Kerewan, where his own Kintekunda villagers had voted. This gave him a total of 160 marbles, and the chiefdom of Lower Baddibu.

Someone pointed out that the total number of marbles was 366, while the number of voters counted at the polling stations was only 365. However, no one was willing to quibble over one marble. Besides, the temperature was now 100 degrees in the little office. Clark went out and announced Kinteh's victory to the assembled crowd. Some cheered, the rest remained silent. It was definitely an upset, for everyone had expected Fatty to win. Clark gave a short speech in English — translated into Mandinka by an interpreter — telling the people that they had all voted fairly, and must take the result in a good spirit. He hoped they would "pull together now behind your new chief, and give him your full support."

Kinteh's people headed back to Kintekunda for a celebration, the rest of the villagers began walking across the fields to their own villages, and Clark, Hardi Fye, John Bishop, Gavin Dudley and I went over to Clark's house for lunch. Bishop estimated the temperature in the sun at somewhere between 130 and 140 degrees. At lunch, everyone expressed surprise at Kinteh's victory. Someone suggested checking the Area Council's books to see whether its treasurer, Kinteh, had partaken of council funds to finance his campaign. Clark said he had already checked. The general conclusion was that Karamo Fatty had come home too late to run an effective campaign. Unlike Singhateh and Kinteh, he had been living outside Lower Baddibu for the past few years, and had worked at Mansa Konko right up till the day before the election.

On his way back to Mansa Konko that afternoon, after inviting me to join him, Commissioner Dudley passed through Kintekunda, where everyone was dancing and drumming around Sherif Janko Kinteh's compound. Dudley also stopped off at Karamo Fatty's compound to offer consolation. Fatty came out with a grim expression and spoke to Dudley. "I think something happen here. I don't want to say, but I think something happen." He would go no further.

"I am sorry you lost the election," said Dudley. "I think you would have made an excellent chief. But that is Allah's will. Anyway, I am glad to have you back as my interpreter. You are my right hand man."

## GAVIN DUDLEY AND THE DUTCHMAN

As WE DROVE along the rutted dirt road from Kerewan in Gavin Dudley's windowless Land Rover, the breeze felt as though it was coming from an open blast furnace. The passing countryside was parched and flat, a series of dull browns and greens broken by patches of fruiting mango trees. Dozens of "strange farmers" from Senegal, in search of land, walked along the road carrying their belongings on their heads in tin suitcases or cloth bundles. During the hour-and-a-half drive to the Trans-Gambian Ferry, we passed only two tractors and a government Land Rover. The ferry was full when we arrived at the landing, and about to leave. When the crewmen saw the Commissioner's flag on our fender they moved two cows and another Land Rover, and made room for us. The ferry did not sound well. It was five years old, and for any mechanical device in Gambia this is a ripe old age. The instrument panel consisted of several meters and gauges, none of which worked. The captain of the ferry told us, "This ferry, she be too old. The engines they both tired."

As we pulled into the Commissioner's compound at Mansa Konko, a few miles from the South Bank ferry landing, Dudley yelled "Bakary!" From within, the houseboy answered, "Yes mastah." When the garden boy came up to take our bags, Dudley introduced him as Moussa, a Hausa tribesman from Nigeria, and greeted him with a long torrent of jovial Hausa. The garden boy looked up at Dudley with an impassive expression . . . Bakary came out and told Dudley that this was Yusapha, not Moussa, and that Yusapha did not savvy Hausa.

Dudley learned Hausa during his thirteen years in the Colonial Service as a District Officer in Northern Nigeria. Upon Nigeria's independence, in 1960, he returned to England, bought a farm in Devon, and tried his hand at breeding riding ponies and saddleback pigs. When the offer came to serve a tour on contract in Gambia, he took it immediately. He has served in several positions, both up-river and in the Secretariat in Bathurst, coming to Mansa Konko only a short time ago.

"I'm just an old retread," he is fond of saying, "patching up holes until the Gambians are ready to fill them." At fifty, he looks anything but a retread. His blue eyes, rimmed by tortoise shell glasses, sparkle in a tanned, freckled face, topped by thinning black hair. He wears the standard colonial uniform — open white shirt, khaki shorts and knee socks. He gives orders to Gambians in the slow serious manner of a schoolmaster dealing with young children, and sprinkles his conversation with "Well dones," "Jolly goods" and "good shows."

Because of his bluff, hearty, paternal manner, Bathurst officials consider Dudley the perfect model of the old style colonial officer. This would please him greatly, for he is proud of being a colonial official, pointing out that "the Dudleys have always been colonialists." His great, great, great-uncle, Sir Thomas Dudley, came over on the second or third *Mayflower* voyage and served four terms as Governor of Massachusetts. Sir Thomas's son, Joseph, was Chief Justice of New York, and later Governor of Massachusetts. Joseph's son, Paul, was Attorney General and later

Chief Justice of Massachusetts. Gavin Dudley's father was a tea planter who went out to Ceylon in 1880, and Gavin grew up there until he was sent to school in England.

That evening a police constable rode up on a bicycle to report that a taxi had turned over near the Trans-Gambian Highway. One passenger was dead, and several others had been "very feared and left the scene." The driver and another passenger were unconscious, and would be driven to Victoria Hospital in Bathurst, two hours away. The constable needed Dudley's signature for a post mortem on the dead passenger, whose body would also be taken to Bathurst. As he signed the forms, Dudley said, "Whew! That's wonderful. In Nigeria we had to hold an inquest right away when someone was killed. It's jolly hot there, and bodies go very quickly."

As the houseboy Bakary prepared dinner, he asked me, "How you like Gambia?" Assured of my approval, he said, "Yes, Gambia small small, but good country. No palava, no fighting, no people kill each other like Congo." As he placed a basket of fresh rolls on the table, I asked him if he had made them himself. "Yes, yes. You come to bush, you got to make everything. If you no get yeast, I use palm wine." Like most houseboys brought up-river from Bathurst by their employers, Bakary did not hide his feelings about life "in the bush." It was something to be endured.

Despite the intense heat of the day, the night was cool, and blankets were necessary. In the morning, after breakfast and the BBC Overseas Service news broadcast, we drove over to the Commissioner's office, a large cement building a few hundred yards from the residence. The Lower River Division is the largest in Gambia, with a population of 96,000 spread over twelve districts. This does not seem awesome to Dudley, however, whose district in Nigeria contained 700,000 people — nearly twice Gambia's total population. The whitewashed walls of his office were decorated with detailed maps of the Division, a portrait of the Queen and an ancient green wall safe. Files lay piled on desks, tables, shelves and the floor. Assistant Commissioner Hardi Fye sat working at one table, beneath a Mobil Oil wall thermometer that already, at 9:00 A.M. pointed to 84 degrees.

Dudley went about his morning's work with cheerful dispatch. He put away the trays of blue marbles used in the Lower Baddibu election, sent for a missing pair of scissors, and dealt with a man who had recently retired after working six years at Victoria Hospital and had not received his gratuity pay. There were several letters requesting employment at the Commissioner's office. One read:

> Honoured Sir:
> I am applying for a post under your consideration. My qualifications for this post are: My big brother is in Georgetown gaol and my sister is the mistress of the Treasury Scribe at Kuntaur, and I too would fain enter Government service.

All government officials, both in Bathurst and up-river, receive a steady stream of such letters from untrained and uneducated Gambians, asking for "any job." One prospective employee wrote a Commissioner, "I would be grateful if you could do me a famous favour, and that is to be my backstay." Another closed his application with, "I put my trust in Christ, whom you so closely resemble." The similarity of many of these letters is due to the fact that most of them are written by professional letter writers, at a cost of one shilling each. The main qualifications of these men are typewriters or fountain pens, and a vague knowledge of English. While this vagueness frequently results in incomprehensible letters, it is sufficient to impress their illiterate clients. Even letters written by government officials, many of whom progressed no further than primary school, display flashes of candor and graphic description unusual in official correspondence elsewhere. A police report of an accident informed Bathurst Headquarters that "the driver suffered from instant tooth extraction, which was caused by the impact of an anthill with the lorry." One up-river inspector reported that "the groundnut crop looks good in my district, by the grace of God and with the permission of the Commissioner."

When Dudley was finished with the morning's correspondence, an assistant brought in a young farmer named Demba Sanyang, who had allegedly abducted a girl from her home in the Casamance, the Senegalese province just south of Gambia. The Senegalese *prefet* at Ziguinchor had written to Dudley, asking him to make inquiries, and the girl's mother had come to Mansa Konko to bring her back.

The abduction of a daughter is a serious affair in Gambia. Not only does it violate normal human relations, it deprives the girl's father of the customary dowry and a useful worker about the compound. As one student of Gambian culture put it, "They don't look on a wife or daughter as another mouth to feed. It's another bod' to plant rice and grind coos." This is one reason why polygamy flourishes in Gambia, as well as the basis for the high price of wives.

These dowries are fairly rigid, varying only with different tribes, and in cases of extreme beauty or ugliness. Mandinka wives cost about $70, and Woloff wives run anywhere from $140 to $196. The relative beauty of Woloff women is one reason for this difference. Fula fathers, who are more accustomed to bargaining with livestock than money, generally receive something like a cow, a sheep and two goats for each daughter. Serahuli women, partly because of their profitable ability to make clay water urns, are the most expensive, running approximately $280. In all cases, non-virgin or "second-hand" wives cost considerably less. While marriage negotiations up-river are exceedingly complex, divorce is relatively simple. The petitioner, in the presence of a marabout or at a Chief's District Tribunal, merely says on three different occasions, "In the name of Allah I divorce thee." Given the pace of modern life, however, even up-river in Gambia, this custom is gradually being reduced to the oath, "Thrice in the name of Allah I divorce thee."

Demba Sanyang stood before Dudley's desk now, shuffling his feet and clasping his hands. He was a good-looking boy, and neatly dressed. Through an interpreter he said he had met the girl, Fatamata Touray, while working in the Casamance as a "strange farmer." Although he and Fatamata were both Mandinkas, her father had rejected Demba's proposal of marriage, saying, "I'm not giving my daughter to a British subject." According to Demba, Fatamata told her parents that she wanted to go away with him and "die in Gambia." (Some of Demba's recital struck me as overly nationalistic melodrama designed to appeal to Commissioner Dudley.) Demba had left the Casamance "on the moon after Ramadan," and Fatamata had followed him a month later. He said he had given her father all his money and presents, and that they would be wasted if she returned to her home. Dudley asked Demba about his farming and his family. The boy seemed intelligent and responsible. Dudley told him Fatamata would have to be taken back to her father. However, he promised to give Demba a letter to the official in Ziguinchor, telling him that Demba was of good character, and could support a wife, and asking the *prefet* to intercede with the father on the young man's behalf. This seemed to satisfy Demba. As Dudley wrote the letter, Demba asked for permission to go and relieve himself. Dudley nodded. The boy walked over to the office door, and was about to urinate on it when the assistant hustled him out.

Next on the morning's agenda was an old gentleman who had
been sending letters to the Prime Minister and the Ministry of
Local Government, urging them to remove from office the members of the local Area Council. At the bottom of these letters,
which had all found their way back to Commissioner Dudley's
desk, the man had signed the names of all the headmen of the
villages of Jarra West District. Dudley had checked with several
of them and learned that they had never seen or heard of the
letters. When Dudley questioned him, the old man produced
several more crumpled letters from the folds of his robe, accusing
the members of the Area Council of various horrendous mis-
deeds. All had typed signatures of district officials who undoubtedly had no knowledge of them. Dudley chastised the old man
for deceiving the officials in Bathurst. He said to the interpreter,
"Tell him that anyone can write to a Minister, but he must have
the courage of his convictions to sign the letter himself, and not
type in the names of Alkalis he has never spoken to." The old
man nodded, and walked out.

At 10:15, it was time for Commissioner's Court. Dudley rose,
put on a tie, gathered up some papers and a large red leather-
bound court record, and walked into the courtroom adjoining his
office. He sat down at a table beside a substitute interpreter sitting in for Karamo Fatty, who was still home in Kerewan licking
his wounds from the election. Facing Dudley at another table
were Police Inspector Secka, an assistant, and a constable. Two
observers sat on wooden chairs at the back of the room. The first
case on the morning's docket was that of Massary N'Jie, charged
with stealing. When the clerk-interpreter called his name, Inspector Secka rose to inform the court that Massary N'Jie who
had been released on bail, had "disappeared." Dudley put the
case over till whenever the police could find him.

The most important case of the morning was the trial of

Lamin Jallow, a 23-year-old Fula cattle herder charged with attempted suicide. Sitting in the defendant's box with his hands clasped between his knees, Lamin Jallow did not look like a dangerous criminal. His coal-black face was bovine and expressionless. He wore dirty, Moslem-style, baggy trousers and a fluorescent blue sport shirt. His feet were bare. Magistrate Dudley read the charge, which the interpreter rendered into Mandinka. Judging by the blank look on Jallow's face, even this translation of case #LL-7-165 and section 206 of the Criminal Code seemed like a foreign language to him. He pleaded guilty.

For many years, Lamin Jallow's elderly father, who lived in Niorro village, had looked after the cattle of a rich Mandinka farmer named Juka Sey. (Fulas customarily perform this labor for Mandinka cattle owners.) When the old man grew too feeble to herd the cattle, he turned them over to his son, Lamin. According to Lamin — and this was disputed by Juka Sey — the understanding between the Jallows and Juka Sey was that in exchange for tending the herd, the Jallows would receive one cow each year (worth about $42) plus half the herd's milk to sell.

Lamin looked after Juka Sey's cattle for six years. The arrangement on the milk worked out satisfactorily, but somehow Juka Sey never got around to giving Lamin any cattle. Meanwhile, Lamin was getting into debt because he wanted a wife. In order to make gifts to the girl's father, he borrowed a sheep and some goats from several Niorro villagers, promising to repay them when he harvested his own peanuts or when Juka Sey gave him a cow. Lamin eventually fell so deeply in debt that he stole two cows from Juka Sey's herd. He slaughtered one for his family, and gave the other to the man from whom he had borrowed a sheep. This man traded it to another man for two loads of tin roofing material. A few days later, Juka Sey happened to stroll by this man's compound and recognized his cow. He traced it back

to Jallow and confronted him with the evidence. Jallow con-
fessed to the theft and begged Juka Sey to give him another
chance. According to Jallow, Juka Sey agreed, giving him a few
months to pay for the stolen cattle.

Either Lamin Jallow misunderstood, or invented this agreement, or else Juka Sey went back on his word, for the rich cattle
owner immediately reported the theft to the seyfu of Kiang
Central District. The seyfu sent one of his badge messengers to
bring Jallow to the police station at Mansa Konko, eight miles
away. This presented a problem, since the badge messenger,
who rode a bicycle, did not wish to demean himself by dismount-
ing to trudge eight miles along a dirt path beside a common
thief. Seeking a solution to the problem, the messenger brought
the accused to the bantaba in the center of Niorro village to put
the issue before the village elders reclining there. While they
debated how to get two people to Mansa Konko with only one
bike, Lamin Jallow went to get a drink at the nearby well. According to the minutely detailed testimony of several witnesses,
Jallow walked quickly to the well, removed his hat, placed it
carefully on the ground, and jumped head first into the well.

All the witnesses agreed that the well was at least eighty feet
deep. They held to this estimate even when the skeptical Magistrate Dudley fetched a measuring tape and showed them how
long eighty feet was on the ground outside the courtroom. They
testified that when they rushed to the well and looked down,
they saw Jallow standing upright in three feet of water at the
bottom. They made a crude ladder of grass and sticks and lowered it into the well. Jallow climbed up and emerged muddy,
wet, shaken and crying — but without a scratch.

The chief and the badge messenger escorted Jallow to the
Mansa Konko police station — on foot. The police booked him
for the theft of the two cows and for attempted suicide, a mis-

demeanor under section 206 of the Gambia Criminal Code. In an earlier trial, he had received a sentence of nine months on the charge of stealing cattle. The present charge of attempted suicide carried a maximum of three years. (Acting as local magistrates, Commissioners can only levy fines up to $280 and sentence up to three years. More serious cases automatically go to Bathurst for trial.) Lamin Jallow's defense consisted entirely of his statement to the police when he had been arrested. In it, he claimed that "Juka Sey had said there would be no pay, but that he would do a good thing. Our [Fula] custom is that if someone looks after cattle for twelve months, the owner will pay by giving one cow. My father told me about this agreement. These past six years, rain and dry season, I have been looking after these cows. Except for the milk, I received nothing for my troubles. I never asked for a stick or a rope.

"I am the one who must feed my compound, because my father is too old and my brother is farming in Senegal. But I could not feed them because I spent all my time caring for the cows. Thus I went into debt. I asked Juka Sey for a bag of coos, but he said 'No.' I almost thought of those cattle as my own, since I had looked after them so well. So I stole two of them. I was very much ashamed when they came for me, and I threw myself into the well. If I had died, it would have been Juka Sey who had killed me."

Commissioner Dudley, who was taking all the testimony down in long hand, filling many pages of the large leather court record, questioned Inspector Secka about the custom of paying one cow per year to a herdsman. Secka replied that it was the general custom of the area, although it was by no means a formal arrangement. He pointed out, in mitigation, that Lamin Jallow had already spent a month in police custody during the trials, and that as the main supporter of his compound, it would be a great hardship on his family if he were in prison for a long time.

After a brief recess, Dudley took nearly twenty minutes to write out the court's decision, pausing several times to rub his chin, ponder and tap his pen on the desk. Finally, he looked up and addressed the court. "Right. This has been an unusual case. It involves a young man, heavily in debt, who steals to pay his debts. There are mitigating circumstances affecting his actions. The lack of payment for six years of work caused great distress in his mind. In passing sentence, therefore, I make a strong request to the seyfu of Kiang Central to assist in persuading Juka Sey to put aside three cattle for the father of the accused. These will be handed over to the accused upon completion of his sentence. [This "request" for the seyfu's "assistance" in carrying out a decision illustrates a central principle of British Colonial policy — utilizing whenever possible already existing political institutions.]

"As for the attempted suicide, only Allah gives life, and only Allah should take it away. Besides, even if the accused didn't attempt suicide, he did try to escape from custody, which is equally serious. Lamin Jallow is a young man of sound mind, and has — or should have — a great future as a good Gambian. I don't want to waste his time in prison, since he has already been convicted of a previous charge. I therefore find the accused guilty as charged, and sentence him to a fine of $140 or one year in prison — to be served concurrently with his other nine month term."

Asked whether the award of three cows was a "compensation ruled by the court," Dudley replied, "I can not force Juka Sey, and the seyfu can not legally force him to give the cattle on the basis of my recommendation. But I have confidence that he will do this out of the goodness of his heart. The purpose of this court is to sow a seed of mercy in the heart of Juka Sey." Just then, a tiny red bird flew in one side of the open courtroom, fluttered briefly over Dudley's desk, and flew out the other side.

At lunch, Dudley said, "What you have seen here today is — or should be — a minor part of my functions. The real work of a Commissioner is going out on trek, talking with chiefs and headmen, inspecting the roads and the farms. You should go out and stay in each village — pitch a tent or use a rest house. In Nigeria, District Officers were ordered to spend at least fifteen nights a month out in the district."

After lunch, we took a stroll about the compound. Perched atop one of the few bits of high ground in Gambia, the Commissioner's residence at Mansa Konko overlooks a broad plain divided by the Gambia River. "That's *the view*," a friend had told me on an earlier visit. "It's the main reason for Mansa Konko, and it's why they built it here. [Mansa Konko's proximity to the Trans-Gambian Highway is another reason for its location.] It's a completely artificial town — no village, no market, no nothing. Just a great bunch of whacking government buildings in the middle of nowhere."

Walking about the compound with Dudley, it did seem barren. A brace of old ceremonial cannons faced forlornly out over the plain. Whitewashed stones marked unnecessary pathways about the dusty grounds. Dudley spoke of a plan to plant trees in the compound. "I believe every administrative officer should leave something behind him. You should leave a mark. I try to get my Gambian Assistant Commissioners to do this also. I built a park in Jos, when I was D. O. in Nigeria, but nobody uses it now. It's known as Dudley's White Elephant. The natives use it as a public lavatory."

*

That afternoon, a Land Rover with "Community Development" marked on its door pulled up to Division Headquarters. The driver entered the office and gave Dudley a note signed "Van

Der Plas." The hastily scrawled message was a demand for several hundred dollars' worth of supplies. Dudley exploded. "He expects me to get him money for this?"

The driver, assuming the outburst was directed at him, shuffled his feet and mumbled, "Well, I don't know. I think Mr. Van Der Plas be under you."

"Yes he is," said Dudley, "but I wonder whether Mr. Van Der Plas is aware of that. He comes into my office every few days and asks for something new."

Before the driver left, I arranged to go with him the next morning to Kwinella, a village about twenty miles from Mansa Konko. There, he informed us, "Mr. Van Der Plas, he make big poison."

I had first seen Van Der Plas back in October, just as the rains reached their hot, sticky end. He had entered the Atlantic Hotel one day like some ghostly apparition. A small, fragile old man, he sat out on the dining terrace looking on the verge of expiration. Skin shriveled like yellow parchment inadequately covered jutting bones and knobby joints. Beady, steel-gray eyes peered out of shrunken sockets in an emaciated face surrounded by wispy gray hair and a full, scraggly beard. The hotel boys said the old man was "Pa Van Der Plas. He be fine fine man. He know de ribba [up-river country] better past all. He help Gambians too much."

Charles Olke Van Der Plas is a seventy-four-year-old Dutchman who has spent most of his years out in a hot sun helping people. Since 1963, he has been doing this in Gambia, where he started the Community Development Department. A man of prodigious energy and eccentricity, he is venerated by most Gambians and endured by those British advisers and officials of whom he has run afoul. One of the latter describes Van Der Plas as "a kind of Schweitzer who never got any publicity." Upon graduat-

ing from the University of Leiden in 1911, Van Der Plas joined
the Dutch Colonial Service as a regional administrator (similar
to a district commissioner) of the Kangean Islands, a distant
outpost of the Dutch East Indies. Of his work there, he says,
"We had almost no communication with the capital. They used
to make wonderful regulations, and had no idea of the results of
our attempts to apply them." After eight years in assorted islands of Java, Van Der Plas returned to Leiden for a degree in
social science and economics. This, along with some Arabic
studies, led to diplomatic appointments in Saudi Arabia and
Ethiopia. In 1927, he returned to Indonesia, where he eventually
rose to become Governor of East Java. He left Djakarta two days
before the Japanese arrived, and returned in 1943 when it was
liberated. His tales of those days include such phrases as
"Mountbatten said to me . . ." and "MacArthur gave me a free
hand." Though one of Holland's highest-ranking colonial officials, he urged the Dutch to move toward independence for Indonesia. "I insisted on complete autonomy for them, but our
people in The Hague missed every chance to come to a real
understanding. The result was absurd. The Dutch tried military
suppression, and this finally led to independence with bad feelings."

In 1950, at the age of sixty, Van Der Plas began working for
the United Nations, heading technical missions to Saudi Arabia,
Jordan, Tunisia, Greece, India, Laos and Yugoslavia. He first
came to Gambia in 1954, to make a survey of post-war unemployment and economic depression in Bathurst. "I took the job
because I thought it would be interesting, and I had never been
to West Africa. I found that with their typical suppleness, the
people had solved the problem themselves. There was not much
work after the war, so they just went back to the land." In 1963,
Van Der Plas talked the Gambian government into creating a

Department of Community Development, of which he has the title "Honorary Organizer." He wheedled about $560 and a Land Rover out of the Ministry of Local Government, and another $560 out of NOVIB, a private Dutch foreign aid foundation he helped organize. Since then, the contributions from both sources have increased annually under his incessant prodding. Because Community Development work cuts across the affairs of several different ministries (Health, Education, Local Government, Agriculture), Van Der Plas makes frequent trips in from the bush to haggle with various Bathurst officials about the operations of his department and theirs. His semiautonomous status enables him to criticize them publicly, which he does with some relish.

In March, Van Der Plas appeared again at the Atlantic Hotel dining terrace, this time looking more brown than yellow. He had put on some weight, but had not lost the scarecrow effect. One still noticed his bony arms as he ate, the watchband loose on the tiny wrist. Veins stood out on his face like markings on a faded road map. He had spent the past few months in Holland, raising funds for NOVIB. "I stayed away longer than I had planned, trying to finalize our assistance program here. I spoke at fund-raising gatherings at churches, universities, labor and business groups. We did very well."

Van Der Plas is not a conversationalist. He prefers monologues, fixing his listener with the piercing stare of the Ancient Mariner. He sprinkles his discussion of Community Development in Gambia with long digressions on Greek philosophy, Mandinka music (on which he has written a book), Arabic poetry, Javanese "shadow plays," and schemes for flushing rats out of urban slums. As he talked, he cut his food into tiny pieces as one does for a child, chewing each morsel for several minutes. When he rose from the table, there were bread crumbs in his gray beard and on his gray flannel trousers. Despite the 90 degree midday heat, he donned a bulky tweed jacket. "I have to see the Prime Minister, and I have nothing else to wear. When I arrived from Holland, they sent my trunk up-river by mistake. Then when they sent it back here, they forgot the key."

Now two months later, as we drove out to meet Van Der Plas at Kwinella, his driver explained that the old Dutchman was attempting to poison the herds of bush pigs, baboons and monkeys that roam throughout the country. While pigs, baboons and monkeys may not have much to do with community development, they have long been a curse on Gambia's agricultural development. Like their counterparts in American zoos, the baboons and monkeys are fond of peanuts. In Gambia, however, they have the good fortune to live in a country that produces little else.

In 1950, the government launched a massive anti-baboon campaign, offering two shillings (28 cents) for each baboon tail handed in to the Commissioners. Since two shillings was a princely bounty to farmers who averaged no more than $78 a year, the campaign was a great boon to those regions fortunate enough to be infested. So great a boon in fact, that regions less well-endowed protested. Under pressure, the government agreed to include bush pigs and monkeys in the campaign. After two years, the government proclaimed the campaign a huge success. Gambians had produced a total of 50,000 baboon tails, 26,000 monkey tails, and 25,000 bush pig tails. Despite this awesome slaughter, officials discovered that they may have made a mistake in assuming that each tail accounted for one animal. Since the tails frequently arrived in advanced stages of decomposition, the Commissioners had been loathe to store them in their offices, and had thrown them out. Somehow, many of them apparently found their way back to the office again and again, smelling a bit

worse each time. Other crafty Gambians had successfully managed to split the tails in two without attracting any attention.
(In Tanganyika, some time before, a campaign to rid Dar es
Salaam of rats produced a similar result of thousands of rat tails
without an apparent drop in the capital's rodent populations.
Officials finally discovered that one enterprising gentleman had
been making a fortune breeding rats on a farm up in the hills.)

Since the pests continue to make major inroads on Gambia's
peanut crop, the government still wages occasional war against
them, organizing "pest hunts" from time to time. During my
stay, the Gambia Field Force sent its crack musketry team up-
river for a month-long pig shoot. They returned after one week,
having killed too few to justify their continued encampment.
This form of pest control was costing the government roughly
$47 per pig.

Van Der Plas's driver headed through the village of Kwinella
to a grove of mango trees, where the Dutchman was "making big
poison" at the government rest house. (There are about two
dozen of these bungalows scattered around the country in the
towns and larger villages.) On a wooden table lay an open toilet
kit, an Olivetti typewriter, a bottle of red pills and the remains of
a grapefruit. I could hear the old man in the bedroom, singing to
himself as he dressed. His "boy," who was busy setting the table
for breakfast, informed me that "Pa Van Der Plas he go come
small time." At about 9:00, Van Der Plas emerged. "I over-
slept. Almost collapsed yesterday. It was too much, tramping
around all day in the sun." He looked thin and sallow in his
white shirt. Olive drab shorts flapped about his knobby knees,
and knee socks encased his broomstick legs. Nevertheless, he
bustled spryly about, clearing off the table.

After breakfast, a procession of villagers appeared for what
seemed to be regular morning office hours. Several needed minor

medication, which Van Der Plas cheerfully dispensed. "We offer daily care for wounds and simple ailments with medicines donated by the Ministry of Health." While he treated his patients, the room filled with village children with no visible ailment other than curiosity about the old man's activities. A huge, buxom woman billowed into the bungalow, causing a stir among the assembled onlookers. Van Der Plas greeted her in a rapid chain of Mandinka. (Along with passable Mandinka and Woloff, he is fluent in Dutch, English, German, French, Italian, Arabic and four Indonesian languages, and gets along well in Spanish and modern Greek.) "This is N'Gansimba," he said. "She's the head of the local women's society, secretary of the Kwinella branch of the PPP and leader of the initiation ceremony for the young girls of the village. They still practice complete excision of the clitoris here. This is one of the things that must be gradually ended. It produces psychological strains, and greatly diminishes the sexual pleasure of the women."

When N'Gansimba had left, Van Der Plas shooed the small fry out of the room and began supervising his two assistants, good-looking young Gambian girls from Bathurst. They set to work on two burlap sacks full of cassava roots. First, they cut them into six-inch cylindrical chunks, then cut plugs out of one end with apple corers. These flimsy tin utensils were no match for the tough cassava, and the girls were having a hard time. "I told you to put the rubber gloves on!" the old man yelled at them. "You mustn't touch them with your hands. The pigs can smell you."

"We're trying to use the cassava chunks as bait, since pigs love cassava. [It is also favored by many Gambians as a source of virility.] We're using a zinc phosphide poison. It's a paste which we put into the holes the girls are making with the apple corers. Then we plug them up. Yesterday we put out a load of unpoisoned cassava chunks to get the pigs used to it. We'll go out this morning to see if they've eaten them, and perhaps put out some more unpoisoned bait."

"Much of Gambia, and particularly this area, is overrun with these small wild pigs. The government has tried several times to eradicate them, but they've gotten nowhere. If this method works around Kwinella, I may be able to convince them to try it in other districts. There's a constant Darwinian struggle here. In 1932, the government stopped an outbreak of rabies in one region by having all the dogs in that region killed. These dogs, however, used to kill rats. When they were gone, the rats multiplied rapidly, and the government had a new problem on its hands. You must be careful when you tamper with Nature's equilibrium."

About 10:30, we loaded up the Land Rover with unpoisoned cassava chunks. At a nearby well, a group of boys were furiously turning the large pump wheel. "They're just playing," said Van Der Plas. "That well has been dry for several weeks. Many wells have dried up over the years. At the end of the dry season, about this time, many of these villages literally run out of water." As we drove out of Kwinella, we scattered a flock of vultures surrounding another old well.

We drove to Jalinding, a small village twenty minutes from Kwinella, then turned off the sandy road into the low bush. After bouncing along for several hundred yards, we stopped in the middle of a heavily wooded area and set out on foot. The bush here was alive with large tsetse flies, called "jolo" by the Mandinkas. Their bite can bring trypanosomiasis, or African sleeping sickness. Van Der Plas ignored them, despite his bare arms and legs. "Clothes make little difference to them. They can bite through heavy pants or a shirt." As we tramped through the bush, we upset a flock of monkeys that had been sitting in the trees. They swung noisily away from tree to tree, screaming and chattering. "They're very destructive. They ruin the rice, coos and groundnut crops. The baboon eats more, but those brutes pull things out of the ground just for the joy of it."

Descending a small hill, we came out onto a broad, open, dried-out marsh. We walked across the brown reed grass until we came to a series of empty water holes, where the C.D. team had placed chunks of cassava root the day before. They lay in the dry mud now, with hornets swarming about them. A few had been nibbled, and a Gambian assistant identified the toothmarks as those of monkeys. After inspecting all the holes, we returned to the Land Rover. Van Der Plas was disappointed, for he was mainly after pigs this time. "If a pig eats the poisoned root, he gets terribly thirsty and hunts for water. The river is still salty at this point, so the swamps are no good. They try for these water holes, or crawl away to die in the shade of the bush. You never find them, usually."

"Then how do you know when you have killed one?"

"You never really know. You can count the missing cassava chunks and hope that each one killed a pig."

"Are the pigs edible, when poisoned by zinc phosphide?"

"No, but the Gambians here are all Moslems, and wouldn't eat them anyway."

At Jalinding, we stopped to pay our respects to Landing M'Binkinding Sanyang, Seyfu of Kiang West District. Chief Sanyang is an enormous, cheerful man, weighing close to 300 pounds. On the walls of his tin-roofed hut were photographs of his three wives, a picture of Queen Elizabeth, and illustrations of scenes in Swaziland. Children ran about everywhere in the compound. Chief Sanyang presented a few of them to us proudly as "my picken. I get plenty picken." He told us that a village woman had just died, and left a sick baby. Van Der Plas promised to send over some medicine. The Chief thanked us profusely for our visit, and gave us a guide to the second spot where the C.D. team had dropped cassava.

Following the guide's directions, we drove along a narrow dirt road that became a dirt path that became a rut in the rocks. This time, instead of getting out, we drove down the hillside onto the dry marsh flats. From the Land Rover we could see several herds of bush pigs grazing at the far end of the marsh, about three hundred yards away. As we walked along, we found entire acres turned up by the rooting pigs, as though a fleet of tractor plows had just been through. "They dig for worms and insects," said Van Der Plas. Vultures circled overhead in the blazing sun as we went from one dried-out water hole to another, searching for sign of the pigs. Again, the cassava had been nibbled, but probably by the monkeys.

When we approached one large water hole near the edge of the marsh, a pack of baboons jumped out and scurried away. They seemed more like small gorrillas than the baboons I had seen in zoos. I asked Van Der Plas if they were dangerous. "Yes. You see, we have invaded their private water hole. They occasionally attrack children, but rarely adults. If you corner them, however, they will, and I wouldn't give you a one per cent chance." The displaced baboons had now taken up position in a clump of trees on the nearby hillside, from which they raised a great hue and cry. They have a fearsome bark which defies the English alphabet, but which sounds something like "nyung." When I walked over to the edge of the hill and started up toward the trees, they all climbed or dropped down and went galloping up to the crest at an astonishing speed. Mothers carried their babies under their arms. Some of the bigger males stood well over six feet on their hind legs, and flashed impressive teeth when they barked. I returned to the marsh.

Back at the Kwinella rest house, we found the two girls — gloveless — still cutting and coring chunks of cassava root. A Gambian Agricultural Officer named Darbo drove up with news of the other two baiting sites. The cassava at one of them had not been touched. At the other, it had been nibbled, and Darbo had found pig dung nearby. Darbo concluded that the pigs were uninterested in the cassava chunks because they were too dry. He recommended boiling them, or at least soaking them in water overnight.

During a lunch of chicken and rice, Van Der Plas launched into one of his shotgun monologues. Highlights were the siege of Gallipoli, United States involvement in Laos, tame baboons in Northern Greece, land tenure under the Ottoman Empire, Haitian poetry, riots in Java, skiing in Cortina and skating in Rockefeller Center. Behind the bungalow, little boys threw sticks and stones up into the mango trees and tried to avoid the falling sticks, stones and mangoes. Out front, other children happily threw cassava chunks at each other. Cows walked among them, eating the stray pieces. Though dry, the heat in the bungalow was oppressive. The temperature must have been close to 100 degrees. I asked Van Der Plas whether he felt it was wise for him, at the age of seventy-four to go tramping about the bush at midday, without a hat. He snorted. "I have spent the greater part of these seventy-four years of mine in the tropics. The sun is my greatest friend. I'll be seventy-five this Saturday, but years are just numbers."

Two messages spoiled the Dutchman's good humor. One came from Darbo, who reported that he would be unable to repair the Community Development headquarters at Massembi, because C.D. was under the Ministry of Local Government, not the Ministry of Agriculture. Therefore the repairs would have to be made by the Public Works Department. Another note from

Commissioner Dudley warned Van Der Plas not to order any supplies without his approval. The old man was furious, ranting for twenty minutes about stupid government officials trying to run his affairs. From his views, I could easily understand why many officials in Bathurst found him as difficult as he found them insensitive and incompetent. He bounded to the table and wrote a sarcastic reply to Commissioner Dudley. Then he spoke of another British official in Bathurst, whom he considered the sharpest thorn in his side. "He is insane. He distinguishes all men into two categories — the criminals he has found out and humiliated, and the criminals he has not yet found out."

When I asked about the failure of previous development schemes in Gambia, Van Der Plas scoffed and said the failures were all due to poor administration. "I've been an administrator all my life, and I know the dangers of poor administration. There's a holy trinity for any development project — research, experimentation and demonstration. If you do these three things, the people will jump to action. The people are extremely keen to try something new, despite what you hear to the contrary. You must only show them how and why it is done.

"In Bathurst, they say you must egg them on, but this is not true. Never have I seen harder work done anywhere in the world than in the race against time in the Gambian farming season. They also say the morals of the village people are low. On the contrary, there are almost no illegitimate children born here. But the Bathurst Woloffs have them every day. Many of the politicians there are corrupt, but these people — at least the farmers — are scrupulously honest. Many of the people sent up here to the provinces from Bathurst have an abominable attitude. One teacher who came to Kwinella said to me, 'You don't seem to realize how horrible it is for me, a civilized man, to live here among these savages.' He was entirely wrong. It is Bathurst that is uncivilized. These villagers are the civilized people."

Exhausted by this tirade, Van Der Plas slumped in a fragile canvas camp chair and discoursed on the theory of Community Development. The two girls and the other assistants gathered about him on the floor, listening raptly. The old man resembled a bearded mystic, expounding his philosophy to the disciples at his feet. "Community Development is the only way to real progress here. But it can not work if it is part of the forces of law and order. There must be a complete separation of powers. Government is forced on the people. We must not order anyone to do anything. Our work must come from the people themselves. Only then will they acquire a sense of responsibility."

## THE "LADY WRIGHT"

THE GAMBIA RIVER rises in the rain-soaked Futa Jallon mountains of nearby Guinea, which also give birth to the much longer Niger. In its 1100-mile journey to the coast, it rushes down from the Guinea highlands onto the dry savannah of Eastern Senegal. Then, encased by Gambia, it meanders across the coastal lowlands to Bathurst, where it flows into the Atlantic. The Gambia should be bustling with traffic, since it is the only river for hundreds of miles along the coast that is navigable year-round by ocean-going freighters. Freighters are few, however, for the river is cut off from its natural economic hinterland by the Senegambian border.

Traffic on the Gambia, like most activities in the country, is leisurely. During the winter "trade season," motor launches from the Bathurst trading firms carry money up-river to their peanut-buying agents. In the spring, small Dutch and German freighters steam up-river to Kaur and Kuntaur, where they load peanuts shelled at the government decorticating stations. In every season, Serere fishermen from Senegal flit about the river in their fragile, gaily-decorated boats that look something like New England dories. The most common vessels on the river are the "groundnutters"— creaky old wooden hulks that carry peanuts from the up-river trading stations down to Kuntaur and the oil mills at Bathurst. Modeled after the early Portuguese sailing ships, groundnutters are built in Bathurst. Many of the older ones are unseaworthy, and several sink each year. This, plus the torpor of those still afloat, has created a serious bottleneck in Gambia's economy. While the peanut crop has increased steadily over the past few years, the groundnutter fleet has decreased, and peanuts sit for weeks at trading stations awaiting transport down-river. Despite this pressure, the groundnutter crews are in no hurry. The peanuts will wait, because there is no one else to carry them. Besides, their ships are not designed for speed. They drift along peacefully in the tidal currents, raising their grimy patched sails only if a breeze comes up and if the crews feel energetic. They rarely do, for it is easier to anchor during the flow tide and wait for the ebb to carry them down-river.

Groundnutter crews are mostly Manjagos or Jahunkas from Portuguese Guinea, people distinguished from Gambians by an addiction to Christianity and alcohol. When under the influence of the latter, they are noted for weaving back and forth before oncoming vessels, and running aground. Asked why the government allows the Manjagos and Jahunkas to operate the groundnutters if they are such a menace to river traffic, one official explained, "Well, the Gambians don't drink like these chaps, but then they aren't worth a damn on the river either." I asked a Woloff shipwright named Ismaila (Ishmael) Jallow, who has worked fifteen years at the Marine Department, and whose father had been a foreman there, if the Manjagos and Jahunkas also worked in the shipyards. "They no work in shipyards," said Jallow. "Only Woloff work in shipyards. Manjago dey be bush people. Dey no civilized enough to work in shipyards."

The queen of the Gambia River, and the flagship of the Gambian navy, is the government's only passenger steamer, the *Lady*

*Wright.* Named after the wife of a former governor, this 540-ton vessel bears a striking resemblance to the one featured in the movie, *African Queen.* Like most forms of transport in Gambia, the *Lady Wright,* though only fifteen years old, has aged rapidly and shows it. Its peeling white paint fights a losing battle with encroaching rust and grime. Underway, it is alive with creaks and groans from aching timbers and plates. The *Lady Wright* makes a five-day round trip to Basse every ten days, carrying passengers, freight and mail. (A much smaller launch, the *Lady Stanhope,* also made mail runs up-river until it sank in 1966.) Despite Gambia's slowly improving network of roads, the *Lady Wright* is still the main link with the outside world for many of its twenty ports along the river, and its arrival is a ceremonial occasion. Along with its normal cargo, it brings the latest gossip and fashions from Bathurst.

Though the *Lady Wright* was already jammed hours before sailing on the April afternoon I boarded, dozens more would-be passengers pressed on from the wharf, carrying suitcases, furniture, chickens and sacks of vegetables. Myriad smells of the marketplace wafted about the ship as wives began preparing the evening meal along the crowded passageways. A winch loaded the forward hold, swinging cargo breathlessly close to the scrambling passengers. There were cases of soap, ketchup, cube sugar, candles, cigarettes, gunpowder and jam; sacks of sugar, onions and cement; crates of curry dishes "Made in Japan," medical supplies for the dispensary at Farrafenni, drums of fuel oil and bales of empty burlap peanut sacks. Piled on the foredeck were steel-frame beds with burlap-covered straw mattresses, sheets of corrugated tin roofing material, two rice-hulling machines and pipes for the Georgetown water system.

At 4:30, with the temperature near 100 degrees, a Gambian passenger approached the steward with the swiftly melting remains of a stick of butter dripping through his fingers. He pointed to the refrigerator in the dining room and asked if he could "put 'im in dere?" The steward looked scornfully at the man for some time, and then asked "How long you be travelin' with that?" Someone up on the bridge dumped the remains of his supper over the side, but the breeze blew a generous helping of rice and vegetables onto the head of a gentleman leaning over the railing of the lower deck. A Gambian trying to descend from one deck to another with three heavy sacks of fruit, yelled "Pig! Pig!" at the horde trying to ascend the same stairs. The purser yelled at him, "Hey man! You travelin' on dis ship?"

"No."

"Well, den, walk off, please."

In the passageways and out on the wharf, the crowd was milling and heaving and yelling. As the deckhands began to loosen the lines, the ship tugged against its moorings and pulled a few feet away from the wharf. Fat, heavily laden Woloff women and bent old men scrambled across the void with wondrous agility, falling upon those already aboard and others attempting to get off. Children and furniture were tossed from wharf to ship. Chickens squawked, goats bleated, people yelled and the ship's whistle gave a final blast. Dozens of onlookers on the wharf seemed to decide they had forgotten something on board, while others on board appeared to be only visiting. Somehow, everyone made it, and at 6:15 the *Lady Wright* pulled slowly upstream, against a powerful ebb tide.

Before dinner, the first class passengers occupying the *Lady Wright's* seven cabins sat on canvas deck chairs, taking the breeze on the quarterdeck. An elderly man in a white robe, baggy trousers, woolen cap and laceless canvas shoes sat picking his toes and spitting down onto the main deck. He introduced himself as Demba Seydou Cham, a PPP Member of Parliament for Niani

District (not to be confused with young Momodou Cham, the U.P. Member from Tumana whose father, Cherno Cham, was also on board). "I was in England last year at this time," said Mr. Cham. "I was at a conference on parliamentary procedure. I saw the late Sir Winston Churchill. I was at Jersey also. Very nice islands. I visited a strong and nice dam there." Asked how he had gotten into politics, Mr. Cham replied, "I was the first Leprosy Officer in Gambia. I trained all the leprosy inspectors that are working now."

About 8:00, we came to Albreda, our first stop. Out in the river, James Island glistened under a rising full moon. There was no one on the pier to take a line except a group of small boys. A deckhand threw one nevertheless, and the boys looked at it while the *Lady Wright* drifted back in the current. One of the boys picked the rope up and examined it more closely. The deckhand yelled at him to slip it over a piling. The little boy continued to hold the rope in his hand. The current pulled us farther away. Someone turned the ship's searchlight on the boy, the First Mate blew his whistle at him and passengers screamed at him. Whereupon he dropped the line and went back to his friends, who stood gazing raptly at the ship. After another try, we managed to tie up, and within a few minutes, hundreds of people crowded onto the pier, coming and going. Little girls held up fresh eggs for sale at three pence each. Little boys climbed about the main deck selling "paw-paw" (papaya).

After dinner, the *Lady Wright*'s cabin passengers gathered on the quarterdeck again. A group of high school students stood at the starboard rail discussing girls, dating, and love. ("But I say, man, girl friends are just too much trouble.") Near them, another group discussed politics. Mansa Jagne, a Yundum College student, professed himself a "N'Krumahist," and spoke at length about "Africanism" versus "Nationalism," advocating the Pan-

African concept of Ghana's President Kwame N'Krumah (since deposed). Mr. Jagne said that "most of Africa's leaders today — except for N'Krumah — are stooges." Asked what he thought of South Africa's Prime Minister Verwoerd (assassinated in 1966), Jagne shouted, "We will cannibalize him! Things will change there. The longest night has an end."

"Do you have any ideas about developing Gambia?" I asked.

"Gambia can be developed very rapidly, if at all we get the chance. We can invite the Communists to come. We have ilmenite and diamonds. We can get help from our fellow Africans. Africans always help each other. We could go to Nigeria and get ten thousand pounds [$28,000] right away. In three years' time and come and see Gambia — it will be a paradise."

Abdoulaye M'Baki, a young customs officer, supported Mr. Jagne's remarks, and stated that Gambia's lack of progress was mainly due to the British-run Agriculture Department. "They've done nothing here. That experimental station at Yundum spends thousands of pounds every year, and nothing has happened. It should be abolished."

Across the deck, a cost clerk, an accountant and an education officer set together, discussing the plight of "modern youth." All three were senior civil servants, men in their fifties. They bewailed the fate of their country, to be left in the hands of the present younger generation. "Young people today expect to move up too quickly. They don't want to work their way up like we did."

Up on the bridge, Captain Nian had donned a white shirt, and First Mate Jobe was bundled into a fur-lined jacket, to ward off the chill of the night air. As the ship pulled alongside each wharf, the searchlight picked it out of the darkness. Because of the strong down-stream current, the ship would steam past the wharf, drop anchor, and then work its way back alongside by means of the lines, turning against the anchor. Standing in the glow of the searchlight, Captain Nian croaked gravel-voiced commands to his engine room, helmsman and deck hands: "Ahead starboard . . . Slow astern . . . Heave . . . Hold on forward . . . Slack away the chain . . . Heave." Many of the wharves were so rotten and shaky from years of haphazard dockings that the *Lady Wright* sort of merged into them. Even after midnight, large crowds appeared at the wharves in festive dress to greet the *Lady Wright*. Village officials came on board to converse with friends traveling up-river. The ship's postal officer distributed mail to each village by calling out the names. People and goods were handed on and off, the whistle blew, crewmen cast off the lines, visitors leaped onto the wharf, the Captain shouted and the *Lady Wright* moved back into the river.

At 7:00 the next morning, the deck passengers still huddled under blankets beneath large canvas awnings hanging from the winch boom. Unaccustomed to chilling nights on the river, they were subdued. Two griots, on their way home from the Tobaski celebrations in Bathurst, tried to revive everyone's spirits. Squatting on the deck, they played "balafongs"— xylophones made of bamboo shoots tied together with leather thongs. Someone explained that they were playing "Alpha Yaya," the tale of an ancient Guinean king. "They say, 'Kings are different, kings are different. Alpha Yaya is different from other kings.' Later, Alpha Yaya dies, and all his followers scatter across West Africa, singing, 'A big tree has fallen, and all the birds have gone.' " As they played, two Nigerian peddlers went about the crowd selling gaudy, plastic jewelry from wooden trays. Other vendors on board sold smoked "bonga" (a fish), fresh fish, eggs, bread, kola nuts and coconuts.

In the galley, Captain Baboucar Nian sat with a huge bowl in his lap, eating his breakfast — meat, potatoes and vegetable stew.

An enormous coalblack Woloff, Captain Nian is a most impressive man. He weighs close to 300 pounds, and in a land of relatively small men this awesome bulk commands immediate respect. During the days, he generally wears white trousers, rubber shower clogs, and a net undershirt that vainly attempts to encase his bulging torso, exposing a trunk-like bare midriff and shoulders like giant hams. Leather ju-ju bands around his biceps seem in constant danger of breaking each time he bends his arms.

Captain Nian enjoys his work immensely, and takes pride in his ability. In a land where technical competence is rare, he has risen to the top of a demanding craft. He started with the Marine Department in 1933 as a shipwright, after working a short time as a carpenter. By 1948, he was second mate on Governor Sir Hilary Blood's launch, the *Prince of Wales*. He has been a master river pilot since 1953. So much better is Captain Nian than his colleagues that when he retired at fifty-five, the marine department quickly rehired him, after discovering by means of several unfortunate experiments that there was no one qualified to replace him. Though his $2,268 salary does not seem high for the master of Gambia's only passenger vessel, it compares quite favorably with that of other senior government employees. Besides, there are other compensations. Baboucar Nian is probably the most popular man on the river. At every port, his familiar bulk up on the bridge brings shouts of greeting from the assembled villagers. He has a word for nearly everyone at every wharf, and they often have gifts of fruit or kola nuts for him. Women send their children aboard with hot meals for him in covered bowls. At one stop he threw down a soiled uniform to a woman who brought him a freshly cleaned and pressed one, dropped off on the previous trip.

About 11:00, with the sun hot enough to send all the passengers in search of shade, the *Lady Wright* pulled into Bambaly, a central trading station for a mid-river rice-growing region. Though the village itself is several hundred yards from the wharf, a few blasts on the ship's horn brought most of the inhabitants scurrying down to the waterfront. At the end of the procession straggled the village elders, shielding themselves from the sun with multi-colored golf umbrellas. Many of the women carried calabash gourd bowls full of rice, coos or red peppers. One old lady sported a gaily colored dress that announced: WELCOME TO GAMBIA. A buxom Woloff woman, perspiring profusely, tumbled onto the ship and up to the bridge, where she slapped Captain Nian on his stomach and exchanged enthusiastic greetings. The two Nigerian peddlers pushed about the crowd on the wharf hawking balloons, plastic hairpins, noisemakers and other trinkets from their wooden trays. The women and children of Bambaly were enthralled. When everything was unloaded and loaded, the Captain told First Mate Jobe to blow the horn. Jobe pulled the horn's handle, but nothing happened. Captain Nian yelled "Cast off!" Jobe whistled, and we pulled slowly away from Bambaly as the last of the villagers scrambled off the stern.

Far from the ocean breezes that cool the river's mouth and lower stretches, the cabin passengers wilted in canvas deck chairs. From time to time they retired to their stifling cabins, where bathed in sweat, they twisted and turned on bunks only to return once more to the deck chairs. Under the glaring sun, the river villages seemed to merge into a continuity of horn blasts, heaving lines, and blazes of colorful attire gathered at the wharves. By this point, the river had narrowed from several miles at Bathurst to a few hundred yards. "Bolons," or creeks, branched off the main stream, reaching in to other villages. We passed several islands, all named for animals: Dog Island, Deer Island, Elephant Island, Baboon Island and Sea Horse Island. Elephant Island acquired its name in the days when elephants were common in West Africa. They no longer are. Crocodiles and hippopotamuses inhabit the upper regions of the river now, along with an unlikely monster called a "saw fish." Occasionally more than twenty feet long, the saw fish is noted for the jagged, long saw-toothed sword extending from its snout. Fortunately for the fishermen who frequently capsize in the river, the saw fish is a vegetarian, using its awesome proboscis merely to stir up plankton from the weeds on the river bottom.

At 3:00, we reached Kaur, one of the biggest river ports, and the first of the two up-river decorticating stations. Ocean-going freighters up to 3,000 tons come up the river to Kaur and Kuntaur. Here they load thousands of sacks of shelled peanuts for Holland and Italy, where they are pressed into oil. At Kaur, the crew unloaded bales of burlap peanut sacks. While the *Lady Wright* was at the pier, all work stopped at the decorticating mill, as the workers crowded around to hear the latest news from Bathurst. At 4:00, the steward served tea to the cabin passengers. Questioned about the point of hot tea in the middle of a broiling afternoon, he replied, "Yes, yes. You drink 'im when hot, he go make you cold. True, true, I mean it."

After we left Kaur, I climbed up to the bridge and glanced into the radio room. The radio operator was reclining on his desk, trying to get some music on a Japanese transistor radio. A young female passenger sat in the radioman's chair, while a friend attempted to straighten her hair. Out on the bridge, one mate sat in a canvas deck chair, listening to Arab music from Dakar on his transistor, while another picked dead insects off the searchlight. Shortly after 5:00, as though at a signal, straw prayer mats sprouted all over the ship, and everyone faced east for the afternoon prayer. The cabin passengers knelt down on their deck, the deck passengers below knelt in the corridors and on the piled freight. The officers knelt on the bridge above, the stewards on the dining room floor and the cook in the galley. A Christian, presumably, was at the helm.

The next stops were Jisady, on Pappa Bolon, and Carrol's wharf, on the main river. At Kudang, there was no village, just a trading station huddled down at the river's edge, beneath a clump of palm trees. Several old groundnutters were tied up along the bank, loading peanuts. Two local gentlemen stood at the bank, next to the wharf, urinating into the river. Villagers sold heavy woven straw floor mats with colorful patterns for one shilling (15 cents). Others offered wicker chairs made with wooden nails at one and sixpence each. At every stop, bargaining does not really take place until the ship begins to pull away. Then prices come down to what Gambian petty traders call "serious price, not joking price." By the time the ship is several feet from the wharf, people get down to final prices. Amid peals of laughter from the passengers, the traders throw floor mats, chairs, eggs, fish and bread across the widening gap, and the buyers throw change down onto the wharf. A certain amount of produce and money ends up in the river under this system, but it is obviously so enjoyable to all concerned that no sensible person would think of changing it.

As the *Lady Wright* pulled away from Kudang, the moon rose and the steward rang the dinner bell. The cabin passengers went in to a dinner of groundnut soup, roast meat and potatoes and thin pancakes for dessert. At three shillings sixpence (50 cents) this seemed to be a bargain, but it apparently did not satisfy the accountant from the Agriculture Department. He told the steward his portion was too small, yelling, "You can not treat Africans this way!"

That evening we pulled into Kuntaur, 176 river miles from Bathurst, and the second major river station for peanuts. A big crowd gathered at the wharf, bathed in the *Lady Wright's* searchlight. Frogs croaked from beneath the wharf. A German freighter, the *Schwennau*, out of Flensburg, was loading peanuts for Taranto, Italy, at another pier. I signaled to a little girl on the wharf who was selling cake from a wicker tray. She threw a piece up to me and I tossed a coin down to her. It fell through the planks of the wharf. I had no more coins. The little girl grinned and told me to keep the cake.

At 4:30 the next morning, the *Lady Wright* reached Georgetown, the second largest town in Gambia, and the administrative center of MacCarthy Island Division. This was the biggest cargo stop of the trip, and Captain Nian's whale-like bulk folded over the railing of the forward hold as he supervised the winch operator. The winch handled the sacks and crates, but much of the cargo had to be unloaded by hand. This was performed by prisoners from the Georgetown jail, who formed a human chain and passed the cargo up to the shore. The transistor radio on the bridge featured Tammy Grimes, singing "Hold On, Hold On." The Voice of America news broadcast announced that Prime Minister Wilson and President Johnson had just held "a fruitful and cordial talk."

As the sun rose that morning, we rounded the point known to generations of Gambia rivermen as "Arse Hill." Bartholomew Stibbs, in his *Journal of a Voyage up the Gambia*, in 1723, wrote: "This Hill takes its name from the obscene Superstition of the Natives, who never pass it without showing their bare Breeches to it, with dancing, singing and clapping of Hands, believing that if they should omit it, they should die before they return. Accordingly ours did the same, which made us laugh heartily." The practice did not evoke laughter a century later, in 1845, when the Reverend Thomas Eyre Poole observed it: "The ceremonial, to describe it as inoffensively as language can do, was that every passenger should . . . present the more honourable part of his body over the ship's side." As the *Lady Wright* steamed by Arse Hill, none of its passengers saw fit to perform the age-old ritual.

After Georgetown, the river narrowed considerably, the foliage along the banks grew more luxurious, and the banks began to climb steeply up from the river. As the river bottom became trickier, we frequently passed close to shore, where we could see and hear monkeys and baboons jumping about in the trees and barking at us. They reportedly throw sticks at some passing ships. On the North Bank, about thirty miles above George-town, there is a flat-topped hill known as "Monkey Court." Here, a large herd of dog-faced baboons reportedly gathers in solemn assembly every Friday evening, to discuss various matters of import.

At Bansang, a sizable river town with the only up-river hospi-tal, there was the usual rush to get on and off the *Lady Wright*. For a people noted for their extreme tranquillity even in the face of apparent necessity, the passengers showed an amazing, if un-necessary, alacrity in boarding and disembarking. From the time the ship was within four feet of each wharf, people began to tumble on and off, teetering over the diminishing gap with seem-ing unconcern. People from shore, in search of mail or cargo, rushed on board and met the departing passengers like a defen-sive line. Despite the cries of Captain Nian and his crew, people climbed about the piled goods on the foredeck in search of their belongings, narrowly missing the yawing winch. By the time the ship was close enough to put the ladder over the side, there was no longer any demand for it. Only after it was up, and the ship was pulling away from the wharf, did visitors begin to think about getting off.

As we docked at Bansang, one old man leaped successfully to the wharf, but spilled a paper bag full of hot peppers. They fell on the deck, in the river and on the wharf. He picked up what he could from the wharf, stuffed them in the ripped paper bag, and sauntered happily off. The winch deposited several crates of Kent cigarettes for a Lebanese trader. A petty trader from the *Lady Wright* strolled about hawking garish independence cloth. Another sold coarse-grained salt from a wicker basket, measuring it out in a tin cup and wrapping it in scraps of paper.

At Karantaba, the next stop, a weathered gentleman named Fily Fofana stood in the village square, grasping an ancient rifle in one hand and two balloons just purchased from the Nigerian peddler in the other. Fily Fofana is a 'hunter." This does not merely mean that he hunts. Hunters are a distinct social caste in Gambia, and there are very few of them. Their rifles are called "Dane guns," after the first weapons brought by the Duke of Courland's men centuries ago. Gambian hunters make their own Dane guns out of odd lengths of rusty pipe and assorted pieces of wood, tied together with bits of wire and string. As a result of such construction, the Dane guns explode from the breech as frequently as they do from the muzzle, which is one reason why there are so few hunters in Gambia.

Like many hunters of the Upper River Region, Fily Fofana is a Sussu, one of the Madinka sub-tribes. Besides his Dane gun, he carried the various implements of his trade — a rope, cartridge pouch, machete and knife. Also hanging about his person were more exotic paraphernalia — ju-jus designed especially for hunters. These included a string of seashells, a small animal's horn, leather squares and a fly whisk. Although most hunters have similar ju-jus, the amulets do not seem to keep the Dane guns from taking nearly as high a toll of hunters as they do of beasts of prey.

\*

Later that afternoon, we reached Basse, 244 river miles from Bathurst, and the end of the line for the *Lady Wright*. Smaller launches can continue up-river another forty-five miles or so to Fatoto. During the high waters of the rainy season, the *Lady Wright* can also make this trip, if there is sufficient cargo. There rarely is. A fellow known as "Amadou," described by crewmen as "the village idiot of Basse," met the ship at the wharf. A good-natured, scraggly haired old man, he reportedly "went round the bend" while serving with the Gambia Regiment in Burma, during World War II. Now he does nothing but meet the *Lady Wright* every ten days with pieces of paper purporting to be bills of lading for his cargo. The crew humors him, examining the slips of paper carefully, and explaining that his cargo will probably arrive the next trip. This time, Amadou's bill of lading was a torn-out magazine ad for cod liver oil. After discussing it for some time with the crew, he sat down on a few cartons of Guinness Stout, claiming they were his.

While the ship unloaded the last of its cargo, I hitched a ride on a Public Works Department truck out to the Commissioner's compound at Mansajang, where I had stayed with Gordon Edwards two months before. He was on leave now, and his house was closed up, awaiting a new Gambian commissioner. The mango trees in the garden were beginning to fruit, and a duck squatted on the welcome mat. Next door, I found the Development Officer, an Englishman named John Coombe, who was serving as Acting Commissioner. Before coming to Gambia in 1958, Mr. Coombe had managed a large tea plantation in British East Africa. On this sweltering Good Friday, a national holiday, he and his wife were taking an afternoon siesta. Despite shades drawn against the sun, his bungalow was stifling. The electric refrigerator (a gas model had been "on the way" for some weeks) only worked when the compound generator did — from 7 A.M. to 1 P.M., and from 6 till 11:00 P.M. This daily defrosting meant that no meats or other perishables could be kept longer than one day. The generator produced so little current that the Coombes played their long-playing records at forty-five rpm.

Up-river temperatures at this time of year, often more than 130 degrees in the sun, make life challenging for officials accustomed to standard European creature comforts. The water pipes in the Coombes' bungalow ran from a small stand-pipe across the top of the corrugated tin roof, which baked all day in the sun. As a result, the faucets became untouchable late in the day, and there was rarely a difference between the "hot" and the "cold." A tepid shower at best could be taken early in the morning, before the sun struck the roof. At Mansa Konko, the Development Officer burned himself once with water from the garden hose that had been lying in the sun. The Gambian Assistant Commissioner there, Hardi Fye, puts ice cubes into his bath to cool the water enough to sit in it.

That evening, I joined the Coombes for Good Friday evening mass at the Catholic mission. Four bare bulbs lit up the small chapel, disclosing pictures of the saints along the walls. Father Fleming, the young Irish priest, stood at the altar between two Gambian altar boys. Of the fifty people in the audience, all but ten were small children. Flies buzzed angrily at the chapel door as Father Fleming read from Exodus the passage about Abraham's sacrifice of the lamb. He explained that this was why Moslems hold Tobaski at this time, and sacrifice a lamb. Father Fleming had only recently arrived from Ireland, and his brogue was still heavy. Reading a passage about the Crucifixion, he spoke of "the mordorers of Jesus." Afterwards, he paraphrased the passage in simple English for those in the audience not yet proficient enough to follow the Biblical reading: "Pilate was a very important man. He had a big job. But he knew that if he ordered Jesus to be crucified, he would be sacked."

After the service, we stood outside the chapel for a moment, swatting flies and watching the smoke from fields where farmers were burning off dead brush. From the nearby village of Mansajang came the sounds of drumming, donkeys braying, cows lowing and roosters crowing. The spell was broken by a messenger who came running up to tell Mr. Coombe that "somebody shoot somebody near de border." Coombe left to investigate.

When the crew stumbled down to the wharf about midnight, they were in high spirits after a bit of palm wine and a movie at the Basse open-air theater. This establishment, known as "Sam's Cinema," is owned by a Lebanese, Sami Zoghib, and seats there range from one to three shillings (15-45 cents). I asked one of the crewmen what film they had seen. He did not recall the name, but said, "He be about one man against hundred men. Plenty fighting."

"What language was it in?"

"He be American film, but he get French talk. No matter, we just watch de action."

During a stroll about Basse Wharf Town the next morning, I met Aniz Salleh, a Lebanese merchant who serves as buying agent in Basse for S. Madi Ltd. Salleh is an ageless, heavy-set, swarthy man who has lived in Gambia since he was a boy. Like many other Lebanese traders, he speaks fluent Woloff, Mandinka, Fula and Serahuli, acquired in the days when he used to travel about the bush himself, buying peanuts. Now he has agents he calls "coaxers" who perform this chore for him. Out behind Salleh's cavernous dry season shop was his "secco," a fenced-in compound where his trucks dumped their loads of peanuts. Now, at the end of the buying season, the mound of peanuts towered above the shop. "When I have sold all these nuts," Salleh explained, "I pull the crinting fence down and invite women from my best (most productive) village to come and pick up all the nuts from the ground. Sometimes they go down ten inches deep. When I have finished shipping the groundnuts from this secco, I go and draw my commission from Madi in Bathurst. Then I buy rice and bring it back here. I sell some, and give some out on credit. The farmers pay me back when they harvest their nuts. Some never pay me back. They die, or leave the country."

The reason that Salleh and the other up-river Lebanese traders prosper, despite such unpromising conditions, is that they too buy on credit from the big firms in Bathurst, for whom they work as agents. However, while they buy and pay interest at wholesale rates, they give out rice and money and charge interest at retail rates. As long as everyone in this chain makes good at the end of the season, both the traders and the firms in Bathurst do well. Trouble comes when the farmers have a bad season and default on their payments to the traders. If the trader has over-extended himself, and can not cover his losses, he goes bankrupt. This happened frequently in the past, but the excellent crops of the last few years have brought good fortune to the farmers and the traders. Occasionally, if a bankrupt trader has served his Bathurst firm well in the past, the firm will bail him out by extending more credit — at interest, of course. A former British Governor, who had vainly attempted to break the credit cycle, told Gambians in his farewell speech, "You were born in debt, you've always been in debt and you'll die in debt."

Another source of profit for many of the Lebanese traders is what the government refers to as "the re-export trade." At the beginning of each trade season, Salleh buys — on credit — about $140,000 worth of cotton cloth. Although Basse is certainly a large town by Gambian standards, it is hardly populous enough to account for such a huge amount of cloth. About 95 per cent of it finds its way across the border to Senegal, where it is considerably cheaper than cloth imported via Dakar's high tariffs. Salleh shrugs at talk of smuggling. "I am a trader. My job is to sell cloth. It is not my concern if most of my customers are petty traders from Senegal. It is not my concern where they sell the cloth."

Aniz Salleh's successful longevity as a trader is due to more than merely business acumen. He also dabbles in politics. Despite perennially fluid political conditions in the Basse area, where power shifts back and forth between the UP and the PPP, Salleh generally manages to emerge from each election standing solidly on his feet. In 1962, the United Party held five of the six parliamentary seats from the Basse area. At that time Salleh was a pillar of the local branch of the UP. Recently, power shifted to the PPP, and with it shifted the ever-nimble Salleh. It is this political agility that has enabled the Lebanese to conduct their affairs without interruption for generations along the West African coast, regardless of independence, revolutions and other disturbances. Asked what form his political support takes, Salleh replied, "During the campaigns, I go around with my lorry, bringing villagers to the PPP rallies. I usually give a bull to the crowd for chop. But they don't understand politics here. Today, one man comes with big propaganda, and everyone is for him. Next day, another man, and they are all for him. They don't have any policies. It's almost a game here in the Upper River Division."

As evidence of how well he played the game, Salleh brought me into his shop and introduced me to his friend, Michael Baldeh, M.P. Mr. Baldeh was elected Member for Basse in 1963, as a candidate of the UP, but switched over to the PPP shortly after its dominance in the House became apparent. Since he was standing behind the counter of the shop, I asked Mr. Baldeh if he worked for Mr. Salleh. "No, politics is my career. I don't work."

That afternoon, the *Lady Wright* began loading cargo for Bathurst. As the ship was about to leave, a passenger climbed up to the bridge and demanded that the purser do something about a woman who was screaming at him from the lower deck. According to his story, he had married the woman in Basse a year ago, and brought her down to live with him in Bathurst, where he was a laborer with the Public Works Department. When he returned to Basse this time, he had brought her back to her father's compound, a customary form of divorce in Gambia. But the wife was having none of it, and insisted on coming back to Bathurst with him. The crowd that had gathered on the wharf found this situation highly amusing. The husband kept pushing the woman away, gesturing to the laughing crowd that he and she were through — finished. She screamed hysterically, threw herself on the deck, and broke into a long animal-like moan. Her relatives came to drag her away, but she fought them off, kicking and screaming. After twenty minutes, she finally decided to leave, when the man agreed to give her a blanket and several other items of their communal belongings.

One hour after its scheduled departure time, the *Lady Wright* gave a few blasts on its horn and pulled away from the Basse wharf. Up on the bridge, Captain Nian put on an impressive display of nautical skill as he brought the ship around to head down-stream. Standing in front of the pilot house, and looking ahead, he reached through one window behind him and rang the changes for both engines while turning the wheel through another window with his other hand. When he had brought the ship around, he turned the wheel over to a mate, chomped on his chewing stick, folded himself over the bridge rail and gazed down at the river.

The first stop on the return trip was Kowsemar, a Serahuli village on the South Bank. A group of Serahuli women, distinguished by their large, hand-wrought gold earrings and braided hair, sold red earthenware water jugs just up from the wharf. At five shillings (75 cents) each, the crew felt they were a bargain, and rushed off the ship to buy them. One crewman explained that they could easily resell these jugs in Bathurst, where they are standard items in every household, for ten to fourteen shillings each. The Serahuli women also offered live chickens at forty cents each, and one-penny patties of a spicy peanut butter. Word about the Nigerian peddlers must have spread during our trip up-river, for the Serahuli women besieged them, spending the money they had just made for their jugs on gaudy sequined plastic jewelry, balloons and hair straighteners.

At Diabugu, the next Serahuli village, everyone was carried away by the pottery fever. Passengers and crew converged on the women sitting beside their clay jugs. Even the Nigerian peddlers dropped their nearly empty wooden trays and reinvested their profits in urns. While the crew was immersed in negotiation with the Serahuli women, the loading of cargo ceased. When they returned to the ship, staggering under several heavy urns each, Captain Nian gave them a tongue-lashing from the bridge. For the rest of the trip, the water jugs took up every available spare corner of the ship. Chief Engineer Percy Ebenezer Bankolay Coker had jugs piled up to the ceiling of his tiny cabin. His assistants stacked theirs along the catwalks of the engine room.

Early Sunday morning, we docked again at Kuntaur, to take on 560 sacks of unshelled peanuts. These were high-grade seed nuts being sold to Sierra Leone. Down the quay, the *Schwennau* was still loading sacks of shelled nuts for Italy. Each of its 32,-000 sacks was carried on board by local laborers. They earned eight pence (10 cents) for carrying each 160-pound sack from the storeyard to the wharf and up a long gangway to the *Schwennau*'s hold. A strong man can earn up to $5.60 per day at this work, but the season is short and the ships are few.

While the *Lady Wright* loaded its peanuts, I took a stroll with Baboucar Sanneh, a Yundum College student home on vacation. He took me to meet his uncle, Doudou N'Dow, Chief of Niani District. Chief N'Dow sat on the steps of a Lebanese trader's shop, along with several other village elders. "He fought for the British as a corporal in Burma," said young Baboucar, "and now look at him. They've done nothing for him. They only gave him a medal." Uncle Doudou, who spoke little English despite his years of military service, just sat there smiling, and said nothing. Baboucar Sanneh led me on a tour of Kuntaur, pointing out a local weaver at work on an ancient loom, a vegetable "plantation" down by the river, and an old man making bamboo fences. We stopped off at a Gambian trader's shop for a soft drink, and the owner showed me a letter from his son who was studying in England. I asked Baboucar if he planned to return to Kuntaur to teach after graduating from Yundum College. "No, I would be worried by my family. You know, in Gambia, the moment they know you are working, they think you make plenty of money. I would rather work somewhere else."

At Kudang, one of the passengers who came on board was Momodou Cham, the opposition M.P. from Tumana, whose father, Cherno Cham, had made the trip up-river. Cham is a tall, slender young man, with a small pinched face, large brown eyes and a small goatee. He wore narrow black trousers, pointed black patent leather boots, a sport jacket and an olive green fez. In a loquacious mood, he relaxed in a deck chair and chatted with the other passengers about his start in politics. After high school, Cham worked for two years as a minor civilian clerk at Police Headquarters, then left when the Department decided to make all civilian employees enter the uniformed service. While some officials recall other reasons for his departure, Cham claims it was a point of honor. "I refused to put on the uniform. Our police force was a place where young people with some education wanted to work. But I worked under semi-literate bosses who were jealous of me. As a civilian, I was not subject to them, so I refused to join the uniform force. About that time, my people in Tumana wrote to me, inviting me to resign and stand for election to Parliament. I did, and I won."

Besides their annual salary of $1,340, up-river Members receive small travel and hotel allowances to cover the expense of attending Parliament sessions in Bathurst. Since all districts are only a day's trip by Land Rover from Bathurst, and since M.P.'s can usually wrangle free passage on the *Lady Wright*, the government considers their travel allowance ample. Momodou Cham does not. "We M.P.'s incur more expenses than Ministers, because we are not stationed in Bathurst. [This was odd, since the cost of living in the provinces is negligible compared to that in Bathurst.] We live with our people, and we have a lot of expenses doing things for our constituents in Bathurst." Asked if he supplemented his salary with any other work, he replied, "Some M.P.'s have extra jobs, others do not choose to have them. I do not choose to. You see, the only place you could look for employment would be with the government or else the commercial firms. I would not want to work for them, since I would want to criticize them."

"Are you satisfied with the way Parliament runs now?"

"I think the House sittings should be more often, for we have much to say. But that would take an act of Parliament, and it won't happen because most of the members do not vote sincerely, according to their heart."

"You say that most politicians in Gambia are not sincere?"

"Some of them may be sincere, but politics in Gambia is not properly organized. They call people 'party chairmen' in a district, and all they do is a little paper work. In Basse, Georgetown and Bathurst, where you have a sufficiently sophisticated area, party members pay dues. The rest of the people pay nothing. The PPP sells party cards each year to raise money, but some of their boys are corrupt. They sell some people many cards. They tell them they will be better qualified members if they have several cards."

Asked for his views on the prospects of a merger with Senegal, Cham was uncertain. "In fact this Senegambia business, I can't make out a thing." He did offer one suggestion, as a means of pressuring Senegal in any negotiating — closing down the Trans-Gambian Highway. If implemented, this move would undoubtedly be effective. It would cut Senegal off from its agriculturally rich Casamance region, and probably bring the Force Armée Senegalaise down upon Bathurst.

When a group of students returning to Bathurst from their spring vacation gathered around Mr. Cham, he asked them what they planned to study. Most said they wanted to study politics, in order to work in the administration. This roused Cham to anger. He told the boys they were foolish. "We have so many administrators who have nothing to administrate." Several students complained that they were unable to get a proper education because the government did not offer enough scholarships for study in England. This also displeased Mr. Cham. "By education, you mean purifying yourselves in Britain. All our students go off and get their heads stuffed with Western ideologies. This country is already too full of Western ideologies. Even our African universities are Western. Their systems have been introduced by Westerners. We have been condemning these foreign advisers, yet you are all trying to copy them by studying under their people. Do you think that people who go to U.K. and study English law and what not should come back here and tell our fathers in Basse how they should live?

"This is all part of English imperialism, Britain's policy of retarding the development of Gambia. There must be many changes of the system left over from colonial days. But with our present leader they won't be changed quickly. We [the United Party] don't like his ideas, but we have no hatred for him. The question of revolution does not depend on hatred. If we have a revolution here, it will be peaceful."

Momodou Cham's revolutionary ardor was dampened when the purser came over and berated him for having signed his father on for the up-river trip as "Cham, M.P." so that the old man traveled free. Though caught red-handed, Cham remained unruffled. He explained to the students that all M.P.'s have the right to authorize free transportation on the *Lady Wright* for legislative purposes. "It is taken for granted that we will not abuse the privilege."

The rest of the trip down to Bathurst was uneventful. Passengers wilting in the heat were not even able to summon sufficient energy for conversation. They slumped in deck chairs, staring out at the river. On the return trip, the *Lady Wright* had gradually taken on the air of a refugee ship. On the foredeck, piled in considerable abandon, were the personal possessions of many families moving to the capital — bicycles, chairs, tables, suitcases, calabash gourds, clay urns and mattresses. On Sunday night, the last of the trip, Atlantic breezes brought a chill to the river, and on the exposed foredeck, the temperature fell more than 60 degrees. Wrapped in blankets, shawls and prayer mats, the deck passengers huddled together, trying to find a level spot to sleep among the cargo.

At noon, Monday, the *Lady Wright* steamed up to the wharf at Bathurst. As soon as a few lines were secured the jumping, pushing and scrambling began again.

# 10

## CITY COUNCIL

THE BATHURST CITY COUNCIL does not have much to do with the affairs of the city of Bathurst. Because it is Gambia's only city, only port, and only commercial center, most of the capital's affairs are interrelated with those of the entire country, and for this reason, the central government has traditionally directed the commerce, labor, public works, police, courts, electricity, health, education and welfare of the city's 30,000 inhabitants. This does not leave much for the City Council. It handles the city's water supply, street cleaning, garbage collection and public rest rooms. The BCC supports these operations with license fees and rents from the city's residential property, and the stalls at Albert Market. The British Colonial rulers originally formed the Bathurst City Council not to run the city, but to allow its Gambian residents a representative body through which they could make their views known to the central government. Though the Council would like to increase its powers now that the country is independent, the new Gambian leaders are content to leave things as they are. This conflict came to light recently when the Council voted to take over the operations of the Bathurst-Barra Ferry and the Bathurst Electricity Department. Both are notable among government departments for showing an annual profit. Asked what the chances of such a takeover were, an official at the Ministry of Local Government (which must approve most BCC decisions) said, "Not bloody likely."

While the central government does not relish giving up control over municipal affairs, the main reason for its policy seems to be a lack of confidence in the Council. "They've achieved absolutely nothing," said one Administration official. "They don't even collect enough rents to pay their own staff. They only run the market, the water and the sanitary service, and they make a complete balls of that." To illustrate the need for limiting the BCC's powers, critics cite the affair of the City Hall loan. Some time ago, the Council heard of an organization in Sierra Leone called the "Economic Intelligence Unit" that reportedly loans money to African governments. Wishing to build a new City Hall, the City Council applied for a $112,000 loan. E.I.U.'s immediately favorable response was astounding, since any reputable investment institution would hesitate before making a loan to a city that already has great difficulty meeting its meager expenses. E.I.U. not only agreed to a loan, but said that $112,000 was too small a request for it to consider, and asked whether the BCC would be interested instead in a $11,200,000 loan, more than fifty times the BCC's annual budget. The Council solemnly debated the offer, and voted to accept it. The Ministry of Local Government vetoed the plan, and no one has since heard from the Economic Intelligence Unit.

The City Council has twenty members, five of whom are appointed by the Ministry of Local Government. The rest are elected, and show the dominance of the Akus and the United Party in Bathurst. The UP has seven representatives on the Council, the PPP four, and four others belong to the Gambia Congress Party, a small movement whose leader, Ibrimah Momodou Garba-Jahumpa, is one of the Councillors. The Mayor and

Chairman of the Council, Baboucar Ousman Semega-Janneh, is one of Gambia's leading citizens. Tall, poised and distinguished, he was trained in England and recently retired as head of the government's Survey Department. A noted athlete in his youth, Mayor Janneh, at fifty-five, is still an excellent tennis player. Semega-Janneh is a name to conjure with in Gambia, for the Mayor's brother Hoswoon is a Member of Parliament and a former Minister of Agriculture, while another brother, Kesemar, is one of the City Councillors.

Just before the April meeting of the Council began, Mayor Janneh attended a small ceremony in the Town Clerk's office, where he greeted D. B. Bartlett, an English education official on a brief visit to Gambia, sponsored by the British government. On behalf of his own city, Southend-on-Sea, Mr. Bartlett presented Mayor Janneh with "a few tokens of good will" from E. E. Morris, Mayor of Southend-on-Sea, including a booklet by Southend-on-Sea's Chamber of Commerce, a wooden plaque showing its coat of arms, and a leather-bound history of the city autographed by Mayor Morris. Mayor Janneh thanked Mr. Bartlett, told him to thank Mayor Morris, and showed him Bathurst's coat of arms. This design contains a rampant ram and elephant, two crescents, a cross, a ship, cannons, peanut plants, a dolphin and a helmet with bent plumes. The ash tray on the Town Clerk's desk announced that "Guinness is good for you."

After exchanging a few pleasantries, Mayor Janneh, Mr. Bartlett and Town Clerk Jagne walked across the dirt yard to the Bathurst City Council Chamber. Americans would call this building a Quonset hut; the British call it a Nissen hut. Gambians, particularly the City Councillors, call it an eyesore. The tin sheets of its roof do not fit perfectly, moistening meetings during the rainy season. Behind the Chamber lie the remains of a severely cannibalized motor vehicle. Inside the long Chamber hall, some of the rain-stained panel boards are peeling away from the curved walls. Hanging along the walls are a portrait of William Pitt, rotogravure photographs of the Queen and her family, and an autographed photograph of the Duchess of Kent. The twenty City Councillors sit around a long table covered in maroon felt, at the head of which, on a raised platform, sits the Mayor's throne-like chair.

At 3:45, Mayor Janneh opened the meeting with a brief prayer. He presented Mr. Bartlett, and passed around the gifts from Southend-on-Sea. Mr. Bartlett told the Councillors that "city council work seems to be very much the same here in Gambia as it is in England," and wished them the best of luck. Deputy Mayor I. A. S. Burang-John thanked Mr. Bartlett on behalf of the Council, and said he was happy to learn that the work of the BCC was identical with that of city councils in England. Mayor Janneh announced that Mr. Bartlett had kindly consented to answer questions, but urged Councillors to remember that he is an education officer, not a city councillor. The first question was "Does Mr. Bartlett, as an education officer, sit as a city councillor?" The Councillors, who serve without pay, were particularly interested to know whether city councillors in Southend-on-Sea receive a salary. Mr. Bartlett said they do not, but the Mayor receives $3,360. At this news, an excited murmur rippled around the table, since a salary for the mayor has long been one of the BCC's battle cries in its endless skirmish with the Ministry of Local Government. They ignored the fact that Southend-on-Sea's population is six times that of Bathurst. (That evening at the hotel, Mr. Bartlett said, "In a place this size at home, the mayor wouldn't get a sausage.")

When Mr. Bartlett had withdrawn, to warm applause, Gambia's Postmaster, A. J. Senghore, announced a forthcoming commemorative issue of stamps in honor of the 150th anniversary of the founding of Bathurst. He explained that the major purpose of this special issue was to attract philatelists. (Sales of Gambia's stamps to dealers abroad constitute one of the country's most lucrative sources of revenue.) Mr. Senghore asked the Councillors if they had any suggestions for the design of the Bathurst commemorative stamps. They did not.

At 4:30, with the business meeting not yet under way, attendants served the Councillors tea and cookies on blue china. The tin-roofed Quonset hut, having baked all day in the sun, was now stifling. The city's ancient green water truck/street sprinkler came wheezing into the yard and sputtered to a stop beside the Council Chamber. The Mayor read a letter from General H. K. Lee, South Korean Ambassador to London, who had passed through Gambia recently and, according to his letter, had enjoyed his stay.

Reviewing the minutes of the previous meetings, the Councillors discovered to their dismay that on March 17 they had voted not to raise the salaries of the property assessors, and that two weeks later they had voted to raise them 33 per cent. When Mayor Janneh pointed out that "we can not have both these decisions on the record," the Council decided to raise the salaries and strike out the earlier vote. Reading the previous minutes also brought up the unsettled issue of wages for the city's street cleaners, called "Sanitary Night Service Laborers." These men had been getting ten shillings ($1.40) per night for three hours of work. In a display of fiscal ingenuity, the Council decided to lay off half the workers, double the hours of the rest, and pay them the same nightly rate. Another unsettled case from the last meeting was that of Alhadji Basiru Onifade, a Nigerian who had constructed a stall on Allen Street without a permit. The Councillors debated various forms of punishment for this malefactor until Councillor Green-Harris informed them that since their last meeting Alhadji Onifade had returned to Nigeria.

An appeal from the senior butchers at Albert Market opened

the meeting's new business. Threatened with losing their stalls for non-payment of rent, they were asking the Council for a delay in payment because of what they termed "an administrative misunderstanding." These senior butchers do not work at the market themselves, but control the stalls and sublet them to the younger butchers. They sat now in a row at the back of the hall, five old gentlemen in Moslem robes, with pith helmets or fezzes in their laps. Two of them leaned on umbrellas, one on a cane. Their cadaverous faces watched the speakers intently, although it is doubtful if any of them understood enough English to follow the proceedings. Councillor Faal-Taal, a commercial clerk, supported their plea. "Your Worship," he said, addressing the Mayor, "I know all members of the Council will be interested in this matter because all of us eat meat every day. These men are Gambians. Let us treat them as our brothers."

Councillor Gomez, a United Party official, disagreed. "Your Lordship, these people are my fathers and my brothers — fellow Gambians. But if we don't uphold our laws they will not respect us. If they don't respect us, how will foreigners respect us? Let them pay their arrears." (The talk of "foreigners" refers to the many Woloffs from Senegal who rent stalls in Albert Market. They are known as Woloffs, however, rather than Senegalese.)

Kesemar Janneh, the Mayor's younger brother, stood up for the petitioners. "We should encourage these people, for they are Gambians. Gambians in Senegal are not treated well at all. Gambians can not get stalls in Dakar. These people are Gambians and we are independent now. Let us not encourage foreigners."

Councillor Oliver, described as "a private gentleman" yelled, "Should we let foreigners have the run of our markets while our Gambians, born and bred, are turned out of their stalls?"

An extended and animated debate developed, in which nearly

every member took simultaneous part. The issue of foreigners in the markets seemed to eclipse the original point of whether the petitioners should be made to pay their arrears. Members began shouting at each other: "I know what I'm saying" . . . "This thing is being done by bribes." Councillor Samba, a clerk at the Marine Department, read a passage from *The Laws of The Gambia*.

"To what book are you reading from?" asked Councillor George, another U.P. official.

Mr. Samba replied with considerable emotion that although he was reading, he did not really need the book, since he "knew all this fifty years ago."

"We don't care what you know!" yelled Mr. George.

Mayor Janneh sat tapping a pack of Players cigarettes with his pencil. After enduring a half hour of this debate, he broke in with some advice to the anti-foreigner faction: "If we were to weed out all foreigners from Albert Market, there would be almost no one left in the market." He recommended that the issue be turned over to the Council's Albert Market Committee. The Council so moved. The five old men in back slipped into their sandals, picked up their pith helmets, fezzes, canes and umbrellas, and padded out, muttering.

The Licensing Committee, which sets fees for such trades as palm wine tappers (five shillings — 70 cents), reported on some recommended increases. After a short debate, Council voted to raise the cost of a "haircutter's license" from ten shillings to one pound. A dispute then arose over the license fee for bands and orchestras, which Councillor Faal-Taal claimed were "monstrously high." He moved to decrease them from five pounds to two pounds, making up the loss in revenue by raising the fee for bankers "because they make more money than orchestras." Since there is only one commercial bank in Gambia, this did not seem a fruitful source of income, but since there are more orchestras than banks, the motion proved popular. An acrimonious debate followed, over the quality of Gambian bands and the price of dance tickets. When one member said that most bands charge £70 ($196) per dance, Councillor Janneh jumped to his feet and yelled, "The question of 70 pounds is out of it! I am sure on my leg!"

Councillor Dennis, also described as "a private gentleman," said, "I am a youth, and my interest is to protect the youths of Gambia. The bands give me pleasure every time they play, but — fellow councillors — let us remember the masses." Mr. Dennis sat down without telling the Councillors why they should remember the masses. After another twenty minutes of heated discussion, the issue was settled when M. M. Sosseh, a bright young Gambian representing the Ministry of Local Government, managed to break in. He informed the Council that debate on new license fees was pointless because they had already been set for this year by the previous year's Council.

The Mayor then read a letter from the Secretary of the Executive Committee of the Independence Drive Mosque Extension Work Fund, appealing for a contribution. Shouts of "No money!" came from several Councillors. Rather than put their devotion to a test, the Mayor decided to ask the Ministry of Local Government if the BCC is allowed to give money to such appeals. The next letter came from Henry Oliver, the British adviser to the Ministry of Local Government. He wrote that with no money in that year's budget for a mayor's salary or allowances, any money the council wished to vote him would have to come from the Council's entertainment fund. "He is playing with the Council!" yelled M. H. N'Jie, an employee of Elder Dempster Lines. "He has no respect for us. The Ministry is challenging our integrity. We feel so, and the masses support us.

I'm fed up with this thing. Let's act!" This brought cheers from his colleagues.

An elderly member joined the attack. "I think it is high time we let the Ministry of Local Government know that the days of colonialism are over. We have just been told by Mr. Bartlett that his mayor gets one thousand two hundred pounds. Can we not have five hundred pounds for our own mayor? We have been given a city charter by royalty. We should be able to act. I am with these young men here. We are just like donkeys and cattle."

Councillor Green-Harris, also a UP official, noted that "this is the fourth time we have sent a letter to the Ministry about the mayor's salary. Our mayor must receive foreign guests and ambassadors. Can we have him receive them in rags? It is high time we acted according to the way things are in U.K. We don't have the right to call ourselves Councillors. We have an overlord over our heads — Henry Oliver. He is an obstacle between the Council and the Minister."

(Similar accusations are frequently leveled at several other senior British advisers. By being British, as well as advisers, they perform the additional function of whipping boys, absorbing criticism that would otherwise fall upon their Gambian Ministers. When they are gone or replaced — which many Gambians would like to see happen soon — the Ministers themselves will have to bear the brunt of the abuse resulting from their decisions.)

Councillor George moved to "march on the Minister and show him we are human beings and have been elected, just as he is." After considering this and other alternatives, the Council voted unanimously to send a six-man delegation to the Minister of Local Government. Competition for a place on the delegation was not very keen, many of the Councillors finding they had

other pressing business. Threatening to march on various Ministries is a standard BCC response to government opposition. Few
of the marches take place.

Mayor Janneh read a letter from the Edward Small Memorial
Committee, seeking approval for a bronze plaque and memorial
they planned to erect at Cameron Street, honoring the former
Bathurst political leader. A crude hand drawing of the proposed
memorial accompanied the letter, but neither the Mayor nor
those sitting near him could make out the details. They voted to
send it back to the Committee, requesting a more accurate drawing. Someone urged that a refuse bin, presently located near the
site of Fort Louvel, an historic landmark, be moved to a more
appropriate location. Councillors seconded the motion, and
were about to vote when the Mayor broke in: "Wait a moment.
We can not just rush into this thing. Where will we move it
to?" No one offered any suggestions. The Mayor appointed a
three-man committee of members from the affected wards to
make a report on a new site for the refuse bin.

Councillor Alasan N'Dure, editor of the Congress Party's
newsletter, *African Unity*, rose to offer the evening's major piece
of legislation. "Your Lordship, with the attainment of independence by The Gambia, I move that Council recommend to
the central government the renaming of all streets in the city to
become purely African names." Nationalistic Gambians had
been talking about such a move since independence, and the
City Council, in its last meeting, had already voted to change
Bathurst to "Banjul," the former Mandinka name for the capital.

In putting forth his motion, Councillor N'Dure banged his fist
on the table and yelled, "The days of colonialism are over! The
street names must be changed now!" "Hear, hear!" shouted his
colleagues. Before they got carried away, Mayor Janneh broke in
and urged that the streets be renamed gradually. "If we do this

thing overnight, people will not be able to find their way home."

The reason for Bathurst's English street names is that when Captain Alexander Grant — who had served with Wellington — laid out the city in 1816, his mind turned, like that of any loyal officer, to the recent British victory at Waterloo. Thus six of the city's major thoroughfares bear the names of Wellington's generals — Picton, Anglesea, Blücher, Hill, Orange and Cotton. Other streets named then and later include Leman, Hagen, Rankin, Ingram, Dobson, Clarkson, Llewelyn, Peel, Stanley, McDonnell, Bedford, Gloucester, Lancaster and Perseverance. Only one street, at Crab Island, carries a Gambian name, and it is one reason British authorities were loathe to allow the practice to flourish. To honor a former Bathurst Moslem leader, Gambians submitted the name "Imam Alhadji Sheik Omar Sowe, M.B.E. Avenue." The government cut this down to a crisp "Imam Omar Sowe Avenue." When a representative of a Dutch sign company had passed through Gambia and paid a call on the Public Works Department, he told guests at the hotel that his firm specialized in street signs, and that he expected to do some business in Gambia after independence. Informed that no one had mentioned changing street names at that time, he said cheerfully, "Oh, that's all right. They will. They always do. I'll be back."

The next item on the Council's agenda was the deployment of its eight drivers. At that time, five of them drove the refuse collection tractors, while the other three were assigned to the sewage truck, the water truck and the municipal funeral van. At ten shillings per trip, the funeral van is one of the Council's most dependable sources of revenue. On ceremonial occasions, it also doubles as a vehicle for the living. One Councillor asked, "Why do we have one man drive the funeral van all day? People do not die all day." Town Clerk Jagne explained, "We tried other systems, but you can never tell when people will die. When they do, they want a funeral right away. You know these Moslems."

The Council then took up the issue of the city's new slaughterhouse, and its modern method of killing cattle with a small pistol which fires a blunt steel bolt into the animal's brain. Since the standard Moslem method is to kill by slitting the throat, an issue had arisen. Town Clerk Jagne reported, "This is a delicate religious matter. We must have actual demonstrations, and show the Imam what will be done." (A British official commenting later said that the whole issue of the slaughterhouse was one of patronage, not religion. "The Imam will agree to the new method, on the condition that they have someone of sufficient holiness in attendance to give a short prayer as each cow is killed. That someone will most likely be a friend of the Imam.")

At 7:30, Mayor Janneh reported on plans for a fender flag to be flown on his car at ceremonial occasions. Quotations and samples were being sought from London. Councillor Faal-Taal moved that the King George Memorial Ground at Half Die be changed to a "garden of rest" for the citizens of Bathurst. Mayor Janneh informed him that "garden of rest" meant a cemetery. Mr. Faal-Taal said he meant a park. The Mayor told him it already was a park. Councillor Faal-Taal, who did not seem particularly committed to the idea anyway, sat down. Deputy Mayor Burang-John, the UP's General Secretary, recommended that every compound in Bathurst be provided with running water and a refuse container. While this proposal met with general approval, its enactment, because of the city's financial state, is unlikely in the near future. Less than one-tenth of the compounds in the city presently have running water. The rest got theirs from the many public taps. Although the City Council maintains a number of large refuse containers about the town, many residents prefer to dump their garbage into the open sewers.

Council then took up several applications for credit from the BCC staff. Town Clerk Jagne wanted $1,540 to purchase a car, and several other members of the staff wanted credit for everything from uniforms to refrigerators. A later check of the BCC's records showed that Mr. Jagne had already drawn $6,328, nearly three times his salary, to buy a house. Mr. B. E. John, assistant Town Clerk, had drawn $3,116, and Council Treasurer R. H. Joof had drawn $4,777. Nearly all these debts were still outstanding. One often hears educated Gambian officials in Bathurst bemoaning the up-river farmers' unfortunate dependence on credit, and discussing means of educating or forcing them into austerity and solvency. These officials themselves, however, despite their emergence from village civilization, somehow manage to carry on the budgetary traditions of their rural countrymen.

Councillor Samba suggested creating a new city post of Security Officer, to insure the safety of rent collections. He felt that "our country is expanding and we can afford these extra expenses." Mr. Samba assumed that if the population and administrative affairs of the country were expanding, its revenues must be also. This does not follow as the night the day, especially for the Bathurst City Council. The Council approved the idea of a Security Officer, but immediately got hung up on the question of his transport. It was apparent to all that the BCC could not afford another car. One member suggested a motor bike, but another wondered what effect this would have if the new officer had a hernia. The question of transport was finally turned over to a committee.

By nine o'clock, the hall was beginning to fill with mosquitos, attracted by the bare overhead bulbs. Several Councillors had left, lured by dinner. The topic now under consideration was whether the city should give some land to the central government for an annex to the Technical School. Opinions flew back and forth until the representative of the government, Mr. Sosseh, told them that the land had only been loaned to the city by the central government, and that if the BCC would not give it back, the government would simply take it. This brought Councillor Oliver springing to his feet: "We must take a stand! We can not let the government push us around."

A letter from Winton Lane criticizing the work of the city's street cleaners roused the nearly slumbering members to yelling and banging on the table. Mr. Lane, the Prime Minister's British adviser, had written that "unless they are constantly kept on their toes, they have a tendency to slack off." By "they," he had meant the street cleaners. But an ambiguous syntax led the Councillors to assume he was talking about them. Mayor Janneh allowed the insults and threats against Lane to run their course, and then tried to calm the Councillors. He pointed out that regardless of Lane's letter, the street cleaning had indeed deteriorated since independence. "Many of the workers felt that now they are independent they need not work as hard." For the irate Councillors, however, the question of cleanliness ran a long second to what they considered Lane's pompous attitude. "Who does he think he is, sitting up there in his luxurious office, telling us how to clean our streets . . . What cheek! . . . What does he think we are, a bunch of barbarians?"

With several of the still-fuming members threatening to march on Lane, the meeting finally broke up about 9:45. When congratulated later for his conduct of the meeting, Mayor Janneh shrugged, and said it had gone better than some.

# 11

## RICH MAN, POOR MAN

THERE IS considerable dispute among the regulars at the Atlantic lounge over who is the richest man in Gambia. Some say the Madi brothers are the richest, and a drive around Bathurst will supply considerable evidence for this opinion. Founded by Sarkis Madi, a shrewd Lebanese merchant who came to Gambia early in this century and traded in peanuts, S. Madi Ltd., is by far the most pervasive economic entity in the country. Along with buying a sizable share of the peanut crop, the Madis own the largest of the two peanut oil mills, the Atlantic Hotel, the Gambia Construction Company, a large wholesale and retail trading firm, the most lucrative auto dealership and garage and a partnership in a recently opened gin bottling plant.

The Madis are unusual only in the degree of their success, for in every city in West Africa, much of the local commerce is in the hands of the Lebanese. Like the Indians and Greeks along the coast of East Africa, they serve as midwives to the African economy. They buy local products and sell them to the large European import-export firms, and import dry goods themselves to sell to the Africans. They handle most of the African retail trade in the cities, and run networks of shops in up-country towns and villages. Often, in the absence of resident government administrators, their little bush village shops constitute the only permanent link with the distant capital. While African leaders bemoan the grip these foreigners have on local commerce, they admit that without them there would be a vacuum. Africans educated enough to operate retail shops generally do not deign to enter commerce, preferring the security and prestige of minor government jobs, no matter how unpromising.

The Lebanese arrived in West Africa during the first two decades of this century, impelled by political turmoil at home to seek their fortunes abroad. Actually, many of them were Syrian, but with Lebanon's present prominence, most now call themselves Lebanese. Today, there are more Lebanese abroad than at home, but their patriotism is undiminished. They send their children back to school in Beirut (as well as London and Paris) and their investments in the otherwise poor homeland have made Beirut a world banking capital. This fact is particularly grating to local banks in Africa, with whom the Lebanese have as little contact as possible, for reasons of financial privacy. Their financial privacy is important because they buy entirely on credit from the large firms and from British exporters. When, as frequently happens, their debts weigh heavily upon them, they often simply "go out of business," leaving their creditors holding worthless claims upon thousands of pounds of merchandise.

Going out of business is unusually common and painless in Gambia because there are no bankruptcy laws. While this discourages wary foreign investment, it provides the Bathurst commercial world with a suspense and excitement unknown in more sophisticated financial circles. Wellington Street rings every few weeks with the auctioneer's ball, signaling the demise of another commercial enterprise. Checks bounce with such regularity that the Bank of West Africa is almost the only place that will cash one.

One prominent reason why Gambia has no bankruptcy law is that the Constitution forbids anyone to sit as a Member of Parliament who has been adjudged bankrupt by a court. In the absence of a bankruptcy law, this provision is of course meaningless. Otherwise, many of the seats in the House would be empty, for M.P.'s seem to find themselves in financial straits with greater frequency than other Gambians. "We've tried three times to pass one," says a high government official, speaking of a bankruptcy act, "but we don't have a chance. The P.M. doesn't want half his House thrown out."

Bathurst's Lebanese traders are happy with the present laws. I observed an illustration of this in April, when one closed his shop leaving claims outstanding for at least $168,000, spread among the city's large firms and a few London textile exporters. The auction of his goods brought only $19,600, which went on a first-come-first-served basis to his creditors. "He's got no troubles," said one observer at the auction. "He's got forty-five thousand quid [$126,000] in his pocket and he's off having a ball in Switzerland. You see they've all folded up here — Hosheimie, Ede, Milky, Salma — some of them several times. They just transfer the ownership to a brother or cousin, take a reasonable amount of money out of the business — you don't take everything; it's not considered cricket — and go off for a brief holiday. Then you come back and start again. Only it's then A. B. Bensouda, instead of E. M. Bensouda. You see, insolvency is not considered commercially embarrassing in Gambia. As far as the businessmen are concerned, it's just another deal. You win some, you lose some. It's a respectable way to make money when you need some for a new business venture. You don't lose any social status upon going bust here. On the contrary, I would say that your status rises among fellow businessmen for having successfully pulled a coup."

Between "folding up" and other disruptions, the Lebanese sit above the daily turmoil in their long, dark, cavernous shops, watching their Gambian clerks, translating into Arabic, Fula or Serahuli, converting from Senegalese francs to Gambian pounds with the help of a pocket converter, and mentally computing bulk rates for petty traders from Senegal and Mauritanian shop-keepers from Bathurst. In the evening, when the shops are closed, and Wellington Street is quiet, they sit bent over their counting desks in the dim light, tallying the day's sales and dreaming of retirement in Lebanon. Up-river, their cousins and brothers close their shops earlier and sit in the back rooms, sip-ping beer and planning Land Rover trips down to the capital for supplies. Each shop up-river is related by blood and commerce to a larger one in Bathurst, just as these are related to large Leba-nese export houses in London. As one French competitor in Bathurst said, in grudging admiration, "The Lebanese don't need large corporations — just large families."

One morning in May, I dropped in at Rachid's Novelty Store, the corner shop in the Madi building next to MacCarthy Square. Antoine Rachid has been trading in Gambia since the 1930's, and has Lebanese relatives and friends up and down the West African coast. His shop is a jumble of packing cases, crates, sacks and bundles. The shelves are filled with straw prayer mats and flashlights from Hong Kong, shirts and shorts from West Germany, and rubber and plastic sandals from Japan. Piles of corrugated tin sheets clutter the floor. The sandals seemed to be the fastest-selling item. "These are new to this country," said Mr. Rachid. "Few years ago, majority they walk around with no shoes. They just start wearing them last two years. Now you can get rubber or plastic sandals from two to five shillings. He and Kamal Milky and Jimmy Hosheimie and my cousin all get to-gether and buy these sandals. None of us alone is big enough to buy at good price."

A Mauritanian in a dirty white robe, black turban and leather thong sandals came in with a huge shotgun and began haggling with Rachid in Arabic. Finally, Rachid separated the stock from the barrel and gave the stock to the Mauritanian, who walked out in a huff. "I gave it to him to fix for a friend. He's a gunsmith. He only repaired the spring and he wants three pounds. You can buy a new spring for ten shillings. I would give him one pound for the job, but he doesn't agree. I'll let him keep the stock until my friend decides what to do." A woman came in with a baby strapped to her back with a shawl, in the Gambian fashion. Rachid gave her a pair of rubber sandals. "She's the mother of my house girl. She just come from far away, so I dash her sandals." Another Mauritanian entered the shop and began piling green Senegalese francs on the counter. He had 22,500, worth $90. Rachid had his shop boy open a crate of sandals with a crowbar, and the Mauritanian stuffed the sandals in a burlap bag.

As each customer entered, he would haggle for a time with Rachid in Woloff, French or Arabic. The haggling was not so much over prices, which are fairly standard around town, but over the exchange rate of pounds to francs. (Most Lebanese do their money changing with George Isaac, a Lebanese trader whose rates are lower than those at the bank, and whose transactions are less public.) Most of Rachid's business that morning was with petty traders from Senegal, who bought cartons full of sandals with bags full of francs. He counted out the francs, haggled over the exchange rate, then stuffed them into the bottom right hand drawer of his desk. The drawer was nearly full. I asked why sandals were moving so briskly. "Now is the time for sandals," said Rachid. "I have these sandals in stock for twelve months in my warehouse. Now I sell them. Next month, something else. One month you sell sandals, one month you sell textiles. I have all these jerseys here, but they won't sell until next year, in the cold season. It's all seasonal. Many times you order the goods and they don't come until after the season for them is over. Then you are stuck with them till next season. You can get hurt easily."

At 1:00, Antoine Rachid took all the morning's francs from the desk drawer, stuffed them into a plastic briefcase and closed the shop for lunch. As he pulled down the corrugated tin front to the shop, and locked it, I asked why the Lebanese are so successful in Africa, where business is so mercurial. "We are not like other businessmen," he replied. "We don't just come to a country and do business there. We become part of the country, speak the languages, marry the people. Everywhere you go today, you find Lebanese. You see, we are the Phoenicians. Since four thousand years before Jesus Christ we have been traveling to all parts of the world. Today we are everywhere."

The reason that Mr. Rachid's lower right hand desk drawer is daily stuffed with Senegalese francs is that most of his trade, as well as that of other Bathurst wholesalers, is with petty traders from Senegal who carry the goods through or around the Senegalese customs posts. This is known as the "re-export trade," and accounts for a sizable share of Gambia's economy. Asked if he had an idea just how large a share, a Bathurst businessman replied, "Well, it's really quite simple. Gambia's only export is groundnuts. The annual value of groundnut exports is about three million pounds. Imports run about four and a half million. You figure it out." Gambian government officials do not know how much is "re-exported" to Senegal, and are not particularly anxious to find out. Senegalese officials may have an idea, but cynics feel they have good reasons to see that the flow continues. There is little visible evidence of who is involved in the smuggling, since the shopowners themselves deny all knowledge of what happens to their goods after they sell them. It may be notable, however, that Aliou Jeng, a Gambian trader in the border village of Fass, drives a gray Rolls Royce. One Bathurst official says that "if you stood at the customs post, you'd find that some money changed hands now and again. It's one of the most ancient forms of smuggling. When you hand your passport over, you just see to it that there are a few extra pages in it."

Much of the re-export trade goes by "mammy wagons," the small rickety buses that carry most of the overland traffic in West Africa. Teeming with passengers inside and produce and bundles on top, they teeter along rutted dirt roads at incredible speeds and on unpredictable schedules. A recent voyager by mammy wagon from Bathurst to Dakar was surprised when the driver stopped about half a mile from the customs post, and a band of ragged little men emerged from the thick bush at the edge of the road. The women passengers took their carefully covered baskets down off the roof. The little men took the baskets on their heads and melted back into the bush. The bus then proceeded through customs, where the driver presented the inspector with a case of bottled soda. About half a mile up the road from the post, the driver stopped again. The little men appeared out of the bush, handed the baskets up to the roof, and the bus headed on to Dakar.

Actually, complicity on the part of Senegalese customs officials is hardly necessary, since the border is largely unmarked and unpatrolled bush. At night, travelers along the roads are never sure whether they hear leaves rustling in the breeze, or hordes of petty traders gliding through the underbrush. Another common method of transport is the motorized dories which load up in the evening on the beach at Bathurst, run up the coast about twenty miles, and unload their cargo on the lonely beaches of Senegal. The most common items smuggled into Senegal are transistor radios, cigarettes, liquor, cloth and sandals. All of these are priced much higher in Senegal because of Dakar's high import duties, while Bathurst's are the lowest on the West African coast. For example, a bottle of Scotch that sells for $4.20 in Bathurst will fetch up to $14 in Dakar, where the French have acquired a strong taste for this beverage. The cigarette trade is rather complex, because while the Senegalese dote on British-made "Craven A's," the average Gambian smoker prefers the cruder "Camelias" manufactured in Senegal. This cultural quirk provides smugglers with a brisk trade. One smuggled item that has nothing to do with import duties or customs men in "jamba," a local growth of Indian hemp from which the knowledgeable can brew a narcotic much in favor in Dakar.

The one smuggling activity that Gambian officials neither condone nor ignore is the diamond trade. Little is heard about this, for no one involved wishes to discuss his activities, and the government would rather the whole thing simply did not exist. Most of the diamonds come up from Sierra Leone, where nearly as many leave the country illegally as legally. Others come from as far as Leopoldville, the outlet for the Congo's loosely patrolled diamond fields. Much of the diamond transport within Africa is traditionally performed by Serahuli traders from Gambia, who over the years have set up way stations run by relatives in most cities along the coast. While the Serahulis do trade in other commodities, it would be difficult to imagine why any sane man would travel more than 2,500 miles down the coast just to sell a dozen pairs of sandals or a few bolts of cloth. The Serahulis often carry no goods at all when they go off on their missions. They sometimes come into the British United Airways office in Bathurst, dressed in rags, and lay down ($280) for a round trip ticket. While Bathurst traders joke freely about most smuggling, they are extremely reticent whenever diamonds are mentioned. Once, over a drink at the Atlantic lounge, I happened to ask a

Lebanese shopkeeper for some information about smuggling, knowing he dealt heavily in transistors bound for Senegal. Despite a swarthy complexion, he paled considerably, and rushed out of the lounge. I learned later that only that morning he had taped a packet of diamonds to the inside of his left front hubcap.

For those Gambians disinclined to smuggling either by prudence or virtue, the "pools" represent an equally exciting if less dependable source of wealth. Based on the results of games played in British football (soccer) leagues, the pools offer bettors a chance to win thousands of pounds each week for bets of a few shillings. Large English betting firms license local agents in cities of British culture around the world. Of the several agents in Bathurst, Sam Bidwell, a Gambian Aku who represents the Littlewoods system, is by far the most successful. Every Wednesday, his newspaper shop on Wellington Street overflows onto the sidewalk with eager bettors crowding toward the caged counter. In the words of a steward at the Atlantic Hotel, "This man Bidwell, he get plenty profit."

Knowledgeable observers in Bathurst estimate that three out of four men in the city and surrounding areas bet regularly, while bettors in the up-river towns send their marked forms down weekly by Land Rover. With average bets of five shillings (70 cents) estimates of the weekly action range anywhere from $14,000 to $20,000. In a city the size of Bathurst, this is not peanuts. The surprising thing about the pools in Bathurst is the size of the bets. Dockers who earn less than ten shillings a day will lay down five each week on the pool. Minor office clerks earning a few pounds a week will borrow from their friends to place a one-pound bet every Wednesday. Work in government and commercial offices slows to a standstill each Wednesday morning, as employees ponder their selections and pore over copies of *News of the World* to check the teams' records. The betting forms are airmailed to London the following morning on the weekly BUA flight. The teams play on Saturday, and those with powerful radios can pick up the scores that evening. The rest wait for the arrival of next week's *News of the World*. Whenever someone "wins big," his name and system of picking are discussed heatedly for several weeks afterward.

The biggest winner in recent years was Mr. Joseph Forster, O.B.E., a rotund, jovial Aku who had risen to the top of the civil service as Comptroller of Customs. Twelve days before independence, Mr. Forster won $25,760, which represented more than five times his annual salary. "Thus I became independent before my country," he said happily. The windfall came at an opportune time, for his scheduled retirement was only a few months away. Unlike most Gambian bettors, Mr. Forster began playing the pools late in life. "I started in England, in fifty-eight, during a customs course I was taking there. I stayed with a Nigerian chap who indoctrinated me into this affair. I now bet an average of one pound-ten [$4.20] a week. It affords some amusement, and you get a sensation of belonging to the sports world. You have something to look forward to on Saturday." Mr. Forster makes no claims to exceptional intelligence in his betting, feeling that success at the pools is mostly a matter of luck. "I have seen a chap who won two thousand pounds [$5,600] a few years ago. He's illiterate. He had a literate friend who had made a forecast for him the week before. He couldn't find his friend this time, so he simply copied the previous week's selections. He could only make the X's — he can't write." Asked what he had done with his new fortune, Mr. Forster said, "I haven't done anything with it yet. When you have so much money you don't let it change your plans. I've left it all in a bank in England. I'm clogged up here with office work now. I must wait till it is off my shoulders before I sit down and think and plan." Six months later, Mr. Forster died.

*

If the energy and expense devoted to the weekly pools amazes a visitor to Bathurst, he must remember that unlike more developed or commercially active countries, Gambia offers few other prospects for getting rich quick. With peanuts the only export, there is not much loose money floating around the country, despite the amount that flows weekly into the pools. Most of the money goes to large firms like the Madis, United Africa Company and the major French trading concerns. Individual success stories are exceedingly rare. There is one Gambian, however, who has achieved such success, and many feel he is the richest man in the country today. His name is Alhadji Momodou Moussa N'Jie.

Although Mr. N'Jie can neither read nor write, he has amassed a fortune by simply doing well what hundreds of other Gambian traders do — buying and selling. Rumors abound in Bathurst about his dealings and the extent of his wealth, and one can always hear of his latest coup over a beer in the Atlantic lounge. His independence gift of $2,800, though larger than that from many countries, startled no one. "Momodou," as he is commonly known, appears frequently throughout the country, looking after his affairs. An up-river official says, "He extends credit to all the Serahulis in the provinces." A bank official says, "He's used as a business agent by Gambians who haven't a clue about formal transactions." I once saw him in the bank, assisting a Mauritanian cattleman from Senegal who spoke only Arabic. The dark-skinned Moor had piles of dirty Senegalese francs tied up in a piece of cloth, and Mr. N'Jie was helping him fill out some forms to transfer the money to an associate in Senegal.

Managers of the large trading firms speak with awe of their relations with him. "He started out as a clerk," says one of them. "He's never been to school, but he's got what you might call a bent for making money. He signs his checks with a thumbprint and 'M. M. N'Jie,' but the signature is never the same. It's the thumbprint that counts. Old Momodou's very highly respected by the Bank of West Africa. He's one of their best customers on the coast. Unlike the Lebanese and many of the Africans, he uses the bank. The rest of them stuff their money in mattresses or send it out of the country. He'll come in to us about June, and buy a hundred tons of rice at five pounds a bag. We don't ask him to pay until next November, when the trade season starts, and we don't charge any interest on the credit either. Old Momodou will go out and flog that rice at up to ten pounds a bag. It's none of our business what he does with it as long as he pays — and he always pays."

One government official who has followed Mr. N'Jie's career with interest over the years, says, "Momodou made piles on diamond smuggling from Sierra Leone, and money changing down the coast. Years ago, before any of the British territories were independent, there used to be absolutely free movement of currency between the four British West African colonies. CFA [French West African] francs used to be much cheaper in the Gold Coast than elsewhere. You could sail down to the Gold Coast on the *Apapa* with a suitcase full of West African pound notes. You changed them there for a suitcase full of CFA francs, and then brought those illegally into one of the nearby French territories."

Philip Bridges, the British Attorney General, has acquired grudging respect for Mr. N'Jie's business acumen closer to home. "When I was Lands Officer," says Bridges, "I went over near Crab Island one day and found an entire block of crinting huts thrown up on Crown land. I inquired whose they were, and was told they belonged to Alhadji Momodou Moussa N'Jie. I went down to his office and told him they'd have to come down. He suggested I think about it for a while, but I told him it was all settled — finish. He then claimed it was a charitable affair, built for all the Fulas and Serahulis from up-river who come down to Bathurst with nowhere to stay. He said their rents were only donations to the charity. I told him they would still have to come down. I went back to check up a week or so later and the huts were all gone — everything. Two weeks after that, I happened to be driving by and saw the whole development up again, with people settled in as if nothing had happened. I went down to see old Momodou and asked what the hell was going on. He said, 'Oh sah! I be make mistake.' "

I arranged to meet Mr. N'Jie one morning down at his Buckle Street office in the Nigeria Airways Building. He came roaring up in a big 1962 Dodge sedan, with flashing chrome and jutting tail fins. He climbed out, wearing a chartreuse robe, white silk scarf, embroidered white Moslem cap and white plastic slippers. A tall, slender man with a relaxed manner and a charming smile, he greeted me warmly and led me into his outer office, where a dozen business "associates" sprawled in low chairs or reclined on straw floor mats, intently rubbing their teeth with chewing sticks. They all mustered the traditional Moslem greeting, "Salaam Aleikum" as we entered. We passed on to the inner office, partitioned off from the outer room by wood and glass panels. There were cans of paint in the corner, plumbing connections in a glass cabinet, two clocks on the wall and three on the desk. Dozens of fountain pens littered the desk, along with currency conversion booklets and a transistor radio. Behind the desk, piled one atop the other, were three ancient green safes.

N'Jie told me he was born fifty-one years ago in Basse, where his father was a horse trader. He worked with his father for a few years, then entered the shop of a Lebanese trader there as a clerk. Later he worked at a Madi shop in Basse. "After nineteen forty, I leave Madi. I go buy goods here, I buy 'em, sell 'em, buy more goods, buy 'em, sell 'em, buy cattle and sell 'em. I travel all over — Nigeria, Gold Coast, Sierra Leone. Now I no travel. I sit down here and buy property."

The phone rang. He picked it up and carried on an energetic multilingual conversation with several people on the other end of the line. When he put the phone down, he apologized for the interruption and sent an assistant out for a bottle of Tennants beer and a dirty glass, which he offered me. At 10:00 on a hot, sticky June morning in Bathurst, room temperature is warmer than I customarily like my beer, but since Mr. N'Jie was a strict Moslem, it was all mine. "Thank you very much," I said.

"For nothing," said Momodou.

I asked him why he no longer traded down the coast, and he replied, "I no travel now because I get plenty picken."

"How many do you have?"

"I think I get thirty-one . . . maybe thirty-two. I get four wives. I get one boy picken, he learning I think economics in England at Oxford school. I get three picken in Freetown at school, and one boy picken, he study in Amerique, in Philadelphia. He go learn for teaching. Amerique, dey give 'im scholarship."

"Is your son at Oxford also on scholarship?"

"No, I send 'im, but now de government dey go help small."

Throughout our chat, young boys invaded the office from time to time, and I presumed they were his. When I asked, he said they were, and stopped the next one. "Dis be Brimah. Say hello dis mastah, Brimah." When the boy had made his greeting and left, Mr. N'Jie said, "Dis boy, he be smart too much. Since he be born, he never get second. All time in school he get first."

"How old is Brimah?"

"I don' know — maybe 'leven, twelve."

When I asked if Mr. N'Jie had ever dealt in diamonds during his travels to Sierra Leone, he became excited. "No! No! I never do diamonds. Me never do it at all. Sometimes, maybe I bring kola nuts from Sierra Leone. I get some cattle too. I buy some and sell 'em."

"How many cattle do you have?"

"Maybe few hundred. You know, dey some dying, some living."

"Do you deal in groundnuts also?"

"Not now. I want to buy groundnuts. All de Gambians want me to buy dere nuts because all farmers my friend. Anything I want dey give me. But de bank no let me buy groundnuts. First de bank say dey go let me have hundred thousand pounds [$280,000] to buy groundnuts, but de big firms no 'gree. Dey tell bank no give me money for buy groundnuts. Dese firms can do anything. Bank he promise me money, but after two weeks of trade season, he say no. If I get money to buy groundnuts I must make big profit — hundred thousand pounds — because all farmers want me to buy. Now I maybe start small, small."

Mr. N'Jie stopped to light up what looked like an incense taper stuck in a long black cigarette holder. He leaned back in his chair and drew contentedly on it. "Dis be 'choorai Mecca' [a cheroot stick]. My wife bring 'im to me. I send five people dis year to Mecca — cost fifteen hundred pounds [$4,200]. I send two wives, my daughter, daughter husband and daughter picken. I go Mecca nineteen fifty-one. Me build mosque on Picton Street. Fine, fine mosque — cost about four thousand pound [$11,200]. I building also Mohammedan School."

"What other property do you have in Bathurst?"

"Well, I get dis Nigeria Airways Building. I build 'im for seventy thousand pound. He get ten shops and six flats. De Chellerams building, I buy 'im for eighteen thousand. I get another building on Wellington Street, I buy 'im for twenty thousand. I no get much money, but de bank he like me too much. Dey give me anything. Last year I build fine building near Crab Island School. He get plenty apartments. He called 'London Corner.' "

During the morning, a steady stream of visitors entered the office — Fula cattlemen from up-river, Mauritanian cattlemen from Senegal, Hausa traders from Nigeria and Serahuli traders from down the coast. Mr. N'Jie dealt quickly with all of them, speaking fluently to each in his own language. I asked if perhaps I was taking up too much of his time, but he insisted that I stay. "No, no. You no go. Me no get worry." Seeing that I was only halfway through the pint of tepid beer, he said, "Finish 'im. Me no use 'im. Me drink lemonade."

As I rose to leave, later, I asked if he agreed with the talk about town that he is the wealthiest man in Gambia. "No! No!" he yelled, jumping to his feet. "I no believe. Plenty people dey hide de money. When I get small, I go build small. I still be small, small."

\*

If there is doubt about the richest man in Gambia, finding the poorest is nearly impossible. Measuring poverty is difficult in Africa, since accurate economic statistics are scarce, and many self-sufficient villagers live almost outside the money economy. They barter whenever they need something, and show up badly in statistical reports on per capita income. The average Gambian farmer earns approximately $70 to $85 a year from the sale of his peanut crop, supplementing this by growing some of his own rice and most of his vegetables. With his money, he buys rice,

The *Lady Wright*

Loading Peanuts on a German Freighter Up-River

The Captain of the *Lady Wright*

Wrestlers

Voting Drums

Fisherman

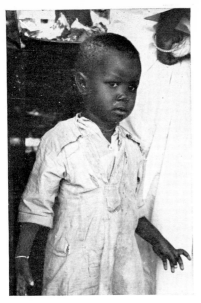

Up-River Boy

Mother and Child

Women Pounding Coos

Boy at Tobaski Celebration

Winnowing Peanuts

A Loaded "Groundnutter"

Remains of the Old Fort at James Island

Food for Sale at an Up-River Port

Robin Mulholland

Johnny Rollings

Pa Van Der Plas

Pumping Water at the Village Well

occasional bits of meat or fish, cloth and other necessities. This may not seem like much of a life, but he is better off than most of the residents of Dakar's Medina, a teeming, tin-shack suburb where low-salaried and part-time workers struggle vainly to stretch their meager funds enough to buy all the family's necessities.

Though Bathurst is not a wealthy city, it has none of the poverty or foul slums common to most other African capitals. The poorest families live in relatively clean one-room wood or tin houses, clustered together like village compounds with central dirt courtyards. The women do their cooking, washing and other chores at each compound's communal fire and water tap. The different families living in each compound are frequently related, or come from the same up-river village. Because of these ties, they try to help each other out in times of financial strain. Help is often needed, for day-laborers earn only $14 to $20 per month, and steward-waiters at the hotel earn $25 to $30. After paying a few pounds a month for rent, there is not much left. Since most of their fellow compound dwellers are in similar positions, everyone eventually ends up in debt to the Mauritanian and Lebanese shopkeepers.

There is one Bathurst resident who does not fit into this pattern. He never works, has no friends or relatives to help him out, pays no rent, never has more than a shilling or two, and is never in debt. He is called "Mad Johnny" Rollings, and he lives in a hole in the ground with a pack of stray dogs. No one would mind where Johnny lived if his hole didn't happen to be in the center of the Crab Island housing development. He moved in years ago, and claims that former Governor Sir Hilary Blood gave him the land. When the government reclaimed swampy Crab Island and began laying out housing plots, they found Mad Johnny nestled snugly in the middle. "We've been trying to move him out for years," says Attorney General Bridges, "but he won't go. He won't even pay taxes. We set aside a piece of land for him out in the Kombo [the area just beyond Bathurst] but he won't have any part of it. 'I like it here,' he says, 'and besides, the dogs wouldn't like it out there. You can offer me Government House if you like — I'll stay here.' He's extremely well-read. Always has the latest copies of the *Times* and *The New Statesman*. He's up to date on everything. Once, when I had him brought into the office to discuss his refusal to move, I told him, 'Look Johnny, there's something important I'd like to discuss with you.' 'Fine,' he says, 'there are several important things I'd like to discuss with you too. What's going to happen if Britain doesn't join the Common Market?' "

As these remarks suggest, Mad Johnny's madness is selective. Few other Gambians are prepared to discuss the Common Market, or spend their time reading *The New Statesman*. There are many others around Bathurst, however, who exhibit signs of mental turmoil. For some reason, they seem to congregate around the government secretariat. One gentleman who calls himself "the Crown Prince of Gambia" makes the rounds of senior officials each day with scraps of paper, envelopes, napkins or old *Lady Wright* sailing schedules. He claims that these are the documents proving his ownership of the "crown jewels," which he says the government has taken from him. He insists that each official certify his documents with a stamp and signature. "We've tried throwing him out," says one administrator, "but he keeps coming back. It's easier to just sign his paper, stamp it several times with official-looking seals, and send him on to the next office.

"There's a blind man named Henry Bolingbroke-Fowlis who comes into the courtyard annually and sings 'God Save the Queen.' Then he comes around for contributions. He's a retired schoolmaster who used to run a brothel during the war. There's another chap, a former policeman, who occasionally storms into the secretariat screaming '*Down with the Prime Minister!*' We just lead him quietly away each time."

Whether Bathurst has an unusually large proportion of such gentlemen, or whether they are simply more noticeable in a small city, is open to question. Dakar, which is ten times the size of Bathurst, also has its share. Embassy officials there report frequent visitations from Senegalese of various aberrations. One known as "Prince Nana" calls regularly on the British Embassy, demanding an urgent interview with the ambassador. He carries a voluminous manuscript which he calls "The Plan." Written in exquisite longhand, it outlines a detailed proposal for a British takeover and recolonization of Africa. Another gentleman calls periodically at the United States Embasssy trying to see the ambassador about "the word." Says one official there, "We can't tell if he's a Rosicrucian or if he's doing a crossword puzzle."

Many of the mentally disturbed in Africa are well-educated men who have studied at European universities. An unusually high percentage of them "go 'round the bend" while they are abroad, and have to be brought quietly home. A former Bathurst judge explained, "I think it's a matter of putting too great a strain on their minds. They leave here and get a severe cultural shock when they have to get along in a greatly different world. On top of that, you throw them into a difficult school and pile a load of work on them. It's too much, and they crack under the strain. Many of them go 'round after they return here. Having acquired a superficial knowledge in England, they come back with a profound belief in their own wisdom, and react violently when people here disagree with them about anything. It's like putting too great a load of seed in virgin soil."

A young man named N'Jie, no kin to Momodou, is a prime example of the effects of such strain. An excellent student, he won a government scholarship to Edinburgh University, where he graduated with honors. The government wanted him to study education next, but by the time they approached him he was already " 'round the bend," and had to be brought home. Now he rides slowly about Bathurst on his bicycle, with one arm hanging by his side, staring blankly before him. He spends the afternoon in the lounge of the Atlantic Hotel, reading British newspapers and staring out the window. A pleasant fellow, N'Jie is happy to engage in conversation with anyone, ranging freely over Hegel, Kant and Freud with only occasional incoherence. When asked what his plans are, he says, "Well, I may take an appointment some time, but not just now. I'm still trying to organize things."

Compared to Mr. N'Jie, old Johnny Rollings has things fairly well organized. He spends his days strolling about Bathurst looking for odd pieces of wood or tin, caring for his dogs, and puttering around his yard full of scraggly shrubs. A Gambian who brings Johnny newspapers took me to Crab Island one morning to meet him. As we arrived, he said, "That old pa is the happiest bloke in Gambia." Johnny's plot of ground off Spalding Street was overgrown with briers, weeds and seemingly dead bushes. Smoke curled up from a tangle of old scrap metal, where he was brewing his midmorning tea. Around him lay old pots, paint cans, a car door, an iron bedstead, and a rusty old tin water tank that serves as a roof over his hole. When we yelled, Johnny came out to greet us, wearing a faded torn shirt, fastened with a safety pin, and a pair of oversized trousers held up with a knotted tie. His eyes were rheumy and glazed, but piercing. Bits of straw were caught in his scraggly gray hair and beard.

Johnny Rollings is an Aku, and says his full name is John Timothy William Orocolagbeh Ijebumuray Boi Manley-Rollings. He was born in Bathurst in 1892, where his mother's family had property. When his father, a policeman, died six years later, his mother brought Johnny back to Freetown, Sierra Leone, where he attended mission schools. When his mother died, he had to leave school, and took up tailoring. In 1919, he moved to Bathurst and ran his own tailor shop until he retired ten years ago. Now seventy-two, he moves about spryly, despite his scarecrow appearance.

"I am royal blood," he says. "I can trace my ancestors to Solomon and David. I should be king in Nigeria by this time if there was no English to intervene. My mother was a Cummings from Freetown — an old family. She was whiter than you. My father had plenty of property in Bathurst when he died. I paid a lawyer seventy-three pounds, but the English took my property and squandered it. They've stolen everything. I came to this place in nineteen-forty, and I was entitled to it by law — the statute of limitations — after seven years. I have been here twenty-six years now, but the English and people here are all against me. They tried to get me out by changing the law. They changed the law just to get me. They try and try, all sort of dirty tricks, but I am too strong for them. They even try to kill my dogs."

"Where are your dogs now?"

"Some of them they killed. The rest are out walking on the beach. Now that the hot days are here they like to go down to the beach and take the air. I take walks downtown sometimes, but I don't mix with people. I keep aloof. I don't hobnob. You see, the people thieve me here all the time. They kill my dogs, they stone me, they try to break my house and give me heart failure. They have tried all they know to get me out, but they find I'm a tough guy." Johnny cited the parallel persecutions suffered by Christ, and made appropriate quotations from the Bible. He recounted stories about the times the Health and Police Departments had tried to get him declared insane. Upon examination, the doctors at Victoria Hospital refused to sign. "They couldn't find anything wrong with me. I am perfectly sound. I can tell anything that happened in the eighteen-nineties."

Since it is the only empty lot in Crab Island, people use Johnny's plot as a garbage dump, throwing bottles, cans and refuse onto it as they walk by. Johnny collects the bottles and cans. He also does a bit of farming, and since his is also the only farm in Bathurst, his produce is popular with neighborhood women. "I have okra, peppers, tomatoes, sweet potatoes, maize, jockatoo, and cassava. [Some of these vegetables grow only in Johnny's fertile imagination.] If I am not here, they come and take them without paying."

Along with his farming, Johnny Rollings has acquired considerable local renown as a medicine man, doing a brisk trade in leaves and stalks from the underbrush growing in his yard. Though local women consider him mad, they seem to feel his affliction gives him arcane medical powers. As we walked about the dead stalks and parched bushes, Johnny stopped to point out their various uses. "When the rains come, these grow leaves right away. This one is 'Sierra Leone tea bush.' That one is 'bush tea bush.' If you have blackwater fever, or bile, you boil these seeds and extract the oil. Put two drops of it on a lump of sugar and eat it. Then cover yourself. The fever will sweat right away, sir. If you continue to drink it, fever will never attack you."

The next bush looked like an overgrown weed. "You can't get any chemical in the hospital that will relieve you like this one," said Johnny. "You take the leaves and grind them with a mortar to take out the juice. Then you add salt, a little bit of fireside ashes — they have potassium, you know — and mix it with water. It cures diarrhea and bellyache." Pointing to a tired-looking cotton bush, he said, "If you are passing blood in your stool . . ." I told him I was not so afflicted.

"Over here I have castor oil leaves. The women come for them at all times. After they deliver a child, they make a brew of these leaves and sit in a pan of it. These are chile peppers. In five minutes they will cure diseases that doctors would never attempt. That prickly bush there is 'loo bush.' They tie it around the head when they have a headache." He pointed to a pile of old leaves and stalks on the ground. "That is 'offo oodoo.' It cures all kinds of internal diseases. It is very powerful, and few people know about it. If the doctors really knew about the powers of this, all the causes of mortality would stop."

As we approached the edge of the next yard, a group of young boys stood at the fence and laughed at Johnny. "The children here all throw stones at me. Their parents do not take care of them. Oh, I could do things to them if I wished." He told a tale of an old man who had been tormented by two little girls. "He put a curse on them, and turned them into palm trees. I can show you the place. If you stick a pin in the trees, blood will come out."

Back at his house, Johnny placed two paint cans upside down for seats, and offered to brew me some tea. Nearby, several rotting fish heads hung from the branches of an otherwise barren tree. "I am experimenting with that," said Johnny.

"Were you ever married?" I asked, as we sipped the tea.

"No. I don't believe in telling any woman 'I worship your body and give you all my worldly goods.' I don't believe in it at all."

"What would you have done if you had received the income from your father's property?"

"I would have gone for law and medicine, and preach. I would have protected people from swindlers. I still study and read all the time. I read anything — economics, sociology, war. I had a big volume on palmistry, but it's stolen. I read anything, even if it's written by the devil. I read about Confucianism, Taoism, Buddhism, Zoaism — that's from Persia. It lasted until the birth of Christ."

Asked if he had any thoughts about Gambia's future development, Johnny grew angry. "Gambia was once much bigger than this, but the English cut it up and sold it. If I was Prime Minister, I would tell all the African nations and the world that they must return our land to us. But this country is still rich. There is gold everywhere in Gambia. In the river they used to get gold easily. There is another way. You bury a body in a trench — it must be a yellow body, a Chinaman — and cover it up. After some time, you dig it up. All that was blood, the heart, the . . . what do you call it . . . the pancreas, the liver and the arteries — they will all be gold."

As I rose to leave, Johnny quoted a passage from the Bible: "Take off thy shoes from off thy feet, for whereon thou standest is holy ground. Everywhere is holy ground." Johnny stood barefoot among the rubble in his yard — broken baskets, bricks, parts of an auto chassis, scraps of burlap and tin. "All this will be used up," he said. "I will use it to patch my house. I only try to patch up life."

# 12

## ALHAMDULLAH

WHEN EUROPEAN MISSIONARIES first came to Africa, they and the societies that sent them looked upon "the dark continent" as a vast collection of heathen souls awaiting salvation. Despite centuries of energetic missionary work, however, the souls are still waiting. Except for a few isolated outposts, Christianity never spread much further than the edge of European civilization, penetrating only as far from the coastal settlements as the river boats could carry the missionaries. For a time, this state of affairs bothered no one, for the slave trade provided ample spiritual fodder. Looking on Africa as a province of the devil, the Church was content to have its priests and bishops stand on the fortified walls of coastal slaving depots, blessing the ships full of black cargo on their way to salvation in the New World. The missionaries' reports home cheered Church authorities, and their blessings soothed the rarely ruffled consciences of the slave dealers. Relations between the merchants and the Church grew cooler as the slave trade enlarged to the point that it became embarrassing to the Church and highly profitable for the merchants. For a time, they settled their differences by an agreement that forbade the sale of any baptized African. This policy brought baptism into immediate favor among captured tribesmen about to be sold into slavery. Satisfied with the mass conversions that resulted from this system, the priests forsook blessing the ships full of Africans so insensitive as to refuse baptism.

The end of the slave trade in the nineteenth century caused a sharp decline in applications for baptism, and Christianity never again managed to find an equally compelling argument for conversion. Catholics, Quakers, Wesleyans, Anglicans, Seventh Day Adventists and Holy Rollers have all tried their hands at the Black Continent, with little success. For many years they had all they could do to endure what were exceedingly trying physical conditions, many of the missionaries dying in their twenties of malaria and other tropical diseases. When they had the energy, they built small mission schools, tried to help the natives, and translated portions of the Bible. Pidgen English Bibles used on the West Coast told how "de Lord he dash Gabriel one trumpet an give 'im license to blow." In the time of the flood, "de Lord say to Noah, 'You build an ark, an' I go make you my number one man like Elder Dempster agent.'"

In Africa today, there are only small Christian congregations in the cities and large towns, and scattered mission posts out in the bush. Gambia has only a few thousand Christians, most of them centered in Bathurst. Every Sunday, the Akus attend the Wesleyan Methodist Church on Dobson Street, dressed in Victorian finery. In the afternoon, the Aku children in their church best — the girls carrying dainty parasols — stroll up and down Marina Street from Government House to the Atlantic Hotel, in what other Gambians refer to as the "Aku parade." The British and a few Gambians support the little Anglican Church of St. Mary, just off MacCarthy Square. Petunias, daisies and hollyhocks grow in the little garden out back. The Nigerian who superintends spiritual affairs at St. Mary's bears the title, "Bishop of the Gambia and the Rio Pongas." No one in Gambia seems to know the location of the Rio Pongas.

The Catholics are the largest Christian group in Gambia, numbering about 2,000, most of whom are Bathurst Woloffs. The influence of Christianity on their lives can be seen in such names as Faithful Oogoo and Mary Magdalen N'Dong. Ministering to this flock are the Holy Ghost Fathers, an Irish missionary order that opened its first mission in Gambia in 1849. There are now fifteen priests and fourteen sisters who operate a number of village missions and schools, along with their secondary schools in Bathurst. Despite this extensive apparatus, however, the Holy Ghost Fathers have not made many converts in the last few decades. Asked why, Bishop Maloney, who arrived in Gambia in 1937, simply shrugs and says, "We just can't seem to keep up with the Moslems."

The race between Christianity and Islam in Africa has never really been in doubt. When the two have come in direct conflict, Islam has usually emerged victorious. The decline of Christianity in recent years of nationalism and independence has been hastened by its association with white colonial culture. Perhaps for this reason, Islam has recently expanded rapidly throughout the continent. As a North African religion it carries no foreign taint, and many political leaders raised in Christian mission schools have publicly espoused the Moslem faith partly to solidify their power.

Islam's spread from Arab North Africa through Black Africa began long before independence. Bending to local customs, it adapted itself to tribal and regional traditions, taking varying forms in various countries. Until the twentieth century, Islam stopped at the edge of Africa's jungles. In the words of one writer, "the only thing that has slowed the advance of the faith of the Prophet is the tsetse fly, the only thing that has stopped it is the rain forest." Modern roads and communication systems have removed most of these obstacles to Islam's propagation, and many observers now feel that it is only a matter of time before the entire continent will follow the faith of the Prophet.

Gambia is a good illustration of the flux between Moslem and pagan practices in a nominally Moslem country. Relatively close to the Sahara, the Senegambian region fell under the influence of Islam in the Marabout-Soninki religious struggles in the nineteenth century. Headmen and chiefs who expressed reluctance at adopting the new faith were offered a choice of accepting it or losing their power — and occasionally their heads. Given this option, most of them chose spiritual discretion over a posthumous reputation for valor.

Today, Gambia is about 85 per cent Moslem, but the degree of devotion and observance varies widely. The dominant Mandinkas are nearly all Moslem, although they are lax in such matters as the proper number of wives. (Islam allows four.) The Serahuli, who live furthest up-river, and have thus had the least contact with Bathurst and other spiritually contaminating influences, are also completely Moslem. Up-river Woloffs are mostly Moslem, while many of those in Bathurst are Catholic. The Fulas are mostly Moslem, although several sub-tribes are still pagan. The Jolas have remained proudly pagan, only a few succumbing to Catholic missionaries. Actually, the rice-growing Jolas do not care much for religion, being more addicted to palm wine and wrestling.

The distinction between Moslem and non-Moslem is often quite hazy. Many pagan practices are combined with those of Islam by toning down the uninhibited parts and interspersing the rest with suitable Moslem prayers. While most Gambians limit themselves to four or fewer wives — through strict observance of Moslem law or for financial reasons — polygamy in excess of the proper number is common. The extra wives are generally given euphemistic classifications such as "helpers" or "sub-wives."

Though a relatively uncomplex religion, Islam nevertheless represents a considerable leap into the abstract for the average African villager. Sophisticated concepts like Mohammed (or Christ) and a holy Koran (or Bible) stretch his imagination. His own spiritual world is always about him in his daily life. Unaware that he is an animist, he sees spiritual significance in normal events, and infuses inanimate objects with being. His world is alive, full of gods and devils, sacred animals and trees. To the African, it is a richer and more immediate world than the spiritual austerity offered by Islam or Christianity.

Gambians, for example, consider owls to be witches in disguise. They have a "plenty bad devil" named Ninky Nanka, who lives in the ground, or under the water, and is responsible for fires, accidents and shipwrecks. He often walks about at night, and anyone looking directly at the large diamond in his head will die immediately. Mumbo Jumbo, despite its present world-wide exposure, originated in this part of West Africa, and still exists as a leaf-clad devil in Mandinka villages who appears whenever there has been "women palava." Actually a villager dressed in a suit of leaves, Mumbo Jumbo comes at night, accompanied by fearsome drumming. After a violent dance before the assembled villagers, he points out the woman who has been causing trouble. She then receives suitable punishment. While the gods and devils only appear from time to time, the sacred pools, animals and trees are ever-present. Villagers in suburban Bakau, only ten miles from Bathurst, refused to let government anti-malaria workers drain their sacred Ketchikali pool. Though infested with mosquitos, it is also the home of a sacred crocodile. No one has spotted the crocodile for several years now, but the villagers are sure he is still there.

At Kartung, a coastal village near the southern border, another sacred crocodile makes his home in a small pool. I went out to Kartung with a police officer once to visit this crocodile. At first, the villagers were unwilling to show us the pool, saying, "You can't shoot dis crocodile. You no go kill 'im." After a long pa-laver, and assured of our good intentions, two men climbed into our Land Rover and led us to the pool, a mile or so outside the village. At the top of a slight hill, we got out and walked down to a low swampy area. As we approached the pool, one of the guides held out his hand and said, "You must give charity for de croco-dile."

Since we had some eggs in the car, I asked if they would do. "No," said our guide, "He no like eggs. He like money."

We gave him three-pence and asked, "What are you going to do with the money?"

"I go keep 'im. Man who bring you to de crocodile he get de money."

"But what about the crocodile?"

"Shhh. We close by now."

We had come to a small swampy pool hidden under thick overhanging bushes. At the far end we could see a small, five-foot crocodile placidly sunning itself in the mud. Mud and leaves were caked on his back. He looked neither ferocious nor sacred. "Some time you come here, de pool be all full for croco-dile," said our guide. "He get plenty picken. You no go near him now — he go chop you." At our edge of the pool, there were several large bowls, cups and shells, in which villagers from Kar-tung placed bits of food for the crocodile. "When dere is any-thing dey want, dey come here and giv 'im something. Den dey say de prayers and drink some pool water. De prophet Moham-med come here long time ago, when he was traveling. [Moham-med apparently stopped in as many places in Africa as George Washington did in the United States.] He take some water an' bless de place. Ever since, de people come here."

While the casual visitor to Gambia may not have the opportu-

nity to observe gods, devils and sacred crocodiles, he will undoubtedly come in contact with "ju-ju" — the leather amulets
worn around the wrist, neck, waist, ankle, arm and chest. Ju-ju
amulets are still worn throughout Africa, elephant hairs being
the customary version in East Africa, while leather is used in the
West. As popular in Bathurst as they are up-river, there are special ju-ju for hunting, wrestling, fishing and other vocations. Students who claim not to believe in ju-ju bring them to exams;
policemen have them inside their caps; even the most "emerged"
citizens of the capital may keep a ju-ju wrist band, explaining it
off-handedly as "merely for luck."

Moslem leaders, with typical suppleness, never tried to suppress
ju-ju, though the Koran expressly forbids the wearing of such
charms. Instead, recognizing an immovable and potentially
profitable obstacle, the marabouts took over its distribution.
Today, Gambians buy all their ju-ju from village marabouts, at
prices ranging from a few shillings for a leather bracelet of limited efficacy to ten pounds or more for one of superior powers.
Since nearly everyone has at least one ju-ju, the marabouts make
a tidy income from this trade. The most common ju-ju is a
leather amulet tied to the arm by a leather band. The amulet
will theoretically contain a verse from the Koran, but since it is
never opened — on pain of some awesome retribution — its con-
tents are debatable. Belief in the power of ju-ju is impressive. I
saw a houseboy dare his English master to stick a kitchen knife in
him while he held his ju-ju. Hoping to cure the boy of his folly,
the Englishman held the tip of the knife at the boy's throat.
The boy did not flinch, and the Englishman gave in. The boy
then explained that his ju-ju had prevented the knife from going
in.

Seeking more information about ju-ju, I once asked my hotel
steward Moussa to tell me about the one he wore on his arm.

Moussa's ju-ju consisted of two pieces of leather, attached by a string and a safety pin. One piece was a square of solid leather, and the other was a pair of rusty scissors encased in leather, with the ends sticking out. "You see dis ju-ju?" said Moussa. "If you get dis ju-ju an' I vex for you, an' I say I going to fight with you now, you get dis ju-ju you see I fall down. I go fall down here. I can't reach to you. I get no powah. If people say, 'We vex for you, we want to fight you,' when we meet you, you take de ju-ju an' go like dis an' we fall down. We can't go up.

"When a man try to cut you like dis, he never go in. He get big big knife, go cut, cut, cut — nothing happen. De ju-ju make de knife never go inside your body. Same with de gun. He go out, he shoot people, you know? With dis ju-ju you be all right. De bullet he go dis way, he go pass. You know, during de army time, de black man dey going to de fight. When you go shoot dem, you go pass — you never kill 'em." [During the Congo rebellion, mercenary government troops encountered hordes of rebel Congolese tribesmen who charged in the face of heavy fire, convinced the bullets could not hurt them. They were wrong.]

"When I fight with you," Moussa continued, "I put dis ju-ju like dis three times [drawing an imaginary line on the floor, and mumbling an Arabic incantation]. Now your foot is no good for walking on. I make 'im foot no good, or de hand spoil, or do something like dat [waving the ju-ju at me] an' you never wake up, or you can't sleep in de bed. Very bad."

"But that's just a pair of scissors. You can do all those things with that?"

"Yes, if I'm vex, if I like."

"What is that other ju-ju you wear around your waist?"

"Dis be traveling ju-ju. Wherever I go, nothing happen. If I go on de ship, an' de ship fall down an' de water go inside, I no go in de water. I never go in. De fish dere, dey see you, dey try to chop you, but dey can't. Dey can't chop you if you get dat ju-ju. Nothing go chop me. I just standing dere in de water. People come in de motor launch, dey say, 'Oh, dis accident happen. Many people die.' But you don't die. You get dat ju-ju."

"Can any marabout make these ju-ju, even in Bathurst?"

"Yes, but dey no get good marabouts here in Bathurst. De ribbah get de best marabouts. Fula and Mandingo marabouts better past all."

"Can anyone go to the marabout and get a ju-ju?"

"Yes, yes. He can do it. But de marabout he no give ju-ju to anybody. When he see you are serious man, an' you never bring fight all de time, den he give you. Small boys no can have it, because every time dey vex dey go kill somebody, and dat is very bad from God. Dat is why dey only give ju-ju to old man, you know, somebody who get thirty years."

"How much do they cost?"

"Oh, twenty poun', forty poun', ninety poun'. I tell you, de ju-ju like de book. You know de book? Dey get many different kind. Some of dem cost much money, some of dem be cheap price."

"How much did you pay for the one you have?"

"I not know dis. My fadda he buy 'im for me. Get 'im from big marabout. My fadda give him two cows."

\*

While Islam has reconciled itself to ju-ju and other pagan practices in Gambia, its several sects are not reconciled to each other. There are four competing factions — Tijan, Cadi, Mooride, and Ahmadiyya. The Tijan sect is by far the most numerous, with adherents in Bathurst and up-river towns, while the Cadi sect is limited to villages in a few areas. Most of Bathurst's 500 Mauritanian traders belong to the Mooride sect. Up in Dakar, where the Moorides are more numerous, they recently fought a pitched battle with stones against the Tijani over which group would control the magnificent new mosque the Senegalese government had just built. The battle was a draw, but the Tijani won control of the mosque.

Though fairly new to Gambia, the Pakistan-based Ahmadiyya sect has been around for more than 130 years, and claims a membership of two million in Pakistan alone. It has sixty-four foreign missions, including ones in London, New York, Chicago, and Washington. The founder of the movement was a Pakistani named Hazrat Mirza Ahmad, who never attended school and failed a legal examination before receiving instructions from the spirit of Mohammed that he was to be the Redeemer of his age. Originally, Hazrat Ahmad planned to save the entire world, but he weakened his appeal to Christians by claiming private information that Jesus had not died upon the cross but merely fallen into a "swoon." According to Hazrat Ahmad, Jesus was taken down from the cross, and eventually traveled to Kashmir, where he died a natural death. An Ahmadiyya pamphlet entitled *Jesus in Kashmir* refutes the doctrines of resurrection and ascension, and tells how Hazrat Mirza Ahmad, "through divine revelation and research," located Jesus's actual tomb on Khanyar Street in Srinagar, Kashmir.

At 75 Lancaster Street, in Bathurst, a lively sixty-four-year-old Pakistani named Ghulam Ahmad now runs the Ahmadiyya mission in Gambia. Unlike the founder of the movement, he is a well-educated man, with a degree in Arabic studies from the University of Lahore, Pakistan. He claims 400 members in Gambia, with small groups organized in Basse, Georgetown, Farrafenni, Bakau and Bathurst. He gives instruction in the Koran every day at his Bathurst headquarters, and has classes each Tuesday out at Bakau. The marabouts look upon Ghulam

Ahmad as an intruder, and put pressure on their flocks to avoid
him. On Fridays, the Tijan Imam of Bathurst leads the faithful
in prayer at the official Moslem prayer ground near Gambia High
School. The followers of Ahmadiyya hold their services behind a
row of cannons near Government House.

One morning a Gambian houseboy named Bacary took me to
the mission to visit Ghulam Ahmad. We entered a sandy courtyard off Lancaster Street, where several lines of laundry impeded
our progress. Hens scratched in the sand for scraps, and two
scrawny goats walked about in search of shade. We found
Ghulam Ahmad reclining in a canvas beach chair up on the second floor terrace, his yellow-brown face creased in thought as he
studied an arabic text. He jumped up spryly to greet us, smiling
a "Salaam Aleikum" through his few remaining yellow teeth.
He wore an open Pakistani jacket over a full-length robe but-
toned to the chin, embellished by slippers and an enormous
white turban. Bacary and I removed our shoes and followed
Ghulam Ahmad into his sitting room. Seeing that we were tired
from walking about town under the blazing sun, he went into his
bedroom-office and emerged a few moments later with dirty glass
beer mugs in which he poured us tea. As we sipped the tea, he
brought out a pile of magazines illustrating the Ahmadiyya
movement's activities. There were pictures of Ahmadiyya banquets and committee meetings during the annual convention at
Karachi, Pakistan, showing bearded worthies in huge turbans.

"We are everywhere," said Ghulam Ahmad, pointing to a list
of Ahmadiyya foreign missions. "Japan, Fiji, Argentine, U.S.A.
Only in countries like Afghanistan and Gamal Nasser and the
Russians, where people are narrow minded, do we have trouble.
We have two Islamic colleges in Sierra Leone, two in Ghana
and three in Nigeria. The marabouts in Senegal forced the government not to allow us there." He pulled out two photographs

of himself, taken while he read a prayer during the independence celebrations at MacCarthy Square. "Here is the prayer I gave," he said, handing me two badly typed pages. "The Imam of Bathurst only spoke for one minute and a half. He did not even read from the Koran. The people clapped for me, and did not clap for him."

"Do you get along well with the Imam?" I asked.

"Our last man here, he gone to see him three times, and the Imam never came here to visit. I gone to see him once, and he did not come here."

"What about the rest of the marabouts here in Gambia? What do you think of them?"

"These people have no knowledge of Koran as our members of Ahmadiyya have. Only they have beads in their hands, and long robes, and show themselves as scholars. There are many wrong things they believe. They go to the villages and give them some writings and say they are from Koran, and sell them as ju-ju. Many people come to me for ju-ju, but I say 'Go on, go on!' Holy Prophet not use that. When the Angel of Death comes, even if man have many ju-ju, ju-ju be nothing."

When we were through with our tea, Ghulam Ahmad led Bacary and me into his office, a small room containing his desk, bed, and three chairs. Islamic books lay in piles on the floor, on shelves, and in wooden crates marked "Bowbilt Brand Sun Helmets." As we talked, he sent Bacary several times to get books from the shelves. Since Bacary was unable to tell one title from another, he frequently brought the wrong book. The missionary rose each time in a huff to get the book himself, muttering about Bacary's incompetence. Asked what sort of teaching he did, Ghulam Ahmad said, "I teach my people the Koran."

"How do you teach the Koran?"

"I teach them to recite the verses and prayers."

Since Bacary was supposedly one of his better pupils, I asked
him to read to me from the Koran. The thirty-year-old houseboy, who worked at the home of a British official, took the volume and successfully negotiated a few verses in halting arabic.
When I asked him to translate it into English he said, "I can't."
Ghulam Ahmad broke in, saying he had not taught Bacary to
translate yet. I asked Bacary if he could tell me generally what
the passage was about. He could not. The Pakistani broke in
again, this time rather testily, and said that he had taught some
of his followers to recite the entire Koran in six months, while
many students in the local Tijan Koranic schools spent years
plodding through a few pages. "I have one man who spend seventeen years learning only this much of Koran from Tijan marabout," he said, indicating about 100 pages. "I teach him this
much [about 300 pages] in five months."

"But if they don't understand what they are reciting, what is
the value in their learning the Koran?"

"The Koran is the word of Allah. One must know the Koran
to be a good Moslem."

Since he was beginning to get a bit huffy over the distinction
between "recite" and "understand," I dropped the subject. As I
put my shoes back on, out on the terrace, he gave me a small
pamphlet entitled *Why I Believe in Islam*, by Hazrat Mirza
Bashiruddin Mahmud Ahmad Khalifatul Masih II. "Read this,"
said Ghulam Ahmad. "It will answer all your questions." In the
pamphlet, the present leader of the Ahmadiyya sect wrote that
he believed in Islam "because it is the truth, and the truth of a
faith is surely a sufficient reason for believing in it . . . One of
the ways in which we come to believe in God is by studying the
life of a person to whom God has revealed Himself. As by the
grace of God I happen to be one of those people to whom God
has on many occasions and in a supernatural way revealed Him-

self, I stand in need of no further reason for believing in the truth of Islam than that I have experienced the truth of Islam in my own person. For the benefit of people who have had no similar experience, however, I proceed to relate . . ." At this point I stopped reading.

Whatever the reasons for their faith, many of Gambia's Moslems go about their devotions with admirable fervor. Following Islamic law, they forego alcohol, attend Mosque every Friday, and pray five times a day. Before each of the prayer sessions, the most devout wash themselves carefully, an impressive feat in a country in which regular ablutions are rare. At government offices, private shops, peanut fields and the river's edge, work stops as the faithful face Mecca and kneel on their straw prayer mats, fingering their praying beads and chanting, "Lah illah, Mohammedu rasul lullah." — "There is no god except Allah, and Mohammed is his prophet."

The five pillars of Islam are the Declaration of Faith, Prayer, Charity, Fasting during the month of Ramadan, and the Pilgrimage to Mecca. Most Gambian Moslems can fulfill the first four requirements, but only those of considerable wealth can afford to make the trip to Mecca, in Saudi Arabia. The round trip, lasting nearly a month, costs about $700–$800 per person, and some pilgrims bring their wives and children. Each year, about 150 to 200 pilgrims who have saved for years make the trip by chartered planes. Known as the "Hadji," the pilgrimage qualifies them to bear the honorific title of "Alhadji."

Those who can not afford the trip to Mecca save their energy and money for Tobaski, the April feast marking the close of the "Hadj," and the biggest, most joyful Moslem holiday. On this day, the pilgrims at Mecca, the farmers up-river and the Moslems in Bathurst buy cows, sheep, or goats and slaughter them as a sacrifice to Allah. (This practice relates to the Jewish Passover custom of the sacrificial lamb.) For days before Tobaski, the bleating of tethered sheep and goats disturbs Bathurst's normal calm. On the last day before Tobaski, I asked several Gambians around the hotel about the significance of the holiday. Kemo, the itinerant barber, said, "Tomorrow, all men sitting down in prayer ground — women and men, small picken, all. Dey all quiet, looking to North Bank [facing Mecca], waiting for Imam. When Imam come, all men get up an' stan' by. When Imam say, 'Allah Kebaro' all men say 'Allah Kebaro.' "

"What does that mean?"

"You call God to bless you."

Momodou, the ubiquitous seller of leatherwork and wood carvings, said, "Many people from de bush bring many sheep here to sell. Some people use goat — many, many. Some people use cow. Dey kill sheep an' eat 'im. Take half de sheep an' dash him [give it away] for charity. I just buy sheep yesterday — big one, cost seven pound. Tomorrow, you come to my compound, you go chop plenty. Maybe de man side my compound he no get money. I go dash him. Anybody who come to my compound, he want to chop, he eat for free. Like you Christians. You know de Christmas time? Dis be our Christmas."

M'Boge, the young former teacher who works as desk clerk at the hotel, pointed out another facet of the giving of meat. "Each person sends a gift of raw meat to his friends, Moslem dignitaries, and the Imam. Most people give away most of their own animal because they prefer the one they are given rather than the one they kill themselves. Young men like me don't start this killing business, because once you start, it becomes compulsory after that every year. People with two wives normally kill two sheep — one for each wife. The Imam is supposed to kill the first sheep. Anybody who kills a sheep before the Imam, that's not Tobaski — he wastes his sheep. God doesn't start accepting sacrifices until after the Imam kills a sheep. The head of the family normally eats the heart and the liver. The elders of the family eat the rest of the innards. Afterward, the head of the compound uses the animal skin as a prayer mat."

Inside the hotel, at lunch, Minister of Local Government Sherif Dibba, a Moslem, took a more critical view of the To- baski sacrificial feasting. "This slaughtering of animals is one thing that is not in my philosophy. It is very wasteful. All year the people go without enough meat. Then they waste it all in one day. This is something I would like to see changed. I don't think this sort of thing will get anyone to heaven."

Next morning at dawn, children from each compound led their sheep or goats down to the river for a purifying wash. Little boys, shivering, waded into the river with bleating sheep or goats slung across their backs, while others tried to drag the unwilling animals in by their tethers. By seven o'clock, all the sacrificial animals in the city had been bathed and returned to their com- pounds, to await their moment of glory. Later that morning, several thousand Moslem men (the women never seem to take part in Moslem ceremonies), dressed in freshly laundered white robes, tried to push their way into the walled prayer grounds. Many had to spread their straw prayer mats outside the walls, on the sidewalk or the street. Blind or crippled beggars moved briskly about the crowd, rattling their wooden boxes full of shil- lings and six-pence. Two Catholic priests stood on a nearby bal- cony, taking motion pictures. A faulty loudspeaker blared unin- telligible prayers.

Finally the Imam of Bathurst, Alhadji Muhammadou Lamin Bah, began the Tobaski service. As he droned on, reciting from the Koran, a bystander told me, "De Imam, he be very learned in de Moslem business." After many lengthy prayers, the Imam ended the ceremony. Then he walked over to the compound next to the prayer ground and slit the throat of a small sheep. Everyone returned to their own compounds to perform the same function on their own animals. For the rest of the morning, knives flashed in the sun, animals screamed and writhed, and blood gushed out, staining the hot sand.

That evening, a few friends and I joined Alhadji Muhammadou Lamin Bah at his home for Tobaski dinner. After quite a search, we found the house tucked away behind the Half Die Mosque, off Cameron Street. The Imam's twelve-year-old son, Tijan, led us up the stairs, and Sherif, Tijan's elder brother, greeted us and went to get his father. The Imam emerged from an inner room, in a soiled white robe and bare feet. A tall, bulky man, with graying hair, rheumy eyes and a large hooked nose, the Imam led us into a crowded sitting room, where several of his relatives and children had gathered. One of his wives appeared with a platter of heavily peppered lamb, potatoes and beans, and a large bowl of "chereh" — corn meal with cassava, cabbage, beans, peppers and a fiery hot sauce. We sat around a low table scooping the food from the communal bowls and putting out the fire with water.

Seeing all the children gathered, I asked the Imam how many he had. A lawyer named Drameh, who serves as his assistant, translated my question into Woloff, although the Imam understands English fairly well. The Imam would not answer my question about the number of his children. "He reserves that to himself," said lawyer Drameh. Asked how many wives he had, the Imam answered himself: "I have three in Bathurst and one in Dakar. Two live here in my compound and one lives in my father's compound."

Alhadji Lamin Bah had recently returned from a trip abroad, and was anxious to tell about it. "I been to England," he said. "I know England all — Exeter, Manchester, Leeds. I stay ten days in Birmingham. I was guest of Lord Mayor of Liverpool, and I have lunch with Archbishop of Canterbury." He passed around some photographs of his trip, including one showing him looking at insect models in a Liverpool museum. "I have also been to Lagos to a conference of Imams. Last year I went to Mecca."

Noticing that he wore a large leather ju-ju, I asked the Imam how he had come by it. "I get him from big marabout in Senegal," he said. "If there is something you fear, he can make you ju-ju that will make you all right. This not ju-ju as you know them — not like those they make up-river here. This protect you from knife and snake."

At forty-five, Lamin Bah claims to be the youngest Imam in Bathurst's history, and is the fourth generation of his family to hold the position. When he was a young boy, his father sent him off to a Koranic school in Senegal to train to be a marabout. There he spent twenty years studying the Koran and Islamic law.

"How is a new Imam chosen?" I asked.

"To be Imam you must know the Koran thoroughly. You must be free of all bad habits. The Council of Moslem elders in Bathurst selects each new Imam. Your birth is the most important thing. If you are descendant of a slave, you are out of it. You must also have certain qualities to be selected. I have all these qualities."

# 13

## STUDENTS AND POLITICIANS

ON PAPER, Gambia's educational system is fairly impressive for a small, underdeveloped country. The government operates more than fifty primary schools with an enrollment of about 10,000. These figures, however, do not tell the whole story, particularly for the schools up-river. Only one-tenth of the teachers in the primary schools completed high school themselves, and they conduct classes in English, a language with which few of them are on intimate terms. This makes things difficult for the students, for whom English is virtually a foreign tongue. Because of such difficulties, attendance is a sometime thing. Students stay home for weeks at a time to help out in the fields or around the home. They drift cheerfully in and out of school, depending on whether village life or the classroom is more diverting on any particular day. There are no truant officers. Because of such problems, some up-river primary schools have been shut down for what the Education Department refers to as "lack of support."

Obstacles to education abound in the home as well as the classroom. Up-river, none of the students learning to read and write can get assistance from their illiterate parents, and they almost never see books and magazines. In the towns and in Bathurst, there are other problems. According to one observer, "No-where in the world is there an atmosphere so inimical to scholar-ship as that which prevails in the average African home: there is a constant hubbub, lighting is either poor or non-existent, food is sketchy, regular study periods and bed times are unknown." There are few mirrors, magnets, motors or museums to intrigue the mind, and travel is a luxury enjoyed only by the lucky. The "head boy" of a recent graduating class from Gambia High School, for example, had never been outside of Bathurst before 1e left for Oxford.

Those who manage to complete primary school, depending on their success in an exam, can go on to either high school or "sec-ondary modern school," which runs four years and prepares one for minor clerical positions. There are approximately 2,500 stu-dents enrolled in "secondary modern schools," and about 1,000 in "grammar" or high schools. In Bathurst, the Catholic mission runs separate five-year high schools for boys and girls. Gambia High School is the only secondary school offering a relatively complete curriculum and from which one can enter a college or university abroad. The principal and most of the twenty-man staff are British. Virtually all the 450 students are Gambians, since all the British and most of the Lebanese send their children abroad for school.

While graduates of the primary schools can go on to Gambia High School, graduates of high school are in a bit of a bind, for Gambia is one of the only countries in Africa with no form of higher education. Many of the several hundred graduates each year have to settle for menial jobs, and some find none at all. Everyone talks of scholarships, but only a dozen or so of the top graduates of Gambia High School manage to win them. Those who do generally major in history or politics, rather than the fields in which Gambia has more pressing need of specialists.

For this reason, the government has begun to exert pressure on scholarship candidates to study these fields. For several years after they finish or drop out of school, ex-students in search of scholarships approach visiting foreigners on the streets of Bathurst and ask for help. They sit in the British Council Library, pouring over the three-year-old, dog-eared copy of the UNESCO guide to foreign study, and write heart-rending letters to the United States Embassy in Dakar.

When I visited the official in charge of such affairs at the Dakar Embassy, there were several letters from Gambia in his morning mail. "We get ten to twenty of these each week," he said. He pulled out a bulging file marked "Gambia" and handed me a pile of letters. One was addressed to the late President Kennedy: "Dear Sir, My name is Saihou Sumarreh. Sir, I entreat you to grant me a Scholarship to study Civil Engineering either in America or anywhere else (excepting the Communist World)." A letter addressed to the Ambassador told him, "Since I left school two years ago I have been looking out for ways of advance study but *being a poor boy, I found none* . . . The field of studies that I would rather prefer will be medicine. I have a little experience in it for it is my present occupation." In response to a negative reply from the Embassy official, one correspondent wrote back: "Sir: Thank you very much indeed for your most thrilling letter . . ." He told of taking an exam after leaving school, "but I was unfortunate to get a pass. Howbeit, I can assure you that I have a sound knowledge of Secondary education because I have been taught there for at least four years."

Unfortunately, few of the letter-writers are even minimally qualified to pursue college-level studies either in England or the United States. Many have not finished school, and those that have are not well prepared, even in comparison to students of neighboring countries. When a team of examiners from the African Students Program of American Universities (ASPAU) administered the Scholastic Aptitude Test to Gambian scholarship candidates in 1965, the results were discouraging. While in other West African countries enough candidates scored above the minimum grade of 80 to enable ASPAU to select thirty-one Nigerians, fifteen Ghanaians and two Liberians, the highest score in Gambia was 78. Said one of the examiners: "It was a pretty dramatic illustration of the state of Gambia's education system."

While Gambia has no institution of higher learning, it does have a two-year teacher training school generously referred to as Yundum College. Yundum trains teachers for primary schools, and draws its students from those who have finished four or more years of high school, and from practicing but unqualified teachers. About 250 to 300 youths apply to Yundum each year for the sixty openings, although no high school graduates deign to apply. Yundum's students, who range in age from sixteen to twenty-one, receive monthly allowances from the government to cover school expenses and a little spending money. The principal and most of the ten-man staff are British, and only four have university degrees. The College is located about fifteen miles from Bathurst, out near the airport. It consists of a few small classrooms and administration buildings, plus a dozen or so dormitories that formerly served as hen houses for an ill-fated poultry project. A sign at the entrance displays the school motto: *Per Ardua Ad Praemium* — "Through hard work, success."

On my visit to Yundum, I first sat in on an English class for a group of first year students who averaged about seventeen years old. Half of them were from Bathurst and its surrounding area, and the other half were from up-river. Their teacher, a young English girl named Carol Lawson, was assigning three-minute extemporaneous speeches to the students. She asked the first boy, named Kebba, to talk about his recent visit to Yundum Airport. "I had a nice visit with a friend of mine for about ten minutes," said Kebba. "We saw a nice plane coming. When the plane came down we went into the plane and saw all the places of the plane and the engine room."

Miss Lawson asked the next student, Sulayman Cham, to speak about "Grammar." "I am not interested in that subject," said Mr. Cham. After a few moments of awkward silence, a classmate yelled to Miss Lawson, "He's not interested, man. Don't waste our time. Call someone else." She asked another youth to speak on "Hunting," but he replied, "In fact, I can't say anything about hunting."

Hassan Joof, asked to talk about "story-reading," said, "Well, about story-reading, you have different types of stories and story-reading. Well, you see, you have these novels. It's very difficult to understand novels. They are speaking slangs, and that is very difficult."

Francis Wilson, speaking on "My Situation at Yundum College," said, "Well now, to say about my situation at Yundum College, I have to say you all know there are some difficulties I have to face. There are worries, and exams. These exams, and all these things, they frighten me, but success came my way."

A classmate broke in, "I don't think these exams are fair. You know, some people are not good on exams. The only fair way is to pass everybody."

My next stop was a history class of Yundum seniors, who joined me in a free-wheeling discussion. With a rare opportunity to talk to a foreigner, they launched a barrage of questions: "What are your impressions of Gambia? . . . How do you compare Gambians and Americans? . . . Why are the Americans fighting in Vietnam? . . . Compare Prime Minister Jawara and President Johnson . . . Why do Americans trade with

South Africa? . . . What do you think about what the British have done to us?" When I had a chance, I asked them what they thought about Gambia's development as an independent nation. One student replied, "The government is doing very little to develop the country. They are not taking an active part in African unity. Most of them are just sleeping or filling their pockets. All those fine houses at Box Bar are going to the Ministers. The Opposition is not doing anything. Gambian politics just means doing business."

A second student said, "The majority of our people are illiterate, and don't know what independence means. The leaders don't explain what it means to them. They only tell them to work harder."

"The government is very selfish to youths," said another classmate. "Some people here should have scholarships to study abroad. All the money that goes to these expatriates should go to students for scholarships."

When I asked how many of them planned to go into teaching, only a few raised their hands. The rest talked vaguely of getting scholarships, working for the government, or "going into politics." One said he would go into teaching "only if there is an improvement in the educational system." Another said he wanted to be a soldier. Asked why he came to Yundum College if he wanted to be a soldier, he said that he had been unable to get a job, and Yundum's government allowance at least supplied him with money.

After classes, I dropped in on a British faculty member, and told him about the students' comments on independence. "All our students here are politicians," he said. "They write and speak much better about politics than about their class work. Very few of them do much studying. They have no respect for their books. You should see what they do to the ones in the library."

"Why do you think they aren't interested in studying?"

"It's a question of morale, partly. You see, they have no determination. They look at the teachers working in the schools now, and get discouraged. Most of the primary school teachers are unqualified. Some are rejects from Yundum College, but the government needs teachers so badly that they'll hire almost anyone."

"Isn't Yundum having some effect on the standard of teaching?"

"Oh, I suppose so. Whatever these students are — and they're a bolshie lot — they're better than what's out there now. But the program is expanding so fast that the standards will have to lower. There's tremendous pressure here at Yundum to pass almost everyone because they're needed so badly. But if you don't keep up the standards, the classification 'qualified' won't mean anything. If there was a pool of qualified students available for Yundum College, we could raise the standards here. Hopefully, as Gambia High School and other secondary school graduates begin to realize there aren't enough government jobs to go around, they'll begin to think about teaching."

*

It is true that most Gambian students are "politicians," but if political discourse among Gambia's leaders rarely goes beyond the most general consideration of the nation's problems, political dialogue among educated Gambian youths rarely descends to even the national level. Concerned, though ill-informed, mainly about events on the world scene, they are more knowledgeable about racial policies in Mississippi than tribal policies up-river; more aroused by a successful moon shot than an increase in the peanut crop. Throughout Africa, the situation is the same. At youth rallies, leaders argue at great length and emotion to hammer out their stands on various world issues, ignoring the more pressing if prosaic problems of development at home. They denounce colonialism with more vehemence than their elders who experienced it, and chafe at their own inability to prevent what they consider the neo-colonialism of independence.

Though they constitute the most vocal segment of the African public, these young students, labor leaders and government workers have comparatively little influence on government policy. Many are not old enough to vote; those who are are vastly outnumbered by illiterate villagers; and those who have entered government service have not yet risen to positions of prominence. Because opportunities for rapid advancement in government are no longer as limitless as they were just a few years ago, today's young civil servants can only foresee a slow unglamorous climb — a prospect they face with ill-concealed impatience. Young clerks with degrees from Paris or London resent less-educated superiors fortunate enough to have climbed when the climbing was quicker. Perhaps because of their inability to influence government policy, their attacks on it are all the more vehement. They give vent to their often uninformed or misdirected enthusiasm in poorly mimeographed bulletins and manifestos, and at disorderly political gatherings. Though few of them have ever worked with their hands, or have any desire to do so, they speak constantly about "the working class." Despite their feverish desire to study or travel in London or Paris or the United States, they repeatedly denounce the "imperialist culture" they expect to encounter there.

By dint of hasty readings in Marxist literature and world history, they have acquired an impressively awkward political vocabulary of little relevance to Africa. In heated discussions and impassioned speeches, they stumble over misunderstood slogans and try on various exotic and conflicting ideologies like ill-fitting suits. They devote so much conversational energy to such questions as "Can democracy live in the shadow of one-class domination?" that they rarely have time or energy left for questions of local economics.

One evening in April, Bathurst students held a meeting to debate "Whether democracy is the best system of government for Africa." The sponsor of the debate was something called BESECO — the Board for Emerging Social, Educational and Cultural Organizations, made up of representatives from three Bathurst student groups: The Raylets, the Inseparable Teenagers and the Black Born Rovers. Baboucar Foon, BESECO's sixteen-year-old "Organizing Secretary," told me, "It was I who brought these youth groups together, because independence was fast approaching, and we thought it necessary to come together." The site of the meeting was the British Council Library, where rows of folding canvas chairs were set up in the main reading room beneath British Information Service posters of the English countryside. The audience was made up mostly of high school students from thirteen to seventeen, with a scattering of adults. Most of the students smoked, wore dark sunglasses, and INDE-PENDENCE buttons.

A Gambia Workers Union youth leader named Amadou Bah, serving as moderator, opened the meeting by explaining that everyone should pay attention to the evening's debate because democracy "is a subject that is very important." He then introduced the first speaker, Moussa Gaye, a young man in a bright yellow polo shirt. Mr. Gaye opened the debate with a fiery attack on democracy. "I address you tonight as a true African nationalist, not a political marionette. For us Africans, democracy has been a system of government given to us by our colonial masters. But what the white man instituted in Africa is not good government or democracy. [Applause] Democracy in Africa has meant exploitation of man by man — the rich getting richer and the poor getting poorer.

"We are not saying democracy is not a good system of government. It is just not the best system. We feel that the best form of government for Africa is a synthesis of many forms." Mr. Gaye did not specify the components of such a synthesis. He claimed that "revolutionary changes are going on in the world today," and that something called "evolutionary socialism" was the form of government best designed to meet them. In conclusion, Mr. Gaye stated: "It is only under democracy that workers have no status in society." He called for a "dictatorship of the proletariat," drawing cheers of "Hear! Hear!" from several union officials in the audience.

The second speaker of the evening was Cherno Joof, who led off the defense of democracy. Mr. Joof began his discourse with some background information that sounded as if he had been hastily studying the encyclopedia that afternoon. "Socialism and capitalism are not forms of government. They are policies. There are only two forms of government — communism and democracy. Communism means the state can take over everything owned by the individuals. But if a man is poor, and wants to be rich, can the government make him rich? Let him work as the rich man did and he will get rich too. Democracy is the form of government based on self-rule, equal rights and equal opportunity. There are three kinds of democracy — parliamentary, representative, and — I think — direct democracy. African leaders are running away from democracy today because they are afraid of losing their jobs. Many of them are useless and incompetent." Mr. Joof ended by urging, "Let us make our own form of African democracy," but did not specify what such a system of government would entail.

By the time Abdoulaye Loum, the second anti-democracy speaker, rose, the hall had filled with nearly 100 youths who responded enthusiastically, if indiscriminately, to each oratorical sally. Like the audience at meetings of Parliament, they laughed when speakers made serious points and applauded before the points were made. They seemed to appreciate the debate more as a general entertainment than as a political dialogue. When asked what a speaker had just said, one wildly applauding youth sitting next to me replied happily, "I don't know."

Mr. Loum, wearing a blue Moslem robe, began by noting that "mankind has never succeeded in governing by rational agreement. Rule by the people means anarchy. Aristotle placed democracy among the lowest forms of government. It lends itself to disorder. Democracy is only to suit the governing classes, and to gratify their personal desires. Democracy goes hand in hand with capitalism. It draws on the proletariat for its means of life. The capitalist class is rolling in wealth based on the labor of workers and extortions from the working class."

Recommending socialism, Mr. Loum said it is "a movement aimed at a classless society. Its historic mission is to bring class society to an end. It is a movement of the working class who are our fathers." Though urging his listeners to adopt socialism, Mr. Loum warned that it would be "foolish to Westernize ourselves completely. We should use the traditions we have had for centuries." He did not say what these traditions were.

The next speaker, Samba Faye, seemed to be a favorite with the audience, judging by the applause that greeted him when he rose to defend democracy. "Africa is the land of rising people," said Mr. Faye, "but those on the other side of the table would like to take us back to Communist style practiced in Russia today. [The audience broke into wild applause, either because it favored or opposed such a move.] Dictatorship is not the desire of Africans today. It is a barrier to African unity. Ladies and gentlemen, as Africans you should not be instigated by these people out of your principles. For democracy is a state of mind, the operation of the majority's will. Any government outside of democratic principles will eventually bring you to dictatorship."

After the last two speakers had offered their opposing views of democracy, the moderator opened the meeting to questions from the audience. Many spoke, but few asked questions. A young man in a Moslem robe and dark sunglasses stood up and proceeded to read a long prepared speech of his own: "Mr. Chairman, what kind of democracy are we talking about — parliamentary, direct, representative, economic or social? [Laughter and applause] Mr. Chairman, what kind of government do they recommend for our beloved African states — Jacobinism, Communism, Socialism?" [Wild laughter]

A young man wearing a cowboy shirt, Levis and dark blue sunglasses said, "Do you want to tell me that the democratic states of Africa have been strengthened by democracy? Democracy is an alien system forced upon us by our colonial masters. Most democratic nations in the world do not have these freedoms you talk about. We must formulate our own system of government for ourselves. We must change the system of government completely to form a united Africa." The young man sat down without outlining the nature of this new system of government.

The next "question" came from a lad named Senghore, who criticized the speakers at length. "If democracy is not suitable, what is? Do not tell us what is not good for Africa. Tell us what *is*." Mr. Senghore claimed the audience was disappointed with the speakers because they had "abused the topic. It is one thing to speak sense. It's another to speak something which does not make sense. If it does not make sense, it is nonsense."

A Fourth Former at St. Augustine's school said that "the wind of change is blowing over Africa and smashing the yoke of British imperialism. My brothers, democracy was brought to Africa by our white masters to divide us into Black Africa, White Africa, Tropical Africa, et cetera. Now we are in the decade of African socialism. Socialism does not necessarily lead to Communism. There are democratic socialism, communist socialism, Christian socialism, African socialism." In conclusion, the speaker misquoted Karl Marx: "Democracy is the opium of the people."

From this point on, the meeting grew increasingly disorganized, with questions or proclamations coming at random from the floor. One youth defended democracy, saying, "Any government can get up and practice any kind of nonsense and call it democracy. If real principles of democracy are not abused, democracy is the best form of government for Africa."

Across the hall, another student jumped up to dispute the point, stating that democracy was "a political football introduced into Africa by imperialists."

An old man yelled through a window: "We should join together the virtues of both democracy and communism, and merge them into a new form for the emerging states of Africa."

When another gentleman criticized democracy, a fellow behind him said, "According to the last speaker, I believe he is nowhere. So let's just leave him in the air."

A young Police Department detective rose and said, "Democracy has failed in Africa because African heads of state have failed to apply its principles. [Laughter] These critics of democracy are just trying to cajole you. Without democracy there will be no happiness in the world."

An older man in the back of the hall said, "If you study democracy, it is very vague. All governments claim to be practicing it, but whether they are really practicing it, well God only knows. Democracy has failed in Africa and everybody knows about it. Democracy is just corruption and useless and hopeless government. Most countries who are practicing it are simply filling their own pockets. It is just horrible. What is socialism? It is very good. It is sharing everything. So my brothers, let us not speak sentiments. Let us come to conclusions."

After an hour or so of random discussion from the floor, the moderator called upon the chief debaters from both sides for their final statements. When they had spoken, he called for a vote from the audience. The issue was definitely democracy, rather than the effectiveness of either debating team. Voting by a show of hands, the audience rejected democracy 37 to 33. When someone suggested recording the many abstentions, Mr. Bah refused. "Do we need abstentions? These are just people who do not have the power to make a decision."

# 14

## PARLIAMENT

"SPEAKAH!" The audience rose as A. Sam Jack, Speaker of the House, lumbered past the long mahogany table, up onto the blue felt dais, and stood before his maroon-draped throne. Mr. Jack resembled a rotund Sonny Liston. His baleful visage hidden behind blue sunglasses, the burly Gambian wore the Speaker's black robe and three-cornered hat. Following him came the clerk, and a khaki-uniformed sergeant at arms, bearing the three-foot golden mace. The mace represents the British crown, under whose royal authority Gambia, as a constitutional monarchy, conducts its affairs of state. A similar instrument was recently used by an irate Nigerian legislator to enforce his views on selected members of the Opposition.

Because the House meets only three or four times a year, for two- or three-day sessions, Gambians look forward to each meeting as a dramatic highlight of the year. Because they have few other official duties, the Members of Parliament also enjoy the sessions. Such pleasure is important because they receive only $1,344 as their salary for the year. (Senegalese *deputees* earn a more respectable $10,000.) Considering that Gambian M.P.'s normally meet for a total of only ten to fifteen days a year, and that the average Gambian farmer earns less than one-tenth as much, they are paid fairly well. Of the thirty-two elected Members, seven are Ministers and four are "Parliamentary Secretaries," or assistants to the Ministers. Both positions are full time jobs. Most other M.P.'s from Bathurst hold regular jobs in the city, while those from up-river are generally petty traders, or operate taxis, or raise peanuts.

Gambia's legislature meets in the ballroom of the former Bathurst Club, a low, one-story cement building which the government purchased because it was the only suitable edifice available. Despite Bathurst's severe shortage of public buildings, it is only used for the sessions of Parliament and occasional conferences — a total of perhaps twenty days a year. Next door to the House are the Bathurst Club's two tennis courts, where play is curtailed during each session. Gambians attending the meetings park their black Raleigh bicycles against the tennis court fence.

Twenty minutes before this steaming June session began, the hall was filled with Akus in their Sunday best, and other Bathurst citizenry in embroidered Moslem robes that created a blaze of indigo, lemon, violet and tangerine. Headgear ranged from turbans to skull caps and fezzes. Some youthful onlookers were less formally attired in open polo shirts or T-shirts. British advisers huddled behind their respective Ministers in a reserved section, along with a few wives and guests of officials. Mrs. Jawara, Mrs. Sisay (Finance) and Mrs. Dibba (Local Government) sat together, resplendent in bright sequined gowns and fashionable wigs from Dakar. Mrs. Sisay wore flashing gold baubles on her ears, neck and fingers. On the walls hung pictures of Queen Elizabeth and of several Westminster coronations.

The first business of the House was "Questions." These are submitted to the relevant Ministries some time before the session, and are printed for the session with the Ministers' answers, often written by the British advisers. This system allows Members to get the beefs of particular constituents on the record, and allows the Ministers to give presumably considered and detailed replies, occasionally sprinkled with heavy wit. The first Question of this session came from Mr. Kalilou Singhateh, of Lower Baddibu, who objected to an article in *Newsweek* about Gambia's independence. He wished to know "what action, if any," the government planned to take against the still-resident correspondent. (There had been rumors about deportation.) The Prime Minister answered that he had discussed the article with the correspondent, and that in view of his apology for any displeasure caused, the Government did not "consider that any useful purpose would be served by pursuing the matter further." This did not satisfy Mr. Singhateh. He demanded that the correspondent be "immigrated."

Mr. Howsoon Ousman Semega-Janneh, Member for Serrekunda, asked the Minister of Education, Paul Baldeh, what steps the government was taking to provide transportation for schoolchildren coming to Bathurst from the outlying areas. Mr. Baldeh replied that the government had made an unsuccessful application to UNICEF for help on this problem, and while the search continued, the government had decided to authorize the use of Public Works Department trucks for this purpose. After Questions, the administration offered several technical motions such as "the suspension of standing orders 72(2) and (6)," which passed in a general air of incomprehension. Various Ministers "laid papers" reporting the activities of their various departments. Two overhead fans turned slowly in a vain attempt to combat the afternoon's sticky heat. Many of the audience fanned themselves with the mimeographed programs.

Prime Minister Jawara, wearing a white and baby-blue checked Moslem robe, white cap and white plastic slippers, rose to offer the most important resolution of this session: "Be it resolved, that subject to the outcome of a national referendum, The Gambia should become a Republic within the Commonwealth on the first anniversary of the country's Independence, the 18th of February, 1966." This resolution came as no surprise, for it had been discussed publicly for several weeks prior to this session. Nor was it unusual. Nearly all former African colonies have become republics since independence, governed by a President alone, or, as in Nigeria and the Congo, both a President and a Prime Minister (Premier). Under the proposed republic, Mr. Jawara would assume the Presidency, combining his present political powers as Prime Minister with the ceremonial powers of the Governor-General. By changing from a monarchy to a republic, Gambia would no longer recognize Elizabeth as its Queen, and therefore her representative, the Governor-General, would withdraw. When Gambia attained self-government in 1963, Governor-General Paul's authority became largely nominal. Since independence it has become almost completely so. While Sir John, as head of state, theoretically makes all major government decisions "upon the advice of the Prime Minister," it is the Prime Minister who actually rules, with very occasional advice from the Governor-General. When foreign dignitaries arrive, however, Sir John, as head of state, meets them first. These differences between appearance and reality rankle the breasts of fervent Gambian nationalists. Their mutterings have become increasingly audible at state functions, where the dashing Sir John frequently upstages the Prime Minister. They also resent Sir John Paul's $11,480 salary and his palatial residence, Government House, both of which dwarf those of the P.M. Lately, their resentment has led to chalked recommendations on the streets near Government House: JOHN PAUL MUST GO.

In stating his reasons for changing to a republic, Mr. Jawara emphasized the issue of authority. He pointed out that Gambians traditionally vest both ceremonial and real power in the same person. "The division between real authority and formal authority is not easily understood. The institutions of government must be able to be understood by the people. To us in Africa, honor and respect are accorded to a chief, monarch or president, not because of symbolism, but because of the authority and responsibility that he holds." Mr. Jawara also mentioned that it was embarrassing for him, during state visits to Senegal and other African neighbors, to be placed by protocol on a lower level than their presidents.

Debate on the issue began with a spiritless attack by the Opposition. UP leader P. S. N'Jie pointed out that the country had "decided on a monarchy after two years of discussions. Why should we suddenly change now, a few months after becoming one?" He suggested that Prime Minister Jawara was motivated by "misguided ambition." He had no doubt that the people of Gambia would reject the motion in a referendum, and thanked the P.M. for this opportunity to test the administration's prestige. Mr. N'Jie felt that the idea of a republic was "premature," since "the philosophy of the people is not yet in line with it."

Young Momodou Cham, another UP man, said that despite what everyone felt about Mr. Jawara, you could never tell whether a Prime Minister, upon becoming President, "will become a different kind of person." Howsoon Janneh, a staunch administration supporter, assured the audience that "everyone in the Gambia will vote 'yes' for this referendum, absolutely everyone." He said that the government should "strike while the iron is red," and that "haste makes waste." Another PPP Member said that "if all the other countries in Africa are republics, we should be a republic too." This brought cheers from the audience. Hulking former Minister of Agriculture Musa Darbo also spoke in favor of the motion, citing a blunt political axiom: "It is use-

less to be ruler when you don't have hundred per cent power."
Nominated Member M. D. Sallah, former principal of Armitage
School at Georgetown, said, "There is no one here who knows
the Prime Minister as well as I do. I know that he will not misuse this power. We have just emerged from a long period of
colonial domination. We are still a backward country, and we
have much to do. We will never get things going under the present system of government, not for hundreds of years. We need
this system to allow the Prime Minister to start moving ahead."
(The language of the New Frontier has caught on quickly
among African statesmen.)

When everyone had said his piece on the republic issue, the
Speaker called for a voice vote on the motion. All those in favor
said "Aye," and all those opposed sat silently with sour expressions. The House then adjourned for the evening.

Like Mr. Sallah, many Gambian public officials and private
citizens assume the country's lack of progress is due to the form
of its government, rather than its appalling lack of natural and
human resources. In 1963, public speeches forecast that with
self-government would come a new age of prosperity. It didn't.
In the fall of 1964, Members of the House claimed that once
they had thrown off the shackles of colonialism and gained independence, the country would begin to prosper. It didn't. Now
some officials feel the reason nothing is happening is that the
country is still not "really independent." Once Gambia becomes
a republic, they feel, things will really start to move. This fallacy
has a discouraging effect, for as the inadequacy of each change
becomes evident, a period of disillusion follows. The dissatisfied
waste their energies on the changing of forms, instead of such
concrete problems as agricultural development.

Next morning at 9:00, the House reconvened as a Committee
of Supply to consider departmental requests for additional funds.

In a budget speech, Finance Minister Sherif Sisay informed the
House that due to some clerical errors in previous reports, the
budget deficit would be $660,800, rather than $336,000. This
news drew some grousing from Members, but no questions. The
first item up for approval was the sum of $154,000 to purchase and
alter a building in Kensington for the Gambia High Commission
(embassy) in London. One Member rose in support of the ap-
propriation, stating that last year, as a member of a Gambian
Parliamentary delegation to London, he had been unable to locate the old High Commission building. (It was his first visit to
London.) He felt that Gambia should certainly have a building
everyone could find easily. Supporters of the new building in
Kensington assured him that it was easy to find. The item
passed unanimously.

The next budget request was $140,000 for minting a distinc-
tive Gambian coinage. The coins currently in use are those of
the British West African Currency Board, which is anxious to go
out of business now that its last member, Gambia, is independent. Other items up for House approval included: $39.20 for
additional furniture for Gambia High School; several thousand
pounds for an armored vehicle for the Gambia Field Force;
$11.20 for additional equipment for the Pest Control Laboratory;
$5.60 for protective clothing for Pest Control workers; and $12,-
600 for an accounting machine for the Treasury Department.
The latter item brought mutterings of disbelief from Members
who could not believe so much money was necessary for one machine.

Much of the discussion on these items involved complex
financial terms such as "revotes," "indent liabilities" and "capital funds versus development funds." Members tossed this un-
familiar jargon about with the earnest abandon and appropriate
precision of children at play with new toys. If some of their talk

was confused, this is understandable, since few have had any economic training, and aside from the Ministers, their average educational level is not much beyond primary school. Speaker Jack, a director of S. Madi Ltd. during the 350 days a year that Parliament is not in session, has had extensive financial experience, and showed obvious impatience with his colleagues. After allowing ten minutes or so of generally irrelevant or misinformed debate on each item, he would call for a vote and ram the measure through. Few Members bothered to voice their votes.

During one desultory discussion, a group of British advisers stepped out back for a smoke. One of them recalled that in Kenya, the Colonial administration got so fed up with the M.P.'s inability to handle government and financial details that it organized a course in government affairs for them. They refused to come. Finance adviser Frank Williams, who formerly held the same position in Nigeria, Jamaica and the short-lived West Indies Federation, said, "This is a hangover from Colonial days, when the M.P.'s were allowed to have a whack at the Colonial officials. But these people are totally incapable of launching an attack on government policy. You can't really blame them for not having enough education to cope with these things. That's the fault of the British Colonial system. In Jamaica we had two Rhodes Scholars as Ministers, and the Parliament had some excellent people. Here, it's all an unfortunate historical mistake."

Back in the hall, Members were arguing about the expense of $1,400 for construction of a latrine at the Yellitenda Ferry Terminal. The matter was settled when they learned that this sum was for the entire terminal. Mr. Cham and others protested violently at the sum of $9,800 for consultant fees on proposed improvements at Yundum Airport — "And they haven't even built anything yet?" Mr. Cham was so incensed that he moved to cut the fees down to $840. Debate raged on for about ten minutes until a more knowledgeable Member attempted to mollify Mr. Cham by explaining that the money was a grant from the British government, and had already been spent anyway. This did not mollify Mr. Cham. He broke into the discussion of the next item and asked for an explanation — something the others rarely did. "I am not an expert in accounts, and I think I have a right to be enlightened." He sat down, draped one leg over the arm of his chair, and ignored the forthcoming explanation.

At twenty-seven, Momodou C. Cham is the youngest Member of the House, a great favorite of the audience, and the most articulate Member of the Opposition. While recent legislative sessions have been difficult for the rapidly diminishing United Party in general, they have been particularly turbulent for this slender young former Police Department clerk. Young Cham distinguishes himself in Parliamentary debate by periodically interrupting the proceedings with penetrating irrelevancies and minute points of order. Long-suffering British cabinet advisers often accuse him of purposely delaying the affairs of the House in order to stretch the session out an extra day, and thereby collect another $5.60 per diem — considerably more than they feel he is worth on the open market. When shunted aside by the normally patient Speaker, Mr. Cham is given to violent temper tantrums. So energetically did he conduct himself during one recent session that he was bodily removed from the House — after considerable struggle — and later suspended for the duration of that session. This event appeared as follows in the minutes of the meeting:

> The Honourable M. Cham persistently and unnecessarily interrupted the proceedings of the House during committee, and on several occasions challenged the Chairman's rulings. He also refused to obey the Chairman on several occasions when called to order. In view of the Honourable M. Cham's behavior the Chairman requested him to withdraw from the precincts of the

House. This the Honourable Member did with much reluctance, and the Sergeant-at-Arms had to assist in seeing him out.

*

That evening, Parliament resumed at five o'clock. During the rest of the session, nearly half the audience — and certainly the most attentive half — consisted of high school students. A group of them who publish a mimeographed journal of opinion called *Tonya* (Truth) included a critique of the House in one of their issues. They described the atmosphere as very discouraging, "with some people slowly falling asleep, others going out and coming in, and most of the Members lost in wondering." *Tonya* considered only five of the M.P.'s "dynamic," declaring that most of them were "not fit to be what they are." The students felt that the "root cause" of Parliament's "regrettable atmosphere" lay in the fact that "most of the members are uneducated."

The evening's business began with discussion of several minor bills, including an "Amendment to the Prevention of Damage by Pests Act." This elicited a brief tirade from Momodou Cham, a traditional scourge of the Agriculture Department. "It is high time to do something about the Agriculture Ministry. They have done nothing for twenty years. It should be scrapped. They should get us an insecticide that will rid us of all pests forever."

Agriculture Minister Amang Kanyi replied calmly, "It's quite impossible to make the Gambia an earthly paradise overnight."

Several bills followed, revising acts whose wording had become obsolete with independence. Other bills set quality standards for peanuts, prohibited unofficial or unlicensed use of Gambia's coat of arms, and set procedures for price controls on essential foodstuffs. "This is a nice bill," said Momodou Cham of the latter. A "Continental Shelf Act" brought the coastal waters and ocean floor resources under the laws of Gambia. Mr. Sallah felt that the law was not enough. He proposed that if the country could not afford a man-of-war, it should at least acquire a coastal patrol boat to protect Gambia's offshore rights. "All sorts of things go on out there and we know nothing about it." Mr. J. H. Joof, Member for Bathurst's Half Die ward, said that government should inform the House "as soon as oil or anything else is discovered."

When the Prime Minister rose to read the new "Emergency Powers Act," debate began to heat up. "This government," said the P.M., "although tolerant and liberal, will not stand for any nonsense when it comes to maintaining law and order in the national interest." In view of the increasingly rabid street rallies being held by the Gambia Workers Union, some felt the bill was primarily aimed at controlling it. Lamin M'Boge, whose speech at a GWU rally had led to his dismissal as Deputy Speaker, said the bill was "an insult to the peaceful people of Gambia. This is the most oppressive bill ever brought into this House." The Prime Minister replied that the bill "is a routine matter which allows government to protect its citizens, and is found in any government in the world."

The biggest debate of the evening, lasting much longer than that over the proposed change to a republic, came on a government plan to change Gambia's traditional English custom of driving on the left to conform to surrounding Senegal's custom of driving on the right. First to speak to the motion was Howsoon Janneh, who recalled that such a measure had been suggested and defeated "during colonial days," and wondered why it should be brought up again now. Kalilou Singhateh pointed out that all motor vehicles in Gambia were designed for left side driving, and that a change would increase the number of accidents. He felt that if the change did take place, the government should set a twenty-five-mile-per-hour speed limit during the first six months. "If we don't do this there will be chaos." (Considering the carefree abandon with which most of Gambia's traffic hurtles along its few roads serviceable enough for hurtling, the prospect was indeed awesome.) Momodou Cham opposed the bill, appealing to latent Gambian nationalism with talk of "preserving our own laws and customs." Despite his claim that "since time immemorial Gambians have been driving on the left," he felt that "our drivers have still not assimilated the existing traffic laws." Mr. Sallah, supporting the bill, felt that an initial twenty-five mph speed limit would curb "Gambia's notoriously dangerous drivers." He offered a novel traffic code to punish drivers involved in fatal accidents — "Those who kill should be killed."

"Point of order," broke in Cham. "The Honorable Nominated Member is not a competent driver."

Sallah replied that the Member for Tumana was not qualified to speak, as he "has had several accidents too numerous to mention."

When Sam Jack had quieted them down, Mr. M'Boge spoke in favor of the bill. He suggested that "since Gambia is changing its laws to conform to Senegal's, and since Senegal is rich and Gambia is poor, Senegal should pay for the change." If not, he proposed that Senegal, whose population is ten times larger than Gambia's, should change its laws to conform to those of Gambia. Minister of Works and Communications Andrew Camara, whose Ministry would handle the changeover, rose to defend the bill. "Driving on the right or driving on the left, it's just a matter of convenience." He demonstrated this point by confusing the right and left in his discussion of the change, until it became difficult to tell whether he was supporting or opposing the bill. At 7:30, Prime Minister Jawara rose to end the evening with a

final defense of the bill. "Today, relations between Senegal and
Gambia are much closer. Everyone except those who refuse to
see the light can see this. Gambia is surrounded by the larger
Senegal which drives on the right. We are a small island in the
vast area around us, including Senegal, Mauritania, Mali and
Guinea, where we still drive on the left." He cited as an example
Canada's change from left to right because of its proximity to the
United States. Appealing to African unity, he said, "We must
not seek to isolate ourselves and look inward, but we should seek
to harmonize ourselves with our neighbors."

The following morning the House reconvened as a Committee
of Supply to finish the supplemental appropriations. Things
were late getting started, as Speaker Sam Jack did not appear till
9:45, several Ministers and Members arrived well after the opening, and a half-dozen M.P.'s, including Opposition leader P. S.
N'Jie, did not show up at all. The audience was down to a smat-
tering. While they waited for the meeting to begin, Finance
adviser Williams raced through the London *Times* crossword
puzzle, and Winton Lane, adviser to the P.M., read the *Times
Sunday Magazine*.

Business got off to a roaring start when Howsoon Janneh and
Kalilou Singhateh squabbled over the first item, a $1,260 com-
pensation to the out-going British Audit Director. Their debate concluded when Mr. Janneh forsook logic, and told Mr.
Singhateh to "Sit down!" Alphonso Demba, whose suburban
Bakau constituency includes most of the senior British officials,
broke in to protest the drawing of this sum from the Development Fund. He sat down in a huff when Speaker Jack explained
to him that it was not being drawn from the Development Fund.

The next debate arose over "inducement pay," a bonus paid to
foreign (generally British) officials and technicians who work for
the Gambian government. A traditional Colonial practice, it has

been continued by most ex-colonies. Some Gambians, however, fail to see why a foreigner should receive extra money to come and take a job that might have gone to a Gambian. They also resent the implication that Gambia is some sort of hardship post. Momodou Cham jumped to his feet and exclaimed, "It is high time we considered doing away with inducement pay." When someone informed him that inducement pay was paid by Her Majesty's Government, he replied, "It is high time, if the British government is going to give us money, they should let us decide how we will spend it."

When the Parliamentarians came to a $140 item for an underestimation in the Prime Minister's transport and travel allowance, Cham rose again and demanded to know why the government had underestimated. A. B. N'Jie, Gambia's Foreign Minister, and the most experienced member of the cabinet, attempted an explanation. "The Honorable Member from Tumana should know that at the beginning of the year we make estimates. They are rough estimates. You can never predict exactly." Looking directly at Mr. Cham, he added, "For example, the Government has made provision for allowances for M.P.'s for two days this session, but now it is going on three or more days."

Another item that caused a minor dispute was $280 for Gambia's High Commissioner in London to fly to Geneva to sign the General Agreement on Tariffs & Trade (GATT). Several M.P.'s objected to this, and asked if the $280 was for hotel bills or transportation. They were told it was for both. They then argued over whether hotel rates in Geneva were reasonable. No one asked what GATT was. At one point in the next debate, J. H. Joof demanded irately that the Minister of Works and Communications "explain this." "Explain what?" asked Speaker Jack. Joof didn't know. He mumbled inaudibly for a

few moments, and sat down. Head Chiefs' Member Landing
Sonko, who till then had not said a word, asked if the House was
now discussing bills. Speaker Jack told him the House was discussing appropriations, and would not take up bills until the afternoon session. Chief Sonko nodded, and returned to his silent
reverie. Several other Members sat throughout the entire four
days without saying a word. They laughed nervously at inappro-
priate moments, gazed cheerfully about the hall, walked in and
out, and chatted with friends in the audience. Numakunda
Darbo, who had appeared at Commissioner's court at Basse,
slouched in his chair, peering wide-eyed out of the top of his
robe. Many M.P.'s and a few Ministers who did address the
House spoke so inaudibly or with such poor enunciation that
their remarks were lost on the audience. This did not seem to
bother anyone.

When the House came to approving Economic Adviser David
Percival's $5,880 salary, Cham again objected strenuously. "I
think now that we are independent, we can rely on international groups like the UN and others. This man is not doing
anything. We have plenty of reports — FAO, UN. We don't
need any more reports. We have all been told by the Minister of
Agriculture that our economy is based completely on groundnuts.
It is not that complicated. It must be very simple. Why do we
need an economic adviser with his fabulous salary?" As each department's budget came up for approval, Cham, Janneh or Singhateh brought up petty or irrelevant points which dragged the
morning's work out, and insured another day to this meeting of
Parliament. By the intermission at noon, several of the advisers
had had enough, and went home for lunch. As they left, one of
them sighed, "Ah, democracy. It's a wonderful thing."

That afternoon, the House reached the stage at which M.P.'s
could offer their revisions to any of the bills. Sam Jack, his deep

bass voice by now a weak, grating rasp, went through them, calling for approval of each separate clause in each bill. Mr. Cham,
who had raised many points the previous evening and been told
to save them for this time, was absent. Opposition leader P. S.
N'Jie was absent. No one brought up any of the changes suggested in the previous debates. Despite all their earlier comments,
Members did not offer one revision or cast one negative vote during the entire session on any motion or bill. Their silence was
due to lack of interest and comprehension, rather than any back-
room horse-trading. Were they more learned in or concerned
about matters of finance or law, they might have put up more of a
fight. This condition is not without benefit, however. A great
deal of excellent legislation empowering the administration to
act for the common weal is thus pushed through the House with
uncomprehending approval by the elected representatives of the
people. While this may not be ideal democratic procedure, it
has enabled Mr. Jawara's enlightened and well-advised regime to
build a solid legislative foundation for the country.

On Friday afternoon at 4:00, Parliament met for its final session. This was the "Adjournment Debate," a free-for-all in which
M.P.'s, who rarely stick to the point at issue anyhow, are allowed
to ramble indiscriminately over any aspect of government policy
or local needs that captures their fancy. The hall was hot, sticky
and breezeless. The overhead fans turned slowly. Many of those
wearing suits had taken off their jackets, loosened their ties, and
rolled up their shirt sleeves. Moist handkerchiefs mopped perspiring brows. June in Gambia is neither the time nor the place
for extended legislative debate. The Prime Minister opened the
Adjournment Debate with a brief summary of the highlights of
his recent West African tour. He said his visits had strengthened
the numerous bonds of friendship and historical ties which bind
Gambia to its neighboring countries, and that he had been

warmly received wherever he had gone. He was particularly impressed by Nigeria's ability to weld its fifty-six million diverse
people into a regional grouping that enabled a single federal government to function. This, he felt, should serve as a model for
all Africa. (Nigeria's federal government, plagued by regional
and tribal strife, has begun to show signs of imminent collapse.)

Lamin M'Boge recommended instead a "continental government" for Africa. Regionalism, he said, was regression, and in-
terfered with African unity by breeding neo-colonialism. He also
felt that Gambia should not stand by and wait for other African
nations to take a stand on Rhodesia. It should take a stand *now*.
He criticized Gambia's educational system for being "out of line
with the aspirations of our people." He did not specify what
these aspirations were. He urged the government to bring forth
"sound economic and educational plans," because these were
very important. He offered no suggestions as to the nature of
such plans.

Numakunda Darbo, in his maiden speech of the session, stuck
to specifics in listing the needs of his constituency: Bansang
needed electricity; Bansang needed a second ambulance because
Basse had two; the Georgetown-Basse road needed grading. Michael Baldeh, a former UP Member who had crossed over to the
PPP, rose to offer a shotgun analysis of Gambia's problems.
"Gambianization of the civil service is proceeding too slowly,"
said Mr. Baldeh; he suggested darkly that there was something
"deliberate" about this. He also felt that development works
were progressing too slowly, fisheries should be encouraged, the
Agriculture Department should develop a second crop, the Economic Adviser is "no good," accommodations on the *Lady
Wright* were not good and its lavatories were out of order.

Howsoon Janneh, wearing a new gold-embroidered white robe
and a tall red felt hat, spoke next. After a series of florid intro-

ductory remarks, he praised the Speaker effusively for his work, and promised to have him knighted, but did not say whether he had discussed this matter with the Queen. He praised the independence gifts from United Africa Company, S. Madi Ltd., and the Bank of West Africa, and said that the other firms, particularly the French companies, should have given more.

In his attack on the government, Mr. Janneh moved systematically from one Ministry to the next: "I have finished with the Minister of Finance. Now I will take the Minister of Local Government, Labor and Lands." He urged the Ministry of Finance to increase the size of its Revolving Loan Fund, since "the only way to help this country is to have more money." He hinted that the Gambia Oilseeds Marketing Board was still "under the control of colonial powers." Later, he said that the Minister of Local Government, Labor and Lands "must see what can be done about unemployment. For it is only employment which can help the Gambia." He felt the Ministry of Agriculture should be given more funds, but did not say where these would come from. He felt a second cash crop should be developed. "We know the Minister of Agriculture's fingers are green, but what we want is that his body be green too. The only way to do this is more money."

The volume of Mr. Janneh's tirade awoke P. S. N'Jie, who had arrived late and gone immediately to sleep. He scowled at Janneh. Janneh, oblivious to P. S. N'Jie and anyone else, went on for another twenty minutes. He recommended a government housing scheme, water and electricity for the villages of his district, a new sea wall at Mile Three, free education, higher scholarships for Gambian students studying abroad and a dispensary at Serrekunda. He urged the government to do something about "the crazy women who are sitting in the street at night," and to do something about "fleas and mosquitos. Every night they are tossing in our bed." Mr. Janneh concluded by urging the audience to show greater respect for the dignity of the House.

Musa Darbo proposed a corps of government "griots" (minstrels) "to amuse the Prime Minister and accompany him everywhere in the provinces." Based on his own experience as a Minister, he felt that "most of the expatriate officers are very loyal," and that Gambianization should not be speeded up too rapidly. Seyfu Kebba Jammeh, speaking for the Chiefs, urged the continuance of the institution of chieftancy, and recommended increasing chiefs' salaries so they could "maintain their position." "As the forefathers of this country," he concluded, "I would like to say that we are very pleased with the work the government is doing."

During Momodou Cham's contribution to the Adjournment Debate he voiced distress about the conditions at Royal Victoria Hospital for mothers whose babies are in the children's ward. (In Africa, mothers would not think of leaving a child at the hospital. They stay with them.) "Charity begins at home," said Mr. Cham. "These mothers while waiting for their children have nowhere to sleep — no beds, et cetera. This is not right." He attempted a Biblical quotation, but gave up in the middle, explaining that the "government should not allow them to stay in such filthy conditions." After several minutes of this tirade, Speaker Jack broke in. "The Honorable Member is repeating himself."

Minister of Health J. L. B. Daffeh testily reminded Mr. Cham that the women do not have to stay at the hospital, and took issue with his estimate of the size of the mothers' waiting room. A lengthy brouhaha ensued between the Minister and Cham over whether Cham had said the room was four feet or four yards square.

"Point of order! Point of order!" yelled Momodou Cham. "I

am an elected Member and I do not expect to be insulted by the Minister."

"What is your point of order?" asked Speaker Jack.

"He says that what I said is not true. He is calling me a liar."

"That may be so, but it is not a point of order. You may be seated."

Cham sat down muttering, in a huff; he picked up a copy of the 1962-63 Gambia handbook and pouted intently at it — upside down — during the rest of the Minister of Health's remarks.

When nominated Member Sallah rose to speak, late in the evening, a groan rose from the audience with him, for his endurance in Parliamentary discourse is legendary. He opened with extended references to Sir Alec Douglas Home, Ahmed Ben Bella, Zambia and Kenya before leading up to the fact that it was he, Sallah, who had originally suggested the idea of a republic in a House speech years ago. He spoke at some length about development, progress and independence. "Our attempt to gain independence has not been smooth. At times it has been very rough, but through many conferences and negotiations we have finally achieved it. It is the duty of every one of us, now that we are free, to decide upon a new way of life. We must be enterprising." Sallah began a florid congratulatory address to the two new Head Chiefs' Members, but when he turned to face them he saw that both had left. By now several British advisers were dozing, and even the Speaker and a few Ministers were nodding. Possibly tiring himself, Sallah launched into a final syrupy praise of the Prime Minister, beginning each sentence with "Sir, I must congratulate you . . ." "He's known as the government's griot," whispered an official near me. When Sallah had finished, the Ministers defended their Ministries against some of the criticisms and promised to "look into" others. The hall was now nearly empty. Many of those who had gone out for a stroll or a smoke had gone home to dinner, unsure of how long Sallah might continue.

In his concluding remarks, the Prime Minister promised a general election in a year or so, then returned to the theme of Nigeria's regional government. He noted that Nigeria's Northern Region alone, with thirty million people, was larger than most other countries in Africa, yet it formed part of a single federal government. If this could be repeated in other areas of the continent, he felt, "we should go a long way towards African unity." He urged greater efforts toward the lifting of regional barriers, practical schemes of cooperation, customs unions and common markets. "It is only in this way that African unity will be achieved — not by dreams of overall unity, but by individual African nations trying to get along and cooperate with their neighbors."

# 15

## CP-UP-PPP AND JALLOW

To THOSE who read only the headlines, African politics may seem a topsy-turvy affair, with presidents and generals stepping on and off the stage like figures in a puppet show. This impression is heightened by the similarity of their roles. As each new leader gains power, he tells the nation of the ruin it faced at the hands of his oppressive or corrupt predecessor. He promises to restore order, lead the country into a period of prosperity, and carry out The Will of the People. What the will of the people is, and how they will express it, are problems left to the new leader.

Few outsiders have an accurate idea of "the people" of Black Africa. Though relatively few are naked savages in the style of early *National Geographic*, 80 to 90 per cent are tribal peasant farmers, generally unconcerned about affairs beyond their own villages. They have little knowledge of other countries, and only the vaguest awareness of the existence of their own. Such ignorance and unconcern have nothing to do with their race or color. Many Polynesians, Peruvians, Burmese and Bedouins, and even some Tennessee mountain people live happily in a similar state of intellectual purity, their minds undefiled by speculation on a national or ideological level.

The African tribesman's ignorance is simply a matter of education. His lack of concern for affairs outside his own village is the result of the fact that years of events, decisions and speeches in distant capitals have proved to have little effect on his own existence. Present-day African rulers, like their colonial forebears, see little point in seeking approval for their policies from the largely uninformed and unconcerned populace. They can not or will not spare the time or energy to explain, and they often feel approval is unnecessary. While colonial rulers were abused for such undemocratic efficiency in dealing with subject peoples, few criticize today's African leaders for dealing similarly with their brothers.

Because of this absence of communication between the leaders and the people, and because African rulers traditionally have ruled for life, most of the new leaders have been reluctant to give up their power in the name of democracy. They have found little difficulty in rigging elections in countries still unaccustomed to them, and sometimes they simply forget to hold them. It is not a coincidence that no ruling party in Africa has lost power at the ballot box. As a result, the coup rather than the election has become the customary means of political change. After France's ex-colonies became independent in 1960 and 1961, opposition forces carried out or attempted more than a dozen coups in the next two years. In 1964, former British East Africa erupted with revolts in Zanzibar, Uganda, Kenya and Tanganyika. Since then, military leaders have seized power in the Congo, Dahomey, Central African Republic, Upper Volta, Nigeria and Ghana. In 1966–67, Uganda, Burundi and tiny Lesotho (formerly Basutoland) also underwent changes of leadership without benefit of due process. With such a record, it is understandable if today's leaders rest uneasy.

One reason why democracy has had trouble catching on in Africa is that no country came to independence with well-formed national political parties. Hastily formed and loosely organized groups in the cities had no time to establish political traditions or contacts at the village level. Since independence, they have had to devote much of their energies to merely remaining in existence. In most cases, the party that came to power upon independence has remained there. Leaders change, but the party stays. The price of what stability there is has been the virtual disappearance of opposition. Most of the countries in Black Africa not under military rule are now one-party states, and the rest are rapidly approaching a similar condition. Nearly every newspaper reflects or is directly controlled by government policy. Political debate, absent from assemblies and parliaments, has been forced into back rooms and the streets.

Gambia is different, because it had a later start than the rest of the continent, and because Gambians take their politics, like everything else, in a more relaxed manner. Until 1960, only residents of Bathurst and the surrounding Kombo St. Mary voted for members of the Legislative Council which "advised" the Governor, and politics was therefore limited to the capital. Four parties competed then, of which only two — the United Party and the Congress Party — have any real power today.

Just before the franchise was extended to the provinces, or "Protectorate," in 1960, a group of young up-river Gambians formed the Protectorate Peoples Party, and chose as its leader a young Glasgow-educated veterinary officer named David Jawara. Changing its name later to the Peoples Progressive Party, the PPP campaigned on a platform of opposition to the traditional dominance of Bathurst political parties. The PPP startled the older politicians in the capital by forming the first really country-wide organization, with subscriptions, cards, and even uniforms. All this work paid off. The PPP won ten of the nineteen elected seats in 1960, and increased its majority at each subsequent election. By 1963, prior to self-government, the race had narrowed down to the United Party, which controlled most of Bathurst, and the PPP, which controlled most of the provinces. Since the voters in the provinces outnumber those of the capital and surrounding area by nearly five to one, the PPP has become the overwhelmingly dominant party.

The PPP's present power doesn't seem to be quite enough to satisfy the Party's leaders, however, for they continue to apply pressure to the diminishing opposition. Upon independence, the PPP's newspaper, *The New Gambia*, stated that "all politicians of all tendencies should rally round the Government of the masses, the PPP, so that the country's concerted efforts will bear golden fruits. We must not allow factions to undermine the real issues of the day." A few weeks later, a reader sent this poem to the editors:

> *How a minority*
> *Reaching majority*
> *Seizing authority*
> *Hates a minority.*

Despite such inter-party bickering, the PPP, UP, and Congress Party continue to conduct their affairs in an atmosphere of British gentility and Rotarian good-fellowship. At their regular monthly meetings, party members deliver discourses on various public issues. Debate is often rather turgid, for members of party "political bureaus" devote so much energy to lofty notions like "revolutionary socialism," "Pan-Africanism" and "neo-colonialist capitalism" that there is often little time left for the more prosaic domestic issues.

In addition to party meetings, there are also dances and other festivities. *The New Gambia* launched a fund-raising campaign shortly after independence with this announcement:

STOP PRESS: All Party Members are informed that Party Badges are available at the PPP National Bureau at 73A Leman Street at a very reasonable price of two shillings each. It is designed in a way that the photo of our renowned Prime Minister is in the center with the initials of the Party. Secure one immediately and keep it to show that you are one of those in the Party that brought or took Gambia to INDEPENDENCE. BRAVO BRAVO!!

I made my first visit to the PPP's National Bureau with an official from the United States Embassy in Dakar who was bringing a donation of paperback books for the Party's library. He had come upon the written request of Abdullah M'Backe N'Jie, who had signed himself "Administrative Secretary of the PPP's Political Bureau." (He is also a reporter for *The New Gambia.*) We had difficulty locating Mr. N'Jie because he had recently converted from the Anglican to the Moslem faith, and was still commonly known as Francis N'Jie. After a lengthy search, we found the Party Headquarters on Leman Street, sharing an old stucco building with an unused Triumph garage. Two Gambians slouched against the counter in the outer room, chewing kola nuts. When we asked if Mr. N'Jie was in, one of them said sharply, "First say good morning!" We said "Good Morning," and asked again for Mr. N'Jie.

"He's out. Maybe later."

We came back an hour later and found Mr. N'Jie, a mousy young man in a dirty blue Moslem robe and dark sunglasses which he wore inside the office. When we had carried the cartons of books into the office, the man from the Embassy asked where the library was. Mr. N'Jie faltered for a moment, shuffled his feet, and explained, "Well, you see, there is no library just yet. We're just getting it started." He then led us into the inner conference room, where the three of us sat around an immense oval table. After exchanging pleasantries, Mr. N'Jie asked whether the Embassy might also see its way to donating some furniture to Party Headquarters. "What we have here," he said, "is not at all suitable." The American official politely turned him down, and after more pleasantries we left. Months later, when I asked about the books, I was told that shortly after we had left town, Mr. N'Jie had held a book sale at Party Headquarters.

Putting the bite on foreigners is not a practice of the PPP alone. A minor official of the United Party sent the following letter to an American visitor he had met briefly several months before:

> I was speaking to the 1st Secretary to the U.S.S.R. Embassy in Dakar last week Monday . . . He tried to convince me to affiliate my Youth Wing to the Communist World by showing all that can be offered me and my Youth Wing in terms of Motor Vehicles, scholarships etc. but I am not interested in Communism and my Party as a whole for that matter.
>
> After our conversation I was really convinced we need help to continue the good work we have started, but as I am not in for Communism I feel now that I have your address I have an other opportunity to push far these Communist. I therefore would be most grateful if you would introduce my Youth Wing to any organization in U.S.A. that you know or feel will be great help to us.

The most notorious case in recent years involving the use of party funds for private gain came to light when Alasan N'Dure, Propaganda Secretary of the Gambia Congress Party, resigned in protest over alleged misuse of party money by its leader, I. M. Garba-Jahumpa. According to Mr. N'Dure, Jahumpa had squandered, among other sums, a large donation from "an international body" (reportedly Red China). He used what was left as a down payment on a Party vehicle, the rental fees from which he kept. When the Party's Executive Board tried to take over the vehicle, Jahumpa sold it to a Party member. The "international body" also made gifts to the Party of a tape recorder, duplicating machine and public address system. Mr. N'Dure accused Jahumpa of selling the tape recorder and duplicator, and of renting out the P.A. system.

Mr. Jahumpa has also acquired a reputation for borrowing titles. During a trip to Dakar in 1953, as Minister without Portfolio, he told officials there that he was mayor of Bathurst. In 1961, when he was Minister of Agriculture, he introduced himself in Ghana as Gambia's Chief Minister. In 1963, when he was no longer a Member of Parliament, he presented himself to the Colonial Office in London as deputy leader of the Opposition.

Despite Mr. Jahumpa's efforts, the Congress Party has fallen on bad times. It has no seats in Parliament, and two of its four members on the Bathurst City Council recently resigned from the Party. Even the Party's idols have had bad luck. Mr. Jahumpa had always urged Party members to follow the teachings of Algeria's Ahmed Ben Bella and Ghana's Kwame N'Krumah, the foremost exponents of his brand of African socialism, both of whom were recently deposed. Despite the Congress Party's decline, Jahumpa still worries the few American officials assigned to worry about Gambia. He is the only avowedly left-wing political figure of any stature in the country, and his frequent trips to Algiers, Cairo, Moscow and Peking raise eyebrows in Washington. Most Bathurst politicians feel such concern is unwarranted. "Jahumpa is a dead issue," says one of them. "He has no power at all."

To learn what a powerless political leader does about such a state of affairs, I went down to Congress Party Headquarters one morning to visit Mr. Jahumpa. Headquarters is at his home, a small cement building on Hagen Street, with a red and white Party flag flying from the gate post. Inside, I found Mr. Jahumpa in a sitting room furnished with a faded Persian rug, a few wooden chairs, a table, refrigerator, a huge console radio, and dozens of photographs on the walls. Most of these showed Mr. Jahumpa on various ceremonial occasions. There were also fading pictures of Egypt's President Nasser, Kwame N'Krumah and John F. Kennedy.

Ibrimah (Abraham) Momodou (Mohammed) Garba-Jahumpa is a heavy, round man, with a pudgy, light-brown face. Gazing out through thick tortoise shell glasses, he looks like a tired, benign owl. On the morning of my visit he wore a rumpled double-breasted blue suit and chomped on a chewing stick throughout our talk. He rose from his low chair with some effort when I entered. Though only in his mid-fifties, Jahumpa is something of a grand-old-man of Gambian politics. As a teacher at Bathurst's Mohammedan School in the 30's, he had as a student a young Mandinka boy from up-river named David Jawara.

After World War II he concentrated on politics. "The year 1945 was very important in my life. I went to London to take part in the Fifth Pan-African Conference. There I met Doctor N'Krumah, and we became friends up to today. Jomo Kenyatta was there as well. After I returned to Gambia I engaged in politics — organizing, and trying to awaken the political consciousness of the Moslem community of Bathurst. Some friends and I founded the Bathurst Young Moslems Society and entered the first election for a Legislative Council, in 1951. I was elected. I am also the longest-serving member of the Bathurst Town Council — from 1946 till now. In 1959, when we were allowed to elect our own chairman, I became the first Chairman of the Council. I was invested with the chain of office. There it is there, hanging on the wall. For many years I was also Minister

of Agriculture. Then in the 1962 election, when we merged with
the Democratic Party to form the DCA, I lost my seat to the
present UP Member for Half Die — Mr. Joof, the most dormant
Member of the House. He's never said a word in the House since
he was elected."

"Why do you think you lost to Mr. Joof?"

"I lost that election because my own party members sabotaged
me. And also, the UP paid for many of its votes. After the election there was great dissatisfaction spread down to the rank and
file of the DCA, culminating in my resignation. I broke away
and organized the Congress Party. Now we are active in reorgan-
izing and spreading in the provinces, in readiness for the next
general election."

"Does the Congress Party have a national program?"

"Yes. We accuse the PPP of practicing tribalism. They have
been indoctrinated by the colonialists. The government now ap-
points only pro-PPP chiefs. They will only be chiefs if they toe
the PPP line."

"What do you spend most of your time on?"

"Well, since withdrawing from the DCA, I have done a great
deal of traveling. I have been everywhere but America — People's Republic of China, North Korea, Algeria, Ghana, Cairo,
USSR, Czechoslovakia. In 1963 I spent three weeks in Russia. I
was invited by the International Institute of Peace to attend the
World Peace Conference. I was invited to attend the Asian Economics Seminar last summer in North Korea. Then I went on to
Peking. I had been expecting to go to Cairo soon, but I'm afraid
it is not going to materialize. I hope to go to Accra in May for
the Afro-Asian Solidarity Conference."

*

A few blocks away from Mr. Jahumpa's office-home, at 19 Buckle
Steet, is the Headquarters of the United Party, the only signifi-

cant opposition force in the country. Back in what UP leaders like to think of as the "good old days," before the vote was extended to the provinces, the UP was a major power. It still has strong support from the Woloffs in Bathurst and the surrounding Kombo, but there are simply many more Mandinkas up-river than Woloffs in Bathurst. This fact became clear in the 1963 election when the PPP won twenty-seven seats in Parliament, to the UP's seven. Observing this impressive imbalance, three of the seven decided to join the PPP. The PPP's *New Gambia* greeted their move joyfully: "With the withdrawal of Janneh, Jones and Jagana, the United Party is fast sinking and will soon close up." The UP has not closed up, and its leader, Pierre Sarr N'Jie, still looks forward to the day when the UP will once again be the ruling party. His appetite was whetted by a one-year term of office he served as Chief Minister, just prior to self-government. British officials who worked with him at the time are not as anxious as he is to see him back in power. "He's a charming chap," says one of them, "but he's impossible to work with — totally disreputable."

The building on Buckle Street houses the UP Headquarters, Mr. N'Jie's residence, and the offices of N'Jie Brothers, a leading Bathurst law firm. The firm specializes in registering foreign designs, patents and trademarks such as Daimler Benz, Coca-Cola and Planters Punch, at $14 each. The two brothers — Sherif Aidera N'Jie and Ebrimah Dowda N'Jie, an M.P. and former Minister — now handle most of the firm's business, since P.S. is busy with Party affairs, and also because he was disbarred several years ago for misuse of a client's funds. "We could easily have thrown him in jail," says an official involved in the case. "It was a clear-cut case of fraud. But by the time it was settled he was Chief Minister. What could we do? You can't throw the bloody head of government in jail. So we just had him disbarred."

To reach P. S. N'Jie's office, I passed through the firm's offices on the first floor, where several young clerks sat copying legal documents by hand and discussing politics. In the compound out back a rooster and three chickens scratched in the sand beneath the Party's blue Land Rover. The Party leader received me upstairs in an outer room, where several Party regulars sprawled in lounge chairs, and led me into a small room overlooking Buckle Street. He wore a beige linen sport jacket, a red checked shirt and a plaid bow tie. Known as one of the sharpest dressers in Bathurst, he buys most of his clothes on his trips to Paris and London.

Like many Bathurst Woloff's, Pierre Sarr N'Jie is a Catholic, and grew up in a fairly prosperous family. "My father was a trader — a successful trader. He was a nephew of the last king of Saloum, Semu Joof. After school here in Bathurst, he sent me to Kings College at London University. I only stayed there a short time. I was to be a doctor, but I don't like blood. So I moved to Lincoln's Inn, where I studied law. All the N'Jies are lawyers — my brothers, my cousins, we even have a niece studying law in Munich. All the N'Jies are educated, but this man Jawara, he is not educated. He's only got a veterinary diploma. I am much more popular than he is. Did you listen to the crowds at independence? They did not cheer him. They always cheer me. He should never have won the election in nineteen sixty-three. We would have won except for a scallywag of a chief who deserted us."

Asked about a short-lived political "understanding" between the PPP and UP, N'Jie became irate. "You can't have an understanding with a man like that. He never means anything he says. He's a liar. He's a rascal — low born, and low bred. You see, the PPP are all Mandinka people, and Mandinkas only understand money, meat and groundnuts. They are all lazy. Character and honor is meaningless to them."

"Do you include people like the Cabinet Ministers Dibba

and Sissay, when you speak about Mandinkas this way?"

"Dibba and Sissay? They're ignoramuses."

"How about the three United Party M.P.'s who crossed over to the PPP?"

"They're not politicians. They were afraid. They put money before party and the country. You don't get politicians in a backward country like this. A real politician has to be able to wait. He must wait twelve or thirteen years, like the Labour Government did."

"What do you think about the prospect of Gambia becoming a republic, with Mr. Jawara as president?"

"That would be all right for someone born with servants in the house and everything, like I was. But these PPP men are all from the bush. This Jawara is a scallywag. When I was P.M. and I said 'yes,' it meant yes. Not this man. It's the result of coming from a low family — the lowest of the low. His Ministers and M.P.'s are the same. Kah forged checks. Daffeh stole from the District Authority treasury. Famara Wassa Touray served a prison term. Singhateh stole money. When the police issued a warrant for him, he ran away to Sierra Leone. Then he came back and stood for election. I know these things because I am a lawyer."

"What about the rest of the Opposition? Do you feel Mr. Jahumpa and the Congress Party have any future?"

"Jahumpa is dead now, for deceiving the people."

"What do you think of the rumors that he receives support from the Communists?"

"He's not a Communist. People here are not ready for Communism. It's too rough and ready."

"How about M. E. Jallow, the union leader? Could he start a national party?"

"Jallow could never start a party. He is a ruffian, and Gambians are dignified. They don't want a ruffian as P.M. Besides, all the workers are members of the UP. None of these people you mention are important. I'm the only man they're afraid of here."

If the PPP and the administration fear any opposition leader, they conceal it well. With a 28 to 4 majority in the House, they do not have much to worry about. Though nominally head of the Party, Prime Minister Jawara now remains somewhat aloof from Party affairs. He speaks at Party rallies, but leaves much of the organizing to Finance Minister Sherif Sissay, the Party's Secretary-General, and Minister of Local Government Sherif Dibba, the Assistant Secretary-General. Sissay is a competent and extremely hardworking young official who does not care for public discourse or private interviews. This leaves Sherif Dibba as the Party's most frequent spokesman.

Though only twenty-eight, and the youngest member of the Cabinet, Dibba is an effective, articulate speaker, and despite his relative lack of experience, a very influential member of the administration. Observers in Bathurst think Sherif Dibba has an excellent future, and the U. S. State Department must agree, for it recently brought him to the United States for a month of travel on a foreign leadership grant. Born in Sallikeni, in Central Baddibu District, Dibba attended Armitage School in Georgetown and Methodist Boys High School in Bathurst. After three years as a minor clerk with the United Africa Company, he resigned in 1959 to enter politics. "We founded the PPP together," he says, "Jawara, Sissay, myself and Sanjali Bojang. We had to expel Bojang later for certain moves contrary to the discipline of the Party. [He campaigned for the UP.]"

Asked about the role of the Opposition in Gambia, Mr. Dibba replied, "I personally am interested in achieving a true democracy here, and that can not be achieved without the two-party system. But I'm not at all happy with the way the UP carries on. Since they lost at the polls it seems they are not very interested in politics any more. They aren't in the House half the time. I hope that they'll soon fall on their feet again, and play the role of an opposing party, which is to criticize the Government policy and so on."

Several months later, the idea of a two-party democracy no longer seemed to hold Mr. Dibba's fancy. He told a reporter, "It seems that Gambia is turning into a one-party state, as the opposition dies. It seems to be the trend all over Africa. We would not force the case here. It should come naturally."

*

The only significant political force besides the three political parties is the Gambia Workers Union, which passes for the "organized labor" in Gambia.

Relations between government and labor in Gambia have become increasingly strained in recent years. Many Gambians expected that independence would somehow mean jobs for everyone. Not only was the government unable to produce new industries upon independence, but, saddled with new expenses and faced with the prospect of gradually diminishing British aid, it was forced to introduce austerity measures. These came at an awkward time, for like most other new countries in Africa, Gambia came to independence with a rapidly growing pool of unemployed. Many Gambians arrive each month in Bathurst, equipped with the scantiest of educations at up-river primary schools, and are unemployable for all but manual labor. Yet because of their slight education, they now scorn the idea of returning to the provinces to work in the fields. Others, having graduated from secondary schools in Bathurst, are educated but untrained. Unfortunately, the country already has a surfeit of the unskilled and untrained.

The lack of government jobs is far more serious in Africa than it would be in more developed parts of the world, for in Africa the government is by far the largest employer. Nearly two-thirds of Gambia's 10,000-man salaried labor force works for the government. With no expansion in sight for the commercial sector of the economy, this leaves the unemployed in a bind. They continually send letters to commercial employers and government officials begging for jobs with painful urgency. The following letter is typical:

> Sir, Kindly help me for I knows anyone to help me except you. Please uncle, only have sympthy on me as were I am today my father and mother are now very old now and I am their elder son. I have no work and has tried since long to get employment but I could not get. To help me as I have no hoping in anywhere except to you and I hope that Sir you will have Sympthy on me and give to me a help.

The bind became tighter when the government laid off more than 500 laborers in 1964, as part of the austerity program. Labor Minister Dibba defended the administration's move, pointing out that "unemployment is a characteristic of most new countries in Africa today." M. E. Jallow, the leader and driving force of the Gambia Workers Union, does not agree. "We feel the government has a moral responsibility for the destiny of everybody, including finding jobs for them. Therefore we are opposed to the concept of retrenchment as a means toward economizing. I think it's not real economy."

Though he has never publicly offered an alternative solution to Gambia's economic problems, Mr. Jallow's disagreement with government policy is significant, for his Gambia Workers Union is the only effective one in the country. It claims a registered membership of 10,000, which is doubtful, and a dues-paying membership of 3,000 to 4,000, not all of whom actually pay. One reason these figures are questionable is that, despite prodding from the government, the GWU keeps no books. Its income is sufficient to support a full-time staff of thirteen officials. Assessing their work is difficult, because there is little evidence of any. They make speeches, hold rallies, and take occasional trips up-river and to other African capitals. They arrange few wage settlements, have not organized a strike for two years, and are generally considered something of a joke.

Their leader, however, is a different matter. If the GWU has risen to dominance in Gambia, its power is primarily attributable to and held by the aggressive and eloquent Mr. Jallow. In fact, some observers consider him the most powerful man in the country today. Others consider him a threat to the continued stability of the government. A tall, husky Woloff, he has a mercurial personality, and can be charming or obnoxious, depending on his mood. One of the few gifted public speakers in Gambia, he can capture a formal meeting or a street full of screaming workers with equal ease. This ability does not endear him to government officials, who consider him an unstable and ill-mannered ruffian. Their views do not worry Jallow, for he thinks little of most government officials. As Secretary General of the African regional body of the International Confederation of Free Trade Unions (ICFTU), Jallow travels more frequently about Africa and Europe than any member of the administration, and is probably more widely known in Africa than Prime Minister Jawara. He is forever flying off to labor congresses in Nairobi, Kampala, Rome or Brussels. When in Bathurst, he and his colleagues spend much of their time cruising around town like middle-management Mafia in his chauffeur-driven Citroën (a gift from the United States AFL-CIO), or drinking in the lounge of the Atlantic Hotel. They rarely order less than double-shots of brandy, and usually drink them down as though prohibition were imminent.

On my first evening in Gambia, I was chatting with two Englishmen in the Atlantic lounge when Jallow strode in. He walked up unsteadily and said "Hello" in a commanding tone. I looked up, nodded a greeting, and turned back to our conversation. My companions did not even look up. He stood there and said "Hello" again, in a more menacing tone. This time one of the Englishmen told him politely, "Excuse me, we're discussing something at the moment."

"Do not treat me like a dog!" yelled Jallow. "I have been to Liverpool."

We tried politely to get him to wait until we had finished, but he was having none of it. Rather than risk a brawl, we invited him to sit down with us. My friends introduced him to me and told me he was a very important person in Gambia. Jallow nodded. I tried to ask him a few civil questions about his union and local politics, but each time I addressed him he cried out, "Do not talk to me like a dog!"

Several days later, Jallow accosted me unaccountably in the lounge again, and said, "You're American, aren't you? Well, if you've come here with your American ideas, you won't last long. I can have you thrown out of the country next week. I can see to it that you don't get another drink in this hotel. Those boys at the bar are my men. I have been all over America — Chicago, Cleveland, Peoria, San Francisco, everywhere. I know America inside out."

Another time, Jallow was sitting in a corner of the lounge with two of his deputies, feverishly tossing off double brandies. They sang several rousing choruses of "Solidarity Forever," amid much laughing and thumping on the table. The British guests in the lounge stared into their pink gins or looked out the window. Finally, one of the deputies jumped up, raised his glass, and shouted, "Today, Gambia is a small, poor, underdeveloped country that everyone spits on. Next year Gambia will be sovereign of all Africa. After that, the world!" The British guests looked startled. One of them muttered, "Balls!" Jallow and his men rose and cheered the proclamation, threw a few pound notes on the table and marched out, bumping into a few chairs and the door as they left.

*

One June morning about ten o'clock, I went down to the GWU Headquarters to meet Jallow. The office is an unpretentious building at 69 Hagen Street named "Rose Ville," with an open front through which passers-by can observe the activity in the front office. There is generally little to observe. The morning I arrived a half dozen individuals were in this outer room, leaning against the walls or sitting at a bare wooden table, the room's only piece of furniture. Told that Jallow was "back there," I passed through a second room containing a broken typewriter on one table and a mimeograph machine on another, covered with smudged mimeo sheets. In a back room I found Jallow in conference with several members of the union's "executive committee," all talking at once. When I entered, Jallow sent most of them out, leaving only Joof, his first deputy, Loum, his second deputy, and a surly fellow who sat at a desk opening mail and never said a word all morning. The mail was from labor organizations around the world, announcing international congresses or enclosing pamphlets. There were booklets on *Peace, Freedom and Socialism* and *What the Communists Stand For*, plus newsletters from the AFL-CIO, the International Transport Workers Federation, and the Freier Deutscher Gewerkschaftsbund. Jallow sat in a wooden chair, leaning against the wall. When I apologized for breaking up the staff meeting, he said, "I feel disorganized this morning anyway, and don't feel like working."

Momodou Ebrimah Jallow was born in Georgetown, where his father was a minor civil servant. When he was ten, the family moved to Bathurst, where he attended the Catholic secondary school, Saint Augustine's. "As a Joloff, I was badly treated by my schoolmates," he says. "Many of them were Methodist Boys School products, the Akus, and here was a young Joloff trying to come up. But then I took the government entrance exam and came out on top. At 25, Jallow won a scholarship to study agricultural cooperatives in Nigeria, and eventually became Gambia's first Cooperative Officer, in 1954. He went rapidly through a series of government and commercial positions, his speed and mobility the result of frequent altercations with his superiors. He was variously accused of insubordination and corruption, but never incompetence. Jallow refers to most of his former superiors as "bulleys," who were "out to get" him. (This is a form of paranoia common to many of today's African leaders when they refer to their former colonial rulers.)

Drifting into labor problems, he organized a successful strike against the Gambia Construction Company, and spent a year at the International Labour College in Uganda. He led Gambia's first general strike in 1960, gaining a 25 per cent wage increase for all workers. Another general strike the following year paralyzed Bathurst for a few days, and caused riots that required the combined efforts of Gambia's police and Field Force, and a troop flown in from Sierra Leone. Jallow was arrested that time, but the workers got another 10 per cent raise.

"Does the fact that there have not been any major strikes in the past few years mean that the workers are satisfied now?" I asked.

"No," said Jallow, "they are very discontented. The cost of living has risen, and the wages are no longer real wages. They have been eroded by this rise in the cost of commodities. The government started a retrenchment last year, and about six hundred workers were thrown out of jobs. Now there are many hundreds of them out in the streets. They are very unhappy."

"You say the government simply threw these people out of work?"

"Yes, into the streets. We could have called a general strike, but we did nothing then. We could have paralyzed the government, but you see, we didn't want to defeat independence. Now we are independent, so . . ."

"Do you have any ideas about how to expand the economy or create more jobs?"

"No. All I know is that things are wrong — seriously wrong. And if we don't do something about it soon we will live to regret it. We will go back to where we were years ago. We've got to head somewhere."

"Why do you think things are going wrong?"

"Basically it's lack of political leadership. You see, we do not have any hero-worshiping here. Government has always been by discussion. The leaders always had to consult the people, and this feeling is still there in the people. Now this was easy for a village headman, but this business of being a political leader is a different thing. The PPP has the support of the provinces, but Jawara is not the man with the sort of personality which he can put into the people so that they come to see him as a leader. He is no Kwame N'Krumah. He's just a very good stick that nobody notices. He's a very nice man, and a hard worker, but basically a civil servant, not a politician."

"Have you considered starting a Labor Party yourself?"

At this point Loum broke in. "They've been expecting the GWU to turn to politics, but that's what happened to all the old unions, and they died. We decided to make the GWU a reality — make it stand firm as a trade union."

"But we must some day convert into a political body," said Jallow.

Loum and Joof both yelled "No!" and they all argued the point for several minutes in a friendly manner.

"You see, said Jallow, "There is no future for a Labor Party here in Gambia yet. Only ten per cent of the people in the country are paid workers. [The figure is actually about three per cent.] The first thing we must do is get rid of this Parliament. It is a farce. People like me are out. That is the trouble."

*

In May, 1966, the government called the first national election since independence. While in other countries of Black Africa this event has normally been accompanied by bloodshed, disorder or fraud, few feared such results in Gambia. Announcing the elections to the country over Radio Gambia, Prime Minister Jawara said, "In the days ahead there will naturally be increased political activity, but I know that I can count on all of you to go about your affairs in a calm and orderly manner, so that once again The Gambia will have justified its reputation for tolerance, discipline and democracy."

Political campaigns in Gambia would not capture the imagination of American or even British voters, hardened to the saturation of posters, billboards, sound trucks and television. Gambian political parties are limited to Land Rover treks up-river and Radio Gambia. Since each party has only one Land Rover, and the government sets the number of campaign broadcasts — three for the PPP, two for the UP and one for the Congress Party — the country does not get very worked up over elections. Besides, May in Gambia is too hot to get worked up about anything.

Minister of Finance Sherif Sissay, Secretary-General of the PPP, made the first of the fifteen-minute broadcasts in English and Mandinka, defending the administration and discretely criticizing the opposition.

Before the PPP came into the scene in 1959, there were three major political parties: namely the United Party, the Congress, the Democratic Party. And you know just as well as I do that these parties did not serve this country adequately. But as these are either defunct now, or on the verge of so becoming, I do not wish to dwell at any length on them. Suffice it to say, however, that the PPP came at the right moment for the salvation of this country.

Replying in the second broadcast, the UP leader, P. S. N'Jie, urged voters to cast their ballots in the "umbrella green colored box" (the umbrella is the UP's symbol). Mr. N'Jie stated that Sherif Sissay "is not, as you know, correct when he told you on Monday that the PPP have fulfilled all their promises. They have broken every promise made to you."

We all, you and I, know what we have suffered during nearly four years of PPP government — deprivation of all sorts at home, in the fields and farms and at shops and offices. There is hardly a home in The Gambia which has not suffered from one activity or other of the PPP. You may say all this is true, but what do the UP offer? First, freedom from fear to your personal liberty and hunger and shelter. UP's are not jealous and envious. UP's want you to have that which they want for themselves.

In a later broadcast, A. B. N'Jie (no relation to P. S. N'Jie), the Minister of State for External Affairs, issued a warning to those who had not yet climbed on the PPP bandwagon. Speaking to the Akus in particular, who had opposed the PPP as an up-river party that destroyed their political power, Mr. N'Jie said, "I want them to realize that the PPP is the party of the people, and is here to stay, and that he who hesitates is lost."

When the election took place later that month, after an energetic campaign by a newly formed alliance between the UP and the Congress Party, Gambians elected twenty-four PPP candidates to Parliament and eight from the opposition coalition. Though this represented a loss of four seats for the PPP, its leaders were quite satisfied, since the election gave them a mandate for a maximum of another five years. Close observers of African politics noted happily that in an election that took one week, there was no bloodshed or disorder, and no allegation of fraud, thereby setting some sort of record for Africa.

Earlier in 1966, Gambians produced another rare example of democracy at work when they voted on the national referendum to change the country's status to a republic, with Mr. Jawara as President. The PPP-dominated House had voted 28 to 4 in favor of the proposed change, and everyone assumed that it would be overwhelmingly approved by the public. Out of 154,626 eligible voters, 93,489 cast ballots — 61,568 for the proposed constitutional revision, 31,921 against. A two-thirds majority being required, the proposal therefore failed by less than one per cent, a margin of loss unheard of in Africa, where parties in power often manage to "repair" losses of more than 30 or 40 per cent. In an article on the referendum, the British weekly, *West Africa*, paid admiring tribute: "Gambians can take pride in this glorious Quixotic assertion of democracy of a kind that is increasingly rare elsewhere on the African continent."

# 16

## TO STAND ON THEIR OWN

WHEN SPEAKING about the new nations of Black Africa, Americans frequently refer to them as "emerging" or "developing," which gives the impression of economic progress. The impression is largely false. Though political independence came easily, most of these countries have made only faltering steps toward economic independence — steps often misdirected, and occasionally backward. Many are worse off now than they were five years ago. While Western nations worry about their rate of economic progress, these countries have all they can do just to keep from falling further behind. Few can balance their budgets, let alone set something aside for development. Many of them, according to the most friendly and optimistic economists, will not become viable economic entities for decades. Some may never be.

At the southern edge of the Sahara, Mali, Upper Volta, Niger, Chad and Sudan must depend on foreign aid for development projects, since unlike their Arab neighbors to the North, they have no oil. Tiny Gambia, Togo, Dahomey, Rwanda, Burundi and Malawi are simply smaller than countries with unimpressive natural resources should be. Of France's fourteen former colonies in West and Equatorial Africa, only two — Ivory

Coast and Gabon — boast a favorable balance of trade. Most Black African countries are dependent on the fluctuations of heartless world commodity markets. By an unfortunate bit of timing, they have come to independence at a time when the trend is toward rising prices for the manufactured goods they must import, and declining prices for the produce and raw materials they export. In other words, they have to run just to stand still. This discouraging prospect prompted an African delegate to complain to a recent UN Conference on World Trade and Development: "You in the West tell us to work hard and we will get rich. Well, we are working hard, and we are getting poorer."

In requesting foreign aid, most African leaders seem to be under the illusion that industrialization is the only road to development. Though this may be so for certain other underdeveloped areas of the world, few economists think it will be true for Black Africa. Most of the new countries there have small populations, and only a tiny fraction of these people have enough money to constitute a domestic market for locally manufactured goods. The cost of manufacturing on a large scale for export is prohibitively high because of the lack of cheap power, efficient transportation and skilled labor and management. Africans accuse their former colonial rulers of having intentionally fostered these conditions in order to assure continued markets for their own manufactured goods. Whether or not such accusations are true, the problem exists, and impedes attempts to industrialize. The labor problem is surprising in that Africa appears to have an unlimited supply of cheap labor. Though these men are cheap — less than a dollar a day for manual laborers — most are so unskilled that European supervisors do not consider them poorly paid. In the long run they can be extremely expensive. The supervisors jokingly say that the African workers' motto is "Give us the job and we'll finish the tools."

In time, the nations of Black Africa will work out some of the problems of industrialization, but they will also have to repay the loans that have financed it. Meanwhile, money is diverted from agriculture. Whether their leaders like it or not — and many are ashamed of the fact — 80 to 90 per cent of the people in Black Africa are engaged in agriculture, and are likely to continue in it. Despite minimal diets and largely subsistence-level farming, however, most of these countries can not even feed themselves. Senegal, which is busy industrializing, still imports 40 per cent of its basic foodstuffs. All over Africa, precious hard-earned foreign currency is spent on imported rice and other foods that could be grown at home. Until these countries can feed themselves and save this currency, they will not have a solid economic base upon which to begin development.

The problems facing agricultural development are only slightly less discouraging than those besetting industrialization. Few Africans have money enough for a team of oxen and a plow, and most still farm with crude hoes. Mechanization will have to wait at least a generation for mechanics, money and a willingness to change. One reason African farming is so inefficient and unsuitable for mechanization is that unlike the landless peasants of Latin America, most Africans *do* own their own plots of land, which are too small to pay for a tractor or make efficient use of it. Agricultural cooperatives offer the only solution to this problem, and fortunately they have thus far been remarkably successful.

Another reason agricultural development will take time is that pitifully few Africans have studied or are studying agriculture. Though it is customary — and somewhat justifiable — to blame the British and French for this state of affairs, blaming them does not solve the problem. In their favor, one can say that they had difficulty finding educated Africans willing to study agriculture. This was true under colonialism, and is still true today.

Back-country parents who scrimp to put their sons through school would consider their efforts wasted if the boys chose to study agriculture. And once the boys have seen the charms of city life, they rarely decide on a career that will take them back to the farms. Even less likely, is a city boy choosing to study agriculture. Because of this lack of interest, and despite the pressing need, many of the countries still do not have schools of agriculture.

Another serious problem is the state of agricultural research. As independence approached, colonial governments devoted some of their energies to experiments in crop improvement and diversification. Since independence, some expatriate researchers have stayed on to continue this work, but they are being dismissed or replaced by generally less-qualified Africans. Faced with growing demands for immediate improvements, the new, financially pressed governments are cutting back on research budgets which promise only long-range rewards.

Foreign agricultural experts often fare no better than the colonialists did. Hundreds of Red Chinese are raising rice yields in Mali's Niger River lowlands, but Western observers see little evidence that any of this oriental knowledge is reaching the Malian onlookers. Rice experts from Formosa set up a demonstration project in Senegal, growing two crops a year, and nearly doubling the normal yield on each one. When planting time came the following year, Senegalese officials invited the Mandinka village elders of the region to come and watch the Chinese. No one showed up. Mandinkas feel that growing rice is women's work, and that men should not demean themselves by becoming involved. Why didn't the women come? They were busy planting their rice — the old way.

There are other agricultural problems more sophisticated than production. In barren Upper Volta, cheek-scarred Mossi tribesmen somehow manage to raise herds of magnificent cattle. The Fulas, cattlemen of West Africa, drive huge herds across the plains of Senegal, Mali, Niger and Nigeria. Despite a shortage of grazing land and the pleas of various governments, neither the Mossi nor the Fulas will sell a cow unless in dire need. Their cattle simply grow old and die. Both tribes consider cattle the only measure of a man's wealth and status. They are not so sure about money.

In Senegal's lush Casamance region, the Jola tribe produces enough rice to feed the entire country, which nevertheless now imports thousands of tons each year. Mountains of rice, some of it more than five years old, pile up behind Jola huts. Exasperated Senegalese officials have tried various means of persuasion to get the Jolas to sell their surplus, but they refuse. For rice, even when too old to be edible, is the only basis for prestige in a Jola village. They will sell only enough to satisfy their meager necessities. "The trouble with these people," says the local Woloff administrator, in an analysis worthy of Madison Avenue, "is that they have too much wealth and not enough needs. The problem is to create some needs for them."

As they gradually realize the years necessary to develop a profitable industry or agriculture, African leaders frequently acquire delusions of mineral wealth. In countries that have been exhaustively surveyed by competent geologists with discouraging results, high officials of otherwise impressive intelligence insist that their mineral deposits are much larger than "the foreigners" say. According to them, vast amounts of diamonds, silver or gold lie undiscovered just beneath the surface. Asked why the surveys fail to confirm their opinions, they speak of a vague "neo-colonialist" plot to keep them from their rightful wealth. Said one high African official, "Why else do you think they stayed here so long?" Surveys have turned up some worthwhile mineral deposits, which European and American companies are now busy extracting, but while mining appeals to the new finance ministers as a source of immediate income, it is unsuitable as a means of long-range development. Since independence, private investors in Black Africa have concentrated on mining because it offers a large and speedy return in countries they consider politically too unstable for more permanent investment. Modern mining, with its huge efficient equipment, solves few employment problems in Africa. It no longer requires hundreds of pick and shovel men, and few Africans are trained to work at a more technical level. One day, the veins will run out, the foreigners and their big machines will leave, and nothing will remain but ugly gashes in the ground.

*

If the rest of Black Africa has found economic independence a difficult goal to achieve, it often seems like an impossible prospect in Gambia, for the problems that impede the progress of its neighbors nearly overwhelm this tiny country. Cursed with a nearly total lack of natural resources, a small, illiterate population, a one-crop economy, few trained technicians, and absurd borders, Gambia is an unfortunate laboratory of Africa's economic ills. As former Governor Sir Edward Windley said, "The accident of history created Gambia too small and too ill-endowed with natural resources to develop economically in isolation."

"Ill-endowed" is an understatement. Other countries have problems with their mineral resources, Gambia does not even have problems. In 1953, prospectors out at Cape St. Mary found traces of ilmenite (also known as "rutile," a heavy black sand used in paint pigments) which induced England's giant Imperial Chemical Industries to begin mining operations. The deposit

proved smaller than expected, however, and the costs of working with untrained local labor under poor conditions was too
high. After three years, I.C.I. closed down, writing off a loss of
nearly $2,800,000, and throwing 650 Gambians — one-tenth of
the nation's salaried labor force — out of work. A year or so later,
British Petroleum Ltd. found traces of oil near the coast. After
seismic and aerial surveys, BP drilled two test holes at Serrekunda
and Brikama. "They found absolutely nothing," says an official
who was around at the time. Pointing to a black rock that served
as a paperweight on his desk, he said, "This is limestone-shale. It
came from the bottom of an eleven-hundred-foot hole. Even this
would have been useful for road surfacing if they had found it
near the surface, but it's not worth much at eleven hundred feet."

While prospecting for offshore oil continues, nothing has
turned up yet. Many Gambians are sure oil is there, however,
and talk of getting "another country" to drill for it. They also
talk seriously of gold, pointing out that early European traders in
the river bought gold from the natives. (Most historians think
the gold came from the interior, far from the river.) The Reverend J. C. Faye, a former Gambian High Commissioner in
London, believes there are "pools of mercury" lying about the
country. As yet, no one has been able to find them. After independence, many Gambians took out licenses for diamond prospecting, but the results have been disheartening. According to a
government announcement, "All samples have proved valueless
and are quartz crystals, except for one very small grain, about the
size of a pinhead."

Even water is in short supply, despite the fact that most of the
country is within a few miles of the river. The lower reaches of
the river are salty, and many of the village wells run dry before
each rainy season. Some years ago, colonial officials attempted to
solve the water shortage by sending to England for a diviner or

"dowser" named Bert Hughes. Officially titled Village Water Supply Superintendent, Bert became known simply as "the government dowser." Along with his official duties, he also worked as a private contractor at ten pounds per well. "He made a packet out of this country," says one of Bert's acquaintances. "He was an absolute charlatan, but somehow he always managed to find water. I suppose he figured if they dug deep enough they'd find it anywhere."

One natural resource that lies up on the surface is Yundum Airport, the closest field in Africa to South America. Because of this strategic position, Germany's Lufthansa Airlines used Gambia as the take-off point for the first transatlantic passenger service from Europe to Brazil, in 1934. In 1940 Britain's BOAC operated a flying boat service from England, via Gambia, to Brazil. Throughout World War II, Yundum was a thriving RAF base, and after the war, most flights heading down the coast made overnight refueling stops in Gambia. Since traffic to Africa has grown, however, and modern planes have increased their range, business at Yundum has fallen off. Today, only one flight a week arrives from Europe. Ghana Airways and Nigeria Airways still compete for the dozen or so passengers that fly up or down the coast each day, but Air Senegal has halted its service from Dakar, leaving a debt of $5,600 in unpaid landing fees.

The only natural resource in any quantity seems to be fish, and Gambians have traditionally had little to do with fishing. Dozens of small motorized fishing dories set out from Bathurst each day, but most of these belong to Serreres from Senegal. Some Gambians go out in smaller sailing dories, and dugout canoes, but they can not go far from shore. In order to keep the fish fresh, they go out at night and have to come in before the heat of midday. To help Gambian fishermen, the government has brought in Austin Thomas, a Jamaican fisheries expert sponsored by the UN's Food and Agricultural Organization. After a careful study of Gambian fishing habits, Mr. Thomas does not advise any radical changes. "In most small developing countries that have fishing, you usually hear people saying, 'Let's bring in big processing plants and boats.' This sort of thing does nothing for the small fishermen who've been slogging along all these years. They would be useless in any mechanized operation. There's no reason why they can't improve the small boat fishing for local consumption, and also begin to develop an export trade. The first thing to do is to assist the fishermen with what they already have. They are as conservative as the farmers, and are very suspicious of any change. We shouldn't change their boats. These small craft are ideal. They need no harbors, or boatyards, and they can be built and docked on the beach. We could work out a system of loaning them money to motorize their boats. The cost of the whole thing — boat, engine and gear — is only about forty pounds [$112] per man, a very low capitalization. This is an advantage in a poor country like this."

Some of Mr. Thomas's wisdom might have prevented a disastrous fisheries scheme about fifteen years ago. Shortly after World War II, Britain's semi-autonomous Colonial Development Corporation launched a project in Gambia to extract oil from the sharks that lurk off the coast. With no pilot project or initial surveys, C.D.C. invested approximately $1.5 million in extensive shore facilities, a team of experts, dozens of small shark boats and a large factory ship called the *African Queen*. The sharks were uncooperative, and the project folded.

A few years earlier, with post-war England short of food, C.D.C. tried a poultry project in Gambia, designed to produce for annual export twenty million eggs and one million pounds of dressed poultry. C.D.C. spent more than $2.5 million on fifty poultry experts, 1,000 Gambian laborers, rows of concrete hen houses, 300,000 imported hens, a refrigeration plant and local feed grain schemes. Misfortune plagued the Yundum poultry project. The 10,000 acres of land cleared, plowed and planted somehow refused to yield a fruitful harvest, and C.D.C. had to import feed grains from down the coast. An outbreak of fowl typhoid killed 30,000 hens. The refrigeration plant broke down repeatedly, spoiling 70,000 pounds of dressed poultry. Under pressure in London from an angry Parliament, C.D.C. fired the project manager. His replacement, a Mr. Graves, had no experience in poultry farming, and told a reporter from the *Daily Telegraph*, "I hate chickens." In two years of operations, the Yundum project produced about 40,000 eggs and 60,000 pounds of chicken. Some wag figured that this came to about $30 an egg. All but ninety of the hens eventually died of something called Newcastle's disease. C.D.C. finally abandoned the Yundum poultry scheme, and today the concrete hen houses serve as dormitories for the students at Yundum College.

Bloody but unbowed, C.D.C. somehow managed to talk Parliament into another try, this time a $3 million scheme designed to cultivate and irrigate 23,000 acres of rice land at Wallikunda. Using heavily mechanized methods, including a giant American combine-harvester that proved too heavy to move through the rice fields, C.D.C. managed to plant 200 acres. The yield was half a ton per acre, about what the average Gambian produces with a hoe. C.D.C. finally abandoned the Wallikunda rice project.

While the C.D.C. projects were hastily conceived and poorly managed, such impressive failures demand further explanation. C.D.C. managers, as well as others who have attempted large-scale operations in West Africa, blame their failures partly on local labor and working conditions. The educational level of the average worker is so low that "unskilled" pretty much means restricted to manual labor of the simplest kind. Even then, supervisors say, their work requires constant attention. When questioned about repeated failures and delayed schedules, they shrug and say "WAWA" — "West Africa Wins Again."

Much of the problem of skilled labor is a matter of education. While most students of African affairs criticize the British and French for not providing enough education in their former colonies, experienced observers feel they provided too much — or at least too much of the wrong kind. Colonial education policies generally aimed at teaching Africans how to read and write, not how to *do* anything. The reason for being able to read and write was that one could then get a minor clerical job in the government. Such a policy worked well in the days when the colonial governments could easily absorb the few who mastered these skills, but today the governments already have more clerks than they can use. What they need are technicians, but the system was never designed to produce them. While these countries busily plan new schools, roads, irrigation canals and buildings, they are not training any masons, carpenters, electricians, mechanics or plumbers.

Technical training alone does not seem to be enough. Given any kind of education, most Africans seem reluctant to get their hands dirty. Students who have studied agriculture abroad are annoyed when superiors suggest that they work in the field as well as the office. Each year in Freetown, Sierra Leone, a large brewery takes on a few students from Fourah Bay College as summer trainees. Three well-dressed engineering students in a recent group objected to wearing work clothes, and flatly refused when the resident Dutch engineer-manager tried to take them on a tour that included crawling about the vats. "After all," one explained, "we *are* engineering students."

Scratch any foreign ministry and you can find doctors and engineers who prefer high government posts to practicing their professions. Doctors who have completed their training in London or Paris often choose to stay there in relatively menial positions rather than return to work in ill-equipped bush dispensaries and clinics. Bright high school graduates in search of scholarships have learned that they should express an interest in such careers as civil engineering and agriculture, but most of them confess that eventually they plan to "go into politics." At a technical training school in Mali, twenty boys were studying refrigeration in order to serve as technicians for a proposed network of slaughterhouses. When the three-year course was nearly through, the government announced a competitive exam for the Foreign Service. Half the refrigeration trainees took the exam, and the few who passed left the course immediately. The Israeli director of the school suggested, with only a trace of humor, that "they should stop teaching these boys how to read and write. Once they have learned, they are useless for any real work."

One man who is trying to do something about preparing Gambians for real work is a forty-two-year-old Englishman named Ted Snead, a UNESCO technical adviser. An electrical engineer, former teacher, and former adviser to the Nigerian government, Snead recently completed a survey of technical training needs and facilities in Gambia. In his report, he went through each government department and examined the number of technically qualified Gambians. The results were grim. In Posts and Telegraph, there was no Gambian qualified at a senior technical level. The Electricity Department had no Gambian electrical engineers. Only one of the five posts for civil engineers in the Public Works Department was filled by a Gambian. Nearly all of PWD's technical superintendents were expatriates. While the Agricultural Department should have 100 extension workers, there were only forty-eight such posts available, and only twenty-eight of these were filled. Fortunately, Snead noted, the demand for technicians is not likely to increase in the near future, since no one expects the economy to make any rapid gains.

As an outgrowth of his report, Snead now runs a small trade school in some ramshackle buildings down near the mud flats at Box Bar. One morning I went down to visit the school and found Snead bent over a Land Rover engine next to a young Gambian. A small, peppery man, his clothes were grimy, and when we shook hands I received a handful of grease. With a budget of only $3,000 and four Gambian assistants, he tries to train young Gambians for specific job openings such as electrical or automotive mechanics. "We don't teach more than there are jobs for," says Snead. "It's nonsense to run these special courses full time, because we'll be turning out blokes who'll sit on the street corner."

"Do you train any boys for the commercial firms?"

"We've offered them our services, but they don't want any part of it. They're dinosaurs."

"What do you think of the education that students receive at Gambia High School?"

"They're educating boys for a way of life that doesn't exist and that never will exist here. It's terrible! Criminal! Let's face it. You've got to take a hard look at what the country has today, and what it's likely to have twenty-five years from now. It's got nothing but agriculture now, and it's not likely to have anything else for the next twenty-five years. It's disgraceful that in such a country the agricultural extension school just started last year."

As we walked over to Snead's small, cluttered office, he said, "I devote my time to getting the tools in their hands, and getting on to the job. There's a tendency in Africa to train to a far higher level of skill than the job to be done demands. They need ordinary mechanics here now far more than they need men with

university degrees. We've set our aims deliberately low. I'm trying to build a project around my Gambian assistants — not
around me. For that reason it lacks glamor and gloss, but it will
run after I leave."

If Gambia's industrial development continues at its present
rate, Mr. Snead's vocational school will not have to train many industrial workers. At various times in the past, investors have lost
money on or abandoned plans for a ketchup factory, butter production, a brick and tile plant, leather curing, and numerous
other enterprises. Only two small peanut oil mills and a few
back-room soda bottling plants have survived over the years. Not
all these ventures were launched by men of sterling character, for
as flies head for honey, disreputable promoters seem to flock to
each newly independent nation with schemes they claim will
revolutionize the economy. Hard-pressed, inexperienced and relatively uncritical African development officials tend to grab at
any possibility of raising revenues. In 1963, a gentleman named
Koslovsky arrived in Bathurst with his wife, three children and
brother-in-law, to promote a coastal fisheries plant. Plans progressed to the point of conferences with the Prime Minister and
appeals to Gambian investors. During these negotiations, the
entire family stayed at the Atlantic Hotel, where they gave dinner parties for interested officials and prospective investors.
When the hotel asked Koslovsky to invest in the payment of his
bill, he left for South America to promote some new venture.
His wife left for Dakar, his brother-in-law went to Ghana, and
the Gambian government had to pay the children's fare back to
England. About a year later, an Englishman named Jeff Morton
appeared in Bathurst, presumably representing an organization
called "Investment Investigators Ltd.," with a financial backing
of more than $25 million. He soon formed the Gambia Develop-
ment Corporation, and drew up plans for the development of a

local cotton industry, whereupon Gambia's Parliament passed legislation granting him a concession for all cotton exports. Mr. Morton also caused a stir by speaking of plans for the development of tourism, a local pottery industry, and the production of a synthetic fiber board made from peanut shells. Before any of these projects got underway, he suddenly disappeared one day, owing three months' salary to his laundress and cook.

While some legitimate promoters blame their failures on the alleged sloth, ignorance, or lack of skill of Gambian workers, their own poor planning and management have been equally responsible. Some Gambians speak of more sinister reasons. As with the failure of various mining ventures, these citizens consider the industrial failures part of a conspiracy to keep Gambia in poverty. An editorial in *The Nation* put forth this view:

> It is strongly suspected and believed that certain commercial and industrial monopolists in The Gambia, opposed . . . to local indigenous projects that are assisted from foreign capital, have been at work to undermine these efforts. The wreckers, afraid of local opposition to these machinations, work clandestinely, in connivance with certain influential individuals and those in responsible positions, to strengthen their vested interests. It is further suspected that these individuals and dupes rake appreciable sums of money from this deal. We have no evidence of this.

Despite such fears, many Gambians hoped that independence would bring a new age of prosperity and industrial growth. My hotel steward, Moussa, came to my room shortly before independence to tell me he would be leaving the hotel soon. Asked why, he replied, "Oh sah. When we get de independence dey go have plenty big factory with good job." I told Moussa it might be wiser to wait until he saw the new factories under construction before quitting. Several months later, still at the hotel, he came to me shaking his head. "I don't know 'bout dis independence business. We no get factory, no get embassy — just get more politics."

Though new factories and new jobs did not appear immediately, independence was a boon to the country's most dependably profitable industry aside from peanuts and smuggling — postage stamps. The Post Office Department estimated its revenues for 1965–66 at about $200,000, all but a tenth of which came from the sale of stamps. That amounts to a great many stamps — far more than Gambians use on their letters and packages. In fact, about 90 per cent of them went to stamp dealers and collectors abroad who seem to prize the philatelic outputs of such out-of-the-way lands.

In order to expand the economy from its base of peanuts, stamps and smuggling, Prime Minister Jawara addressed a luncheon of the African-American Chamber of Commerce during a visit to New York. Admitting his country's lack of natural resources, the P.M. stressed its compensating virtues of political stability and democratic government. He mentioned several areas in which foreign investment might prove fruitful, including fishing, tourism, and diamonds. He invited the forty businessmen present to come to Gambia for a firsthand look at these opportunities, but few have managed to make the trip. When two new industries finally appeared, about a year after independence, they were in the hands of local entrepreneurs. A few miles from Bathurst, an Indian firm built a small Coca-Cola bottling plant. Nearby, the Madis, in association with the Gambian government and the producers of Gilbey's Gin, opened Gambia Distillers Ltd., which now turns out bottles of "Duncan's Whisky," "Tourell Brandy," "Banjul Gin" and "Queen Elizabeth Gin." Some observers were surprised at this venture, since Gambia's small population is made up predominantly of Moslems who abstain from alcohol. At the factory's opening reception, however, official guests sampled the output, and one of the Gambian Directors predicted that "despite man's natural reluctance to change, the new company's products will stand on their own."

*

Standing on its own has been a problem for Gambia for years, and is likely to remain a problem for many years to come. In this respect Gambia is no different from most of its larger neighbors. Nearly all of them depend on foreign aid to balance their budgets. Britain and France continue to make up the budget deficits for many of their former colonies, and also contribute the lion's share of development aid. The Common Market, West Germany, the United States, Israel, Red China and Russia are also engaged in relatively low-cost development projects, but they seem quite willing to let the French and British continue bearing most of the burden. The African policy of the United States Agency for International Development has been to concentrate its assistance on countries "with moderate and stable governments which have demonstrated concern for purposeful economic development, are carefully using their own resources, and are taking vigorous self-help measures to improve living standards." Such criteria are intelligent and admirable, but the problem in Black Africa is finding countries that qualify. Since most givers of economic assistance use — or would like to use — similar criteria, the result has been that the few rich African nations are getting richer, while the many poor ones are getting poorer.

For example, of the $57 million in U.S. development loans to the thirty countries of Black Africa in 1964, more than half went to one country — Nigeria. Already blessed with an abundant, diversified agriculture and a large, relatively literate population,

Nigeria — until the recent breakdown of its federal government — was rapidly outdistancing its neighbors. As more money came to its 55 million people, it became an attractive market for domestic industry. This drew private investment which in turn gave the country the economic stability to attract more foreign aid. (In the ex-French sector, Ivory Coast has a similarly enviable position.)

For many of Nigeria's neighbors, the cycle works in reverse. Lacking Nigeria's basic economic advantages, they are unable to attract the aid or investment necessary to acquire them. So they fall further behind. Asked about their problem, a top A.I.D. official insisted that the United States will gladly give loans or grants to any of these other African countries if they submit carefully thought-out plans. "We have plenty of money available for solid proposals," he said. "But they come in here totally unprepared, and simply say that they want money for this or that, and expect you to give it to them right off."

In the case of Britain and France, most African leaders feel they "owe" their former colonies development aid, to make up for "the years of subjugation." When I asked Gambia's Minister of Local Government, Sherif Dibba, whether he thought the British have a moral obligation to support Gambia, he replied, "Of course they have a moral obligation. Look what they have done to us. They are responsible for our poverty. There should only be one country here — either Gambia or Senegal. The British are the ones who made us this small. There were many opportunities when they could have made an arrangement with the French, but the negotiations always failed. What did they ever do to develop our economy? Before they came here we were self-sufficient. Now we are completely dependent on outside influences. It vexes me, honestly it does!"

While their dependence on Britain vexes many Gambians, they become even more annoyed when they learn that other ex-colonies receive more than Gambia. When Britain granted copper-rich Zambia a $28 million loan, Gambian M.P.'s raised a furor in Parliament. No one mentioned the fact that Zambia has a population ten times that of Gambia, and is seventy times as large. Various M.P.'s have threatened to "turn to the East," but as yet, the East seems unaware of Gambia's existence.

Meanwhile, occasional gifts arrive from abroad. Nationalist China has sent a team of rice experts; West Germany sent 2,000 tons of fertilizer; the Peace Corps sent a track coach for a few weeks; a school in Detroit sent a crate of sports equipment, including a catcher's mask. Over the years, the U.S. government has sent nearly 1,000 tons of powdered milk, to be distributed to the schools and hospitals. The American Red Cross sent a shipment of diapers, which the Gambians refer to as "nappies." "I've seen 'em used as hats," said one up-river official. "I've seen 'em used in the markets to carry rice. I saw a lady selling tomatoes in one once. But I've never seen one yet on a baby's bottom."

One possible source of foreign aid that has not yet been explored is American colleges. Upper Volta, for example, recently fell heir to American intercollegiate munificence, though the practical benefits have thus far been minimal. It all started when a student at New York's City College named Louis Mandel saw a picture of the Voltaic delegate to the UN looking lonely at a General Assembly session. Mr. Mandel, who claims to have been searching for a cause anyway, looked up Upper Volta in several reference works and found it to his liking. From this attraction grew The Friends of Upper Volta, an organization with chapters on twenty-three American campuses, including Harvard, Yale, Columbia, Stanford, and Ohio State. At the first public meeting of the City College chapter, an ex-Peace Corpsman lectured on "Nightlife in Ouagadougou," Upper Volta's capital. Mr. Mandel attributed the club's rapid growth to the virtues of Upper Volta, and to the modest fifteen-cent dues. The club's motto is "For 15 cents, can you afford to be an enemy of Upper Volta?"

Most economists agree that along with foreign aid, Africa's main hope lies in regional groupings for common economic goals. This may happen eventually, through sheer necessity, but the eventuality is not visible at present. Africa's new leaders feel they must unite their own tribes into stable nations before they can join together with their neighbors. Any leader who devotes too much energy to cooperation with a neighboring country may find he is no longer the leader of his own, for the opposition will say he is "selling out our hard-won independence." In many cases, friction between neighbors has proved an effective aid to internal unification. While nationalism becomes entrenched, regionalism must wait.

The British and French are responsible for the present Balkanization of Africa, but they claim that by the time independence seemed imminent, it was too late to put the pieces back together again. It probably would not have worked anyway, for Africa never was together. When the Europeans came, centuries ago, there were no countries, only warring tribes and loosely governed feudal kingdoms. Later colonial entities such as French and British West Africa were united mainly on paper, for administrative purposes.

The few attempts at regional government since independence have all been dismal failures. The seven-month-old Mali Federation of Senegal and Mali broke up upon their independence in 1960. The ten-year-old Central African Federation ended in 1963, with Northern Rhodesia (now Zambia) and Nyasaland (now Malawi) becoming self-governing, and later independent. Attempts to form an East African federation failed in 1963, when Kenya, Tanganyika and Uganda were unable to agree on the site of the federal capital, among other issues. The member countries of all these proposed, attempted and stillborn federations are more sharply separated from each other today than they were five years ago. In the fall of 1965, a meeting of the Organization of African Unity showed that the continent's attempt to unite on a grand scale is faring little better than the regional federations. Ghana's ex-President N'Krumah opened the meeting with his annual appeal for a Pan-African government, but only half the heads of state were there to hear it. Liberia's President Tubman wondered, "With the kind of confusion we have seen among ourselves right here, can we hope to have one government functioning for us all?"

If political federation has been a failure, joint development has been only slightly more successful. Various commissions have been formed, and ministers from various countries continually meet. They issue joint communiqués emphasizing "the strong ties binding our countries together in friendship," but lacking specific proposals. Commissions for the development of the Niger and Senegal Rivers spent several years and dozens of meetings before deciding on the sites of their commission headquarters. Thirteen different Black African countries have national airlines flying to other African capitals and Europe. The overlapping and duplication of routes causes near-empty flights and unbalanced service.

Although Gambia and Senegal have signed agreements for common defense and foreign policies, cooperation has not progressed much beyond this innocuous stage. In 1963, a team of two experts from the UN's Food and Agricultural Organization spent three weeks in Senegal and Gambia, and wrote a report entitled "Integrated Agricultural Development in the Gambia River Basin." The report called for a system of dams and irrigation that would eventually permit "a spectacular expansion of rice growing," and enable both Senegal and Gambia to save the hard-earned foreign currency they now spend to import thousands of tons of rice each year. The report also made recommendations about peanuts, crop diversification, fisheries and transport.

In the three years since the report appeared, little has been done to implement its proposals. The first formal meeting between the two countries to discuss the report did not take place until the summer of 1965 — a year and a half later. The delegates to the meeting issued a joint communiqué hailing "the positive results they had achieved, and the spirit of cooperation and frank cordiality which pervaded their discussions." The positive results consisted of a request to the UN's Special Fund for further "pre-investment" studies, and a resolution "to proceed as soon as possible towards clear objectives and concrete action." Most of the blame for the absence of concrete action at the meeting can be laid to the casual attitude that Senegal has taken toward joint development. This attitude led normally reticent Prime Minister Jawara to issue a cautious criticism in a subsequent meeting of Parliament: "We look forward to closer relations at all levels with our Senegalese friends; although I feel compelled to remark that if only they would show a greater and more prompt response to the matters which are from time to time referred to them, cooperation would be that much easier and more fruitful."

The leader of the Gambian delegation at that joint Senegalo-Gambian meeting was a tall, spare, fifty-year-old Englishmen named David Percival, who holds the position of Economic Adviser. Though his official realm is long-range planning and development, he also has a hand in many of the government's financial affairs. Because of his seemingly pervasive influence, radical

Gambians have made him into an economic whipping boy, holding him responsible for everything from the fluctuating price of peanuts to the lack of mineral resources and the irregular rainfall. One of their frequent peeves is that Mr. Percival has no degree in economics. This does not bother Mr. Percival. When questioned at a cocktail party about charges that he is unqualified for his job, he replied, "Why of course. I'm unqualified in at least seven different fields that I deal with constantly."

Though he has no degree in economics, Percival has a wealth of practical experience in development. For twenty years, he served off and on as economic adviser to Cyprus. For three years he was economic adviser to the ill-fated embryo West Indies Federation. He retired when Cyprus became independent in 1961, only to accept a contract one year later to come to Gambia. Like many of the British officials in Gambia, Percival comes from a tradition of colonial service. "My father was in the civil service in India," he says. "His father was, and my mother's father also. I was never in India myself. I got sick just as I was about to go out there as a boy. I was brought up in England by my grandmother, who acquired her standards and ethics under Queen Victoria. Thus I'm actually a Victorian myself. I started out to be a chartered accountant, but eventually I gravitated into the Colonial Service. Family tradition, and all that."

Just after the June meeting on joint development of the Gambia River basin, I asked Percival why the meeting had not taken place earlier.

"We'd sent them a date ages ago," said Percival, "along with an agenda and other background material. Of course, I didn't really expect them to show up. The day before the meeting was to be held, they called up and said they couldn't come because their 'expert' wasn't available. Actually they have no experts. They proposed a later date which was unacceptable to us be-

cause it fell on the day of our Parliament. So we finally settled
on this week. They showed up with a dozen of their bright
young men, none of whom had ever had any experience with this
joint development plan. When they arrived, I handed them the
agenda and schedule for a two-day meeting, with three working
sessions. Actually the whole thing could have been done in half
an hour if everyone had been prepared. The meeting lasted four
days, and we hardly got to the agenda. We spent the last day
simply formulating the final communiqué. There was a big do
over whether the head of the Senegalese delegation would have
his name in it. I wasn't about to have my name in it, and therefore he couldn't either. He was furious. There was a big dispute
over whether there should be two counterparts — one Gambian
and one Senegalese — for each UN expert. Frank Williams, our
Financial Adviser, pointed out that Gambia couldn't possibly
come up with counterparts in most of the technical fields. I
doubt if the Senegalese could either, though they'd never admit
it.

"Actually, I don't think much of the counterpart idea. It usually means letting a few of the local blokes stand around drawing
a salary for watching. Might just as well let the experts come out
and get on with their work by themselves. At our present stage
of development, nothing of a capital or research nature will get
done unless it's done by people from the outside. All these aid
programs — particularly those of the UN — insist on using local
counterparts. This is the obverse of the old colonial style. I just
don't think this new method works. On paper, the expert comes
out and trains the local counterpart, then leaves. But in actual-
ity, the man comes out and does the job himself. That way it
gets done. But the emerging countries don't want that kind of
aid any more. They don't want the aid people to just come in
and do the job, and then turn it over to them only after it's
done."

"But if they don't work on these projects themselves, how will they ever acquire the technical know-how to stand on their own?"

"Ah, now. You expect them to stand on their own. But you see, I'm quite unashamedly an old-fashioned, brutal colonialist. The old British philosophy of colonial development was to let the chap who could do something do it. If he couldn't, let someone else who could, do it. The modern development policy is to diversify and industrialize, and to become self-sufficient. For this reason Gambia is not typical of Africa. No one here seriously believes that Gambia will be anything but a single-crop agricultural country. This may be an advantage, for Gambia may thus avoid many of the problems that Ghana and India have gone through in trying to become self-sufficient."

"Many Gambians feel that England never even tried to do anything to help this country."

"What the British did here wasn't much, but there was a very good reason for it. There wasn't much hope that Gambia would ever be worth much expense. They mostly tried to preserve stability."

"But you do give money to Gambia now."

"Oh yes. We give them a grant of about a half-million pounds [$1.4 million] a year to balance the budget, plus another eight hundred thousand pounds [$2.2 million] in development loans. Most of the development money isn't really used for development anyhow. It goes for maintenance, repairs of already existing buildings and roads, plus replacement of vehicles. Upon independence, the British said they would taper off the budget grants. It's supposed to phase out around 1967. What they would like to see remaining on the Development Budget is so many hundred thousand pounds worth of Land Rovers and Bedford lorries. She wants to dispose of her capital goods here, not her money. Upon independence, the moral obligation of support tends to disappear, and normal business policy takes over.

"Actually, we're so bloody inefficient here that we never manage to spend the entire eight hundred thousand. We just don't have the infrastructure to absorb it all. In spite of the fantastic expense of the Public Works Department on practically nothing, they can't use up the money offered. This happens all over Africa. Even with the greatest good will in the world, and allowing for enormous rake-offs all down the line, few of these underdeveloped countries can use up the big offers of foreign aid. They just don't have the necessary administrative, technical or transportation facilities."

"Aside from money, isn't there something you can do to diversify the economy? How about the potential of fishing?"

"That's really a pretty difficult situation. Nobody who knows anything about fishing here can read or write, and nobody who can read or write would be bothered fishing."

"How about light industry?"

"We've gotten a surge of potential investors since independence. These chaps come along here with wonderful plans for factories to produce plastic raincoats, shoes, candles, etcetera. We take them all seriously, but we don't expect many of these projects to come to fruition."

"Haven't you been stung several times already by shady promoters?"

"Yes, but our policy has been to let anybody get away with murder, just so long as he gets something moving. Actually, if they really want to make a great deal of money here in a few years, to support the politicians in the manner to which they will have become accustomed, there is only one solution — that's to turn the place into a Miami Beach. Sell off the coastline to some big hotel operators. Or you might turn it into a hideout for deposed but wealthy African heads of state. There's bound to be more and more of them."

"Aside from such speculations, what sort of work does an Economic Adviser do?"

"As Economic Adviser, I don't really *do* anything. My main object here is to keep them from making bloody fool errors. Actually there's not much I can do. All you have here is a bunch of farmers who raise groundnuts six months of the year, and who are almost completely dependent on weather and price — factors over which I have no control. While the price has been good lately, and the crops have been increasing, the government's expenses have been increasing also."

"Do you feel that your work, and that of the other British advisers here, is appreciated by the Gambians?"

"I don't suppose so. You must have noticed all those messages scrawled on the streets and walls, telling Winton Lane and Sir John to 'Go Home.' They annoyed me so much that the other day I sent off a rocket to the acting Prime Minister, pointing it out and recommending that the government or police take stern measures to put a stop to it. That afternoon, as I walked home from the Secretariat, I saw a crude chalk scrawl on the street. It said 'Percival Go Home.'"

\*

Despite independence, the new Coca-Cola and gin plants, and the gradual departure of expatriates like David Percival, some Gambians are still dissatisfied with the country's development. An editorial in the PPP's *New Gambia* claimed that Gambianization is not enough, and propounded a doctrine of "cultural nationalism" called "Gambianizationalism," designed to "shake off Britishness or non-Gambianness." Gambia, according to the editorial, has "a culture and a personality which must be positively projected and more sharply focused. Mere political independence is not enough, for the process of decolonization must have

mental and cultural aspects . . . The doctrine of Gambianizationalism will help to implement and accelerate this change
. . . by projecting the Gambian Personality."

What the up-river farmers think about the doctrine of Gambianizationalism, or in fact, whether they worry about the Gambian Personality at all, is a question better left to sociologists
who have thus far found the question insufficiently pressing to
require investigation. Those who have studied the problem elsewhere in Africa feel that it will take generations before the majority of tribal villagers begin to worry about more than tribal or
village affairs. As for Gambia, it is difficult to see how a greater
appreciation of the Gambian Personality would benefit the peasant farmers who make up about 85 per cent of the population.
They have much more practical problems to worry about, like
peanuts.

With the aid of the Agriculture Department, the farmers have
been making steady progress on peanuts, and the 1965-66 season
brought a high quality harvest of 118,510 tons (unshelled), a
startling gain of nearly 30 per cent. (Latest reports indicate another substantial increase in the 1966–67 crop.) With the world
market price firm, this represented a tremendous boost to the
economy, and brought forth numerous predictions of Gambian
prosperity. Prosperity was not that simple, however, for while the
peanut crop increased, the cost of independence increased also,
and the financial gain was not enough to balance the budget.

Faced with these cold hard economic realities, some Gambians become depressed, and see a murky, neo-colonialist conspiracy aimed at keeping Gambia in poverty. Ironically, some of the
remaining colonial officials are the most optimistic about Gambia's prospects. Compared with other newly independent African nations, they feel that Gambia's political stability, its improving agriculture, and Prime Minister Jawara's good sense may

eventually enable the country to achieve a relative measure of economic independence. Other British officials feel that these assets will never offset Gambia's discouraging lack of human and natural resources enough for it to "get out from under." When asked for his opinion, one British technical adviser who has served twenty years in several African countries, said, "Oh, things will sort themselves out in a hundred years or so." He was not smiling.

It should not take that long, but it will certainly take more than one generation. If this seems like a long time to wait, Gambians might recall one of their own Woloff proverbs: "Danka danka, japa golo." — "Soflee soflee, catchee monkey."

# 17

## A PLACE IN THE WORLD

A FEW MONTHS before independence, Prime Minister Jawara and his wife spent a month traveling around the United States as guests of the State Department. Upon her return, Mrs. Jawara described some of the highlights of the trip in a magazine article: "We travelled extensively by train, by road and by air. The train journey from Denver to San Francisco was particularly delightful, but the most wonderful and fascinating thing we saw was Niagara Falls. . . . Our visit to Puerto Rico was the most useful, as it was an experience relative to our problems here in the Gambia . . . Like us, they are a one-crop country. In their case they produce tobacco as we do groundnuts."

Mrs. Jawara's tour of Puerto Rico must have been brief, for her comparison of that island's economy with Gambia's is neither apt nor accurate. While Gambia does produce little other than its $10–15 million peanut crop, Puerto Rico has a diversified agricultural production in which tobacco ranks third after dairying and livestock, and sugar. In her comparison, Mrs. Jawara neglected to mention that Puerto Rico also earns nearly half a billion dollars a year from manufacturing, plus a tidy sum from its bustling tourist industry.

During her trip through the United States, Mrs. Jawara met

with members of the International Council of Women, to which the Gambia Federation of Women is affiliated. "It was great, after corresponding with the girls there for so many years to actually meet them." She was less pleased to note that the American Negro's struggle for civil rights is still very acute. "This situation is very strange, considering that America is such a great country with such high democratic ideals, and a country that the whole world looks up to . . . However, it appears that a great many Americans are very conscious of this dreadful situation today, and are dedicated to the task of putting it right. I hope it doesn't take long, because in spite of the fact that I have the greatest admiration for America, it's very difficult to look up to a country where all is not right in their own backyard."

While his wife looked in on women's clubs, hospitals and Gambian students, the Prime Minister visited industrial and agricultural sites of interest. At a news conference before leaving for Africa, Mr. Jawara reviewed what he called a "highly successful" tour. "There are warm and friendly American people everywhere you go. They do not wait for a stranger to speak to them first. Even in the streets of New York, people stop you without any inhibitions at all, ask for your name, address and an autograph . . . The tempo here is so stimulating. Your people are so active, and always busy, always going somewhere or doing something." Although there had been no ticker tape parades or state dinners, the Prime Minister said that everywhere he went, he "found Americans vitally interested in Gambian independence."

About a year later, Prime Minister Jawara returned to New York to lead Gambia's delegation to its first United Nations session. On Tuesday, September 25, 1965, Gambia became the UN's 115th member nation. It was a day to make the founding powers stop and meditate. Along with Gambia, two other countries — Singapore and the Maldive Islands — gained votes in the Assembly equal to those of Russia, France, England and the United States. To those who searched in their atlases for the three new countries, tiny Gambia loomed large — eighteen times larger than Singapore and thirty-six times larger than the Maldive Islands. In his speech to the General Assembly on this august occasion, Prime Minister Jawara said that "the honor and privilege of addressing this Assembly" filled him with "a deep sense of pride and humility."

With my people, I take pride in the thought that without ever departing from the path of peaceful and orderly progress, The Gambia has taken its rightful place in the family of nations. But I am all humility when I reflect that in terms of size, population and resources, The Gambia is one of the smallest countries to accede to international sovereignty.

This presents very special problems when a country like The Gambia finds that it is expected to contribute to the expenses of the United Nations Organisation on the basis of a minimum contribution which is out of all proportion to its resources, and to join specialized agencies which intend to assess the country's contribution on the basis of the same minimum rates. This problem has been explained to the Secretary-General, and unless a solution can be found, it may well mean that my country may not be able to participate in the affairs of the United Nations to the extent which we would wish.

Whilst admitting that The Gambia has many problems, particularly economic and financial, I take comfort from the fact that, having regard to the sympathy and impartiality which characterise the brotherhood of nations, my country is no longer alone in her struggles now that she has gained admission to this society.

The Prime Minister was not joking when he said that admission to international society would strain Gambia's economy. Minimal representation in Dakar, London and New York will cost about $210,000. Gambia's annual dues at the UN are about $40,000, plus another $40,000 for special agencies. The Organization of African Unity charges nearly $100,000, with another donation expected for the Committee of Liberation. Though both assessments are based on the lowest category — which includes countries many times larger and wealthier than Gambia — they are simply more than Gambia can afford.

If Gambia's financial state leaves it unable to afford diplomatic presence in most nations, these nations, for other reasons, are equally reluctant about establishing diplomatic presence in Gambia. While thirty-five countries expressed an interest in establishing relations with Gambia upon its independence, after one year only sixteen had bothered to do so, and only four had opened local offices — Great Britain, Nigeria, Senegal and the United States. The others simply gave their ambassadors to Senegal diplomatic jurisdiction over Gambia as well. Every week or so, one of them would appear in Bathurst in full regalia, present his letters of credence at Government House, and hurry back to Dakar. Though many Gambians resent this treatment, the Administration seems to favor it. When one M.P. asked in Parliament why the government was not encouraging foreign embassies to establish in Gambia, the P.M. replied: "The Gambia is ill-equipped for the moment, both in terms of personnel and facilities, to cater for and to cope with, the problems that would arise from the setting up in Bathurst of a large diplomatic corps."

While most countries were only too willing to go along with the P.M.'s desire, the United States found itself in a quandary, for until then it had automatically established an embassy in each new African nation. As the number of these nations grew larger, and their size grew smaller, certain State Department officials began to urge the establishment of consulates instead of embassies in the smaller countries. When Gambia became independent, their view gained considerable favor. It was also advocated by the U.S. Embassy in Dakar, which till then had handled all diplomatic affairs with Gambia. Top officials at State, however, insisted that it would be an insult to Gambia if the U.S. opened only a consulate in Bathurst, while maintaining embassies in the capital of every other independent African state.

Seven months after independence, the State Department settled the issue after a fashion, to the confusion of everyone concerned. The United States opened an "Embassy" in Bathurst, but left it in command of a "Chargé d'Affaires," with the Ambassador to Senegal assuming the title of Ambassador to Gambia as well. The Embassy is a modest affair, consisting of Room 44 at the Atlantic Hotel. The Chargé and his wife, who serves as his secretary, make up the entire staff. The raising of the stars and stripes had to wait several days until a hotel workman could find a few lengths of rusty pipe to make a flagpole. Since the arrival of the Americans had been long and eagerly awaited by unemployed Gambians, the Embassy was something of a disappointment. Nevertheless, they came in droves to volunteer their services as officials, messengers, janitors and "boys." They came in vain. Every week or so, the following notice appeared in the *Gambia News Bulletin:* "No VACANCIES: The American Embassy in Bathurst again announces with regret that it has no present or expected vacancies for employment."

While there isn't much Gambia can do about the diplomatic moves of other countries, some local critics feel it should take a more active role itself on the world scene. *The Nation,* the sporadic left-of-center monthly, urged Gambia to send more delegates to international bodies, "fully armed with positive proposals to speak on behalf of the Gambians. No half-way measures would promote the interests of the people of this country and put across the aspirations of The Gambia." The editorial was not specific about the aspirations of The Gambia or the "positive proposals" it recommended. "As an Independent Nation," it went on, "with equal status with Great Britain in the Commonwealth, and the same status with Senegal in the OAU, the voice of The Gambia must be heard, and forcefully too."

Prime Minister Jawara addressed himself to this subject in a subsequent session of Parliament, marking Gambia's first anniversary. "If outwardly, one year after independence, life is much the same within The Gambia, independence has meant that our little country is able to make its voice heard in the international sphere." He went on to list the various international organizations (UN, OAU, Commonwealth), agencies (FAO), and treaties (GATT) with which Gambia had established some connection, and mentioned several international conferences that he and his ministers had attended. Only that summer, for example, Mr. Jawara and Minister of Works Andrew Camara made a state visit to Lebanon, where a luncheon was held in their honor. The two visitors made a sight-seeing tour which included Tripoli, Ba'albek, and a performance of the Australian Ballet Company. They discussed with private commercial groups the possibility of a Lebanese Trade Mission to Gambia, and talked to government officials about a new City Hall for Bathurst. Before they returned to Gambia, Lebanon's Prime Minister decorated Mr. Jawara with the Grand Order of Lebanon, Green Band, while Mr. Camara received the Order of the Cedar, Red Band.

Gambia also established itself in the world of sports by sending an eight-man team to the first African Games, held in Brazzaville, Republic of the Congo. Most countries sent teams of nearly 100 contestants. Though five of the Gambian athletes made the finals in their events, including Kebba Joiner in the hop, skip and jump, none of them scored any points. In cricket,

Gambia continued its series of Test Matches against Nigeria, beating the team from down the coast by five wickets and four runs. Independence also allowed Gambia to enter Miss N'Dey Jagne, "Miss Gambia 1965," in London's Miss World contest. She tied for seventeenth place, out of forty-three entries.

In the realm of foreign policy, Gambia steered a moderate pro-Western course. When a young camera-laden couple from the Soviet Embassy in Dakar visited Bathurst for a day of apparent sight-seeing, they were ostentatiously tailed by the Assistant Superintendent of Police and two detectives. When an opposition M.P. criticized the Prime Minister for not pursuing a strictly independent foreign policy, the P.M. replied with considerable insight that "there is no government, not even the great powers, with an independent foreign policy." When the Rhodesian crisis arose, upon the unilateral declaration of independence by that country's white minority, some radical political leaders urged the government to break off diplomatic relations with Great Britain in protest. The government issued the following policy statement: "The Gambia government does not see how this [forcing the downfall of the white government] can be achieved by severing relations with Great Britain at this critical stage. To do so would be to shut the door against direct negotiations with the country which is still primarily responsible for the affairs of Rhodesia." When an irate opposition M.P. demanded that Gambia impose economic sanctions, boycotting all trade with Rhodesia, Finance Minister Sherif Sissay pointed out that Gambia had never had any trade with Rhodesia.

While much of the Parliamentary debate on foreign policy concerns affairs in the UN, OAU and Rhodesia, the major issue of practical significance remains the question of Gambia's association with Senegal. Before independence, a UN team of experts spent three months in Senegal and Gambia, and issued a report full of "howevers" and "on the other hands," in which they out-lined three alternatives: integration, federation, or an "entente." They ruled out complete integration of Gambia into Senegal as unrealistic, and viewed complete separation as against the inter-ests of both countries. Their choice was federation, approached by means of successively close stages of association. Federation, the study argued, would reduce administrative expenses in Gam-bia, discourage the smuggling trade, and open the Gambia River to its natural economic hinterland.

As a first step toward federation, in 1964, the two countries signed agreements on foreign affairs and defense. The treaty on foreign affairs merely called for "joint consultation" between the two governments with a view of "harmonizing" their positions. The defense treaty called for mutual defense in the event of ex-ternal aggression. No one in Bathurst, by the wildest possible stretch of the imagination, can conceive of any country wanting to attack Gambia — except possibly Senegal.

Since independence, the two countries have come no closer to political association. There is still no "entente," and federation seems as distant as ever. Various ministers in each country have conferred with their counterparts in the other. Various joint committees have met and issued statements testifying to mutual agreement on innocuous generalities. Not only is federation making little progress, there is not much evidence that the leaders of either country are seriously interested in it. At one meeting, President Leopold Senghore of Senegal reportedly re-ferred to Gambia as "a kid sister which Senegal rocks on its knee." On a visit to London, Gambia's Speaker of the House, the Honorable A. Sam Jack, told reporters asking about an even-tual Senegambia that "we mean to keep our identity and our British way of life." Most Gambian political leaders, now that they are independent, do not want to give up any of their newly

gained sovereignty to surrounding Senegal. Few Gambian Ministers relish the idea of becoming Under Secretaries in a Senegambia. Senegalese officials seem content to wait, assuming that
the realities and hardships of independence will eventually convince Gambians of the benefits of integration. As *Dakar Matin*
put it, "The people of Gambia and Senegal are condemned to
live together."

While such issues as merger with Senegal and Rhodesia's independence cause considerable concern, most of Gambia's foreign affairs involve matters far less critical. The problems of diplomatic recognition, for example, had never bothered anyone in
Bathurst before. Now, suddenly, decisions had to be made on
such matters as accrediting an ambassador from Korea. The official in charge of the negotiations for a time told me, "The question is whether we should recognize the ambassador from South
Korea — they're the good ones, aren't they? — or the man from
North Korea. The file is now up to fifty-seven pages, and I'm
sure it will be up to a hundred before we've finished with the
thing. The South Korean Ambassador to Dakar has been pressing us for a decision, but the P.M.'s away in London at the moment. I just sent a memo off to the acting P.M., saying that since
it is extremely unlikely that we will have any business with either
South or North Korea for the next fifty years, I think this matter
can await the P.M.'s return."

Along with such problems, diplomatic courtesy messages and
goodwill missions take up much of the energies of the two-man
Foreign Ministry. Messages are frequent, since the other African
states are always having independence celebrations or anniver-
saries. When Zambia gained its independence, Prime Minister
Jawara, who was traveling in West Germany at the time, sent
a congratulatory telegram to Zambia's new President, Kenneth
Kaunda. Mr. Kaunda wired back: "I am most touched and

grateful by the fraternal message of good-will you have sent to me and the people of the new Republic of Zambia. We in turn send our greetings to you and your people." When Sir Albert Margai, Prime Minister of Sierra Leone, was sailing down the coast on his way home from a trip to England, he sent a message by ship's radio to Prime Minister Jawara: "As I pass your shores on my way home, I send fraternal greetings to you personally and the people of The Gambia." Prime Minister Jawara wired back: "I am most grateful for your kind message. In return, I send you good wishes on behalf of all in The Gambia."

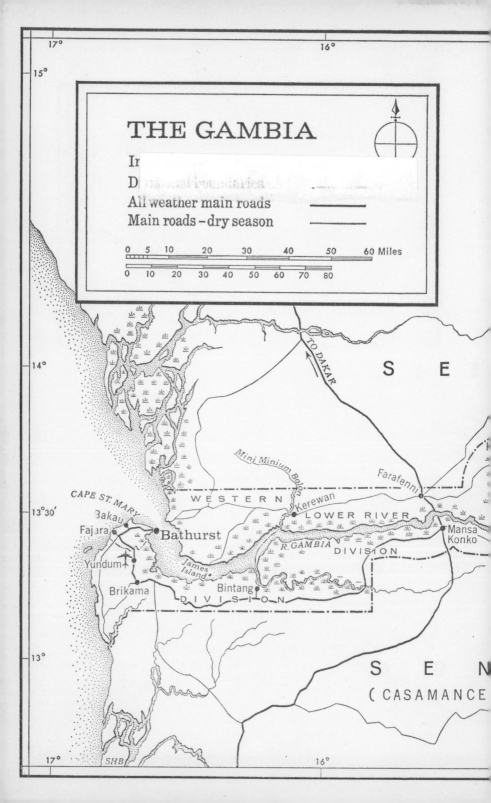

## THE GAMBIA

In
D
All weather main roads
Main roads – dry season

0   5   10      20      30      40      50   60 Miles
0   10   20   30   40   50   60   70   80

TO DAKAR

S E

Mini Minium Bolon

Farafenni

CAPE ST. MARY

WESTERN

Kerewan

LOWER RIVER

Bakau

Fajara

Bathurst

R. GAMBIA

DIVISION

Mansa Konko

Yundum

James Island

Brikama

Bintang

D I V I S I O N

S E N

(CASAMANCE

SHB